PERRO CALLEJERO

STRAY DOG

DARREN HOWMAN

Perro Callejero (Stray Dog) copyright © Darren Howman
First published as a book July 2020 by Everytime Press

ISBN: 978-1-925536-96-6

BP#00092

All rights reserved by the author and publisher. Except for brief excerpts used for review or scholarly purposes, no part of this book may be reproduced in any manner whatsoever without express written consent of the publisher or the author. Any historical inaccuracies are made in error.

Everytime Press
32 Meredith Street
Sefton Park SA 5083
Australia

Email: everytimepress@outlook.com
Website: https://everytimepress.com/
Everytime Press catalogue:
https://everytimepress.com/everytime-press-catalogue/

Front cover original design copyright © Darren Howman
Front cover original layout copyright © Leighton Dyer
Author photograph by David Stevens, used by permission

Also available as an eBook
ISBN: 978-1-925536-97-3

Everytime Press is a member of the
Bequem Publishing collective
https://www.bequempublishing.com/

for

Varsha, Mum, Dad,

Mat, Rachel, Evie, Wilf & Minnie

I would like to thank the following for their inspiration and belief in my writing: Bernadette Rowan, Rachel Sumner, Greg Hammerdown and David Griffin.

I would also like to thank Michelle Elvy for her everlasting patience with my archaic process and annoying idiosyncrasies while expertly editing this manuscript; and Varsha Singh for believing in me, organising me, guiding me and most of all loving me even in my worst moments.

Lastly, I would like to acknowledge all the people I met along the way and thank you all for being a part of my story. I am forever grateful to the Latin American people who took me in and unconditionally shared their lives with me, especially the people of Nicaragua.

CONTENTS

PART I
INTO THE UNKNOWN
CHILE, ARGENTINA, URUGUAY,
BOLIVIA, PERU
APRIL, MAY, JUNE
Page 3

PART II
GROUP DYNAMICS
PERU, ECUADOR, COLOMBIA, SAN BLAS,
PANAMA, COSTA RICA, NICARAGUA
JULY, AUGUST, SEPTEMBER
Page 169

PART III
GOING IT ALONE
NICARAGUA, EL SALVADOR
GUATEMALA, MEXICO
OCTOBER, NOVEMBER, DECEMBER
Page 311

PREFACE

A long-time interest in skateboarding sparked my passion for travel. Between the ages of fourteen and seventeen, I watched countless VHS tapes of my idols rolling around the sunny streets and schoolyards of Los Angeles. At eighteen, I escaped the grey rain-soaked streets of Reading, England, for the warmer climate of southern California, and I spent the first half of the 1990s back and forth between the two, chasing the sponsored skater dream I so desperately hoped to achieve.

During one of these trips, I was invited to visit New Zealand. It was an offer I couldn't refuse and after only a week on New Zealand soil, I grew determined to settle there. It felt like a place I could stay for the rest of my life: a similar feel to England with the bonus of a sub-tropical climate and drastically smaller population. I slipped into a comfortable lifestyle that handed me opportunities that would never have come my way in the UK, and for eight years I became heavily involved in the NZ skateboarding scene while also gaining experience in the film industry. I was living a good life.

In early 2008, I began to feel detached from the life I'd created in New Zealand. Since emigrating, my travel had been mostly restricted to return trips to the UK to visit family and friends, and my passion for more adventurous travel started to itch again. Two other things conspired to set me on a path away from New Zealand: Dan, a native New Zealander and my good friend and flatmate at the time, had just finished a five-year relationship with his Argentinean girlfriend; and my own relationship with a local woman had disintegrated similarly.

Dan's stories of his year in Argentina brought back tales from a UK ex-girlfriend. The colourful picture she'd painted of her travels in Guatemala had always stirred dreams of 'leaving the grid'. I started thinking more seriously about setting out for further shores: travel without computer and phone, leave bills and responsibilities behind.

Two months on, Dan and I were both still single. We were in our mid-thirties, working long hours and living a simple life we'd both become accustomed to. But we both had an urge to move beyond that life. And so began the plan, only loose at first.

Then, after two weeks of winter drizzle and a sure-fire sign of more of the same for the next three months, we impulsively booked two flights, the destination and departing airports 12,000 kilometres apart. The plan: make it from point A to point B in nine months by land.

Point A: Santiago, Chile. Point B: New York, USA.

Leaving New Zealand in April 2009, I was excited but scared of what lay ahead; I knew I was on a quest to find something I'd been unable to find at home. Perhaps I sought answers to the complexities of life, a circuit breaker from the growing stress of living in what was becoming a more selfish society.

Of course, our adventurous plan of hitchhiking and camping at the side of the road through a large stretch of two of the world's continents without the aid of a travel guidebook were swallowed up and destroyed when we found ourselves falling into the rut of the culture-less backpacker trail that we followed. Eventually I had to take steps to climb out of this rut and immerse myself in local life. The lessons I learnt drastically changed me. They can't be taught, of course; they can only be arrived at. In a mere ten months, I went from feeling like a lost child to discovering the key that would unlock a new door – a door that would open and expose me not only to a new language, but to a place of acceptance from a people I had previously no knowledge of, nor interest in. In short, a whole new way of *seeing* and *being in* the world flooded my consciousness.

This book is my story of life on the road and the changes that travel inspired in me. Words alone cannot begin to describe the friendship and love I experienced along the way, and I will forever be grateful for, and humbled by, the humanity that I was shown in what is now, to me, a magical part of the world.

Darren Howman
Auckland, New Zealand
March 2020

PART I
INTO THE UNKNOWN

CHILE, ARGENTINA, URUGUAY, BOLIVIA, PERU

APRIL, MAY, JUNE

CHAPTER ONE
SANTIAGO

A busy pedestrian street. A man to my left carrying a briefcase, a woman to my right in stilettoes. Hundreds of people milling to and fro on the sidewalk. Sun baking our backs.

We could be in any city in the world.

Suddenly, the man throws his briefcase at me and begins chasing a middle-aged fellow wearing dirty jeans and a basketball vest.

"Holy shit! What's he doing?!" I say to my companion, who is startled, also watching this scene unfold.

"I think the dude just ripped a gold chain from his neck," Dan replies nonchalantly, puffing on his cigarette and speaking as if what's unfolding before us is normal.

Catching up with the thief and grabbing him by the arm, the smartly dressed man punches him in the head and snatches the necklace back before dusting himself off and returning to the crossing. I am unable to speak but pass his briefcase back to him.

The green man lights up, and everyone crosses the road like nothing happened.

Welcome to Santiago, Chile. Welcome to South America.

We arrive at our hostel without further incident. The wide-angle lens used to photograph the hostel for the website showed a spacious guesthouse drenched in rays of sunlight – suspiciously different from what we are now staring at. Reality is a dimly lit interior, made up of various-sized broom cupboards.

We check in at the front desk with a pretty girl who takes us up a narrow flight of stairs to another closet-sized room on the first floor – this one over-crowded with rusty framed bunk beds and littered with other travellers belongings. "Esta," the girl says, pointing at the last empty bunk by pursing her lips in its direction. We leave our packs and head back down. In the corner of the courtyard (aka: the roofless cupboard), is a freckly guy in board shorts and round-framed spectacles, swinging in a hammock with his legs dangling either side. Flip-flops hanging from his toes, he winces and rubs his stinging red eyes while nursing the raw grazes that cover his body with a damp piece of kitchen towel.

"What happened to you?" I ask, before introducing myself.

"I was just roaming the streets, taking photos," he begins, dabbing at the cuts on his elbows. "Then this protest rally comes down the street towards me." He continues in what vaguely sounds like a Kiwi accent. "Hundreds of students with placards and flags! I couldn't resist!" He is starting to sound like he's trying to convince himself he made the right decision joining them.

Turns out, this 'good' idea was soon proved wrong when he came into contact with the sharp sting of the riot police's pepper spray smoke bombs and the high-pressure fire-hose that lifted him off his feet and pushed him down the street on his back. He tells us he's been nursing his eyes and fresh wounds all afternoon.

In the opposite corner of the room, slouched on a frayed, well-worn stripy couch, is a scruffily dressed guy from upstate New York, his sun dried-face sprouting a tangled beard of grey barbed-wire stubble. He holds a small audience of younger backpackers captive with tales from his hang gliding adventure in the Andes. Dan and I can't help but get caught up in his adventure, too.

"Yeah, the last few months have been amazing," he tells the semi-circle of avid listeners. "We were flying, like, *this far* away from giant condors." He stretches his arms out to indicate his proximity to the huge birds.

Eagle man's story starts to drag on so at an appropriate point without seeming rude we break away and head to the supermarket around the corner to search for dinner.

The streets are bustling. Pedestrians weave in and out of each other on the overcrowded sidewalk while cars and trucks honk and crawl through the wide city street.

"In here!" Dan calls back across the crowd, raising his arm and pointing towards a large glass entrance. The supermarket is much the same as the sidewalk and we battle our way to the meat fridges at the rear of the store.

"This is cheap as!" Dan exclaims, pulling out a pre-packed slab of chicken marked with the Peso equivalent of $4 and looking at me like he's found gold rather than the shrink-wrapped meat pack.

"Sweet then," I agree, looking for the tinned veg aisle. "Let's add a can of corn to it and cook it up."

Believing we've scored an amazing deal, we head back to the hostel and fire up the gas stove, ransack the tiny kitchen for a pot and throw the ingredients together. The smell emitting during the heating of our meal is a peculiar scent, but not a word is said between us. Famished, we stay silent as the pot boils.

As I pour the grey, deformed, mini-donut-looking chunks flecked with corn into bowls, I'm starting to wonder what this food before us really is. A cleaner walks past and takes a sniff of our dinner. "Mmm," she hums. "Tope."

Dan looks up from his bowl in disgust and spits out his mouthful.

"What? What?" I ask, doing the same.

"It's arsehole! Chicken arsehole!" he splutters.

"What a fucking waste," I confess, picking out the corn before scraping our near-full plates into the kitchen bin. "Who the fuck would want to buy arseholes?"

The culture shock I'm already experiencing after only a couple of hours is something I couldn't have prepared myself for. Listening to a 'Teach yourself Spanish' language CD in my lunch breaks for two months prior to departing was about as helpful as a kick in the teeth, and my mind is now lost as to why I'm here, and, if I stay, what I want to get out of this trip. Dan, on the other hand, is quite content with drinking his way through the next nine months in various hostel courtyards, enlightening new travellers who have not yet had the pleasure of his cuss-heavy – and repetitious – stories of the history of the world according to him. Coming from a farming background in the greenbelt north of New Zealand, Dan is a vision of country boy confidence. A clump of unkempt curly hair sits on his head and sticks out from under a baseball cap that bears dried perspiration salt lines. Perched on his red weathered face are a pair of black, square-rimmed glasses with a coil of wire wrapped around one arm – an ingenious repair made from the copper of an off-cut of electricity cable. Although his clothing shows signs of heavy maltreatment, underneath this dishevelled layer is one of the most patient, carefree, accommodating and relaxed people I've ever met. For the next nine months we're going to be living in each other's pockets and I realise now, considering all the shit we're about to encounter on a daily basis in this crazy jaunt of ours, I can't think of anyone else who would be able to put up with each other like we do.

An undertaking such as this renders everyone equal. Stripped of our individual job titles and lifestyles, we now shit in the same toilet, sleep in the same room and carry our worldly belongings in a backpack or two.

And this lack of privacy extends beyond the small space occupied by Dan and me, I come to learn on our first night in Santiago. At 4am, our night is interrupted by three drunken Israeli guys who enter the dorm and turn on the lights and proceed to talk in phlegmy Hebrew for half an hour at the top of their voices, as if nobody else is there. This inconsiderate behaviour is followed by them hacking up the phlegm they have utilised in their conversation and spitting it into tissues while I lie under the sheet in my bunk, seething at their pig-headedness. *Surely these idiots will tire of their banter soon*, I think to myself. But no such luck. They carry on for another hour while standing in the middle of the dorm room, and then, when they are finally ready to retire, they replace the loud, spittle-hacking conversation with a snoring chorus of chainsaw motors.

Waking up after the little sleep I managed to salvage, I navigate my way to the showers, avoiding the minefield of Israeli snot rags spread out across the dorm floor while my roommates sleep, their hairy legs twisted and hanging off their bunks, unknowingly showing off their trapped genitals suffocating in tiny purple Y-fronts.

"Fuck, those guys were loud last night," Dan says while we stand in line downstairs, barefooted on the wooden floor.

"So fucking inconsiderate," I reply, angry and tired. Three allotted pancakes are plopped on my plate as I shuffle along the prison-like queue of sleepy eyed backpackers that stretches out of the kitchen, and leads to a conversation with some British travellers on their gap year. They complain of the lack of facilities available here. I'm not sure whether they mean this hostel or Santiago in general, but I decide not to ask. I figure all will be revealed in time. It's only my second day, after all.

We soon come to realise that young tourists like us, venturing out on their big overseas experience, want the world to be like it is on TV: they want places to be muted or switched off by remote control, with nothing less than a reliable Wi-Fi signal at all times, plus air-conditioning, laundry service and a fully stocked bar on site. Fortunately for them there are a variety of hostels that cater for these wants and needs. Dan and I decide early on that we will avoid those at all costs.

Full from the prison pancakes, we relax into our morning, taking time to acclimatise to the heat before making the one-hour walk to the Plaza de Armas in the older part of town. The city covers a huge area – far greater than the tamer New Zealand cities we were heretofore accustomed to – and there seem to be fewer foreign travellers on the streets than I'd anticipated. The main square is a place where new meets old: the hulking cathedral dominates over street vendors, buskers and crowds and is sandwiched between taller, mirror-windowed office blocks – and they somehow strangely complement each other. Each side of the modern buildings casts an alternative view of their older counterparts across the plaza, as grey stone turrets and spires are reflected in the dark glass of the taller shiny edifices.

On the return walk we encounter stray dogs – hundreds of the docile creatures wandering the streets, lying in the middle of the now commuter-free pavements and under trees that line the shady city parks. The most fascinating part is watching the dogs wait for the green pedestrian light before crossing roads. Not something you see every day. Surprising to us is that the relationship between the city's people and these canines seems to be anything but hostile: each species goes about its daily routines, without so much as bothering the other. This is something I quickly grow accustomed to, and, being a dog lover, I am comforted by the idea that in this bustling city these harmless creatures are not under the threat of being lassoed and put down by dog catchers.

Arriving back at the hostel, Dan and I are greeted by the pleasant sight of the Israelis checking out at the reception desk – we reckon a good night's sleep is in store. But upon entering the dorm, I'm greeted by a white haired old man dressed in hiking gear and fossicking in his bags on the bunk below mine. Shaking his hand, I introduce myself.

"Malcolm's the name, young chap, how do you do?" he replies with a cheery smile through a military-like moustache.

I learn that Malcolm is preparing to hike into the Andes tomorrow and planning to stay up there for a few weeks. What Dan and I fail to realise (until it is too late) is that a crucial part of Malcolm's routine relies on an old-fashioned alarm clock set for 4am the following morning. The clock in question is one of those classic dial-faced types with two huge bells on top, which starts at 4am sharp and continues to ring sporadically while Malcolm takes a shower.

"For fuck's sake!" Dan groans, awake and livid at the din that the clock is making. Seizing the opportunity, he shuts the thing down but not before taking a photo of it while Malcolm is still in the bathroom. This starts a trend, or should I say a *theme* for Dan's South American photo series, setting the tone for what he decides to choose as worthy subjects to capture during the rest of the trip. He will fill his memory cards with pictures that, if found by a stranger, would give absolutely no inclination to what continent we are on or of the amazing places we visit over the ensuing nine months. Dan's photographic eye seems determined to capture the most irrelevant details possible. Beginning with Malcolm's alarm clock.

Paying in advance for our first five nights abroad before actually researching the city turns out to be a huge mistake, as Dan and I quickly become restless in what is in reality a boring sprawl of concrete jungle. This isn't helped by the fast foot traffic in our hostel; we observe travellers come and go on a daily basis, telling us of their exciting destinations. We feel almost stuck, and we've only just arrived.

One advantage in Santiago is that we have our skateboards, making the geography seem a lot smaller and helping our week pass a lot quicker. Concrete jungle, while not very pretty, offers kilometres of skateboarding routes. The new terrain to explore is endless. Hopping up and down kerbs, weaving in and out of the rush-hour vehicle and foot traffic while dodging the street dogs in an unchartered city is a skater's dream, and one we lose ourselves in.

The Bella Vista district, its walls adorned with huge graffiti bombs and characters, is particularly fun to roll through and we do just this while making our way to a skate park across town.

On arrival, however, we discover it's not the one we were expecting. Resembling a large rough concrete dish, the place is a huge disappointment, especially as we've spent an hour getting here. Sitting down against the fence of the skate park, we share a cigarette with a dreadlocked local who tells us of the park we were originally looking for.

"Yeah, it's about four blocks from your hostel back across the city," he laughs, directing us back the way we came. Then he adds, "You wanna smoke?" And offers us a joint.

"Yeah, cool – thanks," Dan answers before the guy can change his mind. "Just a quick toke."

He takes the joint between his thumb and index finger before sucking a large puff and passing it. In a matter of minutes, we finish the joint with our dreaded friend and leave to re-trace our route, stoned but with the correct directions.

Generally, skate parks are built in places that the average traveller doesn't venture to. This is true for the newer Santiago park which is situated to the north of the city and accessed through a ghetto stretching for four blocks. The ghetto pavements are in such disrepair our only option is to skate in the roadside gutter, inches away from the speeding traffic whizzing by. We arrive at a chaotic scene, a series of deep concrete bowls linked together in a snake-run style construction and ranging from four to twelve feet in depth. These intimidating craters border one side of the giant graffiti-plastered park, while the remainder of the large area is occupied by banked ramps, benches, stairs and handrails. Both sections are packed with speed-hungry Chilean teenagers with no sense of direction, and no courtesy for their fellow skaters.

After ten minutes of watching the mayhem, trying to make a plan of how to enter in to this mess, Dan and I go for broke, dropping into the 6-foot bowl. I take the right side and pop out of the lip, landing on the platform, heading in the direction of the street, but before I have chance to gather my thoughts, I'm blindsided from the left by a kid travelling at warp speed who carries on past me in mid-air while his board digs itself into my shin. Dan, meanwhile, takes the left route and heads down the snake run towards the 12-foot death bowl. Narrowly missing two head-on collisions with a couple of stray skateboard missiles, he does make it down to the giant bowl, only to be thrown out of the top like a rag doll when he loses his balance with the sheer speed he's now picked up.

An hour or so into this frustrating carry on, we stop for a cigarette.

"Fuck this," I exclaim, turning to Dan, hoping he's had enough.

Thinking about it and taking a long drag of his cigarette, he surveys the carnage and, with an exhale of smoke, nods in agreement.

The following morning, feeling sore from the previous day's skate and now growing rather tired of the pancakes we're continually being served, we set out on foot to the centre of the city for more sightseeing. Perched in the sprawl stands a tall hill which is home to the Statue of San Cristobál, its climb rewarding us with 360-degree views of the city which, we discover upon arrival at the summit, are unfortunately rather drab, dominated by a jumbled medley of dirty low-rise apartment blocks and office buildings shrouded in a light grey smog. At ground level, I see Santiago through newcomer eyes, and I'm met with a huge hostile concrete monster that talks a different language and has no interest in where I've come from or where I'm going. But Santiago, seen from above, goes about its daily grind like any other city in the world.

Further up San Cristobál and sitting on the steps at the foot of the giant white Mary statue, we are swarmed by a blue and white uniformed rabble of 6-year-olds, all wanting to practice their English while their teachers appear quite happy that these two foreigners are, for the time being, doing their jobs. The teachers sit on a wall smoking cigarettes and text message on their mobile phones, while Dan and I engage curious children. This interaction with the kids is my first real heartfelt contact with Latin people, and I find myself happy. I ramble on, seeing how these little faces light up with eagerness as they try to replicate everything we say – I am from New Zealand, I say. We like your city, Dan says. They echo, and we laugh: I am from New Zealand; we like your city. It's a defining moment that triggers something in me that has fuelled my trips since, though I'm unaware at the time of the huge part it will play in my future travels.

Our last morning and last serving of the pancakes is upon us. Loading up the backpacks after filling our bellies, Dan and I tackle the six blocks of colourful, bustling, chaotic street stalls that block the pavements en route to the bus station. With our first city encounters behind us, we are keen to be back on the road, and we climb aboard a giant bus that looks far better than what we'd expected. We could not be more excited as the diesel churns to life and we begin to crawl out of the chaos and make our way up the Andes towards Argentina.

The route is like nothing I've ever seen, switchbacking its way all the way up the hill. Squirming back and forth like a giant python, the road turns left then right, every bend revealing a window of the winding asphalt that disappears into the depths of the ranges far below before changing back and climbing the cliff face at each new corner.

As the peaks change from wet and grey to a white carpet dusting of snow, a high stud shed appears in the distance. Sitting at 3250m above sea level, it's shadowed by the mighty snowcapped peaks of Mt. Aconcagua. The bus pulls into the structure, and our bags are taken from the hold and searched thoroughly on a row of metal tables while we line up in the icy wind for our first border crossing.

"¿Propina?" the baggage handler asks me, with his grubby hand held open and fingers curling upward. Confused and staring back at him, I'm not sure what he's asking.

"He wants a tip," Dan calls across to me, seeing that I'm having trouble understanding.

"For what?" I shout back. "Surely it's not for a tip to say thank you for rifling through my bag while I wait here freezing my arse off?"

"Just give him a few pesos. You're not gonna need 'em again," Dan replies, reboarding the bus.

CHAPTER TWO
MENDOZA

The bus pulls out of the border shed and into the fog. Soon we are at the top of the Andes, winding along a wet highway through a hostile no-man's land flanked either side by jagged grey rock faces and white mountain peaks.

No more than ten minutes after leaving the Chilean checkpoint, we arrive at another shed at the Argentinean border – another dingy steel beamed structure, poorly lit and stained with exhaust, much like the previous one. The icy wind whistles through the rafters and bites at any exposed skin that dares to show itself as we go through the tedious luggage-and-tip routine once more. The baggage handler looks at me with disdain and grunts as I place a few coins in his open hand. I offer him the same gormless look I gave the last guy, and he tosses the coins back at me. They bounce off my chest and fall to the floor before I have time to grab for them.

"I guess he doesn't like Chilean pesos," I remark to Dan as we reboard and rumble down the road into our second country.

The bus makes its way down the eastern wall of the Andes and out of the clouds, and the cold, harsh atmosphere of the mountains soon melts away as we descend into vast sun-drenched plains as far as the eye can see. Vineyards outnumber the populace of the countryside and row upon row of grapevines stretch towards the horizon, flashing by in a blur as we make our way towards Mendoza.

Mendoza bus station immediately takes me back to our last morning in Santiago: the chaotic frenzy of human traffic, market stalls and taxis, everyone coming and going. In both places there is a constant crush of people and noise. But we escape the terminal intact and trudge towards the centre of the city on foot. Moments later, a flickering blue neon sign of a Uruguayan-owned hostel welcomes us. The small entry room is tidily maintained, and we step into an atmosphere much more relaxed than the frenetic energy of our previous accommodations in Santiago. Within minutes, we are welcomed by a subdued but conversational group.

"Would you like some tea?" asks a middle-aged man, cleaning a brass trumpet.

"Please," we reply, taking a seat.

The tea-drinkers, it turns out, are all part of an Uruguayan marching band that has played in a street festival earlier in the day; the band members are clearly exhausted from blowing and banging their instruments all day. They clean their brass while sharing a few tips with us regarding their country, urging us to pay it a visit.

"The east coast up near Brazil's border is very tourist-free," says a long-faced girl polishing her trumpet with a white rag.

"Yeah, that's where my brother and I went," Dan says, helping himself to more tea. "It's a beautiful part of the country. There's a national park we camped in."

"Parque Santa Theresa," she replies.

We jot down a few notes in our guidebook and empty our cups, then retire to our refreshingly clean dorm for a sound night's sleep.

After more tea in the morning we bid farewell to our brass band friends and search out another hostel closer to Mendoza's city centre. Situated on a leafy side street drenched in sunshine, the place is welcoming – it feels like we've hit the jackpot. From the outside, the three-storey building exudes a warmth and friendliness. Brightly painted murals that surround the shiny red door and sparkling clean windows beckon us in. But on entering, we start to think we should have stayed where we were.

The desk boy, dressed in a ripped Metallica t-shirt with greasy black fringe and piercings across his spotty face, greets us with a cold stare, muttering, "Dejar sus maletas aqui, hay camas esta tarde." He speaks with an unenthusiastic drawl still holding the cold stare.

Dan explains. "Free beds this arvo; we can leave our bags here."

But neither of us feels convinced this is a safe plan. For one thing, we don't like the greeting we've just been given. And then there's the fact that there's no one else here.

The desk boy unconvincingly assures us that our bags will be safe where they are, and that they will be put on our beds once the maids have been through.

So we do as he says and leave our bags.

We buy empanadas from a stall in the large central park. Children run around us playing while hemp-clothed hippies practice beats and rhythms on bongo drums under the large shady trees.

I'm most struck by the women, who are elegant and sexy. I don't see a single ugly hair out of place. Not a single ugly outfit. Not a single ugly pimply face. The plaza is, in fact, entirely lacking in ugly; these women are, across the board, *beautiful*. Never mind the MILFs of television sitcoms or the botoxed stars of big-screen Hollywood; these women before me are beyond stunning. They are dolled up in their own way, sure – full lips painted with vibrant reds, eyebrows plucked to alluring arches, legs shaved and oiled to shiny perfection. Long dark hair swishes silkily over their shoulders while tight-fitting business suits hug their curvy bodies as they strut tall and confident in strappy high heels. And it's not just the mothers and single women who catch my eye. Patrolling the park is an olive-skinned policewoman in black SWAT gear accompanied by a serious-looking Doberman. Her long plaited hair drapes over the M-16 hanging from her shoulder while tight-fitting black cargo pants cup her perfectly formed buttocks as she circles the area.

"Definitely something in the water here, maybe it's in the wine," Dan says, smiling, as we enjoy the view from the shade of our bench.

And so, after a lazy few hours of people watching, we arrive back at the hostel later that afternoon, where our bags are in exactly the same place at the door, crying out to be stolen. A new desk boy blasts death metal music at a high volume.

We storm down the hallway, angry at their careless attitude, and find the dorm untouched. The bed sheets and pillows look used, and the floor is littered with food wrappers from the previous guests.

"Is this a joke?" I say, unable to believe what I'm looking at.

"The kitchen's no better," Dan says, calling to me from the opposite end of the hallway. I join him to see sauce-stained plates, stacked head-high, and bowls oozing with leftover pasta and other food waste. This kitchen is surely housing a few resident cockroaches – and possibly worse.

The courtyard, we soon discover, is just as uncared for. Ashtrays overflow with cigarette butts and stagnant brown nicotine-stained rainwater – without doubt a breeding ground for the several families of vicious mosquitoes that hover around them. On the opposite side of the courtyard to the mozzie farm, a blonde Swedish girl sits nursing several lines of ferocious tick bites covering her legs.

"After only von night," she starts in her accent, "I hef all deez bites." She points despondently at her lumps. Disgusted by the conditions, and the fact she didn't get a wink of sleep, she has already checked out and is about to leave.

Two more 'staff' appear in the courtyard, both kitted up in the same rock band outfits as the desk boy. I can't tell which is younger – the one with the torn Slayer t-shirt or the boy with jeans falling off his hips. They both are pimply and look as if they need a good wash. I briefly wonder where their mums are, and I feel suddenly a little older.

"You clean you plates in dee kitchen," one says to us sternly, in broken English.

Shocked by this statement – not only because we haven't set foot in there for fear of catching something we'll regret for years to come, and more so because the kid pointing the finger to us is barely out of nappies – Dan shuts them down, answering, "No son nuestros, ya estaban aqui cuando llegamos."

Not ours, they were here when we arrived.

A surprised look crosses their pimply faces on hearing Dan's fluent Spanish, and we see that they know they can't pin this on us – and that we are telling the truth. Slayer-Boy and his sidekick storm off.

We soon meet another dissatisfied guest: a pretty French girl by the name of Marie, who enters the courtyard shortly after our weird exchange with Slayer-boy and sidekick, and lights up a thin cigarette. She tells us how she has had to persistently decline the passes made from the creepy collection of male staff employed at this even creepier hostel. She is leaving this afternoon.

That night, unable to sleep from the death metal that grows louder into the early hours, I peel myself out of bed and enter the reception.

"Turn down, please," I politely ask with hand gestures of turning a volume knob.

"Si, OK, OK," the drunk teenager replies, shooing me away with his hand while giving the volume knob a slight twist.

I return to my bunk and lie back down, but the music steadily creeps to *loud* again and I get very little sleep. I try my hardest to block the sound, but there's only so much a dirty pillow can do.

At the crack of dawn after what is quite possibly the worst night I've ever experienced in paid accommodation, we leave without a word – "I guess it changed hands since my bro was there," Dan says – and check into our third hostel in Mendoza.

Situated right in the heart of the city on a street lined with tourist restaurants, the new hostel is run by one of the more reputable and mainstream chains by the name of 'Campo Base' and, though very busy with extreme backpackers and beer-swilling Brits, it's a damn sight better than the shithole we just came from.

Dumping my backpack on the floor of the reception, I notice the grip tape on top of my skateboard is beginning to sand holes in the material. There is no other way of attaching it to the pack and the abrasive surface needs to be covered to prevent my bag falling apart.

Dan also inspects his, seeing the same wear marks.

"Cheap sweatpants," he says.

"Eh?" I reply confused.

"Let's buy a pair and cut 'em in half. We can use the legs as board condoms."

"That's bloody genius!" I reply, surprised at his ingenuity. "You're not just a pretty face are you!"

"Good to keep 'em out of sight too," he says, unamused at my pretty face comment.

The week ahead is Semana Santa – Holy Week of Easter. It's one of the biggest national holiday celebrations in all of the very Catholic Latin America. Hundreds of families flee the sweltering cities to barbecue in the surrounding hills and parks; it's a week of eating enormous amounts of food and revelling beyond the reach of workaday life. Our plan is to try to ride on the wind of this event and camp somewhere for the weekend in the surrounding countryside. We find an army surplus store a few streets from our hostel and purchase the necessary camping supplies. Dan finds a tatty pair of sweatpants for the board condoms and I bag myself a pair of ex-military pants for a mere 25 pesos. We ask the army surplus staff for directions to a nature reserve with a camping area we've seen on a map and the two Rambo wannabees dressed for combat burst into laughter.

"¡¿Cree que usted conseguirá caminando por ese barrio?! ¡¡Jajajaja!!" They crumple over, saying we won't even make it through the neighbourhoods that surround the campground park alive. We watch silently as they continue to laugh, until they finally calm down enough to be able to give us advice.

Dan relays the directions to me: "They reckon there's a sweet spot near the village of Potrerillos, about fifty kilometres back towards the Andes."

With our destination set, we turn to the task of supplying victuals for our country adventure. I volunteer to get the supplies – much to the disagreement of Dan, who doesn't think I'm equipped with enough Spanish to conquer the supermarket. We argue the whole way there, but on arrival I stubbornly head in, desperately wanting to prove Dan wrong and impress him. For twenty minutes I search the aisles, trying to decipher the labels and ingredients for supplies to keep us fed while camping. I fail to understand the majority of what I'm reading, however, and end up going by the pictures on the wrappers and tins.

Finally armed with my selections, I join the queue at the front of the store. If there is one quality that characterises us Brits, it is our sense of good manners in situations such as queuing. Other people, it seems, do not share our sense of propriety and order. Latin people, I soon learn, have not yet mastered this skill – or just don't care for it. Either way, they choose a different strategy when it comes to establishing a straight and orderly line. As I wait my turn for the next available checkout, I'm passed successively by not just one but *three* small women who not only have the indecency of jumping queue but also rub it in by elbowing me in the hip on their way past. This rude manoeuvring is infuriating and makes me feel as if I shouldn't be here. (During the next nine months I become an expert in this field, reaching the black belt stage of queuing, securing and defending my position in line while deflecting any elbow that comes close – but as of this moment I'm a newbie and utterly lost.)

I finally make it to the counter and pay for my goods, and I exit the sliding doors with six litres of water, five tins of tuna, a bag of carrots, a packet of instant coffee, another of powdered milk, half a kilo of rice and a bag of nuts. I'm pretty impressed with my haul.

"Holy fuck!" Dan shouts, reading the receipt when I meet him on the street. "How much?!!"

I've blown the budget big time, and studying the receipt shows exactly where I've erred: the nut mix medley I've chosen is probably the most expensive item in the store.

"Amateur!" Dan mumbles through an angry I-told-you-so smirk on his face. "Three days over budget on that one."

We return to the hostel with our luxury scroggin and my confidence bruised.

That evening, drunk on local red wine at a small restaurant opposite our place on the main strip, we meet Dean, an embarrassingly loud British cockney, washed up from the early '90s illegal rave scene and one of those people who compares everything to England and speaks constantly of how perfect the Motherland is in comparison to these 'little backward' countries. Dean and his missus could quite easily pass for cast try-outs for an Irvine Welsh urban slum movie. His other half, Mandy, a plump, peroxided blonde woman of seemingly little intelligence, giggles and agrees with him all night long and in all the appropriate places as he splutters through a gruesome set of rotten brown teeth, his shrunken red Arsenal football shirt riding up his fat belly.

"So oi wuz in dis noightclub in Cuba, were'nt oi, Mandoy," he slurs. Mandy sniggers, knowing the story about to unfold. "And me drink gets spoiked wiv Rohypnol but I just drunk me way frew it and carried on til deh erly hours," he recalls with a cackle. It's clear he believes he's impressed us immensely with his immunity to roofies.

Listening to Dean's stories while 'Mandoy' cackles along with him, I find myself laughing a lot, although the laughter feels directed *at* him more than *with* him.

The restaurant staff packs up tables and chairs around us until we get the message that it's time to go home.

CHAPTER THREE
POTRERILLOS

Waking up to a throbbing hangover from the shitty red wine that we'd shared with Dean and Mandy the night before, we check out of the Campo Base hostel and wait at the kerb on the corner of a busy intersection for the bus that will take us back to the countryside. The brown beast finally pulls up noisily, and we spend the next two hours with our backpacks in our laps as it splutters its way through endless fields of grapevines. We alight at a dusty fork in the road, and we're met with a crude wooden arrow nailed to a crooked pole. The sign reads 'Potrerillos 2 kms' and points down a track leading in the direction of the mountains.

"This way then, I guess," I say to Dan, walking off and pulling on my pack. The road follows a clear glacier river upstream that vanishes in the distance into the burnt orange backdrop of the Andes.

"Fuck, I hope there's a shop," Dan says, wiping the sweat from his glasses on his t-shirt while the afternoon sun beats down on us.

First point of call is a small wooden weatherboard structure resembling my granddad's shed in his allotment back home where he spent years hiding from my nan.

"Yes! A shop!" Dan says in relief.

Stepping inside the dimly lit store, we are greeted by dusty shelves supporting tinned fish, beans, a meagre selection of bruised fruit and a couple of bottles of a fiery but cheap liquor known as 'Fernet' which the shopkeeper, a wrinkled old man who can barely see over the planked counter, bags for us as he takes our money.

Tonight is to be the initiation night for our ultra high-tech, two-man tent. Dan and I bought this expensive item in New Zealand in preparation for the trip. This is it: the beginning of our camping days.

With bright orange waterproof ripstop nylon, titanium pegs and an overall weight of two kilograms, the tent virtually erects itself. It makes us look like seasoned pros at the outdoors game. But we've grossly misjudged the shiny tent's capacity: it's too small to accommodate our packs, so they must be left out on the dewy grass (even if they are slightly sheltered under the door flaps) every time we use it; and furthermore, once inside, we are forced to spoon each other all night long. The miscalculation is a real pain in the arse (excuse the pun) when you have a snoring long-haired gorilla who's impossible to wake up snuggled next to you and nowhere to put that free arm that would otherwise be wrapping over the top of your (smaller, softer) partner.

Setting up the tent the first night, we see that the campsite, a flat grass area dotted with large fir trees, seems empty – a surprising fact given that it's Semana Santa.

"Keen on a dip?" Dan asks. "I need to wash off all this dust."

I eagerly agree. But my thoughts of a refreshing dip in the river are cut short the moment I hit the icy cold water.

"ARRRRRGGGHH!!!" My balls disappear up inside my chest and I frantically scramble over the slippery rocks as if a school of piranhas are chasing me. Escaping the frosty rapids that are now burning my skin, I throw a towel around me and crack open the wine, my shivering hands barely managing the twist-off bottle-cap.

The full moon rises majestically over the jagged mountain range, and my nuts slowly sink back down into my sack with every sip of the herbal alcohol, the taste of which I can't quite pin down. Mulled wine, mint liquor and eggnog come to mind. My camp stove delivers us a sumptuous feed of steaming rice, tomato and tuna, and the peace and quiet is only interrupted by the demonic ice river rushing its way downstream over the rocks.

The bottle of Fernet knocks us out, which fortunately helps with the whole spooning problem. That is, until we awake in each other's arms the next morning.

"Fuck man!" I cry, waking and peeling Dan's hairy arm off my face. "This tent is way too small!"

Dan rolls over and grunts while I uncomfortably twist myself 180 degrees and poke my head out the tent. The campground is transformed: the wide grassy area now resembles a music festival.

Peering further out of the tent flap, a sea of older model Peugeots and Fiats parked next to countless multi-coloured tents surrounds us. Teenagers sit around portable stereos while families cook breakfast on camp stoves. A matrix of guy ropes criss-cross each other throughout the site while their ground pegs battle for space in the dry earth.

"*This* is the Semana Santa crowd," Dan says, peering out to survey the area around us. "They must have all arrived late last night!"

"I'll get a brew on," I say, lighting up the camp stove and filling a pot with water.

A scraggly wild dog appears from nowhere and sits down next to us. I offer it cake, but it turns its nose away rejecting the food.

"You not hungry, fella?" Dan says, ruffling its fur. The dog rolls over contented and falls asleep.

"We've got our own guard dog!" I laugh.

My attention is fully on my stove when a leathery cowboy on horseback greets us with a friendly wave. The dog briefly looks up at his horse before going back to sleep.

The cowboy's leathery – sixty or sixty-five – and straight out of a Wild West movie.

"I've been riding this route for thirty years and it's always good to see some gringos taking advantage of this beautiful spot," he explains to Dan through his last few teeth in an incomprehensible Spanish.

Dan does his best to roughly translate the cowboy's stories to me, but mostly they share a few laughs while I stare on like a mute child.

Leaving them to chat, I open the instant coffee and boil up some more water.

The pants I purchased from the army store back in Mendoza are booby-trapped and I can almost hear those two Rambo guys laughing at me now. Pulling one loose thread opens a whole can of worms and the stitching holding the pockets and seams together unravels mercilessly, revealing arse cheeks and other parts of my legs I'd rather have covered up. Pulling out my sewing kit and sitting at the river's edge in my boxer shorts, I begin the task of repairing them. While I'm doing this, an older lady approaches me over the rocks.

"Toma, Toma," she urges, passing me a crumpled ball of tin foil.

Confused, I unwrap it to find a large lump of sponge cake.

"Gracias!" I shout out to the lady who's already making her way back through the sea of tents.

"You gonna share that?" Dan asks, clambering over the rocks after seeing what just happened and taking a chunk before I have chance to reply. The cake is overly dry but sweet and delicious and we wash down the rest with a cup of coffee back at the tent.

"There's some lakes over that hill," Dan recalls the old cowboy saying. "They're linked by a trail that starts across the road from the campground."

I finish my repair job and zip the tent. We head up the path that twists up around the side of the hill before dropping down into a valley. Four lakes of varying sizes are carpeted in lily pads and surrounded by yellow and purple flowers. A few men are pulling in good-sized trout from the largest lake. Dan approaches one of them and asks if they have any for sale. The stern glare we receive indicates the negative to his question, and we return to our tent empty-handed.

We open another can of tuna to accompany our rice.

The wail of portable CD players blasting Latin pop music fill the campsite as groups of campers huddle around their barbecues cooking meat while fireworks whizz and scream through the balmy evening air. The airspace just above our heads resembles a Middle Eastern air strike and we are awed by the sight, and by the miracle that none of the surrounding trees – or, more importantly, our tent – ignite.

As the weekend draws to a close, we witness a mass exodus of campers. Stuffing their unfolded tents into the back of vehicles, they vacate the site en masse, leaving the oil drum litter bins surrounding the site overflowing with rubbish.

One of these groups consists of an older lady and a gaggle of teenage girls who seem to be having trouble getting into their car. The thin, grey-haired lady approaches us to ask for help.

"¿Usted puede abrir la cajuela, por favor?" she says in a frail voice.

"Vamos a ver," Dan answers, following her back to the vehicle.

She tells Dan that the keys are locked in the boot, and for twenty minutes we pick at the lock, trying our best not to scratch her old classic.

"¡Ataque!" she says, making a fist and punching the air.

"She's telling me to attack it," Dan says, grabbing a rock. "I'm gonna punch the fucking barrel through."

Dan smashes the huge rock on the butt of a screwdriver that he's positioned over the key hole. The old lady doesn't flinch.

"¡Es un coche de mierda! ¡Hazlo!" she shouts, informing us it's a piece of shit and encouraging us to keep going. With her blessing, and after a few whacks with the rock, Dan manages to get the barrel to pop, releasing the boot catch and revealing the bunch of keys left inside.

"¡Ai! ¡Gracias! ¡Gracias!" the girls and old lady cry, clapping and handing us a plastic bag.

"De nada," Dan replies, saying it's nothing.

"¡Adios!" they shout back, waving to us and jumping into the car.

"What's in it?" I ask Dan, pointing at the plastic bag the old lady gave us.

"Oh, yeah! Check it out!" he replies, opening the top.

Barbecue ribs, steaks and the remnants of an icing-covered birthday cake taste like heaven after a few days of rice and tuna (and the rationed luxury nut mix). We devour it like starving cavemen, joined by our wiry-haired canine friend who slumps down in front of us in the dirt.

"Where you been, buddy?" Dan asks, patting his back.

Staring at us tearing into the hunks of meat, he quietly sits by, seemingly uninterested.

"Weird dog, eh?" I remark to Dan, confused as to why he'll never eat any of the food we offer him.

"You're probably just full from the other scraps you've been given, eh, buddy?" Dan says to him, patting the dog with one hand while holding a rib in the other.

CHAPTER FOUR
EL SALTO

When we finish the bag of food, the dog gets to its feet, shakes itself off and disappears, leaving us alone in the vacated campsite. Only the ticking noise of bicycle gears breaks the silence a few minutes later. Dan and I look up to see a curly-haired guy on a dusty mountain bike overloaded with panniers. He skids to a halt a few metres from us, then leans his bike against a tree and erects his micro tent next to ours – in, literally, seconds.

"Heya, fellas, nice evening, eh?" he says in a thick Canadian accent, opening a flap on his bag and producing a large bottle of beer. "I'm Rick, and this is from 'Jerome's'." He holds out the bottle. "It's a little microbrewery I stumbled on twelve kilometres up in a small village called El Salto."

Pouring the contents of the brown forty-ounce bottle into three cups, Rick passes two of them our way. We repay his kindness by introducing him to the delights of rice, tuna and the remainder of our Fernet wine.

Scruffy haired and Canadian-born, Rick settles in for the night. His weathered looks and stories of life on the road seem so distant from our fresh faces and the drab hostel-hopping of our trip thus far. His solitary riding experience from Iquique on the northwest coast of Chile and down through Argentina is a far cry from our route so far – but also a great inspiration to aim for in the coming months.

"I just feel so free," he tells us. "There ain't nothing like travelling alone. I don't have to answer to anybody and I can go wherever I want, whenever I want."

"But don't you get lonely?" I ask him.

He looks at me with a smile and shakes his head. "When everywhere you're heading to is a new place, it can never get lonely." The justification regarding his choice of transport seems a little rehearsed, but is also not without truth.

As dusk settles over the empty site, and the night silence reigns supreme over our fizzling conversation, we all retire to our tents and pass out.

Next morning, we say our farewells and step out in to the glaring sun. Dan and I walk in the direction of the scorched brown mountains, our thumbs held high, while Rick rides off in the opposite direction.

After an hour of walking the hot, dusty roadside, we catch up with an old fellow shuffling along in a suit and tie, assisted by a crooked walking stick.

"Hay bus muy pronto," he says through a toothless mouth, informing us that there's a bus due soon.

We wait with him in a lay-by. Dan tries to understand what he's spluttering by answering with a "Si" or "No" at times he feels appropriate.

Five minutes later, his two friends show up in a pick-up truck. The two men inside look like Mario and Luigi from the Nintendo game. Honking the horn, they beckon us to throw our bags on and jump aboard.

Before I can get all the way in to the back tray, the driver puts his foot to the floor and I'm left with my feet dragging along the road.

"¡Vamos! ¡Vamos!" they shout, laughing at me as the driver stops the truck, allowing me to hoist myself in.

"¿A donde va?" the driver asks through the slit in the rear cab window.

"Jerome's!" Dan shouts back.

Letting out a loud laugh, the driver looks to his mates. "¡Los Gringos!" he says. "¡Siempre pensando en la cerveza!" Always thinking of beer.

The mountain men continue to cackle and laugh in the cab while we climb a road that clings to the mountainside. Sitting in the rear tray with no idea of where we'll end up, I'm overcome with a sense of achievement. This very scenario of meeting strangers and hitching a ride was exactly what I'd expected to encounter during this trip when imagining it back home.

Diverting from the main road, we join a dirt track that passes through a set of wrought iron gates before leading us into a ploughed paddock. Slowing to a halt, the truck is rushed by a pack of barking dogs that jump up at the sides, trying to get to us.

"Fuckin' hell!" Dan screams, backing away. "They're mental!"

A farmer appears and calms the dogs down shooing them away before heaving a churn of milk up into the tray. We continue on, twisting and turning up the mountain road.

"This'll be butter by the time it arrives!" I shout to Dan over the whirr of the noisy truck engine pointing at the churn, laughing. Destined for a different location, the driver tells Dan he'll drop us in the village of El Salto near the brewery. Before long, he slows to a halt at a small orange wooden church.

"¡Jerome's, allí!" the men say, refusing our offers of money and pointing us up the road into the village. "¡Adios muchachos!"

The truck speeds away, leaving us once again to fend for ourselves in another unfamiliar location. I remember what Rick said: Everywhere is a new place, never lonely. The heat of the sun is intense and we have no choice but to follow the road so we hoist our backpacks on our backs and start walking. We pass a row of small weatherboard dwellings and soon come to a sign, hanging on a wall, that reads 'JEROME'S'.

We've found our spot.

Vines grow from the trellis and sprout purple and white flowers. They lead into a shady pub garden where we make ourselves comfortable in a pair of beautifully handcrafted log armchairs.

"¿De donde vienen ustedes?" a stoutly built man asks, handing us a beer menu and curious about where we're from.

"Nueva Zelanda," Dan answers, while his eyes scan the extensive tap beer varieties on offer.

"¡Muy lejos! ¡Bienvenidos! Soy Jerome," the rosy-cheeked man replies, welcoming us and clearly surprised by how far we've come to try his beer. "¿Como sabe de mi negocio?" he adds, curious as to how we've learnt of his place.

We tell him about meeting Rick at the campsite. He nods his head – he remembers the guy, yes – and tells us of another site in a national park a little way further up into the mountains. He then starts us off with a dark red beer topped with a creamy head of froth. Making short work of the refreshingly crisp brew and quenching the dryness we're now feeling from the altitude change, Dan and I spend the next few hours trying the majority of the menu and well and truly blow our budget. When we finally step back out onto the road, we're shaded from the late afternoon sun by a blanket of autumn leaves that flutter from the trees in hues of red, gold and orange. It is an altogether surreal experience, our heads now swimming in Jerome's beer.

We walk uphill away from the village for a half hour or so and reach a trail of andesite rock that veers off to the left where a small wooden hut stands. Inside the hut sits a padlocked wooden deposit box on a lone table that asks for a campground fee of eight pesos. Pinned to the walls are posters of an archaeological site of caves containing ancient murals, situated further up into the mountains.

"We should go there!" I suggest, looking to Dan for approval.

"Nah, it's an eight-hour hike," he replies.

So we drop our coins in the slot and follow the trail further uphill through a bright green gorge where snow-capped mountain peaks backdrop the campsite. We erect our tent next to a crystal clear glacier stream that gurgles its way downhill, and we can see now that the site is carpeted in the purple and yellow flowers that surround the lakes in Potrerillos, making the autumn afternoon feel like spring. Heating our food and blanketed by a star-filled sky, we soon snuggle into the tiny tent for a good night's sleep.

Shuffling noises outside the tent wake us at 3 am.

"Dan, Dan!" I whisper, trying to shake him awake. "Dude, there's someone outside."

I fail to rouse Dan from his deep sleep. So, trying to be as quiet as possible, and too scared to turn my headlight on, I nervously unzip a hole in the door to try and get a look at who or what is outside. The shuffling noises seem to have stopped, and I cautiously poke my whole head out.

"FUCK!" I shout suddenly as a clump of hair swishes into my face. "FUCK!" I shout again, falling back into the tent.

"What's happening?" Dan mumbles, waking up.

"We're surrounded by wild horses," I tell him, turning on my headlight. "They've been scaring the shit out of me for the past hour, stamping and stumbling on our guy ropes."

"Turn that fucking light off! You're fucking blinding me!" Dan barks, his forearm covering his eyes. Fumbling for the button, I put out the beam and lie down relieved our intruders are only of the horse kind. Dan is already snoring.

Some hours later, I wake within the sauna heat of the tent. I'm blinded by the sun, as I zip open the door flap. The horses are happily munching away on tufts of green grass on the hillside. They look harmless in the light of day. I fire up the camp stove for a coffee. The nutty trail mix that blew our budget back in Mendoza makes for a sufficient but boring breakfast and I find a comfortable spot on the mossy grass in the sun. Dan surfaces a few hours later and, after a coffee, walks the two kilometres back to the village for cigarettes. During his three-hour absence, I drift away in the crisp air of my idyllic surroundings and stare mesmerised at the snow peaks that tower all around.

Here, in this near-perfect setting, my issues with what I'm expecting out of my trip and my frustrations with the Spanish language resurface. I have to start lessons if I want to build my confidence to talk to and meet locals, but at the current speed we are travelling it's almost impossible to arrange studying more than one lesson in one place. I'm going to have to find somewhere to hole up and settle for a while – but where?

Before I have more time to resolve the internal battle with myself, Dan returns, out of breath and drenched in sweat but happy he's been able to find cigarettes. Our last camp stove dinner of rice and tuna follows, washed down with more Fernet that Dan picked up with the cigarettes as the sun drops behind us.

"Let's hit the road tomorrow," Dan says, turning to me for approval.

"Good idea, bro," I reply. "We should probably leave early though. I hope there's a bus from Potrerillos tomorrow."

Another blazing hot morning in the tent gets us up early and we set out from the campground. The road runs downhill all the way through El Salto. It's the perfect terrain for our boards, and we fly through the village, refreshed by the cool air from the tunnel of willow trees lining the streets. The dropped jaws and stunned faces of the locals follow us as we speed by; they look as though they are seeing UFOs. The wind on our faces soon changes as the road levels out and our boards slow to a stop. Reattaching the boards to our packs, we resume walking, following the roadside with thumbs out just as we did on the way up. Not one single vehicle slows down to pick us up and we drag ourselves along in the blazing midday heat for close to ten kilometres. Around the halfway mark my left ankle swells under the weight of the pack and the length of the walk. I've been having problems with this ankle for years, the result of countless twists and sprains from skateboarding. I have a nasty feeling this is going to be giving me some trouble during the next nine months on the road and I'm not looking forward to the agony it will bring, especially with the hiking I've been looking forward to.

Two hours later we arrive at the bus lay-by, me now wincing with my swollen joint and eager to get the weight off it. The old brown bus conveniently pulls in moments after we take our packs off, and I am more than relieved that I don't have to walk any more. We climb on board, grab a seat and let out a sigh as the bus crunches into gear and continues its journey back to Mendoza.

CHAPTER FIVE
MENDOZA REVISITED

Arriving back in Mendoza in the late afternoon, we stand at the back of a long queue in the reception of the Campo Base hostel. As we inch our way forward, it's not until we reach the desk that we're informed they are full. The desk lady is apologetic and suggests we try their sister hostel five blocks away. Stepping out into the night, I think back to the Potrerillos campsite. The freedom, the fresh air, the ease of finding a place to sleep simply by erecting the micro tent.

The second hostel has vacancies.

Two Irish lads saunter in and join us. Dave, sporting a greasy blond flat-top haircut, owns a face of bright red zits and is wearing a pair of vomit-patterned board shorts coupled with a beer-stained Tottenham Hotspur shirt. Craig, the shorter of the two, has a curly bob and a set of teeth that look like they haven't been brushed for three weeks. A thin gold chain clings to his neck and hangs limply outside of his Manchester United football shirt. They'd tried sleeping on the floor in the Mendoza bus station the night before last, they tell us, but were moved on every hour by police and have since checked into this place.

Leaving the Irish lads in their cloud of cigarette smoke, Dan and I check in and are allocated the top mattress of a four-high bunk bed in a narrow broom cupboard. Jamming the door from the inside are several backpacks on the floor that won't fit into the already full lockers. Squeezing through the crack, I do my best to make enough space for us to get in. As much as I'm loving the nomad lifestyle, it's times like this when I wish I was in a luxury hotel room of my own, ordering room service without this clutter. Even better, I imagine sitting by a fire next to my tent.

We climb halfway up the ladder and toss our bags up onto the bunk, then we take to the streets in search of food.

"We have to find one of those all-you-can-eat 'Parilla' buffets – I'm fucking starving," Dan says.

A staple of Argentinean life, Dan has told me these restaurants consist of a large barbecue grill area, where huge chunks of meat are slowly roasted over a log fire, accompanied by an enormous buffet bar of salads, vegetables and whatever else you care to feast on, all but an arm's length away. When we finally find one of these places, albeit a slightly more up-market establishment – not at all, in fact, as Dan has described. The red neon sign glows above our outside table. We order a bottle of red wine while scanning the menu.

"This is what we want," Dan tells me, pointing at one of the options. "You get a bit of everything with this."

After a week of bland camp meals, I am ready for this meal. My anticipation of the medieval banquet we're about to receive is fuelled more by my hunger pains and a glass of delicious wine. Finally, the feast is placed in front of us. Still sizzling on a hotplate, the food wafts up and I inhale greedily.

Then I open my eyes.

Before us is a collection of animal parts that I've never had the opportunity to try before. In fact, they are unrecognisable.

"Intestines," Dan says, poking a long, charred semi-coiled tube with his knife.

"And that?" I ask, looking at a wobbly, pale pink blob sitting to the side of the coiled intestines.

"Udders." Dan flicks the blob with his fork and it shakes like jelly.

The tubes have a foul taste and seem to be only partially emptied of semi-digested food while the udders have an unusual texture that slips around my plate like they're alive. I find the meal hard to stomach but I am trying to remain composed.

"All the other bits are cuts of meat, just eat those," Dan says, sensing my disinterest and gobbling up the intestines and udder before sawing into a chunk of steak.

Back at the hostel bar, curly-bobbed Manchester United Craig pulls out his camera.

"Do yer fink it's serious?" he says, showing us photos of the red spots he's discovered on his dick. There are too many photographs, from too many angles.

"Nah," I reply, lying. I am shocked this guy I hardly know is showing me photos of his penis like it's nothing, but I add expertly, "You'll be fine; they'll go away in a couple of days."

He continues to examine his photos.

"How d'you get them? The spots?" I ask.

"I fucked dis bird at der hostel in Buenos Aires," he says. "I fink she gave me summink."

Changing the subject and hoping to pry some valuable information from Craig and his companion Dave, I ask about the Uyuni salt flats in Bolivia. "So you got any tips for the Uyuni trip? Didn't you mention you'd just come from there?"

I try to waft away the cigarette smoke Dave keeps blowing in my face.

"Yeah! So wicked, that place!" he exclaims, puffing another grey cloud of smoke towards me. "That salty ground is wicked for football, bit cold up there though, innit." He flicks the long stem of ash from his cigarette. "There's this place in La Paz called Wild Rover, it's an Irish hostel where they serve Guinness and screen football games 24/7."

He's clearly more excited by this than by the Uyuni salt flats.

"That's it?" I remark. I don't know what I was expecting.

"Well, it's nice and all that, but it just gets a bit boring." He lights another cigarette.

Craig returns just then with another round of beers, and excitedly joins in with an equally useless bit of information. "There's this illegal basement bar called 'Route forty six' where you can buy cocaine legally," he says, smiling happily with his chipped brown teeth.

"Where is it?" Dan says. "We gotta check that out!"

Dan turns to me, now with a goal to aim for when we hit Bolivia.

"They moove every monf so der police never find out where dey are until it's too late," Craig adds. "Just ask around at der Rover, someone'll know."

Dan sips his beer eagerly and stores the vital information somewhere in his alcohol-soaked brain.

Dave and Craig slide off their barstools and bid farewell to the mess of empty pint glasses, crushed cigarette packets and over-full ashtrays that cover the table. They grab their backpacks in preparation for the walk to the bus station. "See yer!" they call out, walking away unsteadily, drunk and disappearing into the night.

I meet many such backpackers along the way. I come to anticipate them. I come to know who they are by the backpacks they carry, by the groups they sit in. And by the things that excite them. Cocaine haven over salt flats, for example. You can spot them from across a room if you know what to look for. You can certainly tell after a pint of beer. These are the 'list ticking' backpackers who spend 80% of their time inside hostels; they are not only common but hard to avoid, a different breed to the remote-control travellers who want everything like home. Where those travellers surround themselves with familiarity and security, these travellers launch themselves into risky scenarios with a dangerous sense of confidence (naiveté) wherever they go, be it a swanky part of town or a maze of backstreet alleys looking for cheap drugs.

"I'm tired, I'm off to bed," I tell Dan, getting off my barstool. "See you tomorrow," I add, leaving him with his cigarette.

Retiring to my dorm and squeezing through the crack in the door, I stumble through the layer of backpacks littering the floor like old tyres laid out on an obstacle course. Climbing up the long ladder past the three bunks below, I sink into a spring-less mattress inches from the roof while a noisy, lint-clogged extractor fan blows warm, sweaty air in my face.

CHAPTER SIX
BUENOS AIRES

It is a long bus ride from Mendoza to Buenos Aires. Dan and I stretch our legs one last time in the park near where we landed a mere two weeks prior and gather our things. We've opted for the medium-priced seats, and the next sixteen hours are spent fidgeting and shifting, trying to find a comfortable position to sleep in before the light of dawn slices through the crack in the curtains that keeps the speeding night just out of reach.

I pull back the curtains and peer down on the now sunlit, empty urban streets from above, and I see an endless stream of side streets flash by. We have arrived. And I see now that this is a sprawling city, unlike anything I've seen before. The maze of interlocking corrugated iron shacks neighbouring the Retiro bus terminal is an altogether frightening sight. I momentarily long for the tranquil, picturesque places we've spent camping during the last two weeks. Stray dogs limp along the narrow dirt alleys that separate the makeshift dwellings while shady-looking characters lurk in doorways. On our side of the high-walled fence that separates the ghetto from the terminal, the bus waits for an empty bay while families wait to board buses and smart-suited business folk with briefcases head to work in the morning rush. The terminal is an unnervingly sprawling hub of chaos that connects the length and breadth of South America to Buenos Aires by countless long-distance bus companies. The giant station also provides links to the far fringes of the city via its underground train network and cluttered mess of smog-choking mini-buses and yellow taxi cabs that honk and jostle for business outside in the dirty streets that surround it.

Joining these commuters, Dan and I barge our way down into the bowels of the terminal and jump into a squeaky crowded subway train, navigating our way over to the swankier Palermo area on the northeast side of the city.

"Palermo's way better," Dan assures me. "I stayed there last time."

We ride the subway for three stops, alighting into the confusing mess of Diagonal Norte station before squeezing into another train with a pleasant smell of soap and hair gel from the passengers on their way to work. During the long ride, an assortment of beggars and buskers take their turns to walk the aisle playing instruments, breakdancing on torn sheets of cardboard or simply holding their hands out mumbling 'dinero'. I ignore them all, not wanting to pull out my wallet on the busy train for fear of being followed and robbed.

Ten stops, one saxophone, two bad guitar riffs and a few backspins later, the carriage delivers us to the Palermo district. Surfacing on the sidewalk we are surrounded by noise and a wide-laned street. I'm not so sure about Dan's assertion.

I'm really not so sure this looks any better than the place we've left. But I follow him and his bobbing backpack as he veers off down a side street, leaving the chaos behind us.

Our hostel is one of many four-storey terraced apartment blocks that line either side of a leafy street. This hostel seems to cater for every type. Older couples, families, gap-year students, you name it, come and go along the corridor that passes the narrow, inner courtyard. The courtyard is open-air but walled in, much like a very wide elevator shaft with no roof – and clearly where people meet; as we pass by, I see other guests seated at the many glass-topped tables, smoking cigarettes and playing cards.

Our dorm is three flights up. It is surprisingly clean and has a freshly painted scent. Unpacking his bag on an adjacent bunk is a guy with a fancy haircut wearing short shorts.

"Hey man, have you just arrived too?" I ask him, wanting to break the ice.

"Yes, but I'm not staying for long," he says in a French accent with a troubled glance.

"Why's that?"

"I followed some guys from the street selling tickets to a bar, and they scammed me for three hundred dollars."

"What!" Dan and I both exclaim together. "How?!"

"The flyers he was handing out were for a bar with free drinks where lots of pretty girls go," he says, now with his head in his hands and obviously realising how naïve he's been. "I was talking to a girl when these fucking guys surround me and get heavy, telling me that I have to buy her a drink before I can leave."

"So how did they get three hundred bucks out of you?" Dan asks. I feel bad that we're prying, but we are both dying to know.

"That's how much the drink was. Bastards!" He is now almost in tears.

"Fuck, sorry, man. That sucks," I tell him, now feeling slightly awkward and looking for an escape from the situation.

Dan clears his throat. "You wanna come get some food?" Dan's like that, always wanting to help, trying to change the subject.

"NO!" The force of his angry reply surprises both of us. "I have no fucking money! I have to call my parents in France tonight!"

We leave the poor French fellow in the dorm to sulk and head to a small supermarket around the corner. The streets are pleasantly subdued, away from the main street but quiet enough to feel dangerous. The supermarket is Vietnamese-owned, but the Asian folk running it speak perfect Argentine Spanish and although they have a good variety of vegetables to choose from their manners are rude and their replies short. Shrugging off their vibe, we realise when we arrive back at our hostel how ravenous we are; we cook up the fresh vegetables in a large pot in the hostel kitchen before retiring to bed.

This first night in Buenos Aires, I'm feeling rather low, still carrying the thoughts about not being able to converse in the native language. How can I possibly carry on without communicating properly? I feel absurd relying on Dan as I do. Suddenly, I am unsure why I'm here, trapped within the walls of each hostel we visit. Here, I'm safe but unchallenged; outside, I follow at the heels of Dan like a young puppy. I am unable to communicate with 95% of the people I come into contact with. Surrounded by the chaos of a large city instead of the space and sky of the last few weeks, I realise now how absurd my situation is: I am unable to get by on my own. Dan, meanwhile, is enjoying being back in Buenos Aires where he spent nine months the previous year studying and living with his (now ex) Argentinean girlfriend. Unlike me, meek and afraid to go to the grocery shop, Dan is revelling in using his Spanish skills with the local people. We are changing with every passing day: Dan is uplifted by the city, and I feel dark and brooding.

Like Santiago, Buenos Aires is, for us, an unexplored concrete jungle that Dan and I as skateboarders need to discover. And when we head out into the unknown streets, I feel the blues lift a little. Weaving through the endless city blocks, hopping up and down kerbs and leaping over bollards and anything else in the way, we get a good take on city life and the people who inhabit it. Apart from the mobile phones hidden away in leather belt pouches, the people of this city could be from any of the last three decades, businessmen in dated but smart suits adorning 1980s hairstyles to professional dog walkers in Lycra who block the smooth marble pavements with ten dogs each stretching out from their arms on leashes. We encounter all kinds of city folk in this seemingly timeless and vast, sprawling place.

The city is a melting pot of cultures, with, I soon discover, an almost Italian or European feel to it. Besides the many Vietnamese supermarkets that become our regular suppliers for our home-cooked meals, French and Italian restaurants are in abundance. The marble buildings of the business district strike a deep contrast to the older, more ornate, dark concrete architecture and pastel-coloured apartments that make up the city avenues, their balconies bursting with hanging pot plants.

One day we take our regular route into the downtown area, and when we pop up out of the subway, we find ourselves in the middle of a crowd of protesters riding in the backs of pick-up trucks waving homemade banners. Red- and black-lettered slogans painted onto sheets and stapled to sticks wave in the wind and form part of the scene. People sing and chant in long lines stretching side-to-side across the wide main streets. I am struck by the size of it, and by the peaceful feel of it – not a pepper-spray hose in sight.

We watch the protest march disappear in the distance, its chanting fades away down one of the city's main streets. Then we make our way over to the Recoletta Cemetery, famous for its elaborate tombs that house the deceased upper echelons of Argentinean society – the famous First Lady of Argentina, Eva Perón, among them. A grid of walkways lined with these finely decorated tombs and polished marble shrines fill the gated graveyard that stands in the middle of the downtown area, surrounded by tall office blocks and beautifully appointed apartment buildings. Being a popular tourist spot, it is crowded and does not hold much allure for Dan and me, though I'm glad to have felt the oddly deep pull of history here, wandering through the decaying echelons of Argentinian aristocracy, thinking about these important people in history I've never heard of, contemplating what a tiny speck I am in the grand scale of things.

We spend only a short time inside the Recoletta Cemetery walls. Sitting down outside a café, we are greeted by a gypsy woman who places a playing card-sized holy picture on our table and carries on walking, doing the same to others.

"Don't touch it." Dan orders me. "It's a scam." He explains further: "You pick it up, you pay for it. She'll be back." He finishes with a confidence in his words.

Sure enough she re-treads her route, taking her cards back but not before whining a mild beg for money.

The following day a wooden-panelled subway train shakes its way out to an indoor skate park in the not-so-wealthy district of Flores. As we rattle our way down the blue line for forty-five minutes, the passengers transform from smartly suited businessmen who don't notice us from behind their newspapers to less mainstream individuals who eyeball us curiously. I begin to worry about what type of scenario we're going to be faced with when we emerge above ground from Flores' empty tube station. I could not have anticipated the fright I got.

The street dog is wild and aggressive, and he takes a shine to my board.

"FUCK OFF!" I shout at the mangy mutt, struggling to pull my board from its jaws.

The dog refuses to let go now he has his jaws round the end of my board. He twists his neck and growls, chewing the end ferociously. For a brief moment I think he will win. But I will not give up so easily, and I hold firm and yell again. Just as I wonder if he speaks English – making a mental note that I must learn to tell a dickhead dog (*puto perro?*) to fuck off in Spanish – he finally lets go and disappears down a back alley, leaving my board with teeth marks and us alone in an area of ramshackle houses that sit behind an iron fence under a grey concrete motorway fly-over.

"It's this way," Dan says, throwing down his board and skating off.

We arrive just as the employees are pulling up the squeaky graffiti-covered roller shutters of the skate park. Shaded by the same motorway fly-over shadowing the subway entrance, the huge concrete bowl, with 11-foot transitioned walls lipped with a strip of cobalt blue tiles, is surrounded by a decent wooden street obstacle area with a hot dog kiosk-cum-skate shop at the entrance. The arrangement of the ramps and obstacles allow for seamless flow and continuous runs. This is one of the best and most useable skateboard parks I've had the pleasure of riding.

Soon, however, the flow becomes more of a collision course as the place fills with skaters battling for space. This doesn't deter Dan in the slightest. Quite the contrary: he blazes a trail around the street course while I capture it all on the video setting of his point-and-shoot camera. His boundless energy continues for a good hour. I get my fill, too, though I am less daredevil than Dan and choose often to observe the local kids who know the various lines and angles like the back of their hands.

Only when the day starts to fade do we return to the city with the train – no *puto perro* this time – and arrive back at El Retiro terminal exhausted but in one piece.

The French guy who fell for the $300-a-drink scam has since left, replaced with a mother and daughter who tell us they're from Uruguay.

"Come and stay with us when you arrive," the mother offers on learning we're from New Zealand. "Uruguay is very quiet." She speaks in a good English accent. "Very different to Buenos Aires. Here, you take my number." She hands us her email address and phone number on a piece of paper.

"Thanks!" I reply, folding it and putting it in my wallet. "How long are you here for?" I ask, wanting to know more about them if we're going to stay at their place if we end up going there.

"Ah, just two days," she answers, tying her greying hair in a bun. "I'm just here for business. We are thinking of sending Jaqui to college in New Zealand, so it would be good to talk to you guys again."

In the morning, we venture across the city in the opposite direction to where the Boca Junior football team (made famous by Diego Maradona) are playing River Plate at the huge stadium, which is situated near a tourist attraction shantytown called El Caminito. The streets are filled with supporters heading to the game and the whole area borders the sprawling slums that surround the stadium. Armed police are posted on every corner.

We don't have tickets for the game and really, we're more interested in directions to an antique market a few blocks away, so Dan approaches a group of people and asks, "¿De que dirección es la feria de San Pedro Telmo?"

They argue between themselves and speak in what we've come to view as typically Argentine, all having their own ideas of which way it is, and no one agreeing with the other.

"¡Por allá! ¡Por allá!" they say, pointing in different directions, still arguing with each other, gesticulating vehemently. Looking at them, I think of those poles found at tourist spots adorned with yellow distance arrows that point to various far-off corners of the world. Except my imaginary arrows all say the same destination.

None the wiser, Dan follows his instinct, and we walk off in the direction he thinks he remembers from his previous travels. But I soon realise he's stricken with a thirst for beer, and seems to be focused on finding a liquor store more than our destination.

And that is how we ended up in a situation I'll never forget.

I suppose it was bound to happen sometime on this trip. I suppose if we follow our instincts in strange, sprawling and sometimes wild places long enough, it'll surely end in trouble. I just didn't expect it to happen on this particular Saturday morning.

Dan's wild goose chase through a maze of backstreets brings us out at a busy, heavily policed cross-section of a main road. The street, clogged with taxis, overflows in a sea of blue and yellow football jerseys.

"We should get a taxi," I suggest. "It's starting to look a little sketchy." I am now feeling vulnerable and not afraid to admit it.

"Nah, we'll be sweet, bro, I know the area," Dan assures me. And then: "Sweet! There's a liquor store over there."

Dan is shouting over his shoulder, crossing the road. I follow him reluctantly. What choice do I have, really?

Exiting the store with a cold beer, we walk another block away from the hustle of match day.

"This is getting worse." I say, looking up and down the deserted alley we're in. "Are you sure we're supposed to be here?"

"Aquí no mas," three girls say, walking arm in arm as they pass us, moving quickly in the direction of the stadium.

"What did they say, Dan?"

"Can't go any further with beer," Dan says, tossing his empty bottle into an open dumpster.

But I'm not feeling safe with Dan's decisions, and I put my foot down. "I'm heading to the main road up here at the corner, whether you're coming or not," I say defiantly, sensing with a growing creep of dread that we're now somewhere we shouldn't be.

And then it happens. Suddenly, out of nowhere, three rough-looking characters in trainers, jeans and football shirts surround us and, before we can manage a civil *Excuse me*, they push us around and demand money. Slamming Dan against a car, two of them strip him of his credit card, money and camera while the other pins me against a wall and pulls out a gun from under his grubby t-shirt.

How the fuck did I end up here races through my mind as I feel the cold barrel of his pistol pushing against my head.

"¡¡Munny!! ¡¡Munny!! ¡¡Munny!!" he demands aggressively as one hand rifles through my pockets while the other keeps the pistol pressed against my temple. His giant psychotic pupils are a sure sign he's high on crack and his greasy fingers frantically dig deep for loose notes and change in my pockets. "¡Bolsa! ¡Bolsa!" he shouts, demanding my bag. Violation runs through my veins. Dan is pinned against a car and still being roughed up. Out of the corner of my eye, I can see he's lost his glasses. I see him squinting from the glaring sun.

For some reason, I have a feeling the gun isn't loaded and my split-second reaction is to push the skinny crackhead away from me. I do so with enough force to catch him off guard. He stumbles back, regains his composure and laughs, shouting something to his mates while keeping the pistol trained on me. Seeing my chance, I turn to run, but before I take a step I feel the whack of the gun handle on the top of my head.

"Fuck you!" I shout at him, cowering. "Here's the backpack! I have nothing else! I have nothing else!"

I am screaming now, covering my head with my hands and still cowering against the wall. I am certain he's going to shoot me.

Still laughing, he rips the bag from my hands and they all run off up the street.

"¡Mis anteojos!" Dan shouts to one of them, pleading for his glasses back. Tossing them over his shoulder, the youth laughs as we watch the glasses skid and bounce across the road, stopping at our feet. Dan bends down to pick them up. They are badly scratched but better than nothing.

Our assailants disappear within seconds with their bounty and all I can think about is the roll of film containing the images I've captured so far that I'll never see again.

"Fuck, my head," I groan, now angrier than ever and feeling the eggy lump growing on my skull. We quickly walk up the street in silence and find a policeman back at the cross-section.

"We've been robbed! We've been robbed!" we tell him, shaking and distressed.

"Ustedes tambien," he says – *you two as well* – casually handing us a cigarette each and clearly not surprised by what we're telling him.

We follow the policeman to the station. I'm torn between exploding at Dan for walking us into a loaded gun and shouting in relief that we are still alive.

The police station is of a by-gone era. It reminds me of a scene from a *Dirty Harry* movie. There are missing children posters pinned to a cork board in a room with dusty blinds. There are beams of sunlight leaking through those dusty blinds. And there is a square wooden table where we are asked to sit and file reports. We try to give the officer a description of the thieves, and soon we are joined in the station by a Brazilian guy and his wife, who also had their rental bicycles and cameras snatched. And then, suddenly, the station is full. One by one, more distressed victims arrive with similar stories to ours.

"Bounty day for the Boca scumbags," Dan says, regretting his actions.

Finishing up our reports, we are informed by the officer that we can get a taxi from outside. I rifle around in my deep pocket – where the thief couldn't reach – and find just enough notes to get us home.

Bouncing along in the back of the taxi, I feel like I'm sinking in a place where I can't communicate. It's daunting enough just trying to buy simple things from a store; now, after what just happened, I'm starting to doubt if this trip was really a good idea in the first place.

Fortunately, the busy atmosphere back at the hostel helps to partially wipe away the robbery, and we treat ourselves to a nice meal in an elegant little restaurant to lighten the mood.

But adding to the insult of our already miserable day, the macho Argentinean waiter ignores us for twenty minutes, immediately serving two girls who arrive after us before finally coming to our table.

"¿Si?" he says rudely, as if we've caused him a great inconvenience by interrupting his sleazeball act with the girls and making him walk over to our table.

"Dos vino tintos y dos platos de Albóndigas, gracias," Dan says confidently, asking him for wine and meatballs.

The waiter's shocked reaction to Dan's Spanish can't hide the fact that he thought we didn't understand the menu. He struts away with our order like a naughty child. Infuriating him more, we get chatting to the girls that he's been greasing up since their arrival. The two friendly Chileans have beautiful almond eyes and innocent smiles and seem happy to join us for dinner.

"I'm Dani and this is my friend Dayanara," the more forward one of the two says, holding out her thin hand.

"Hi!" I reply without hesitation and shaking her hand.

We learn they are on a weekend shopping trip from Santiago, Chile, and that they are, coincidentally, also booked in at our hostel. We hit it off with them, chatting for the rest of the meal and kicking a plastic bottle to each other in the street while walking home.

"Something good always comes from bad," Dan says, trying to lighten my mood before booting the bottle over to the girls as they laugh and tackle each other in the gutter for it.

With only a block to go, our fun is ruined by two police officers who take the bottle and throw it in a bin before lecturing us about not running around in the streets making noise after 9pm.

"You smoke?" Dani asks us, while we sit with them between the chimneys on the roof of the hostel.

"Sure do," Dan answers, draining his beer bottle.

"Cool." Dani sticks her hand down her bra and pulls out a little bag of weed. "It's from Santiago. Good hiding place, no?" she says with a wink.

Rolling a joint, she converses with Dan in Spanish to keep Dayanara included before switching to English for a bit to keep me informed. She's nice like that – and I'm grateful after the day we've had to be part of the congenial group.

"This trip is helping me to take my mind off my ex-fiancé," Dani says as the night draws to a close. "He went home to Paris and jumped in front of a subway train."

"Holy shit, I'm sorry to hear that," I remark awkwardly, taking a drag on the joint and hoping that Dan's going to say something to ease the terrible moment.

But we sit in stoned silence and that seems good enough. The only noise for a while is air-conditioning ducts as they belch out white smoke into the night air.

It's Dani who speaks next, and I'm startled by her cheery tone. "We should swap emails?" She hands Dan a pencil and notebook from her bag.

Dan takes the pencil and scribbles our addresses into the book but says, "I don't think we'll be in Santiago again though."

"No, but maybe we will come to New Zealand!" Dani says, unconvincingly.

It is a strange way to end the day, and I have no expectations that we'd cross paths again. And so it is beyond surprising that, a year after returning home, I receive a random email from Dayanara – *Hi it's Dayanara from Chile! We met in Buenos Aires and now I'm in the South Island of New Zealand. Do you remember me? I am coming to Auckland. Can I stay with you?* – which in a few nights on my couch turns into a short-lived and turbulent relationship, ending in tears when I visit her in Chile to meet her family – but that's another story for another time, and for now, the fallout from the robbery are the most immediate and pressing issues.

CHAPTER SEVEN
TIGRE

The next morning, Dan is up early, trying to contact his bank in New Zealand in an effort to get a new credit card sent over.

"It's a pain in the arse!" he moans. "They can't issue me a card unless I go to the bank in person. What sort of shit is that? I'm on the other side of the world, for fuck's sake."

Eventually making some headway with his problem, he is informed by the bank that his father can go in and sign for a new card which he can then send to him.

"It's gonna take a couple of weeks," he says.

"Are you fucking serious?" I explode. He knows I'm dying to leave the city behind after the robbery. I am fuming at this further delay and how complicated our situation has become. I think for a way out of here. "Have you tried to contact Emi?" I ask him over breakfast, already knowing the answer.

On his previous trip to Buenos Aires, Dan met a guy by the name of Emilio through his ex-girlfriend, and I remember he'd mentioned it would be worth making the effort to contact him when we were planning our trip.

"Nah, but I 'spose I should, aye?" he mutters in a half-interested tone. He is more interested in the free cornflakes he's shoving into his mouth than actually solving our situation.

"Well, now that we have to wait for your card, we may as well squeeze that in before we go to Uruguay," I suggest, frustrated at his laziness.

"But I've got no money, bro," he says. "You'll have to lend me some."

I reluctantly agree. "Anything to get out of here, man."

I continue to pester Dan for a few days while we sit around the hostel. Finally, he gets annoyed with me and sits down to email Emilio.

"He's probably not even here anymore." His tone says he's not bothered if we catch up with the guy or not.

"But maybe he is!" I answer, trying to stay calm and positive.

The reply arrives the same day. *'Dan my friend! You came back! You must call me.'* Emilio includes his number.

"This sounds promising," I say excitedly, turning to Dan.

"Yeah, could be," he mutters, still indifferent.

Dialling the number on the telephone at the reception desk, Dan is greeted with the warm welcome of Emi's voice on the other end.

"Hey! You are in my city! This is great! I have missed you, my friend!" he says, excitedly. "I live in Tigre now, I will take you to my holiday cabin by boat!" he continues, sounding more excited with every word.

"Where's that?" Dan asks.

"Tigre is a small town an hour north by train from the city. I'll meet you tomorrow at 2pm outside the station."

"Alright, alright," Dan says to me, putting the phone down and reading my smug 'I told you so' grin.

"A weekend at a holiday house nestled in the back water estuaries of the Rio Plata after what we've just been through?" I exclaim, super excited. "It's exactly what we need to take our minds off the robbery!"

Checking out of the hostel the next day we find ourselves back in the shifty and chaotic atmosphere of the El Retiro terminal. Images of the Boca incident are returning to haunt me as the train bound for Tigre grinds out through the sprawling northern suburbs. From the window, the neighbourhoods become increasingly rundown while the carriage grows emptier at every stop. Thankfully, the scenery gradually changes from unfinished, tatty concrete dwellings to green fields and pastures and eventually terminates at a pretty little town with an elegantly turreted white hotel situated on a riverbank.

In true Argentine style, Emilio shows up an hour late.

"¡Hola muchachos! ¿Como estamos?" he greets us with no mention of or apology for his tardiness. Climbing into the back seat of his small white Fiat, I listen as he and Dan chat away and reminisce while we drive to where his boat is kept.

Navigating the Fiat through a cluster of dry storage boat sheds, Emilio pulls up at his speedboat. It is no more than four metres long: a compact, fine thing. The chrome trim around the windscreen accentuates its glossy white paint job and the polished wooden floorboards.

"¡Tengo comida!" he says, informing us he has food and handing us several heavy bags loaded with hunks of meat, beer and firewood. "¡Prisa! ¡Prisa!" he shouts to the old guy winching the vessel up off the dock.

"He's concerned about the low tide," Dan says, pointing down into the muddy estuary.

"¡Es un poco profundo!" Emi exclaims.

"Too shallow" Dan translates.

"¡¡Vamos!! Vamos!!" Emi continues, waving his arms around like a deranged baboon and convincing the guy to winch his boat into the brown river. With only ten minutes to spare before the inlet is too low, we scale a rotten ladder down off the edge of the dock and he fires up the engine.

Zooming out towards the deeper waters of the Rio Plata with the wind in our hair, we pass half-sunken rusty submarine carcasses and old dredging boats that lie orange, corroding and abandoned on the mud flats before meeting up with the giant brown river. Over a mile wide and separating Argentina from Uruguay, the vast stretch of water is a gurgling mess of currents and waves that smash into our tiny vessel, making for a rough ride. I am relieved when we veer off into the extensive network of narrow estuaries from the main river, and the surface calms.

Soon, we enter a whole other community that exists within the mangrove swamps. Polished high-gloss wood-panelled boats putter along, while adobe houses on sticks and more abandoned boat hulls sit on the banks outside regal mansions boasting manicured hedges and immaculate lawns. As we meander further into the swamplands, a large flatbed barge approaches, overloaded with shrink-wrapped pallets of fizzy drinks and other edible treats.

"¡Parar!" Emi calls out in a bid to stop the floating supermarket, waving his arms again. The vessel slows to a crawl and he jumps aboard, grabbing a few bottles of drinking water and some homemade cakes to accompany the meat and beer.

As we continue on, the estuary shrinks to a narrow tunnel of muddy foliage and thickly entwined mangroves. We're now riding the high tide, and daylight starts to darken. The canopy of leaves and branches above make it more so. I start to wonder when we'll arrive – *if* we'll arrive – and just then, with not a moment to lose before darkness sets in fully, we moor up at a rickety wooden jetty that's now submerged with the tide.

"¡Aqui esta!" Emi shouts with his arms spread out. "My House!"

At the rear of the flooded plain that at low tide is his front garden, stands a dilapidated but quaintly haggard structure. Like a scene from *Huckleberry Finn*, its cracked pink cement-board wall panels and mismatching window frames are perched precariously head high above the ground on old wooden stilts and surrounded by an untamed mangrove forest. *Holiday house,* I think to myself with a silent chuckle, re-envisaging what sort of place I'd thought we were coming to stay at.

Climbing out of the boat, we're greeted by thousands of vicious mosquitoes and a black dog with no collar who follows us as we walk ankle-deep in water across the garden to the house. His coat is matted with swamp mud but the speed his tail is wagging indicates he's clearly pleased to see us. A wooden ladder accesses the front door and the interior is a cramped but cosy little abode with two old couches and a small dining table that take up most of the space in the living area. A sink and a bench make up the kitchen while a small cubicle fashioned from plastic sheeting tucks itself away in the corner.

"What's in there?" I ask Emi, forgetting he knows very little English.

"¡Ducha!" he says, pulling back a strip of the plastic and revealing a cock-stop tap and a pipe sticking out of the wall.

"Shower," Dan translates.

Tending the barbecue pit in the only part of the front yard that seems to have escaped the high tide, Emi waits for his pile of oak chips to burn down before transferring a shovel full of red hot embers to a tabletop grill, spreading a thin layer under it. Splitting a whole chicken, he rubs it with what seems like way too much salt and lays it on the grill beside a large eye fillet roll an inch or two above the heat.

"¡Boca Daniel! ¡¿Que estaba pensando?! ¡¿Que estaba pensando?!" he says in a fatherly tone to Dan, regarding the stupidity of our wandering off from the Boca stadium and suggesting that Dan should've known better, especially since he's lived in Buenos Aires before. Dan shrugs sheepishly and rolls a cigarette while the fire crackles and illuminates us seated around it in a golden hue.

For the next two hours we're engulfed by the hypnotising aroma of the glowing barbecue and watch, drooling, as the fat drips and sizzles into the embers below while the meat is perfectly cooked. The dog that met us when we arrived has re-appeared and arrives at the precise moment Emi pulls the meat from the heat. My mouth is watering as I watch as he slices it on a chopping board. I take a piece of the eye fillet and experience my first real taste and texture of an authentic Argentine Asado. The meat is tender but well cooked, smoky but smooth, and flakes away in succulent strips.

"Holy fuck," I say, chewing a mouthful and taking a leg of chicken that Emi passes to me.

"Try! Try!" he urges, attacking some of the chicken meat himself.

Swallowing the steak, I bite into the leg and once again am hit with a sensory overload of flavour: the salt he was smothering the thing in beforehand – the very thing I thought to be a little overkill – now making complete sense, as the chicken melts in my mouth.

The three of us make it halfway through the joint of meat before we are belching in chorus and unable to eat any more. We sip our merlots with full but contented stomachs while the fire crackles away in the dark. "Gracias, Emi," I thank him, rubbing my belly. I'm revelling in this authentic and precious Argentine moment.

"¡Vamos a caminar!" Emi announces, springing up from his chair. "We explore!"

His rusty English shows just how much he revels in us being here.

Guiding us down a spiky-branched track that skirts the river, he brings us to another rotten jetty where we polish off another bottle of merlot by the light of the full moon.

"I love this place," he says, still trying to speak English. "The city I don't like."

I nod, agreeing while a million frogs chirrup around us. I pull the drawstrings of my raincoat hood in an effort to keep out the relentless mosquitos. With only my eyes now partially exposed, I follow the other two on the treacherous return – but it's not long before I trip on a tree root. I flap my arms in vain, trying to grab a hold of something. I fail miserably and slip down the river bank into the water, soaking a leg up to the groin while the other is now level with my head still on dry land.

"You alright?!" Dan calls from the darkness above.

"Yeah, I think so," I reply, stuck in the ridiculous position but managing to clamber my way up the embankment, more than slightly embarrassed. I squelch my way back, cursing the persistent mosquitoes, who won't give up trying to eat the backs of my hands. I'm beginning to think that Buenos Aires isn't such a bad place after all.

The unpleasantness of the walk brings a deep sleep in my soft, spongy single bed and, with a belly full of red wine and flavoursome meat, I drift off to the rhythmic chirping orchestra of frogs filling the night air across the mangroves.

I wake with a dry mouth and damp clothes. My shoe that had fallen prey to the river last night is still soaked. Breakfast consists of coffee heated over the still burning embers and the leftover beef that crumbles off the bone in my fingers with the texture of fine chocolate. It tastes better than it did at dinner.

There is now a front yard due to the low tide that has crept halfway down the piles of the jetty, and the outboard motor is tilted up out of the shallow water. Using a long pole to manoeuvre the way until the waters rise, Emi chooses the long route home through the muddy mangrove estuaries that pass squealing black pigs and dogs that bark at us from the water's edge, protecting their master's stick and tarpaulin structures that are quite possibly held together with packaging tape. As we once again steer out into the middle of the wide brown river, we're rewarded with dual views of the coasts of Uruguay, a half mile off to our port side, and Argentina, a stone's throw to starboard.

Eventually arriving back in Tigre, we unload the boat, say an emotional farewell to Emi, thanking him profusely for an unforgettable weekend, and catch the last train back to the city with an overwhelming feeling of gratitude for his hospitality.

Back at the hostel, we are quickly engrossed in city life once more. We arrive to find a group of people going out – and we decide to join them, changing our clothes and shifting gears. The evening entertainment is a bongo percussion group called 'La Bomba Tiempo'; they play every Monday at a club by the name of Konex. These sell-out nights fill a large area with a semi-circled amphitheatre of tiered stages at one end, back-dropped by large projector screens.

"I'll get beers!" Dan shouts over the sea of heads as I turn round to see him dart off in the direction of the alcohol vendor. *Here we go again.* I think of the last time he went looking for beer. The group wear matching red track suits and play an explosive set, accompanied by a guest guitar player whose handiwork is highlighted on the overhead screens. The massive energetic crowd is a sea of waving arms and dance in the large open-air courtyard. Although I can't wait to be heading north again and away from this city, the incredible sound these guys create together, not to mention Emi's hospitality over the weekend, wipe away the horrible memory of that gun barrel pushing against my head and leave me with a repaired memory of this giant place that can one minute be so hostile only to then change and give it so much hope.

CHAPTER EIGHT
COLONIA & MONTEVIDEO

"Wake up! Wake up!" I whisper at Dan, shaking him vigorously.

"Yeah, ten minutes," he grunts, rolling over and still wearing his clothes from the day before.

Leaving him to get his shit together, I head downstairs for breakfast, hoping he does actually get up soon so we don't miss our ferry for Uruguay.

Two bowls of cereal and a cup of coffee later, I return to the dorm.

I slap him round the face

"We have to leave!" I say at a slightly more raised volume than the previous whisper. "The ferry leaves in an hour and it takes at least thirty-five minutes to reach the terminal in this traffic!"

The urgency in my voice wakes someone up across the room.

"Shhh!, Too early!" says the scruffy-haired guy peering over the top of the bunk's edge like a mole. "Keep it down for fuck's sake."

Growing ever more impatient, I storm off to the bathroom to brush my teeth. When I return once again, Dan is snoring like a chainsaw. Now infuriated, I grab him by the belt and, with all my strength, pull him off the bunk. He wakes up in mid-air and lands on the floor with a thud. I think that's enough to let him know that the face slap ten minutes ago wasn't part of his dream.

Like an upturned insect, Dan squirms around on the dormitory floor, still trying to figure out where he is. The squirming quickly changes to a frantic flap as he stuffs his backpack. Charger cables, shirt sleeves and other strange useless objects hang out of the undone top. All the while, I am yelling at him, reminding him again that we need to *get moving*.

I believe either magpies or gypsies reared Dan from birth. He has an incredible skill in collecting useless shiny items of junk. I've watched how, on a daily basis, he will spot something glinting on the ground and swoop in to snatch it up to store in one of his many backpack pouches he's designated for these (he claims) useful commodities. Strips of electrical wire, nuts, bolts, screws and other shiny titbits make up his odd collection – all having failed to escape the clutches of gypsy Dan.

A perfect example is the broken car aerial he's now holding.

"I found it at the campsite in Potrerillos. It'll come in handy at some stage," he assures me.

This proclivity to collect shiny objects goes hand-in-hand with Dan's photographic zeal. A typical traveller may include, in his photographic depiction of a journey, wildlife, architecture, smiling children, narrow street scenes or bucolic pastures. Dan's photos begin with Malcolm's alarm clock and include, at this point, three different angles of the chaotic internal wiring of an electricity box in Mendoza, one of his pints of Jerome's beer in El Salto, a couple of the skate park bowl in Flores (both taken with such bad timing that neither has an actual skateboarder captured but merely an empty skateboard bowl) and a blurry shot of the muddy black dog at Emi's place against a pitch black background of mangrove bushes at night.

Dan stuffs the aerial into his bag, and we race across the city via taxi, egging on the driver to take risks as he ducks in and out of the gaps between other vehicles, spinning the wheel through his hands and showing off his Formula One skills, finally swinging the vehicle into the drop-off bay in the nick of time.

Running into the shiny modern ferry terminal at the edge of the Rio Plata, we are met by a row of customs officers, their suspicious beady eyes glaring at us from behind glass-screened grey booths. Due to the recent worldwide swine flu scare, they're all wearing white face-masks. The tension seems to be a little higher than usual.

"Have you been to any places outside the city?"

"What country you live?"

"New Zealand," I reply.

"It's near China?"

"NO," I answer, confused.

"When did you arrive?"

"What country you arrived in?"

We squirm our way through the questions and seem to pass. They wave us through and we proceed to the next counter: Immigration.

After the passport formalities – and managing to avoid being searched – Dan discovers he's lost his ferry ticket that he purchased less than five minutes ago, and while erratically rifling through his unkempt backpack trying to find it he arouses suspicions of the good officers of the ferry terminal. I hold my breath, hoping they'll let us pass anyway, hoping they'll see he's just a nervous and unlucky traveller. But no. They hone in on Magpie Dan, who by now is furiously pulling out shiny bits and throwing them around in a cloud of confusion and frustration, and direct him to step aside, *por favor*. Pulling us aside, the officers empty our bags on to a stainless steel bench top for inspection. We are now minutes away from missing our boat.

"The next boat is in five hours, bro," I say, as Dan continues to rummage through his stuff, this time with a team of interested customs officials looking on. A broken mirror, a broken VHF radio… All useless but highly absorbing to the officers. By now I can't tell what they want with Dan; perhaps they are as amused by his weird collection of things as I am – though I'm not amused at this particular moment. Holding a short coil of fuse wire, the frayed copper ends of a phone charger lead and a cluster of plastic cable ties that he's fished from Dan's bag, the confused custom officer looks at him not knowing what to think or say.

At that moment the ferry blows its horn, and then, Dan finds his ticket. Crumpled up in his pocket but miraculously intact.

We're free to go. Once the ticket is found, the officers lose interest.

We frantically shove our gear into our packs and run down the tunnel that connects to the ferry while the officer we leave behind radioes the boats bridge to let us board.

The old, ex-English Channel vessel is a sad homage to yesterday, with its logos crudely painted out and rust drips leaking down the sides from its steel joints. But it seems to be fully functional, and with an ear-splitting creak, begins to slide its way slowly across the muddy Rio Plata.

Brown waves smash the side of the ferry while the coast of Argentina slowly disappears behind us.

We dock two hours later in Colonia on Uruguayan soil.

And we are in another world.

The quaint little battlement town of Colonia was founded in 1680 by the Portuguese and consequently changed hands several times over the next hundred years. Making our way up into the town, we traverse sleepy streets from a land that time forgot. Old cars in immaculate condition are parked here and there in the maze of narrow cobbled passageways, watched over by ornate Victorian streetlights that hang from their lampposts. Pastel-shaded houses sit silently, as if a mass exodus has taken place only moments before our arrival.

And all the stores are shut up for midday siesta.

A few hours of wandering rather aimlessly leads us to wonder why we are actually here. We end up at an old underground cheese factory on the banks of the river. A series of flooded arched tunnels, made from red brick, are reflected in the still water seeped in from the riverbanks. It's of little modern-day interest – not a wheel of cheese to be seen.

We rest on a large patch of grass overlooking the river's vast expanse of water. We crave surroundings a little more exciting; this town is a little too sleepy.

So we take a bus to Montevideo.

Which also feels abandoned.

Maybe it has to do with our arrival, landing as we do on a windy, overcast, grey public holiday. To its credit, Montevideo is bigger than Colonia, but it, too, seems to offer little in the way of a living pulse. Both Dan and I find this rather odd, as half of the population of

Uruguay supposedly live here. But the only life seems to be coming from a small art market in the plaza and the flat-capped rag and bone men clip-clopping through the cobbled streets, their wooden carts overloaded with mountains of bulging black trash bags and drawn by mangy leather eye-flapped horses that look like they could do with a good meal.

Uruguay is famous for its *mate* drink, a herb that legend has it contains the same effects as caffeine. Almost everybody has their own little personalised metal cup and straw and, whether they are riding a moped or driving a truck, that cup is always firmly wedged in the bend of their arm. Montevideo is no exception to this rule as the stalls in the markets prove, proudly displaying their walls of personalised silver and leather embossed cup-and-straw combos. I buy a hat from a guy brewing some, holding a big gourd with a silver base. The herb smells good, giving off an aroma happily poised between bitter and sweet

"We should try some," Dan says, sniffing the aroma and pointing across the plaza. "There's a stall over there."

After sampling a cup I can understand why they have to drink the muddy tasting stuff all day, as it clearly does not have the same stimulation powers of the mighty coffee bean.

"Dirt," Dan says, sucking on his straw. "It tastes like dirt."

Our hostel is a thin, two-storey building tucked away on a narrow side street in the old town. Our room looks over a dimly lit car park. This car park, we learn, is a hive of activity during the evenings, and heated arguments can be heard during the night behind a row of wheelie dumpsters that sit at the back of it. Studying these interactions from the window, we discover that it's a favourite spot for the local prostitutes. The orange streetlight directly below our window provides us with a clear view of the various (yes, *various*) whores and their customers who frequent the area on a nightly basis. We watch from above as the awkward interactions around the dumpsters unfold.

It's a form of entertainment.

The tear-off 'things to do' map at the tiny reception desk of the hostel mentions a skate park around five miles away, down along the coast. So Dan and I carefully pick the only two functional – though I might add: most embarrassing – bicycles from the bike rack in the reception area, and set out for said park. I'm not sure whether to take the receptionist's speech about how we should look after them seriously or as a joke. My chosen machine is a bright red girl's bike with a wicker handlebar basket that holds the (broken) gear changer while Dan's, a slightly less feminine but far more badly maintained teenager's mountain bike plastered in Power Ranger decals, has a buckled wheel rim that lets out an ear piercing screech every time it passes the brake pad.

We slowly ride for an hour along the beach boardwalk with our boards interlocked to the top crossbars of the bikes – a pleasant experience – and we arrive at a large graffiti-smeared, outer-walled mellow dish. It is built on a concrete pad in the sand.

"Is this it?" I remark, looking at the eroding centrepiece platform that sits in the middle of the dish, sprinkled with a green shimmer of broken beer bottles.

"Well, we rode all this way," Dan says, grabbing a palm branch and sweeping the green shards into a pile.

We skate up and down the ramps and slopes of the park, trying to avoid the glass, for an hour or so. We finish up satisfied and out of breath.

"Time for a beer, I reckon," Dan suggests, as the sweat from the skate drips from his beard.

Just as we reach a small bar at the roadside of the beach, my back tyre pops.

"You're fucking kidding me!" I say, laughing. I am happy we've found a watering hole. I'll deal with the girly bike later.

Two icy cold, sweat-beaded bottles are placed in front of us on the bar and the amber nectar slides down our throats all too easily.

"How you gonna get home?" Dan asks, ordering another two.

"Push it, I guess?" I reply, tipping my second bottle to my mouth.

"It's still too far to walk, bro," he says, obviously not too excited about the thought of walking alongside me.

We soak down the last of our beers and start back to town. I manage alright, developing a technique of leaning over the handlebars in order to keep my weight over the still inflated front wheel. With a good deal of effort, I scratch and spark my way on the metal rim back to the hostel, while Dan wobbles alongside me on his Power Ranger bike.

CHAPTER NINE
PUNTO DEL DIABLO

Tucking the battle-damaged red girl's bike into the hallway cupboard with its now shredded flat tyre conveniently hidden behind the other tatty bicycles, I climb the low-roofed staircase to the second-storey dorm, where a well-groomed, pink polo-shirted American chap is taking up the majority of the floor space. Sitting cross-legged on the floor, he's stocktaking his equipment and clothing, down to the last shoelace, and packing it all in a large duffle bag.

"Hi, I'm Henry," he says, shaking my hand. "Sorry about the mess, I shan't be long." For an American, he sports an unusual and obvious upper-class accent.

"No problem at all." I smile, looking at his gear. "What's all this stuff?"

I point at his strip laid out on the floor.

"I've been here playing polo in a few tournaments over the past few weeks, but I'm leaving tonight," he replies, folding the kit and stacking it in the duffel bag. His tone isn't one of interest in continuing our conversation and Dan and I settle in for a movie in the upstairs common area. The choice is bleak and we settle for a western starring Clint Eastwood, whose lips move out of sync to its Spanish-dubbed soundtrack.

The following morning, the city has had life breathed into it. We spend it jostling with the hordes of Saturday shoppers along Montevideo's main street, engaging in an exhaustive search for a camp stove gas canister that ends in success, before escaping the crowds to the terminal. Next stop: the South Atlantic coast.

For five hours the bus passes through flat green countryside. A drive canopied by a slate grey sky with a few nondescript towns that break the monotony. Finally, we disembark in the small fishing village of Punto del Diablo.

"Hostel! Hostel!" A group of young boys shout, grabbing us by the arms and leading us through the village's four main dirt roads offering up the scarce accommodation options available.

"Hey that woman back in the BA hostel that gave us her number – we should look her up," I remark to Dan, remembering the piece of paper she gave me in my wallet.

"Bit late now." Dan replies, still being tugged by the grubby young kids. "They lived up in the northeast, I think. We won't be going there."

We choose the newish looking building made of telegraph posts, with a glass frontage from where we can see a glimpse of beach, over the uninviting prefab block with views of the village's drainage ditch.

Entering the reception / common area, we find its plush-cushioned round chairs occupied by young rich Americans in Banana Republic and Gap summer season outfits, plugged into and hypnotised by the blue glow of their portable cyber devices.

"Jesus, is this a Starbucks?" Dan mumbles under his breath, looking around. "Let's get a real drink."

The receptionist directs us to a bar that sits on short stilts in the middle of the white sand beach. Constructed entirely of wooden planks, the place is lit by the glow of red bulbs that hang from the walls. It keeps busy with a generous crowd of travellers.

We order a couple of cheap vinegary house reds. The giant wine glasses they're presented in hold practically a half bottle each. We knock back several of these tankards, and the evening becomes a fuzzy blur.

"Let's talk to those two over there," I say to Dan, looking at the women at the table opposite.

Before he has chance to answer, I'm in there. "Ssssoooo…" I start, already ruining my intro. "Hola, chicas." Not a suave opening, I know – but did I mention the wine glasses were huge? I continue, receiving stares that clearly state the girls are not interested. "What's your problem?" I cheerfully slur at them. "I only want some company and conversation."

Dan steps in front of me and, shooting me a look of disgust, apologises to the girls.

"You always do this!" I snap at Dan, now turning on him. "Always belittling me and talking over everything I say, trying to make me look stupid. I'm fucking over it."

"Bro! Those girls didn't speak English, and I was just explaining what you said," he snaps back at me, half smirking.

"Don't fucking smirk, Dan!" I fire back, now lost in my emotions and too far gone to realise I'm the problem. Things have escalated way too fast, but I can't recover enough to right the situation. So, lacking a better plan, I add an angry "Fuck it, I'm going." And storm off.

And now I'm all alone, wasted and making my way back to the hostel on wobbly legs. I pass the empty reception area and fumble around the bunks of the dark dorm for my backpack. As I'm searching, a shriek comes from a top bunk as my hand runs down what I think is a bag but turns out to be a girl's leg.

Suddenly, I realise where I am and scurry down the corridor to the other dorm before she has time to see me. Scaling the ladder to my bunk, I collapse out of breath on the mattress and cuddle up to my backpack and fall fast asleep, well aware already how much the hangover is going to hurt in the morning. When I wake up ten minutes later, I've absolutely no recollection that I'm two beds high and step out in to thin air, landing with a slap in a crumpled heap on the tiled floor. Pushing myself up to my knees, I'm face to face with a girl snoring in the bottom bunk. I get to my feet and find the toilet, but I've no time to find the light switch and frantically fumble around in my boxers for my dick, but before I have a chance to get started, I'm startled from across the darkness.

"Shut the fucking door!"

And then I realise the reality of my situation: *this isn't the toilet!* I'm back in the other dorm again! And so I run away for the second time.

I do manage to eventually find the bathroom. When I do I let go of my grip; the intense pressure on my bladder releases and a high pressure jet of piss fires into the toilet bowl with the force of a firehose.

"*AAAAAAAhhhhhhhh,*" I grunt, letting out a huge sigh of relief while liberating myself and looking at the ceiling in ecstasy.

CHAPTER TEN
PARQUE SANTA TERESA

Waking the following morning with a mouth like a cat's arsehole and a throbbing head from the cheap red wine, I'm met with harsh stares as I sit down for breakfast. The hostel guests, now all awake and plugged back into their laptops in the common area, are clearly unhappy with the events of last night, knowing full well it was either Dan or me who was the phantom groper.

"The sooner we gap it, the better," I tell Dan, who's still unaware of what I've done.

"Why are they all looking at us like that?" he asks, giving me a suspicious glare. "What happened, bro?"

"I'll tell you once we're out of here." I leave him at the table to go pack my stuff.

Paying our one-night accommodation fee, we leave Punto del Diablo behind and make our way along the beach to the national park.

Which turns out to be a terrible plan. The blistering heat is unbearable for our hangovers. But we've no choice but to continue on, hiking the coast north.

Dan chuckles loudly when he learns of the events of the previous night.

"So how far is it, you reckon?" I ask, sipping some water.

"Ah, it's about ten Ks," Dan replies, grabbing the bottle from me and taking a big swig. Cooled by the ocean breeze and walking barefoot in the wash of the tide, we stop every ten minutes for water and shade and to drop our weighty packs from our backs.

"My ankle's giving me shit again. I'm glad it's soft sand the whole way," I remark, feeling the joint starting to swell.

"Not much further, bro, and there's more shade once we get into the park," Dan says unconvincingly. I appreciate that he's trying to reassure me, but I see him sweating buckets, and I sense that we are a miserable pair.

After another two hours, Dan realises we've gone too far. "I think we should've turned inland a while back," he says, unsure as to where we've ended up. "We're in the national park now but not where we want to be."

We cut back inland and find a sealed road that cuts through the forest and leads to a mossy turreted military barracks. We are, by now, very tired.

"This is it!" Dan says, finally gaining his bearings. "This is where we pay."

A grumpy middle-aged woman in camouflage takes our campground fee and we stock up on tinned fish and chocolate in a small store at the rear of the grey stone barracks before walking another twenty minutes to the campsite.

The beach is visible from our pitch and no more than a minute's walk from the campground. A central grass area is surrounded by fifteen or so yellow-and-brown pitched roof cabanas that are set among the trees and resemble a Swiss nativity scene.

"Let's go check out the fort. It's not far," Dan suggests, referring to the Fortaleza Santa Theresa that the national park has been created for.

Zipping up the tent and leaving the campsite, we follow a trail through the forest that opens out to tussock-filled fields flanked by sea cliffs on one side. In the distance, the old military fortress and cemetery dominate the headland and look out to sea. Many battles have been fought between the Portuguese and Uruguayans for ownership of the headland, and the area is steeped in history. The fort's high, stone walls and pointed corner turrets are carpeted in a captivating bright orange lichen moss. A wide stone path leads to a pair of large, arched wooden doors.

The doors are sealed shut.

"It's fucking closed!" Dan says, laughing.

"Well, I'm gonna walk around it at least and get some photos," I remark. "We've walked far enough to get here."

Shooting some photos from the plains of tussock that surround it, we finish our visit by wandering through the tombstones of the small ornate graveyard that overlooks the choppy Atlantic before returning to camp, somewhat disappointed. I wonder what photos Dan has taken, but I'm too tired to ask. I'll be sure to find out later. His collection usually contains items from our urban adventures, but I wonder if he'll add something from this strange fort adventure to the images he has collected along the way. Before I get a chance to ask, he shows me the screen on the back of his camera.

"Check that out," he says, pointing to the photo.

Displayed on the screen are the innards of the lamppost that stood above the cemetery gate, with its crudely taped together wires that supply the light with power.

"The boys will love that one," Dan smiles, referring to his workmates.

Back at the campsite, a group of young Uruguayans have set up next to us. The university sports graduates are taking a long weekend break and inform Dan they're here to holiday before their real jobs start. Collecting wood with them from the surrounding trees, we share a fire as well as shots of their Carperinha, a Brazilian liquor that is both clear and strong, flavoured with slices of lemon that they've brought in plastic bottles. After one too many of these and a few joints, my lack of Spanish takes centre stage for me, again, as I gain confidence and blurt out a few badly matched words.

"¡Mucho bueno!" I say when one asks me if I like his country.

This causes them to erupt in laughter and me to clam up while Dan gets to know the friendly group better. Sitting by like a lame duck, now too embarrassed to open my mouth, I nod and smile at times I feel appropriate, only catching a little of the topics being talked about, while Dan chats away merrily, clearly ecstatic about being fully immersed in his second language again.

The site is a favourite of the Uruguayans and the following day they lead us to a spot around the point where we bob around peeling fresh mussels from the rocks in the nippy but refreshing water. The following days blur into a haze under blue skies with our new friends. The shellfish missions, the flowing Carperinha and the never-ending supply of joints that are constantly rolled around the smouldering campfire keep us happily occupied. We live for several days in an atmosphere akin to being marooned on a desert island – a filmic version of such a thing, that is.

On our fourth day, dark grey clouds slowly engulf the blue of the sky and our friends decide to pack up and leave, urging us to do the same.

"They reckon we should follow them," Dan translates to me.

But I'm not quite ready to leave this idyllic place. "Let's just stay a couple more nights?" I suggest.

"Yeah, I'm sweet with either," Dan says agreeably. "But we'll run out of food by then so we'll have to gap it anyway."

I watch as he high-fives his new friends and accepts the bottle of carperinha they give us before leaving.

The clouds grow darker and angrier as the evening progresses, and Dan follows suit after finishing the gifted bottle of grog and chasing it with another of red wine. His incomprehensible slurring begins to scare me a little as he grows more abrasive with every mouthful of booze. Well into the evening, as the fire slowly dies, I'm experiencing a side of him I've never seen before. Trying to find my way out of the one-way conversation, I'm given a pass when the heavens open and I make a dash for the tent.

"Whurr yerr fuuukin guin!" he shouts at me as I slip into the tiny tent, now unsure if it's a good idea to fall asleep with a madman in our close quarters. Before I have time to zip up the flap, he crawls in, almost collapsing the tent – and immediately passes out with his feet out the door.

A storm of epic proportions unleashes itself on the coastline and the high winds and driving rain imprison us until it blows over. The storm lasts all night and all the next day.

We are all alone. The ten cabanas surrounding the campsite are no longer occupied and all shutters are bolted down.

The only shelter from the ferocious gusts that are sending branches crashing to the ground all over the campsite is behind the toilet block. This is also the only spot where my camp stove will stay lit and that is now being used more for a heat source than as a cooker, due to the drastic temperature drop that the storm has brought with it. We squat around it with our hands outstretched as close to the gas flame as possible.

The weather is relentless and soul-destroying. I am left feeling rather desperate. At the end of the first day, when the rains seem to lift ever so slightly, Dan and I are sitting against the toilet block wall, and I make a bold suggestion.

"Let's break into a cabin tonight after the warden's last round and be out before his first one in the morning."

Dan nods in agreement, his arms crossed and hands tucked into his armpits. I can see that he's fully feeling the effects of his over-indulgent night, that a day of this storm has done nothing to improve his already dark state. So we shelter behind the toilet block a while longer, shivering from the fierce wind, waiting until the campground warden's headlights have disappeared into the darkness. Then, we pry open a shutter of one of the cabanas with our multi tools. Yanking up the ground pegs of the tent, I make a dash across the campsite like a paraglider trying to take off, but mid-way feel the tent snag on an old fencepost. When I reach the shelter of the cabana porch, I stop, gasping for air, and realise I've torn a hole in our tent – our main shelter – on a piece of rogue barbed wire. I stuff it and myself through the window we've pulled ajar, and land with a thud at Dan's feet inside the tiny but dry cabin.

"I ripped it!" I say, gutted and trying to find the hole. Fortunately, I can see, on inspection inside the cabana, that I've only torn the outer door flap.

"Well, at least it's not the roof," Dan says, taking off his wet clothes and lying down on a bed.

Bliss. To have even just a planked wall between us and the ferocious weather outside is such utter relief, we each grow quiet. We change out of our wet clothes to dry ones, even without a shower – and it makes all the difference in the world. Finally, we bed down for an undisturbed sleep while the wind and rain continue to beat down outside.

When we wake early the next morning, the weather outside the tiny log cabin seems to have broken and we quickly gather our belongings and climb back out the window before the warden's first circuit. The campsite now looks a whole lot different to when we arrived: countless snapped branches, downed trees and plant debris litter the flooded site of swampy puddles.

Back at the military barracks, a bus pulls into the lay-by and we discover it is conveniently heading to Montevideo. As we drive back to town, the landscape of inland rolling hills pass by the bus window and is dotted with the odd dairy farm: an untouched place very much like the landscapes of New Zealand. I smile inwardly at how far away New Zealand seems by now.

Switching buses in Montevideo, we arrive back in Colonia and find a hostel for the night. The place is empty and an early night follows. We need to try to catch up on sleep before catching the return ferry to Argentina in the morning.

CHAPTER ELEVEN
BUENOS AIRES REVISITED

Back at the Palermo hostel in Buenos Aires, the receptionist hands Dan a DHL envelope containing a new credit card and a letter informing him that it can only be used with proof of his passport and a bank teller – and it won't function in ATM machines.

"For fuck's sake!" he says angrily, knowing how much grief this is going to give us. In fact, this will become the thorn in our side for the next nine months as Dan's time is increasingly spent with the administrative nightmare of his new credit card. He will spend whole mornings waiting in the long bank lines that stretch out of the doors for an available teller inside. He will come to hate bank lines. And so will I.

"What's op wid him?" says a thick-accented Irish girl from Dublin with brightly-dyed red hair who sits down uninvited at our table.

"Ah, just a credit card card problem," I reply, getting the feeling she wants to hang out.

"Raabbery?" she says, raising her eyebrows and nodding like a chicken before I have chance to answer.

"Darren. Where you off to?" I say, introducing myself and changing the subject, assessing her mountain of stripy Chinese laundry bags, the ones you see on every corner for $2.

"Name's Maria," she says. "Da Bolivian border tomorra noight!"

I glance quickly to Dan, both of us realising we could well get stuck with her for the long bus ride. We do our best to avoid Maria the following day, in fear of her becoming too friendly and tagging along with us for the next leg. Sometimes that happens in these situations. Hostels attract the solo traveller who doesn't like being solo. The ones who travel with a good deal of baggage, both real and metaphorical. The ones who want to talk and talk and talk, usually when you're hungover or achy or just needing to be alone – really alone.

Maria, although probably a nice person, is far too hyper-charged for Dan's and my current mood and continues to follow us around like we're in desperate need of her chit-chat. We successfully evade her for most of the day, feeling hopeful we've given her the slip with no sign of her or her large pile of luggage. But we arrive at the El Retiro terminal in the evening only to find her waving at us, smiling and sitting happily on her mountain of stripy Chinese laundry bags.

"What *is* all this shit you're dragging around with you?" I ask, having no choice but to join her, and pointing at the bags.

"It's stationary equipment and school supploys," she replies, still smiling. "I'm off to teach in an orphanage in Sucre, Bolivia." She pats the pile underneath her.

"Oh! Cool, good on you." I congratulate her sheepishly now feeling a little ashamed at how we've been trying to avoid her. When the bus pulls up, I make amends with my less charitable side by helping her throw the luggage in to the bus's belly locker. "There you go," I say.

The bus pulls out of the terminal and we depart the great city of Buenos Aires. Out the window, scattered groups of homeless people are drying their clothes and bedding in the evening sun. They collect on the slopes of the banked concrete reservoir. This is the place these people dwell; the giant channel that the city's waste flows through is the place they know as home. They sleep at night in the many outlet pipes that feed into it. And they dry their clothes by day.

We roll on by, acre after acre of this scene unfolding before my eyes. Just as we're leaving the outskirts of the city, we are served coffee and a ham and cheese roll. I recline in my comfy seat, a pang of guilt settling in my gut with the tasty snack.

In just two months we've followed the roads that lead from Santiago de Chile to Buenos Aires and the far reaches of Uruguay across the Rio Plata. Now we are u-turning and heading north up through Argentina once again. This next leg is to be the longest bus ride so far. Eighteen hours of films, snacks, coffee, wine and uninterrupted sleep in a bus that seems to glide on thin air. It is also to be the last of its kind for the next eight months – the end of the line for luxury buses.

Images of the poverty-stricken fringes of Buenos Aires linger in my thoughts as I dream the night away.

The highlight of this part of our journey, in the northern Argentine city of Salta, is 'El Tren de los Nubes', something I've been looking forward to since reading about it back in New Zealand in a guidebook. The 'Train to the clouds' is an old steam engine that climbs a rickety track up into the cloud forests of the mountains. Cloud forests! I've been thinking about those for nearly a year. The train trip lasts fifteen hours, and includes twenty-nine bridges, twenty-one tunnels, thirteen viaducts, two spirals and two zigzags before reaching 4220 metres in altitude. This simply is something I cannot miss.

We disembark the bus and proceed to our hostel by foot, helping Maria with the big bags. It is mid-morning and the sun is casting the clear light I've come to expect. The altitude is noticeably higher as we are all short of breath. It's the light that sets every day right for a perfect day in a new place.

On the hostel's pin board we find a note informing us that 'El Tren de los Nubes' is closed for repairs for the next three months.

"Of course it is," Dan says.

CHAPTER TWELVE
SALTA

With the trip to the clouds cancelled, there's not really a good reason for being in Salta. The town itself offers little in the way of attractions. It's a sleepy place, slowed by the thin air and comprised of small stores stocking everyday needs and churches painted in bright colours. Even the pub seems neglected to the point of serving up what seems like questionable spirits. Besides all that, Maria's short timeline for getting to Sucre cements our decision to stay for the day. We leave that evening.

Maria, ever the optimist and now our constant companion, offers a cheery suggestion. "May as well go up der hill den?"

Dan and I shrug our shoulders — "Why not?" — and park our things at the hostel so we can take in the one site the town has to offer.

A bubble-shaped cable car wobbles and whirrs us up the city's hill leaving the tree line and revealing a magnificent view above the city's grid of blocks before dropping us at the summit. A giant wooden cross and its backdrop of distant snow peaks commands the attention of the few people up here with us, mostly local families. We are literally above the clouds. Sating our thirsts at the hilltop café, we sip the cold liquid from tall pilsner glasses, savouring the most expensive drop we've had since Jerome's brewery back in El Salto. An hour is all we need and alighting back down in the city we discover a surprisingly well-presented museum exhibition showcasing the expedition in the nearby Andes that discovered three 500-year-old infant Inca mummies. The mummies sit silently with legs crossed in freeze-chamber glass display cases, their eerie skeletons wrapped in taught dark skin while chunky toenailed feet poke from the bottom of the hemp that wraps them.

"Are they breathing?" Maria asks with a serious face.

I glance at Dan, who reciprocates with a smirk.

As we walk around the city I notice how the locals cannot take their eyes off Maria's ridiculous hair colour, whispering to each other behind their hands and giggling. These people we are now sharing the footpaths with are different to who we've encountered in cities like B.A and Santiago. Shorter and darker skinned, they seem more reserved. The traditional clothing they wear, reminds me of posters I've seen advertising Peru and Bolivia.

Stray dogs lie flattened by the sun while others hide in the cool shade of orange trees that hang with fruit in the central park.

"Don't pet them," Dan warns as we join them on the grass. "They'll get jealous."

No sooner has he said this, I do the opposite and stroke one who then lunges at another sitting right next to me – and sinks its teeth into its side. Yelping and jumping up, the wounded mutt retaliates, sending all the other dogs dotted around the park into frenzy. As if it isn't bad enough that the two fighting over me are now acting like wild savages, I'm now in the middle of a bloodthirsty duel of sharp white teeth and can't seem to escape for fear of also being bitten.

Out of nowhere, four toothless old ladies approach us, yelling angrily and waving their walking sticks at the dogs.

"¡Vayase!" they shout, shooing the dogs apart and bringing the fight to a close.

Relieved and turning to thank them, I'm shocked as they turn their sticks on us and herd us like naughty sheep out of the park, yelling at us just as they reproached the dogs.

"I fucking told you, bro!" Dan says, while being poked by a walking stick.

We hurriedly leave with our tails between our legs, and the park regains its serenity.

Our day finishes in a 'Parilla' on the outskirts of town. With similar principles to the Parilla in Mendoza, the twenty-peso all-you-can-eat offer is way better and impossible to refuse. We join the long queue with what appears to be the rest of the neighbourhood. As the line moves forward, we weave through the thick timber beams that jut out into the street at forty-five-degree angles, supporting the crooked exterior walls. There's time enough in this queue to hear a little more of Maria's story.

"Oive been studying Spanish for a munt in Buenos Aires," she tells us in her rough Irish accent. "Oi tink oive learnt enough dialogue to tackle der teaching jaab in Bolivia."

"It's easier with kids too," says Dan. "You'll be sweet."

"Oi hope so," she answers nervously.

Dan tucks into his third plate of meat. On offer is an enormous variety of meats, vegetables, fruits and desserts, and being able to choose what we eat ensures the wobbly udder and elastic intestines I was subjected to in Bueno Aires stay well clear of my plate. We eat for several hours until eventually the staff becomes overly attentive towards our table in an obvious but polite effort to make us leave.

Back in the hostel, Maria and Dan head to the dorm to get their gear ready to travel while I head to the bathroom.

A word about bathrooms. I've been travelling enough by now to know that no two bathrooms are the same, and that there's a certain art to using South American toilets. I'd be so bold as to say I'm starting to get the hang of it. In this part of the world, the common factors are weak flushes and ancient drainage systems. Most bathrooms have a small waste paper basket positioned next to the lavatory, for discarding your used toilet paper (even if, incidentally, there usually isn't any). And, though necessary, this unfortunately guarantees you a seat next to a pile of shitty paper while doing your business. Depending on the quality of the establishment you're using, that bin can be empty or overflowing.

This hostel is of a poorer quality, with little attention paid to bathroom hygiene. I can't tell when the trash can was last emptied, but, judging by the flies, it certainly wasn't today or even yesterday, and maybe not even since last week. Matters are only made worse when the door lock breaks – and I'm stuck.

"The lock is broken! Get me out! Get me out!" I scream in the direction of the reception from the locked lavatory. The little mountain of turd-smudged paper stares mockingly at me from the bin in the corner. Nobody answers and I start to stress about missing our bus.

Eventually, the desk boy hears my whimpers.

"Stand back, Stand back, I keek een de door!" he shouts excitedly.

"NO! NO!" I shout back. "You find my friend and he fix the lock!" I do not want to be kicked back into the shit bin.

After finishing his cigarette and in no particular hurry, Dan takes the lock apart, setting me free.

"You need to clean this more often!" I say to the desk guy, who gives me a blank stare.

"Todo bien, amigo," he replies, and pats me on the back.

CHAPTER THIRTEEN
LA QUIACA

We arrive at the Salta terminal via taxi in the nick of time. We hurriedly purchase our tickets and are ushered onto the bus by the sub-driver.

I settle into my seat and sleep solidly for the next eight hours. When I wake up, I discover I'm shivering.

I pull back the curtain to find the window glass is iced up and blurring what looks like a red dawn sky. We're now 1400 metres further up into the mountains than where we were in Salta. We disembark and the elevation of 3600 metres hits us hard.

As I step from the bus, the buffeting cold wind of the Andes cuts through my thin puffa vest and underclothing like sharp icicles.

"Fuck me! We're gonna die out here if we don't start moving," Dan says, rubbing his arms and taking hold of one of Maria's bags.

Short of breath, and dragging the laundry bags through the empty streets of the small town of La Quiaca, we are cold to our core. The long shadows slowly shorten between the rows of mud houses that blend into the nearby mountains. We reach the border and wait. Apparently the border is only open during daylight hours.

Slowly, slowly, the rising sun begins to take the edge off the bitter temperature. We are grateful when the street vendors open and we can get a cup of coffee from a steamy little stall with piping hot urns. The women who serve us stare at Maria's hair like she is some sort of apparition. Thank god they don't know her name, as I imagine they'd all be kneeling at her feet, convinced she's a sign from the Virgin Mary.

The border consists of an iron bridge with an armoured immigration enclosure at each end. Spanning the river that once flowed under it and separating the two, it now marks a dry trench of chocolate bar wrappers and discarded condoms. The huts are each painted in the colours of their respective countries: baby blue and white where La Quiaca and Argentina finish; red, green and yellow marking the beginning of Villazon and Bolivia.

The queue for passport stamping has slowed to a painful crawl. We can't quite figure out how so many people have arrived in this remote place for the border crossing but as the day grows lighter the crowds increase. Besides ourselves, others arrive with bags of varying sizes to line up with us. Others arrive on foot – from where, I have no idea. We all stand in the morning cold, inching forward and waiting our turn.

Dan and I tower in height above the line of people that is deathly quiet. Babies swaddled in rainbow-striped blankets hang from their mothers' backs and local men wearing worn baseball caps clutching sandwich boxes on their way to work obediently filter through the building. Inside, two holes in the wall are sealed with chain-link fencing screens, behind which sit border guards in dark green uniforms.

"Pasaporte," the guard says, holding out his hand.

I slip mine to him through the split in the wire, and he carelessly flicks through it, clearly not understanding what he's reading. He whacks an overly inky stamp on to a page.

We emerge through the exit door and on to Bolivian soil. Almost immediately it feels different. Women in bowler hats and frilly dresses shuffle through street scenes straight out of a Wild West movie.

It could be the 1800s. The culture shock is huge.

Old buildings with flaking paint dominate the landscape, while faded Coca-Cola signage and tarps cut from billboard canvas shade the alpaca blanket stalls lining the sides of the main road. The dry altitude is having an effect on us and we all three move slowly through the streets. Our energy flags, and we stop at an old man resting in the shade in a rocking chair at the front of his store.

"How far is the station?" Dan asks him in Spanish.

The wrinkly old fellow points up the hill. "No es lejos, amigos, solo cien metros."

"A hundred metres?" I say to Dan, understanding his answer. "OK, I can manage that."

One hundred metres on, there is no station. Either our calculations are wrong or the altitude is warping our sense of distance. Fifteen minutes later we come to the next group of lazy locals swinging in hammocks, who point up the hill, smiling. Another hundred metres. How the station can be one hundred metres from two different points en route is beyond me, but we continue dragging the laundry bags through the gantlet of women in bowler hats, frills and multi-coloured woollen shawls going about their everyday business while steaming cooking pots emit delicious smells from roadside stalls. The aromas are irresistible, and I buy a bowl of a goulash-type dish. My meal is scooped with a large ladle from a bubbling pot; my mouth waters at the sight of dark red meat chunks and carrots, onions and other goodness floating in the creamy rich brown sauce. Dan and Maria, turning their noses up at the sight, opt for a sandwich at an adjacent stall and I start to wonder if I've bought the right thing. The wrinkled faces of the two women serving it up are a picture of apprehension as they watch me spoon the gravy goodness eagerly into my mouth. I am too hungry to care why they look so concerned. I momentarily wonder if they know something I don't know – if this will flow through the gringo bowels like fire – but I am too hungry to care.

"Gracias," I say. "Gracias."

The goulash is delicious. I feel like I can go another hundred metres and more.

CHAPTER FOURTEEN
VILLAZON

Villazon train station, like the village we've just climbed through, resembles something out of a Wild West movie.

"We're going to buy tickets, Maria, watch the bags," we say to our travelling companion.

"Yaa shure, no praablem," she replies in her Irish drawl.

We create a small mountain of stripes, straps, nylon and mesh in the middle of the waiting room with our bags. Dan and I go to enquire about tickets. We are exhausted and still quite out of breath, and so far my stomach feels fine.

At the rear of the ticket office in a lofty wood-panelled waiting hall, a small man wearing a train conductor's hat pulls open a wooden drawer that masquerades as a till and deposits our money into it. He hands us our tickets, and we return to our spot in the waiting area, where we find Maria lying on the floor like a dried-up starfish, her iPod and wallet lying on the ground next to her. Miraculously, our belongings are still exactly where we left them, although being surrounded by other waiting passengers.

"Fuck, she's luggage," I say to Dan, regarding Maria's blatant negligence.

"In more sense than one," he replies, laughing.

I'm still waiting for the rumblings that will indicate that I'm about to shit myself.

A blue train pulls in between two spotlessly clean cement platforms and the waiting passengers stampede forward, hurriedly stuffing their bulging stripy blankets through the windows and fighting to get a good spot to store them for the ride.

Maria has bought first class tickets all the way to Uyuni. "Ok boys, be good," she says with a smile, stepping onto the train. We watch as she steps up into a clean carriage where she finds her reserved booth with a vase of flowers on the table. We can see her clean cabin from where we stand, and we half-wish we could sit with her while also glad we're moving on. We've stuck to our budget and have opted for the economy fares to Tupiza, so we wave goodbye and head down the platform to the cattle class carriage.

We climb into the car and squeeze onto seats that are already full of locals and their many, many packs. Two twenty-litre drums of corn oil are pushed into our foot well by an old lady who then adds to the discomfort with two sacks of onions and a crate of potatoes.

Sitting back amongst a carriage of bowler hats, with our knees next to our ears and packs up right on our laps like large fidgety dogs, we settle in for the bumpy ride. The train squeaks out of the station and into the Wild West landscapes that Butch Cassidy and the Sundance Kid roamed on horseback a century or so ago, robbing the locomotives of gold bullion.

Wondering why no else has opened a window to give the hot carriage some fresh air, I slide mine down and fill the car with a cloud of swirling red dust that covers everyone in a blanket of grit. The passengers remain silent and reserved but fire me cutting glances. They rub their eyes, now filled with the sandy particles that fill the air in our cabin.

I close the window.

The clickety clack of the train continues its way through the arid red mountains where herds of llama roam the vast plains. We slow to a crawl through a red mud-brick village, and bowler-hatted women appear from the alleyways and squawk up at the windows, offering plastic bags of Coca-Cola and tamales. The windows are slid down and a sea of hands along the train beckon them over while packs of skinny dogs bark and chase the squeaking wheels. Transactions take place while the train continues to move. Then it gains speed again, and we melt back into the arid desert landscape.

And then it's time to venture to the toilet. I am scared of what I'll find. I'm pleasantly surprised, however, when I push open the door and find a spotless, stainless steel floor-to-ceiling room with a toilet bowl in the centre of the floor. It's the cleanest toilet I've seen since Auckland airport. I'm slightly annoyed that I don't need anything more than a piss as this really is the cleanest toilet I've used since New Zealand. But steadying myself I take some pleasure in watching my yellow stream fall through the hole and splash onto the tracks whizzing by underneath me, as we rattle towards the town of Tupiza.

CHAPTER FIFTEEN
TUPIZA

Squealing in to Tupiza's single-platformed station at dusk, we're immediately accosted by a young Bolivian woman with a crooked front tooth.

"Hostel, hostel, hombres," she beckons, pulling us by our sleeves through the dimly lit streets.

"I love the old women in their bowler hats," I say to her.

"Really?" she replies with a glowing smile. "Well, they will cook and clean if you marry one. I can introduce you to many," she giggles in broken English.

A narrow flight of stairs leads to a reception desk next to a roof terrace already coated by a thick carpet of frost. The temperature has plummeted and I struggle with cold hands to get money from my backpack. We pay the fee and fill in the formalities.

Next morning, we wake up early and go up to the rooftop of our hostel in search of sun and a possible view over the town that was so dark last night. Before us now is a sea of red corrugated iron rooftops within a bowl of equally red cliffs.

Shivering, we desperately wait for the cold night air to evaporate with the first golden bolts of sunlight that beam a blanket of warmth from over the cliff top. I roll up a cigarette and watch the sun gradually melt the frozen rooftops where stiff washing hangs like cardboard.

The high altitude is extremely dehydrating, and Dan and I suffer from light headaches.

"Tienes pastillas?" Dan asks the cleaning lady, as she pegs out a few tea towels, hoping she has headache pills.

"No. ¿Pero, has probado Coca?" she replies, digging deep in her frilly pinny and pulling out a few coca leaves.

Dan's eyes light up as he turns to me. "Yeah, bro! Coca!"

She hands him a little nib of a moist black substance, and explains that we should chew it simultaneously with the leaves in order to waken its medicinal properties and combat our altitude headaches.

We both place a small amount of both on our tongues, and a pulp manifests in our mouths. I slide the quid into my cheek with my tongue, and see Dan do the same. We wait.

And, miraculously, the headaches ease and a mild sense of extra energy comes over us. Sold on this new discovery, we make it a mission to find more of this cure in town later that morning. But our enquiries fall on deaf ears – not only that, but they are often met with stern stares.

We wander through town. Gold-toothed puffy skirted women, their long plaits hanging down their backs, their black bowler hats propped properly atop their heads, squat along the kerbs over pyramids of yam, potatoes and tamales. Others in red-stained aprons stand over chattering rusty bandsaw blades that grind through animal flesh and bone in little tin butcher shacks smattered with blood. Dan seizes the opportunity and snaps a picture of an electric saw still plugged in and sitting in a sink – with a tap running next to it.

"Suicide," he mutters, slipping the camera back in his pocket. We buy tamales from a street vendor. "Carne y queso," the old lady says, plopping them in a plastic bag. "Mee en chiss," she translates.

In the park, men reading newspapers and chatting occupy all the flaky yellow and white concrete benches. Not one of them has any information on where we can buy any coca leaves.

The trumpets and drums of a street parade steadily increase in volume and hordes of green-costumed schoolkids, their faces painted black and white, spill from a side alley. They snake past us and through the narrow streets, dancing and waving flags, banging drums and blowing trombones, while the villagers watch from the sidewalks.

The crowds disperse as the parade disappears to the other side of town. When the street is empty, we spy a short man standing on the narrow sidewalk across the little street, shouting at us. "Heeey, amigos! Come my bar pleeze! ¡Aquí! ¡Aquí!" he pleads, beckoning us into his establishment and boasting of his homemade red 'wine'.

So we cross the street and check out his bar.

He seats us at a table and eagerly pours the wine into two goblet-shaped glasses. I take a cautious sip. I am surprised by the flavour: somewhere between blackcurrant and grape juice, and seemingly without alcohol. We drink the glasses he pours. Then two more.

Far more fascinating than his home brew – and something he'd failed to include in his beckoning that would surely reel in any tourist – is his small exhibition of dinosaur skulls that he's found while hunting in the Andes. In excellent condition with full sets of teeth, they line a dusty wide shelf. I can't believe what I'm looking at, let alone being allowed to pick up and hold. Although nothing like the size of a T- Rex, these relics are nevertheless impressive. In any other country they surely would be behind glass in a museum.

Dinosaur skulls in a pub. Only in Bolivia.

Back at the hostel I'm experiencing the complete opposite to what most travellers suffer regarding stomach problems. Traveller's gut? Non-existent for me. But I'm starting to wish I had a little more of it. I sit on the toilet straining for a good twenty minutes, and I'm ready to give up. Nothing, zilch, nada.

Suddenly, I'm startled by a loud bang, a yelp and a thud. Pulling up my pants and stepping into the corridor, I'm met with the slumped naked body of a girl, leaning against the tiled wall.

"Help! Help!" I sing out down the hallway, as two of the hostel workers come running in.

Touching the gaggle of wires that hover precariously above the showerhead, the girl had received a bolt of electricity, throwing her backwards through the shower curtain and into the wall of the hallway. This sends the hostel staff into a panic as they all crowd around her in an emotional frenzy and unsure of what to do. While this commotion is happening, Dan snaps his photo. Apparently he's sure there's little he can do in the way of helping the poor girl. I see him snap a photo of the cluster of wires above the showerhead. His collection has been steadily growing, and this will obviously add something fascinating to show his electrician workmates at home.

I watch the girl trundle away in an ambulance. I'm glad she's all right.

But I'm quite annoyed that none of this has created any positive bowel shifts, and I return to the toilet to try and finish what I'd started. I'm guessing that the dehydration due to extreme altitude, plus the last few days of cheese tamales, Coca-Cola and llama meat have contributed to my state. I'm starting to think the solid stubborn lump that has plugged my sphincter isn't going to shift on its own. I'm starting to think some extra assistance is going to be necessary.

With no other choice, I finally get things moving with a hooked finger and a little wincing.

CHAPTER SIXTEEN
THE ALTI PLANO

Tupiza is the starting point for one of South America's top attractions: the Salt plains of Uyuni. The helpful staff at the hostel show us our options for touring, including schedules and routes.

"Let's go all out and do the four-day mission, bro," I suggest to Dan.

"It's gonna be fucking cold up there." Dan turns to me with a look of fear.

"We better go buy some warm clothes then," I say, sealing the deal.

Next day, we spend the early part of the morning in the cramped alleys of the market, picking out gloves, socks and alpaca sweatshirts. When we return to the hostel, our driver is preparing the 4x4 jeep to leave. Waiting in the foyer are Diane and Bob, a middle-aged American couple who look like they have a keen sense of adventure and are to be our companions for the next few days. We make their acquaintance and climb into the Nissan.

The driver solves our coca leaf drought with a quick stop at the market and we fill our cheeks, melting into a numb but energised state of bliss and following a red dirt road out of the back of town.

Tupiza becomes a dusty dot in the rear view mirror.

We disappear into the heat waves of the high desert plains and begin the 1500-kilometre route into no-man's land.

Diane is considerably younger than Bob – I'm guessing by around fifteen years. Soft-spoken and of thin build with a pointy face and cropped haircut, she could be easily mistaken from a distance for a boy in his late teens. Her attire, made up of branded outdoor clothing is the mandatory fleece top and those ultra lightweight zip-off leg pants that only ever seem to be made in that drab shade of olive. Bob, a slightly quirky and confident forty-five-year-old, with rectangular spectacles perched on his pointy nose and a bright woollen earflap beanie on his head, carries the attitude of someone half his age and is obsessed with taking photos of everything for his travel blog.

Avid hang-gliders and all round adventure seekers, these two are a pleasure to spend four days with in a hot stuffy Land Cruiser. Dan and I find their stories of previous travel experiences utterly inspiring. From what I can make out, they've taken huge voluntary redundancy pay-outs from their desk jobs for the U.S. Army, invested the money wisely and, as far as I'm aware, are still travelling the world now.

Bob's father is a Vietnam veteran who moved to a small village outside of Tulum in the Yucatan in the late 1970s. Bob has been to visit his dad several times. Tulum and its surroundings, he tells us, are still untouched by the outside world and a far cry from the modern feel of life today.

"This one time I was down there," Bob says in his strong American accent, "the whole village stood with jaws gaping as I crushed a garlic clove with my knife." He recounts how, before this moment, they had spent hours peeling the things with their fingers.

Other delightful stories involving local hospitality are such a far cry to what I've experienced so far on this trip, bringing to the surface again my longing to be involved with the people of these foreign lands. And the obvious impediment of the language barrier.

Our driver, Alfonso, is an emaciated leathery-skinned man with greased jet-black hair that hangs limply around his giant oyster shell ears. He sucks at a quid of coca leaves bulging in his cheek, making him appear as though he has a huge tumour on his face. His wife, Mayra, is our cook. She's an amiable lady of a shy nature with bushy ringlet hair that envelopes her round face. She seems to be rather overdressed in a thick sheepskin-lined collared jacket.

I wonder if Mayra knows something we don't.

We slow to a halt at the side of the trail and get out of the jeep. The dry brown plain in front of us is littered with the white skulls and bones of animals as far as the eye can see.

"Alpaca y llama," Alfonso says, informing us of the species these bones once made up.

From the corner of my eye, I see a yellow football hurtling towards us through the cold dry air. It bounces over our bonnet followed by the sound of trashy chart music accompanied by a football anthem chanted loudly.

There, in the middle of this desolate place, is a group of rowdy British gap-year students running around in their football tracksuits. Not exactly fitting with the backdrop we have just arrived at.

"Did we just time warp to East London?" I remark to no one in particular.

Thankfully, Bob persuades Alfonso and Mayra to wait until the group moves on so that we can begin to appreciate the beauty that surrounds us.

"The Bolivian Alti Plano. Some of the highest and most desolate terrain on the planet," Bob says, taking in a deep breath and looking off towards the horizon.

The hooligans drive away, their shit music fading off into the distance, while a feeling of happiness overcomes me. I am glad we have chosen to share the next four days with Bob and Diane rather than the tracksuit gang and their football.

The Alti Plano, floating above the clouds, is a living Salvador Dali oil painting: a vast expanse of active volcanoes that puff white smoke into the deep blue sky, giant multi-coloured rock formations, immense desert plains and flamingo-filled red lakes. As we drive through it, we stare transfixed.

We have entered the world of the surreal.

Driving on, we continue to take in the multi-hued landscape. Every so often we see a shepherd herding his flock of pink ribbon-eared llamas that kick up red dust clouds from their hooves as they are ushered into pens constructed of cut branches and twine.

Our first stop is at the cliff edge of a deep red canyon where we look down on an otherworldly series of jagged vertical rock faces worn and patterned by the wind. This place is known as 'Quebrada de Palala' –

'The broken shovel'. The view is stunning, giving the impression that this landscape was created by a giant chainsaw carving vertical lines into the canyon walls.

We sleep that night in a mud-brick village littered with old rusting wrecks of jeeps balanced on bricks while grubby children in tattered clothing kick a football around. They skip around in worn out shoes as the sun sets.

And then the temperature drops.

The immense night sky turns jet black and is blanketed by millions of stars glinting like light twinkling through the holes in a giant sieve. I breathe the cold crisp air in deeply and exhale.

Seeing shadows of flickering flames dancing on a wall, Bob invites himself through an alpaca skin curtain hung over a narrow doorway into a family's tiny dirt-floored lounge – and beckons us to join him. Dan and I feel slightly intrusive, but we follow and are greeted by a mother and three small children in earflap hats huddling round a roaring fire emitting an almost unbearable heat.

Bob makes Spanish small talk but the family's vacant stares don't seem overly excited that we are cramping their tiny lounge. We retire to our hay bale mattresses and slide under the heavy layers of woollen blankets.

Later, I miss the crowded warmth of their small space. The temperatures as low as -26 degrees during the night are combated by full thermals, alpaca jumpers and thick blankets. I need to piss but decide to hold off till morning, for fear of my dick snapping off like a frozen icicle.

Mayra's sheepskin jacket makes complete sense to me now.

At 5:00am, Alfonso wakes us. Our breath is visible in the beams of our head torches as we follow him to where Mayra has piping hot coffee, eggs and tortilla ready. My freezing cold hands thaw around the hot coffee mug, while my stomach warms with the food. Dawn breaks and the jeep's interior feels like a chest freezer. Desperately, we wait for it to warm up. We follow a set of railroad tracks that define the Chilean border as the sun rises. The cone of volcano Ollagüe stains the deep blue sky with a long plume of white smoke while the baked brown canyons give glimpses of ancient Spanish mine shafts still containing small amounts of gold, silver, and bronze.

Alfonso slows the jeep to a crawl. "Baja, baja," he says, urging us to get out.

We alight and walk up a track of loose rocks, potholes and sand, and I'm wondering how the jeep is going to make it. But without the extra weight from the passengers, and with a push or two from us, Alfonso manages to bounce and clear the obstacle course without too much of a problem.

As we're walking up this section, a wind-burnt, rosy-cheeked girl appears from nowhere. Shaking a plastic bag of gloves and beanies, she squeaks for attention.

"Comprar, comprar, por favor," she says, persuasively making us try on the alpaca wool items that her mother has obviously sent her out to sell. Moments later she is singing a song and skipping back into the high plains with a fist full of coins, her goods now adorning our hands and heads.

Our next village is of the same red mud-brick construction, the only building over two metres high is the tiny church and its bell tower, itself only reaching another metre towards the deep blue sky. Mayra gets straight to cooking and prepares a stack of bean burritos before we retire with full, warm bellies.

Coffee and eggs begin our day the next morning, and soon we're off again in our 4x4, travelling a well-driven track through an immense canyon where the mountainside's red, white and gold veins run across and down its face like waterfalls. In the middle of this canyon stand a group of rocks sculpted over thousands of years by the gritty high winds of sand that constantly blow through, cutting them into strangely shaped statues. Like a small orchard of apple trees, their thick stone trunks sprout from the red dirt and support giant bulbous rock heads of the same hews of the canyon. It's hard to imagine how they support such a great weight. The landscape resembles a moonscape. It's an amazing sight.

Still driving higher and losing more oxygen every metre, we enter a sulphurous field of bubbling holes in the white rock floor. The vapour emitted burns the hairs inside the nostrils. We stand among these steaming geysers for a while. The sound of their blowholes is reminiscent of a pod of whales.

This is a desolate place up here, lost in the sky.

A few kilometres further on we break for lunch at a series of natural thermal pools, eating bean and salsa sandwiches with our feet soaking in the warm water. Before long, we're back on the road again and heading to Laguna Verde, a huge emerald green lake sitting at 5000m – and the highest point of our trip. Its shimmering jade water glistens in the blinding sun; it's hard to describe the neon green water and its crusted salt shoreline. We marvel a while, and soon we notice the lack of oxygen is starting to take hold. The air becomes dry enough to feel our lips crack and the oxygen-starved altitude is beginning to rob us of any hydration we have left. Dan leaves his smokes in his pocket.

So we drop back down through the brown landscape 1000m or so.

Our next accommodation is an edifice made entirely of salt bricks. Joining the guides driving the other groups, we tuck into another sumptuous meal from Mayra, this time a smoky beef broth. We play cards. Or at least try to. Bob, Diane and Dan listen to the rules of the game, while I sit there bewildered and feeling left out as I struggle to pick up the gist of how it's played. Once again, my insecurities and frustrations with the language eat me up from the inside out. I give up, as I can see my lack of the language is slowing things up considerably, and retire to my salt-bricked room where, from the window, I can see our route tomorrow: a dirty brown line that cuts through the middle of the vast salt flats and disappears as the dusky blue night fades to black.

The salt flats of Uyuni are gradually illuminated by the milky pre-dawn light that appears from the horizon as we drive into the vast 10,500 square kilometres of hexagonally crusted tiles of salt plains, where white meets blue in all directions on the distant horizon. Perception is completely lost in this flat, eternal desert, a strangely mystical place where white earth meets blue sky, and sunburn is only a few seconds away for anyone disembarking the 4x4 and not slathered in cream. The photo opportunities here are endless and create incredible illusions in depth perception. Standing twenty metres behind an object makes it possible to appear as if you're standing on top of it, like a Coke can or plastic bottle, for example. Bob and Diane snap photo after photo – they seem to have a knack for this kind of thing. Dan and I, however, with full cheeks of coca leaves and suffering from lack of oxygen, forget about our positioning in relation to our shadows, and – as later evidenced by our series of photos – fail miserably.

In the centre of the flats sits Isla Pescado – 'fish island' – thus named because, from a distance, it looks like a fish. Really, it's a giant rocky 'island' in the middle of the salt plain populated by hundreds of cactus trees. As we pull up at 6am to the base, we pass two mountain bikes parked outside a blue tent pegged into the icy salt cloaked by the dark shadow formed by the rock.

"Holy shit! Are they for real?" I remark.

"Are they alive?" Bob follows.

"Hope they've got thick sleeping bags," Dan mutters.

We wander over the rocky island and weave through its giant cactus trees. I am grateful when the sun slowly gains heat as it rises in the pale blue cloudless sky. We never encounter the two people from the shaded tent. I hope they survived.

The salt flats pass by outside, a view that never changes for an hour or so as we drive mid-morning to a salt farm, its fields covered with waist-high pyramids of the white granules waiting to be bagged and shipped off for export.

Endless stretches of quinoa rows fill fields being hand-harvested by small groups of old, bent, plaited women, as the tyres of the 4x4 crunch along the dry dirt road into in the sun-bleached, wind-worn, Wild West town of Uyuni, its streets lined with little carts offering quinoa juices and hot corn tamales.

We find a hostel, our only criteria after four days of staying in the same clothes being hot showers.

Within the gold-trimmed, burgundy-tiled walls of the shower stall, the steam rises from the hot water as it thaws my filthy body and nurses my joints and parched skin. This is without doubt one of the more memorable showers of my lifetime. Drying off with a burgundy towel, I dress in clean clothes for the first time in close to a week and go to look around the foyer area for a vending machine. I find nothing. The hotel is basically a reception and a hallway of rooms all coated in a dark shade of burgundy and trimmed with gold door knobs and cupboard handles. If I had to describe it, my description would linger somewhere between Bolivian / Arabic chic with faint smells of mildew. It's beyond gaudy but also under-cared-for. But I can't complain since, compared to the last few nights, it's definitely a step up. Apart from Bob and Diane, it appears empty.

Outside town, there is a locomotive graveyard that I'm dying to see. Bob is immersed in his blog writing but Diane and Dan are both eager to see it too and we head there on foot, following the rubbish-strewn train tracks out to the edge of town. We arrive at three long-linked rows of late-19th-century rusty locomotives. Sunken in the dirt and surrounded by randomly scattered twisted train parts, the rusty axles and bent wrecks of crashed carriages are strewn across the landscape and backdropped by the red mountains. Exploring this interesting site, I only wish these eerie giant hunks of neglected history could tell their stories. I feel a spooky curiosity creep over me, wondering about their journeys and the people they've carried. I am left with questions, and I feel something akin to unease settle in my mind. After all the vast natural beauty of the salt landscape and eroded canyons, this small graveyard is a reminder that people's memories and stories are part of the landscape too.

And then we're brought back to modern-day reality by a bunch of local teenagers who add a strange dynamic to the scene, with a bottle of whisky and a portable stereo blasting auto-tuned lyrics from an open-topped gravel car sunken in the sand. With the ambience shattered, we turn to leave. We follow the rusty tracks back to Uyuni, passing a woman and her two children sifting through the town's rubbish piles alongside the rails while another squats and squeezes out a poo. I keep my eyes averted and walk on, not quite knowing what to think or feel. I am suddenly, strangely, ashamed of my upbringing – of the careless attitudes of the land of plenty. We are certainly a long way from home. That night I dream of the hulking skeletal locomotive ghosts, and that kid in the garbage dump.

Back in town, we bid Bob and Diane farewell and purchase our tickets for the following morning's bus. The bus ticket counter is in a rickety corner store, its only furniture an old glass cabinet desk full of dusty plates and candle sticks. The teenage girl, propped on a long wooden bench and cradling a baby in a white shawl, hardly bats an eyelid as she exchanges our money for the tickets. She says nothing to us as we leave. I glance back over my shoulder to see her shift the fuzzy-haired baby, now contentedly sucking away on her large brown nipple.

CHAPTER SEVENTEEN
POTOSÍ

A faded pink deathtrap bus with a web of cracks across its windscreen is parked outside the corner store the next morning. An embarrassment to the Mercedes brand, the bus looks more like it belongs in the locomotive graveyard, or the less picturesque rubbish pile just outside town. Peeling, clear tape holds the headlights together, and the super luxury decals that adorn its dented panels date it to the early 1980s. Our bags have already joined the others on the roof so there's no turning back.

We climb aboard.

Seven hours of torture follow, as the wheezy vehicle winds its way up and down a gut-churning unsealed mountain road. We drive across several ridges with sheer drops either side that disappear into a green abyss below. The bus is overcrowded, and we must have dropped in altitude as the heat is intense. The interior of the bus becomes an inferno as the broken air-conditioning whirrs noisily, clearly not performing as it's meant to. I wonder, briefly, if Dan has photographed the broke-down air-con.

Children cry through their bubbling snotty noses. Sacks of rice and vegetables spill their contents into the aisles as the vehicle leans on broken shock absorbers at every sharp bend. The child sitting on his mother's knee next to me turns a shade of green and his head starts to jerk like a clucking chicken. His mother quickly pulls a black plastic bag from her purse (obviously prepared for this regular occurrence). He fills the bag with a torrent of vile smelling puke. I'm trapped with no escape.

Halfway through this acid trip of a bus ride we have a toilet stop – the icing on the cake. I watch a row of bowler-hatted indigenous women hoist their frills and squat at the side of the road in the dusty lay-by to squirt jets of piss over the cliff's edge.

Another three hours of oven-roasted torture and we arrive,

dehydrated and sweating but now back at altitude, our sweat rapidly cooling due to the colder temperature. Potosí's centre is bustling and our bags are thrown from the roof of the pink shitheap in to it all. I see a sign reading 'Bienvenidos a Potosí – 4100m'.

"Time to restock on the coca leaves," Dan says.

Once the richest town in the world, Potosí is now a shadow of its former glory days. The rotten crumbling 17th-century balconies attached to the facades of the crooked buildings hang precariously over the narrow streets below. A group of women in traditional dress, grubby-faced and armed with crowbars, replace the cobbles in a street. They prise the old ones up before settling the new ones in place with rough, calloused hands.

Dan and I do as we always do upon arrival in a new town: we find a nearby hostel and check in to offload our packs. We meet a weighty, Welsh rugby player by the name of Fred, his partner Laura, and a tall Irish chap called Warren, whom we team up with for the next two weeks. Fred is the outspoken, more forward one of the bunch with a shaved shiny head and a gap between his two front teeth that is constantly on show with his continuous bellowing laughter and smiles. Warren, on the other hand, is the quieter type but speaks with a confidence and wisdom that makes you shut up and want to listen to whatever he has to say, although his grasp of the Spanish language makes me look like a natural. Then last but by no means least is Laura, Fred's girlfriend, who sports a pair of rectangle-framed glasses and, from what I can tell, is just what Fred needs for good balance.

That night, we meet another traveller, who sinks into the worn brown leather couches of the hostel common room and tells a story of a scam he fell for in broad daylight on a busy street in La Paz.

"This old woman squirted ketchup on my shoulder and disappeared into the crowd," he begins. "Then this other geezer comes up and starts cleaning it off with a tissue, but I didn't realise that the old woman had circled back and nicked my wallet while I was occupied with the other dude. They were working as a team."

Such stories are common in every gringo hostel. And they are worrying, too. But one advantage is being aware of them and avoiding the same happening again when someone is trying it on you. Our Buenos Aires incident is a perfect example of how not to avoid trouble.

The giant Cerro Rico mountain looming over the vast sea of terra-cotta tiled roofs that shelter the town is riddled with mine shafts and tunnels. The hill once stood a few hundred metres higher but diminished during the mining period between 1556 and 1783, as the Spanish, by means of slavery and torture, extracted a total of 41,000 metric tonnes of pure silver from its depths. Warren, the quieter Irish guy, surprises me when he relays this information about the mine.

Tours of this labyrinth are advertised on the hostel pin board and we book in for the next morning. Laura decides to stay back and browse the markets but we are joined by an Italian guy staying in our dorm by the name of Gino. We're taken by our guide to a rotund woman with a face like a toad who sits in a small hut surrounded by waist-high sacks of coca leaves and shelves of a nasty pure alcohol by the name of Ciebo. With a grumpy grunt she sells us some of the brew to gift to the miners working in the tunnels. We do as instructed and also cop a bag of the leaves each for ourselves.

In the courtyard of the tour company we are given protective suits to put on. What passes as 'protective' for these tour guides are basically cheap yellow wet-weather coveralls. We are, however, also handed metal miners' helmets with huge headlamps powered by even huger battery packs hanging from thick leather belts that we are also required to wear. I look like a deep sea diver from a past century. After a short tour of the refinery and its poisonous pools of chemicals used to extract the metals from the rock, we follow a mass of tangled wires hung on the rock face that lead into a hand cut tunnel and join Marco, our second guide. Pablo, our main guide, leads us crouching into a very small cave where a life-sized caricature statue of the satanic horned midget-god 'El Tio' stands. Surrounded by miners' offerings of cigarettes and coca leaves the small hole we're crouching in is more like a rubbish tip. Pablo and Dan light up cigarettes before we begin our descent.

The weight of the belts and gear burdens us as we start to descend. The chutes are hard work and they become narrower, so narrow that it's impossible to turn 180 degrees – impossible to even think of going back. Reaching the second level down, the descent into an ever-more restrictive atmosphere becomes all too much for Gino the Italian. He begins to get agitated, and his agitation soon turns to panic attack; he demands to be taken out and back up to the fresh air.

The brochure at the hostel clearly stated that we would always have two guides with us at all times due to the danger present when underground, but the Italian's episode has been resolved with no regard for that rule as we are now left with only Pablo. Another two storeys down into the oxygen-starved depths, our protective clothing is now heavy, drenched in sweat and restricting movement heavily. This is not surprising as the suits are basically made from thick tarpaulin, an utterly non-breathable fabric.

We soon meet a group of miners pushing an overloaded cart by hand. Their faces are blackened with dust and oil; the whites of their eyes are hauntingly bright as they pass pushing the squeaky cart with great difficulty. Our guide informs us that they have a general life expectancy of around thirty-five years and work in these tiny tunnels for up to twelve hours a day, breathing in filthy dust in the 40-degree inferno. The miners in front of us suddenly lose control of the cart, and they can do nothing but watch as, almost in slow motion, it derails and spills its load on a corner.

"OK, it's good time to give gifts now," Pablo instructs, ushering us towards them.

We hand over the coca, alcohol and fizzy drinks we brought. Their defeated looks turn to smiles and they sit down on the upturned cart, swigging back the booze and chasing it with soda before stuffing fistfuls of the coca leaves into their mouths with gusto. As we leave they smile again, white teeth glowing from soot-blackened faces.

The maze of tunnels open out into carved rooms, the silver veins long ago dug out with hand picks and dynamite. An explosion off in the dark distance rattles our nerves and sends us dropping to the floor as the walls of the chasm send small rocks and dust raining down on our helmets.

"Bloody hell!" Fred shouts holding his helmet on. "Mental!"

"Last year alone, sixty child workers died from cave-ins," Pablo informs us, as if it's some kind of reassurance. He continues, "A total of 30,000 African slaves were shipped over and put to work down here during the colonial period, not to mention the countless Bolivians."

Sparking up a cigarette in the sulphurous air, he calls back to us. "¡Ustedes son de buen salud! ¡Vamos!" Thank goodness for that: we are all of good fitness. Surely that will save us from the shuddering walls.

Pablo leads us on an upward climb through cramped vertical shafts and a series of claustrophobic long horizontal crevasses totalling around forty metres that are only passable by crawling, shuffling and basically shoving your face in the arse of the person in front of you. As we pull ourselves through, scraping the floor with our bellies and roof with shoulder blades, the desperate panting of Fred behind me heightens: clearly a sound of fear. Considering his size, it's a wonder he's able to fit in these tight places at all. When we finally exit the mineshaft, blinded by the light and doubling over gasping for breath, I glance around at the group. Each one wears the same look of relief.

We are led to a car park that overlooks the town. Pablo tosses us some plastic wire and a roll of Sellotape.

"Let's make dynamite!" he shouts, looking excited. He fills plastic bags with gunpowder and tapes the wire around the top, and, a little too expertly, demonstrates the home-made bomb by lighting the fuse and throwing it down the hill, where it explodes, sending rocks up into the air. We follow suit, lighting our fuses and throw them towards the town and watch as they detonate, back-dropped by the town's terracotta rooftops.

The evenings we spend with the Irish and Welsh guys in some of the town's underground bars known as 'Whiskerias' are memorable. These low-roofed dingy discotheques, purple and red flashing lights one of their key signatures, are underground basements located at the bottom of steep flights of stairs. The whiskerias are very popular in the evening with the local young crowd. One of these nights ends with the short English guy stumbling back to the hostel solo and getting robbed by a pack of twelve-year-olds along the way. This is the same guy who told the La Paz ketchup story; he now has another to add to his list. On another occasion, I was the one stumbling solo. I was trying to navigate my way back after one too many pitchers of a mixture of blackcurrant syrup and what I'm presuming is the nasty Ciebo alcohol that we'd gifted the miners. Developing 3D vision at the bar, and deciding enough's enough, and that I can get home without Dan and the other three, I climb the stairs, feeling like a man growing paralysed from the waist down, dragging my feet – which soon take on the weight of cinder blocks. I emerge out in to the orange glow of the dimly lit narrow street, but I am completely disorientated as to which way is home, and stumble off across the cobbles in the direction I believe I'm meant to be going. But I wander for a few minutes and realise I should be heading in the opposite direction. I can see my breath in the cold night air and the 3D vision really isn't helping. My guts are starting to rumble as they battle to digest the potent alcohol-syrup mix. The slippery cobbles are becoming more of a challenge, and I have to concentrate even more on staying upright – and now I'm faced with a new problem: either shitting myself or crouching in a driveway to let the rumbling turd escape. So I squat. I choose a good corner – mostly dry and out of the way. I lean with my back against a wall and drop my trousers in the nick of time as something the size of a cowpat slides out. Now relieved, but still paralytic, I shimmy back up the wall with my shoulders while pulling up my pants, and wobble off on my quest for the hostel.

I see the blinking light of the hostel sign: I've made it. I enter through the dark foyer like a puppet on strings and step into the dorm. Before I can catch myself, I lose my balance and fall backwards like a plank of wood, landing flat on my back. I manage to scramble up and into bed, but I am awakened ten minutes later by my stomach. I crawl to the bathroom where I cling to the slimy toilet bowl for what feels like an eternity and throw up a continuous stream of blackcurrant bile.

Opening my eyes the following morning, I see that apart from Dan, who's still snoring, the dorm around me is completely vacated. My head is pounding. Pulling myself together and walking to the shower, I rub my head, suddenly remembering the events of the night before. *Where did I do that shit?* I think to myself, now feeling ashamed and wishing I'd never done it. I venture out into the street, worried at what I'm going to find as I retrace my steps.

And there it is. A few metres from the hostel door. My enormous shit. What I thought, at the time, to be halfway home is actually the house next door, and my excrement has been scooped up and smudged all over the driveway by the automatic garage door I had leant against.

CHAPTER EIGHTEEN
SUCRE

I spend the day – how else? – hung over. I'm ashamed. I am no different to the travellers I despise. I am a disrespectful gringo, drinking my way up the trail named after dickheads like me. I go to the common room to select a few books left behind by other backpackers. Seems like a good morning for a long, quiet read.

Finishing up a photo book on the silver mine history, I browse the hostel notice board, and spy a scrap of paper pinned amongst the other brochures and phone numbers. The small, hand-written sign reads: *'Sucre train every Thursday 7am'*. This seems weird as everyone I ask at the hostel hasn't heard of it before; every visitor has arrived by bus, and will be leaving by bus.

The man at reception sheds some light on the matter. "Siii amigos, pero es como siete horas a Sucre por ese tren." Seven hours – as opposed to three and a half by bus.

"Hey Fred, let's go by train, eh?" I suggest.

"Yep, sounds good to me, boyo, the others'll be up for it, I'm sure."

Thursday morning at 6am, the five of us – Dan, Warren, Laura, Fred and I – walk through town, greeted by brisk -2 temperatures, to book in for the mystery train ride. The frosty platforms are eerily silent like a deserted film set, the crew and lights long since wrapped up and gone. We sit and wait. Gradually, more people arrive and fill the platform in a mist of frosty air. All heads turn as the clunk of a lock unbolts from the inside of a dark blue door to the ticket office. The door opens with a creak, and a short stationmaster is there in the doorway.

"¿Porque quiere viajar en tren?" he asks – confused about our want to travel by rail. "Todos los dias hay buses a Sucre," he tells us. Plenty of buses every day to Sucre. Is this a hint? Not for us – we are determined to try the now-legendary train. The stationmaster shrugs and takes our passport details. We hand over the $4 fare and he hands us each a crumpled pink raffle ticket.

Our group towers over the small sea of bowler hats at the station. We feel them watching, these curious but reserved Bolivians who we will be riding with. Looking down, I wonder what we're getting ourselves into. I can't help but think these train tracks are the old small-gauge type. I figure – hope – that we'll be riding on the larger ones, the ones like those that support the huge locomotive across the other side of the train yard. Never mind that it's ancient – it's large, and that gives me some degree of reassurance. I look again at the thin tracks before us, wondering again what we've got ourselves into.

Suddenly, the wooden doors of an old shed over on the furthest tracks swing open, and out of a thick cloud of exhaust smoke appears a carbon copy of the pink bus in Uyuni, the only difference being its white paint job and that the tyres have been swapped for train wheels. It belches smoke and winds its way over to us, and my companions and I all do a bad job of masking our laughter from the platform. It must be a track maintenance train. But no – our assumptions are challenged, with finality, when our bags are thrown, tarped and roped onto the roof.

Here we go again.

The thirty-two-seat, 1980 Mercedes is an uncomfortable squeeze for the forty people who are all now squashed into the interior of the car that precariously bulges out over each side of the narrow undercarriage it balances on. I have a bag of garlic under my feet and what suspiciously feels like a sack of cocaine (in reality, probably corn flour) in my lap while my neighbour holds two live chickens in a string net that poke and bob their heads up through the holes. With a sound like metal being chopped to bits with an axe, the train jolts out of Potosí and crawls at five miles an hour, chased by a few malnourished barking dogs. We pass through a narrow space between shanty buildings that stand inches from either side of the tracks, and our journey begins.

If the overcrowded bus-on-tracks was not the first indicator that we should rethink the trip, the driver's attire and driving skills should have been the second concern. For some inexplicable reason, he is wearing a red construction site hard hat and is passing the steering wheel through his hands as if he's driving a car, turning when the track veers off to the left or right. This obviously has no effect in the direction we are travelling but he continues to feed the wheel through his hands for the duration of the trip. The wheels grind up the buckled, twisted rails, and, as we sway from side to side, all I can think about is how on earth this top-heavy contraption is going to stay upright. The outskirts of town, and all its pigs and chickens, slowly disappear behind us as our 'train' sways and squeaks up into the lush mountainous countryside like a badly-serviced fairground ride.

Three hours into the trip and the train comes to a halt on an incline as a woman in Victorian dress appears from a bush and hands the driver his lunch through his window in a steaming black plastic bag. Flirting with the woman for five minutes while we sit in silence sweating like dogs, he finally bids her farewell and engages the engine. The train tries to pull away but remains stationary while its back wheels spin and screech on the rails.

"¡Atras! ¡Atras!" our conductor shouts, ordering us to all move to the rear for some weight assistance.

We huddle at the back with the rest of the passengers, and the wheels eventually bite the track. We move off again, following the ridge of the mountains where sweeping gorges fall away to either side.

Collecting a few other country folk and their sacks at random bushes along the way, the train finally pulls in with an ear-piercing squeal alongside an actual platform. Purple and yellow alpine flowers surround us as a buxom woman with a 20-litre paint bucket approaches with a frown. Uncovering a steaming tea towel from the pail, an irresistible aroma hits us. The bucket is full to the brim with hot fried corn cakes. She empties her deep bucket of its contents, and we wolf them down. Then, the plump woman disappears down an alley into the village, her frilly pinny pocket full of bolivianos. I think back to the small girl selling gloves in the Alti Plano. We trundle away from the platform, back in to the purple flowered wilderness, our bellies full.

Three more hours of winding rails that vanish over the crest of each rise and we stop at a large hinged wooden gate, locked across the tracks.

"¡Terminamos!" the conductor shouts.

"This is us," Dan translates.

The passengers begin to gather their belongings from the overhead racks, and we follow suit.

Although we have exited the train into a glorious afternoon, we still don't seem to be in Sucre. In actual fact we don't seem to be anywhere. We walk for twenty minutes along a hedge-lined road, unsure if we're heading in the right direction, when a taxi slows. We tell him we're looking for Sucre, and he takes us the opposite way. We alight the taxi at the kerb edge, and we're left standing on a street flanked by tall whitewashed colonial buildings, all very well kept and maintained.

"This is alright, isn't it?" Fred says sounding impressed.

"Yeah, not bad, oim tirsty," Warren replies in his thick Irish drawl.

We venture on to find refreshment and come to a small boy with a drink cart. We surmise it's a drink cart by the giant plastic Coke bottle that towers over the dirty-faced boy pushing the sack trolley that it's attached to. The boy is no older than eight or nine. We buy a Coke from him, and a security guard in t-shirt and jeans leaning next to the nearby ATM whistles him over. The guard sets his beat up semi-automatic weapon against the huge bottle; boy and guard exchange words and money. The boy opens a little hatch and pulls out an ice-cold Coke for the guard. It's our first encounter with such a scene: armed guard and young boy, in a simple everyday exchange. We are shocked by the sheer pedestrian quality of this scene: there's an *automatic weapon*, for fuck's sake. But such scenes become an everyday occurrence over the following nine months and, strangely, a sight I become comfortable with.

Our timing is just right: Sucre is celebrating their 200-year bicentennial. The city has a joyous air about it and sounds of pan pipes sail along the flag-lined streets and through the windows into the open-air courtyard of the hotel.

Joining the party, we randomly bump into Maria who we'd said goodbye to back in Villazon.

"What der yer tink o me new huur?" She flicks her bright electric blue mop of hair.

"Nice!" I reply, surprised at how stoked I am to see her, and interested to hear how she's going at the orphanage.

She's enjoying the experience of working with the children and proudly shows us a bunch of photos from the school. "Dey're great," she says, beaming with pride and naming them one by one as she scrolls through the photos.

We drink a few beers with Maria at a street stall but become separated in the crowded street scene. I wonder if we'll see her again.

We mingle back in with the street revellers.

Dan, now on the other side of seven beers, jumps behind the smoky barbecue of a street stall to show a plump woman how to cook her meat while a gaggle of her rotund friends cackle at him, laughing and shouting rude innuendos. I feel immersed in the celebrations and the people. I don't realise it at the time but Sucre has put me in a state of ease. The night comes to a close and Fred finishes the evening by pissing in the bath in our room before passing out on a bench in the foyer of the hotel in his underwear – underwear that his big hairy cheeks have swallowed deep into his arse crack. I feel for anyone who has to see this, but also seize the opportunity and take a photo.

Which reminds me of Dan's photo series. Over the past week, he's added a couple of beauties to his album of random images, one being the stack of wires leading into the depths of the Cerro Rico mine shaft and another of a bootleg NZ Rugby jersey hung outside a shop in Potosí. Photos he's sure will be meaningful at the end of our adventure. Photos that chronicle, in no particular order, an underside of our story, no doubt.

How he misses this opportunity I come to discover when I arrive in our dorm: Dan is passed out in equal fashion, prone and, fully clothed apart from one shoe that's almost pulled the sock off the same foot and that dirty baseball cap permanently stuck to his head.

Waking with throbbing hangovers, Laura comes into our room

laughing. "The maids can't stop giggling," she laughs. "Look at him!"

Rubbing my eyes and sitting up, I see Fred on the landing outside our door, leaning against the railing but still in his underpants.

"They swept around him!" Laura says, still laughing.

Dan and I leave Fred, Laura and Warren to sort their shit out while we go in search of the local markets. We find another undercover grotto of plastic tables and steamy kitchens where round women swaddled in woollen shawls beckon us to sit and eat their food. We pick an exceptionally short woman whose face would brighten up the gloomiest of days and sit on beer crate seats waiting for our sausages to be cooked. The sizzling treats that she fries up get me salivating as I sit looking at the mountains of curly sausages in every shade of pink and crimson sitting atop giant sacks of onions.

"Fred and the others are leaving today. What are we gonna do?" Dan asks me, as the round woman toasts two bread rolls for the sausages now placed in front of us.

"May as well just get the night bus and meet them at their hostel then, yeah?" I suggest, stabbing a plump sausage while he shoots ketchup over himself as he bites into his hotdog.

CHAPTER NINETEEN
LA PAZ

The day drags on back in the tired company of each other now that our new friends have left for La Paz. We catch a taxi earlier than needed to the terminal. Stepping from the taxi, the first thing I see is a bleating llama wearing a striped woollen poncho that's lead on a leash and stuffed into the luggage hold of the bus next to ours.

"What the fuck? Did you just see that?!" I remark to Dan in shock.

"Yeah, trippy, eh?" he replies, lighting a cigarette. "I wonder if it'll survive the ride?" He drags a long puff.

"I don't fancy its chances," I conclude, entering the maze of ticket offices.

The Sucre bus station is the most congested and busy of the trip so far. Every seat and most of the floor space is occupied. Sacks of food and new television sets wrapped in string and cardboard are sprawled over the huge wooden waiting room floor, while the odour of hot tamales wafts through the air. Babies wrapped in multi-coloured striped blankets hang from their mothers' backs, and the booths are alive with the loud chanting of destinations.

"¡La Paz! ¡La Paz! ¡La Paz!"

"¡Potosí! ¡Potosí! ¡Potosí! ¡Potosí!"

"¡Cochabamba! ¡Cochabamba!"

The cries fly around the room from all angles.

"Fuck! This is intense!" Dan shouts to me over the din.

We pass our bags to the girl shouting *¡La Paz!* They are hung by the straps on a large hook at the end of a thick twill rope that dangles through a hole in the ceiling behind the cashier's head. We watch as the rope is pulled with a jerk and our bags disappear up through the ceiling, to the floor above. Then, as fast as they disappeared up through the hole, they're lowered again onto the platform and thrown in the hold. This all happens fast, in about thirty seconds. I still have the string security tag in my hand. Somehow it seems wholly unnecessary.

The double-decked coach groans out of the station, while locals continue to climb on board through the door, still not closed, and cram themselves into the aisles – for them, it's a free ride to the outskirts. A barefooted old lady in bowler hat and white frilled black Victorian dress is asleep in the stairwell. The sight stuns me for a moment before the crowd behind pushes me up the stairs over her. Finding a seat, I reflect on what I've just seen and the desperation of it – how this kind of desperation goes unnoticed. But my reflections are shattered by a small boy in an ill-fitting suit, who begins to screech a hymn at the top of his voice while shaking his flat cap in our faces.

"Give him all you got!" Dan says, laughing. "He's doing my head in."

We fill the hat with a few bolivianos, and the boy leaves, descending the stairs still squawking like a maimed baby bird. Within half an hour the commotion dies down as the freeloaders disembark in their respective villages and the bus skids on. We spend the next six hours trying to sleep while our bus makes its determined way around the narrow mountain roads in the pitch dark.

La Paz sits 4000 metres above sea level on a plateau surrounded by the jagged, snow-capped peaks of the Andes. It sounds like a perfect setting, but the city is smog-choked and freezing cold. We step outside the terminal at 4:30 am in -2 degrees, and we find one lone beat-up taxi, its white exhaust smoke twirling up into the cold night air, to take us to our hostel. We shudder in the cold as the taxi rattles up a curling road.

We bang on the iron-barred door for a full five minutes, and finally a sleepy-eyed receptionist unlocks it and we acquire the necessary change for the taxi driver and are shown to our room where we catch a couple of hours sleep.

Fred and the others have arrived earlier. We find them in the cafeteria in the early afternoon after a nap. I'm surprised when reading the menu that the food is of an Israeli / Bolivian fusion. I'm not convinced the combination of tortillas, eggs, middle-eastern salad and falafel will catch on.

"This is weird," I say to Fred, who's already eaten half his meal.

"Well, I reckon it's a far better option than that Wild Rover Irish backpackers that those fellas in Mendoza had been raving to you about," he says through a mouthful of food.

"Hey, don't knock it til ya troid it," Warren pipes up, defending his country.

"I'm calling it Boli fusion!" Fred says, laughing before shoving a fork full in his mouth.

Fred is dead right, of course: the last thing I'm looking for in Bolivia is a pub where I can eat bangers and mash while watching English football.

The hostel, it turns out, is Israeli owned and Bolivian run, which explains the strange choice of food in the canteen, and while we devour our breakfasts, Dan, adamant about his search for the 'Route 36' cocaine den, makes enquiries with a couple of Israeli lads at another table.

"It's been closed down for a while," one tells him. "They have to move every two months to avoid the police."

Which seems reasonable enough to me but is not to Dan's liking.

"Fuckin' bullshit," he says loudly. "Our timing is always so lame."

Next morning, we head off for a long, pleasantly directionless amble. It's maybe not the smartest idea, but after the B.A. incident and the stories we've heard in our hostels so far, we feel slightly more street smart and reckon we're up for this. The mobile phone and sim card stalls spill out in to the gutters on one side while wool yarn and popcorn stalls teeter on the other. The whole scene is dotted, of course, with black bowler hats tilted on the heads of short, dumpy indigenous women going about their daily business.

We reach a place called the witches' market that runs the length of a roughly cobbled street that clings to the side of the city's steep edge. We soon find ourselves sifting through the tat and trinkets on sale. The most bizarre thing we find is baskets of dried Llama foetuses, supposedly for good luck. Their distended facial features and gnarled, hairless skin, dried-out and brown, stretches over tiny unformed bones. These precious items casually sit among the other wares that overflow in the baskets and clutter the sidewalks lining the lane.

Warren is planning on climbing the snowy mountain peak that looms over La Paz from a distance and heads off to book in with a reputable guide company.

"Oil catch youse up laters!" he shouts disappearing into the crowd.

"This alpaca stuff is cheap!" Fred says, calling us over to a store with a front wall blanketed with the woven garments adorned with llama and Inca patterns.

"This is a great idea for presents," I suggest to the others. "Probably be real cheap to post home, too."

Bartering for the clothing and agreeing upon a reasonable price, we follow the steep streets down to the main plaza and on to the post office.

The ornate concrete building, pillared and with polished marble floors, is a time warp back to an era when Bolivia was wealthy and the precious metals that its mountains contained were still in abundance. We are directed down to the basement, and our packages are wrapped in blue tarpaulins and sewn up with white cord and great care, all for a song.

"Well, that takes care of Christmas!" Fred and Laura say together, happy with their purchases.

I feel slightly dubious about the Bolivian postal system, but really I should be more worried about the UK end, as I receive an email from my mother a full two months later to say that my special Christmas package has been opened on arrival at customs and then accidentally sent inside another parcel to someone else in the north of England, some two hundred miles away. Fortunately the receiver is an honest chap and contacts my mum and forwards my package to its rightful home. Lesson learned: never send camera cables and organic materials (in this instance, alpaca clothing) in the same parcel, and from a country such as Bolivia, lest the concerned customs officers mistake the ingredients for an explosive device.

It's only later in the day, when we trundle further into town to see a movie, that Fred remembers he's left his sleeping bag on the bus from Sucre, and we witness with great interest – and some distance – how his mood quickly changes from happy chuckling Welsh fellow to mighty angry rugby player. His inner rage escalates when Laura makes the mistake of saying, "It's just a sleeping bag."

At that very moment, a dirty-faced street beggar aggressively pesters him for money. We stand back.

"Come on then, mate! Come and get it, boyo! You wanna go?" he shouts, puffing up like a self-inflatable mattress and picking up the poor little man by the coat and dangling him horizontally like a surfboard bag. Letting out a squeal and wriggling free, the man quickly runs away down a side street.

"He didn't see dat comin', did he?!" Warren says, laughing.

The tatty cinema, full of young couples and their infants, plays an R18 violent film set in Rome about an Illuminati sect torturing and killing a number of religious figures. The audio static is deafening. Children of all ages, oblivious to the atrocities on screen, chase each other up and down the aisles, throwing handfuls of popcorn at each other and playing tag while their parents stay transfixed by the gore played on the big screen.

We taxi to the hostel with ringing ears. When we arrive, my money is refused by the driver. It takes a moment for me to catch onto what he is saying as he rejects my fifty Boliviano note.

"Es falso."

Seems I've been slipped a fake.

"For fuck's sake!" I bark after getting out. "How am I gonna get rid of this?" I try to remember who I've taken money from.

I've noticed that the hostel's seven floors are connected by a fireman's staircase that runs up through the centre and am curious to where it leads.

"Are we able to get on the roof?" I ask the receptionist.

The young Arab stares at me with his mouth open like a demented goldfish. "Only five minit and quiet please." He hands me a set of keys.

Climbing the dark stairwell is no easy task without lights. We feel our way up via the handrail. In the pitch black, I trip over something and hit my head on what seems to be a dead end. Fumbling around, I unbolt a lock and the door I've face-planted swings open.

"OH SHIT!" we exclaim simultaneously.

Laid out before us is a jaw-dropping 360-degree view over thousands of little brown Lego-like houses on the surrounding mountainsides. A million yellow lights twinkle magically all around.

"That Route 36 place is somewhere out there," Dan says wistfully.

He blows a plume of ciggy smoke into the cold night air and we marvel at the view for a while.

Stepping back into the stairwell, I see what I tripped on. A small girl is asleep on the steps. I take a wide berth.

Up early the next morning, we're on our way to what I've been looking forward to most since the trip began.

San Pedro prison sits awkwardly smack bang in the middle of the city, and since making its debut in Rusty Young's best-selling book, *Marching Powder*, it has been a main attraction on the gringo trail. The prison-tourist attraction is a unique thing in this world, and well worth a look for the multiple layers of corruption on view – not to mention high-grade cocaine.

The bestseller book tells the story of a backpacker who had strapped slabs of hashish to his waist and attempted to clear La Paz airport customs on his way back to England in 1996.

After being sentenced and experiencing daily life within the perimeter walls, Tanzanian-born, UK-raised Thomas McFadden struck a deal with the guards to let him run tours through the prison for travellers visiting the city. The prison, well known for its inmates manufacturing cocaine, became a backpacker hotspot and an attraction that soon featured in all the guidebooks. The story of San Pedro came to light after Aussie Rusty Young visited the jail with the specific purpose of calling on McFadden. The two struck up a friendship, and Young set to writing McFadden's story. His insider look at the San Pedro system was helped especially by the three months he spent in jail, sharing a cell with McFadden. But unlike McFadden and the other prisoners, Young remained there intentionally, bribing the guards to let him *stay*. He completed the book in 2003. I had read it before Dan and I set foot in Bolivia, but San Pedro had certainly been on my mind when we set La Paz as one of our destinations.

As we approach the main gate of the giant square structure, we see how, along its cracked concrete walls, there are patches of plaster cement fallen away, and at each corner, high up atop the wall, armed guards look down into the leafy plaza from their sentry boxes. I am suddenly aware of our vulnerability and feel a bit uneasy, the guards perched high up on those walls, surrounded by rolls of razor wire, and us far below wandering closer to prison. *Prison, for fuck's sake. In Bolivia.* What were we thinking? I'm from a small rural village in greenbelt England, what has turned me in to such a curious traveller, and why so curious for these destinations so far detached from my 'normal' upbringing? Maybe it's just that, to get or at least feel as far detached as I can from where I was raised.

Snapping out of my childhood daydream, we are greeted by a blue uniformed prison guard at the gate, who informs us our timing is poor.

"No hay tours. Vayase," he says, clutching a short-barrelled shotgun and shaking his head. In no uncertain terms, he tells us to go away.

Disappointed, we exit the courtyard and sit on a bench.

"This comes as no surprise really," I remark to Fred and Dan. "The guidebook's 'things to do' lists are starting to follow a pattern here, first the fort in Uruguay, then the train to the clouds in Salta, and the Route 36 drug bar. Now no tours at the prison. I wonder if Machu Picchu will be closed for renovations, too."

"We gotta go pack our stuff," Fred announces, surprising us. "We're on our way tonight."

"Yeah," Laura says. "We want to see as much as we can in Peru before we fly home."

And just like that we hug and vow to catch up at Christmas when I arrive in England.

I do catch up with Fred a few days after his Christmas work party, and upon meeting him, I can't help but notice his face is covered in tiny cuts.

"I thought it would be a great idea to smash a pint glass on me face in front of the managing director," he tells me in his thick Welsh accent. "The worst bit was driving two junctions down the motorway in the wrong direction by accident the next morning with a nasty hangover."

Dan and I, now just the two of us again, follow the street stalls around the corner that cling to the high grey wall of the prison and head up to the stadium, home to the Bolivian national football team. With the advantage of growing up in such a high altitude, they have an excellent record of home game wins, the visiting teams becoming short of breath soon after the game commences. There is no football today; the grounds are empty, but we enjoy the views just the same. We come to a small park above the grounds littered with slides and climbing frames. It is back-dropped by an eye-popping view of the city's millions of houses and apartment blocks that stretch far below and appear to be swallowed by the mountain basin, situated as they are up here in the clouds. We linger for twenty minutes or so, but the altitude starts to feel a trifle thin so we descend back into the city to book a cycling trip for the following day.

Hunting for a bike tour office that will take us down the 'Death road', I stop at an ATM – which tells me that my transaction of 400 bolivianos has been accepted but then fails to issue any money. I leave baffled and empty handed, praying that the machine was faulty and hasn't been rigged by some scam artist.

"Let's go," Dan says. "Try another one, it'll be sweet."

Successfully drawing 400 at a different machine, we find several tour outfits all on the same street, all offering the same tour.

A curly-haired woman in the musty cycle tour office sits at a wooden desk behind an ageing computer screen. She greets us with a confused stare, her right eye fixing us just right, the other – a glass eye that reminds me vaguely of Hogwart's Mad-Eye Moody – twisted to the left and staring at the unanswering wall. She explains the basics of the tour and offers us a price range of bikes that vary in safety. We choose the mid-priced disc brake option, and I hand over 350 bolivianos, slyly sneaking into the wad the fake 50-Boliviano note.

"Gracias amigos," she says, telling us to be outside the office at 04:30 the following day. The glass eye rolls unnaturally in its socket.

Back at the hostel, Fred and Laura have already checked out and Warren is packing his gear in preparation to climb Aconcagua Mountain.

"Crampons?" I say, intrigued as to the difficulty of the hike.

"Yeah, it's icy up dere," he answers, constantly flicking his fine hair from his eyes and stuffing sleeping bags and puffa jackets into a giant backpack. "It's six towsand nine hundrad an sixty two meetas at da top," he adds, specifically. "We do need oxygen tanks fer safety but I don't tink we go dat hoigh up. What toime yer leavin fer yer boike roide in der morning?"

Our seemingly treacherous death road ride now feels like a roll down to the shops compared to Warren's expedition.

"04:30," Dan answers.

"Ah, oil be gaan befere dat," Warren says, shaking our hands and wishing us well before going back to preparing his pack.

CHAPTER TWENTY
THE DEATH ROAD

Through the mist, a silver Mitsubishi twelve-seat van with a strange ticking noise coming from the engine arrives at the bike tour office at a cheery 5am, stacked high with mountain bikes. The driver climbs out and walks right up to me, frowning.

"Es falso amigo. No vale nada." He hands back my fake 50-boliviano note. The guide confirms it's of no value.

I stuff it back in my pocket and pretend to look innocent. I reluctantly hand over a real one and get in the van.

Dan and I, along with ten other cyclists of various nationalities, watch from the van windows as we climb out of the brown-bricked barrios that cling to the hills and up into the misty Andes to a scoria car park sitting at 4670m in the clouds. The guide and driver take the bikes down from the roof and get to serving the group an egg each, and some coffee, most of which goes straight through me. I wander around in circles like dogs do when they can't find the right spot; I'm desperate to find a secluded place but come up with nothing and so crouch behind a small rock, still in full view of the others, and with the same guilty look that dogs give their owners when they poo, I push out what resembles a dollop of refried beans that have been dropped from a great height.

"Which side do they drive on here?" Dan asks as we mount the bikes and look at the mist that swallows our route.

"¡Tuya!" the guide in front says, laughing.

Yours.

The next sixty-seven kilometres are divided into two parts. The first twenty-two is a wide asphalt road, smooth but slippery, winding its way down through the giant mist-shrouded charcoal mountain spikes of the Bolivian Andes. The second section, the next forty-five kilometres, is a twist of blind corners on a narrow, rough gravel trail. With no side barriers, it erodes off the 600-metre cliff edge that sheers away to the left.

For the first twenty kilometres my fingers are frozen solid to the handlebars and I struggle fiercely to claw at the brake levers at each slippery corner. Freezing cold and struggling to stay upright, I'm not particularly enjoying the ride, but I am spurred on by our tiny Bolivian guide, who flies past me straddled over a bike far too big for him and wearing just shorts and a jacket fashioned from a bin liner. I cling on and hope things will improve.

Leaving the tarmac, we stop at the Cotapata checkpoint and still in almost zero visibility, we find a marker that tells us we've already descended the asphalt part of the road. My hands have started to thaw out a little. A rickety wooden row of stores stands at the checkpoint and the guide tells us that a fifty boliviano fee is required to pass. *Finally*, I think: *I can get rid of that damned fake banknote*. I pull it from my wet pocket, pinching it between my numb thumb and forefinger. Never mind that it now looks more like a pre-moistened tissue and the face on it has smudged into a Picasso-like image. Admitting defeat, I do what I should have two days ago and throw it in a rubbish bin before taking out another real note from my wallet to pay.

The death road now becomes a shitty gravel track and we leave the drizzly checkpoint and return to the cold wet blanket of rain.

Seemingly positioned to make the curves all the more dangerous, white wooden crosses are hammered in on virtually every corner to commemorate the tourists and locals who have met their deaths after losing control of their vehicles and bicycles along this stretch of road. The number of crosses we pass is a good indicator of just how dangerous each curve is.

We skid to a stop at one of these crosses. It has fresh bunches of flowers around it. "El chico se murió muy rapido." Our guide informs us, relishing the details of the road's freshest horror story. "Allí." He points down to a large flat rock 100 metres below the crumbling edge of the sharp bend where a twenty-three-year-old British lad became the latest victim of this twisted widow maker, careening off the road to his death only a few days before.

Like obstacles in a Super Mario game, countless waterfalls pepper the jungle road, cutting deep grooves in the surface. The water and slippery bits of gravel desperately try to grab our wheels and derail us over the edge.

"Let's get out in front!" Dan yells to me over his shoulder.

"Just watch where your fucking going!" I yell back, as he slams on his brakes, barely staying on the track when a sharp corner appears from nowhere. My fingers, now completely thawed in the warm air, would've managed better being frozen to the bars right now as my hands are gripping for dear life while the bike chatters over rocks that have fallen from the cliffs above.

I'm on an adrenaline high the whole way, weaving and skidding on the loose surface as my arms judder with the jolting front suspension, all the while desperately trying to keep the bike upright. A French girl from our group finds out how dangerous this trip can be when she is pitched into the air in one of the slippery ruts; she takes a gash to her knee which confines her to the mini-van for the remainder of the descent. Suddenly a bus climbing up the mountain road towards us appears from around a corner, sending us skidding into the edge.

"Holy shit, that was close!" Dan says, gasping for breath and leaning into the cliff face.

Our group hugs the cliff and squeezes past the mini-bus. Looking back, the two vehicles jostle with each other on the thin track, their tyres spinning in the wet mud. The French girl inside the van looks white as a ghost as rock debris crashes into the foliage down below. Miraculously, and with wing mirrors folded in, the two vehicles finally manage to bite the surface and push past each other. We descend further and finally the climate warms and rays of sunshine light up the track ahead of us. We've dropped 3600m through three climates and are now at the far western edges of the Amazon jungle.

Our descent reveals the small town of Coroico further down the valley. It's a welcome site; Coroico is perched prettily on the side of a hill.

The track lulls us into a false sense of security. We increase our speed, pedalling as fast as we can. Neck and neck with Dan, skidding round a sharp corner, I realise it's too late to slow down as we enter a river crossing and come to a stop in knee-deep water. The rest of the group laughs at us as they cycle past through the correct, shallower part without a hitch. I feel like I'm in a Charlie Brown cartoon.

"¡Ya llegamos!" our guide shouts as we arrive at a row of run-down timber shacks otherwise known as the village of Yolosa. Cloaked in humidity, the small place has a restaurant where we sit down in the tropical heat and drink a cold beer.

"Now that's a good beer," Dan says, savouring the cold brew and chinking bottles with me while our clothes dry. I'm exhilarated. What we just achieved was no small feat. I buy us another round as the bikes are loaded on to the roof for the drive back to La Paz.

"Let's go stay in that village we saw," I suggest, as I slug back the rest of my beer.

"Yep, keen," he replies.

The van leaves our bags and the two of us at a crossroads on the edge of the village with rough directions to a local hotel.

CHAPTER TWENTY-ONE
COROICO

"Veinte minutos a caminar. ¡No mas!"

That's the last we hear from our mini-van driver. We are once again on our own, hoping his instructions are accurate. The van speeds away in a cloud of dust.

"Twenty minutes, eh?" Dan translates, unconvinced.

The single-track road is flanked by thick jungle on either side and alive with the sounds of bird life. We are more than a little surprised when, twenty minutes later, we enter the grounds of the hotel.

The pool area and bar is alive with the deafening sounds of crickets and surrounded by leafy tropical plants. The lounge is adorned with dusty stuffed snakes, herons and flamingos. The whole place is pleasant enough but eerily quiet save for a couple of Bolivian families lounging by the pool outside. It feels very Agatha Christie. The hotel proprietor who floats shiftily in and around the property is a short, round sweaty man with a small-brimmed straw fedora perched on his head and a ratty thin moustache that sprouts from under his nose.

"You come with me in car tomorrow, forty bolivianos," he suggests, wiping the sweat from his brow after Dan asks him about buses to Coroico. As the sun disappears for the night, we retire to our room and fall asleep hard. Who knew cycling – and surviving to tell the tale – would make us so tired?

Next morning, waking to an amplified volume of jungle birdsong, we are served some dry scrambled egg and climb into the hotel manager's metallic green Peugeot that climbs a slippery cobbled road up through terraced coca fields. As the bald tyres spin on the steep incline, we pass two machete-wielding farmers.

Moments later, the car runs out of fuel.

Dan and I swap a worried glance. We are now beginning to feel slightly uncomfortable with our situation, seeing as we are clearly stranded in what could quite possibly be the first stages of a cocaine growing operation run by small men with large knives. Muttering and cursing to himself, our driver suddenly remembers he has a spare gas can, which is sitting in the boot next to a lawnmower he is delivering. He hurriedly jumps out to grab it.

Our driver empties the can into the tank and we are off again, now running on the fumes of an oily rag. The Peugeot hisses a sigh of relief as it reaches the top of the hill and enters into a small, square central plaza where it stops outside a tiny tour office. Snatching our notes without a word, the hotel manager splutters off in the old French automobile, up one of the many steep lanes that branch off from the square.

The only thing we know about this place is the name. We've never read about it in any guidebook; we've never met anyone who's been here.

But at least we're not in the middle of a coca plantation anymore.

Giant condors swoop through the air streams above, their great wings casting huge shadows that ripple across the gigantic green mountains and their gentle lower slopes carpeted in banana, orange and coca plantations. The way these birds silently glide commands attention; the condor is something to behold. From a distance, that is. Close up, they are in fact terribly ugly creatures with a head and neck resembling a grey condom half rolled over an old man's flaccid wrinkly penis.

These creatures surround the town.

While deciding which way to head, I notice a hand-written advertisement for Spanish classes flapping in the breeze on a lamppost.

"I'm gonna do a few lessons while we're here," I tell Dan, nodding at the flapping paper. Dan is busy rummaging in his bag for cigarettes, so he gives an absent-minded shrug.

Halfway up a steep street we find a two-storey hotel and check in. Covered in brown wall tiles, it's a gloomy place that's had the life drained from it. Apart from us, we find the grandly named Castillo de Amazonas to be entirely bereft of guests.

In the main plaza that evening, a group of resident barefooted artisans, sporting foul-smelling dreadlocks and baggy hemp pants, sit on the sidewalk and sell colourful tat. These nomadic travellers will become a permanent fixture of most of the towns we pass through during our trip. They are always of the same appearance, complete with crusty dogs scratching themselves under their trestle tables laden with woven bracelets and other useless items. Next to these hippies is a round-faced smooth-skinned girl sitting in her food stand that is dimly lit by a string of yellow bulbs. Her face is so pretty I'm mesmerised, but – alas! – I am unable to talk to her as she clearly knows no English. I am not easily deterred, however, as I order one after another small servings of her sixty-five cent chicken and chips. I will keep ordering her chicken forever if it keeps the gleam in her enormous brown eyes alive. I am soon overstuffed but I think my heart is bursting, too.

"Come on, bro, let's hit the sack." Dan breaks my reverie. "My guts are feeling weird." I turn to him, annoyed that he is taking my gaze from the girl. "I dunno about that chicken," he adds, holding his stomach.

Fuckin' chicken. I am still thinking of the girl – *those eyes!* – even as I listen to Dan toss and turn. Sure enough, he ruins my mood and any chance of colourful dreaming, as he's back and forth to the toilet all night with a nasty case of the runs. It seems my gorgeous Bolivian queen sells a bad bird.

"How you feeling?" I ask him the next morning, knowing full well he's in bad shape.

"Just need rest," he struggles to say, his head in the pillow. "Get me some water."

I dutifully retrieve Dan a few bottles of water from town. Then I'm left to my own for the rest of the morning. I call about the lessons from the village payphone in the plaza.

"¡Si!" an excited woman answers on the other end of the line. "We can start now." She gives me her address.

I meet Elisa, my teacher, an hour later. She opens the door of a little house clinging to the cliff's edge, teetering over the deep gorge like all the other houses, with a cheery "¡Hola!" Her wiry figure is draped in an over-sized hand-knitted sweater, slippers and pyjama bottoms.

Elisa welcomes me inside and closes the front door. We enter her lounge. The view of the mountain valley from her window is indescribable: a deep, bottomless dark green abyss that stretches into the receding depths of the mountains.

But Elisa could care less about her view. She starts right in with the bare basics. "OK, you please write every word you know in Spanish in de book please."

Surprising myself, I fill two pages of an exercise book. I've obviously picked up more than I realise, and Elisa's patience with me is a comfort as she sits through my string of failed attempts at trying to link sentences together. She sends me away with a few homework challenges and I walk through the village feeling triumphant, not so much for my disastrous efforts at grammar but more for finally taking the plunge and at least trying to get a handle on the language.

Back at the hotel, Dan is still in bed and looks in no better shape.

"Here I got you some fruit, you gotta try to eat something," I tell him, putting a mango, an apple and a banana on his bed.

"I'll just puke it up, bro. I couldn't even keep that water down," he says, rolling over towards me and pushing the fruit away.

I leave him to it and sit alone in the piercing midday heat on the kerb in the central plaza. I hope he'll recover quickly as this little town, as peaceful as it is, is boring without my trusty companion. I sip my third ice-cold Coke through a straw, and a small dog runs past me, chased by a larger one. As I look up, I see Dan teetering – he's just ventured out to find me as the dogs race by, nearly knocking him over.

"Hey!" I say, happy to see him.

"Cheers for the fruit," he answers, joining me on the kerb.

"Check out these dogs, man," I say, as we watch the bigger dog bullying the small one into submission. Flipping the tiny yelping mongrel over with its nose, it pins it in the gutter and goes about giving it a serious licking – literally. No part of the small dog is left untouched, and certain parts are particularly sniffed out and slobbered over. It is strangely compelling, and we can't stop watching. We burst into fits of laughter.

When we regain our composure, I see that Dan is clearly looking better and has regained some colour in his cheeks.

As if the dog sex isn't enough entertainment, the notes of a brass band float on the wind from a side street. A small crowd form a wedding party, dressed in elegant dresses and top and tail suits. We watch them disappear into the plaza's church. Arranging ourselves back in the hostel, I partake in a cigarette with Dan and watch from our second-storey window as a mist of confetti blankets the church entrance while the happy couple pass bottles of champagne around.

Dan wakes early the next morning with the appetite of a dinosaur, after consuming next to nothing over the last day or so. The perfect place for breakfast turns out to be a shack tucked away down a side street, sheltered by a low iron roof with an edge that slopes dangerously into the lane at eye level. An extremely short and unusually round old woman serves us up a plate of beans and eggs, along with a wafer-thin slice of gristly steak. Demolishing his first plate, Dan orders seconds while a squinty-eyed old man sitting opposite sprays our food with spittle and laughs through the remaining teeth that poke out from his pink gums.

"¡Hay que caminar al cascada!" he spits, telling Dan about a track to a waterfall at the edge of town. "Vistas muy lindas." He wipes his lips with a serviette.

Dan probes the old man for info and we pay the round lady for the meal.

"I got a lesson," I remind Dan. "I'll see you in an hour." We head off in opposite directions, planning to meet back at the hotel after.

The second lesson is much the same as the first, and although Elisa seems to be running out of ideas, she's given me more than enough paperwork to keep me occupied in my studies if I don't see her again.

"OK, we see us tomorrow?" she asks, once the lesson is over.

"I will call you," I tell her, lying through my teeth.

"I've found us another place," Dan says when I return to the hotel. "It's half the price of this dive."

"OK, sounds good," I reply, without even seeing our new dwelling.

But I should have looked. Our room, looking over the same plaza as our former hotel room, but from the opposite side, is reached by a tiny staircase that branches off from the main one – and resembles a broom cupboard. As a matter of fact, I think it was the broom cupboard before the shitty beds were pushed in there. The toilet is by far the worst we've experienced yet, with a lid-less cistern and a sink plug chain attached to the flush mechanism that sits inside.

"Thank fuck I didn't get sick here," Dan says, staring at the toilet.

The wide wooden staircase spirals down through the centre of the hostel, giving views of the reception and bar area.

"Let's wash some clothes before the walk," I suggest. "We can hang them all up here on the railings."

Scrubbing what little clothing we have with soap and water on concrete washboard sinks, we then drape our washing out to dry over the top banisters and set out to the waterfall.

Wind currents support the huge condors that circle above, while their giant wingspans cast great shadows as they pass between us and the sun.

"You sure you've got the energy for this, bro?" I ask Dan, listening to him wheezing as we start up the narrow path that skirts the mountains.

"Yeah, I'll be sweet, just need fresh air," he replies unconvincingly.

The track leads us through wide green hills of tiered coca plantations where farmhands glare at us from the hillsides as if to say we're trespassing. I think back to our journey in the green Peugeot.

"Are we allowed here?" I wonder aloud while we take a water break.

"Hope so," Dan answers. "That old man at breakfast said it was sweet," he adds, looking up at the farmers tending their plants.

The trail is a pleasant variety of Andes back-dropped vistas and before long we arrive at the plunging wall of water rushing down the palisade. But as we come closer, we see that it is unfortunately ruined by a cluster of dirty grey PVC pipes that stick out of it to supply the coca fields. It is not the refreshing Andes scene we'd imagined. It resembles a sewer plant.

"What a letdown," I complain. What an ugly mess.

"They gotta make money somehow, bro," Dan says, much more accommodating.

I can tell he's exhausted so we rest there, despite the unfortunate view, before descending down the side of the waterfall and clambering under and over the pipes, to pop out of the undergrowth onto a dusty road. We make our way back towards town. The route is skirted with numerous cinderblock structures, the hardened masonry cement that holds them together oozing from between the bricks. One of these has a Coke sign sticking out from the wall and a few plastic household cleaning items hanging outside.

"Cold Coke!" Dan gasps. "I need cold Coke!"

We pop the tops off our Cokes with a cigarette lighter, and the young girl behind the counter can't believe what she's just seen; she asks us to do it again. Dan demonstrates and we leave her trying to pry her cap from her bottle.

Upon our return to the hostel, we find our laundry all over the floor of the dining area like soggy leaves. We look up to find the cleaning lady's children giggling as they lurk on the stairs. Seems they've found a source of entertainment and have been pushing our garments off the banisters.

"Una semana mas de este clima hombres," the hostel owner informs us with a wry smile, pointing at our wet clothes on the floor and telling us that we have a further week of fog to come.

The fog turns to rain over the next twenty-four hours and we are trapped in the hostel with the owner and his evil spawn. We exhaust the kids' entire DVD collection of the Pink Panther cartoon series and make a plan to leave early the following morning, whether our soggy laundry is wet or dry.

CHAPTER TWENTY-TWO
COPACABANA

I am awoken at 3am by a strange noise. I peer down into the plaza from our room window and can just make out a dark figure stumbling around in the drizzle.

"¡La Paz! ¡La Paz! ¡LaPaz!" he shouts, in a drunken slur, repeating the words and wandering aimlessly.

Dan continues to snore while I lie for the next two hours staring at the ceiling listening to the drunk outside. At 5am we rise to collect our damp laundry from the handrails but find it all back on the floor again. I silently curse the kids as we stuff it into our bags. Heavy rain verifies that our remaining dry clothing is also drenched by the time we reach the station. The micro bus is already stuffed to bursting when we climb aboard.

The bus starts its early morning journey back to the city, winding up through the clouds and rain on the newly asphalted version of the old death road. The interior of the bus smells like a cheap bar of soap.

"At least everyone's clean," Dan comments, squashed against a lady's freshly washed hair.

The condensation from the packed vehicle is beyond bearable but eventually we reach the top of the Andes and roll back into the brown-bricked neighbourhoods and clogged streets of La Paz. The drab colour and the steady noise of the traffic is almost a welcome change from the quiet of our little mountainside excursion.

Disembarking at the terminal on the fringes of the city, we've just enough time to grab some tamales for lunch before racing across the city by taxi to the El Alto bus station.

"¡¿A donde va?!" a persistent ticket tout asks us as we alight the taxi into the crowds.

"¡Copacabana!" Dan slings his backpack over his shoulder.

"¡Aquí! ¡Aquí!" the guy shouts, pushing us up into the stairwell of an old bus before we have a chance to think.

The buses in Latin America never set off until they are full, and there are always cheaper tickets just before they leave. Which means two things: no seat is guaranteed but a late departure is. A bus that says it leaves at 7:00 will be crowded to standing room only and then leave at 8:00. And so, forty-five minutes after we're shoved on, we begin rumbling up through the dry west side of the Bolivian Andes and finally reach the shore of Lake Titicaca several sweltering hours later.

"That was quick. We're already here!" I say, disembarking the bus with the rest of the passengers.

A young boy in a sailor's cap greets us. "¡Adelante! ¡Adelante! ¡Rápido! ¡Rápido!" He ushers us all on foot into the two small wooden boats that bob at the shoreline of the lake. Small waves lap up on shore one after the other and the vast body of water disappears over the horizon.

"This thing is huge," I think out loud, gazing out across what could quite easily be mistaken for an ocean.

Spluttering out into the lake, the bus, still loaded with our bags, drives onto a large flat-decked rusty barge. The weight of the vehicle near submerges it. We can't believe our eyes: this boat, with our overloaded bus, looks like it's going to sink.

"What the fuck?" I say to Dan, laughing. Watching from our little boat, the deck hand furiously bails water with a paint tin as the vessel creaks out across the choppy lake alongside us.

Somehow, miraculously, it survives the crossing. The two little boats skid up on to the mud bank and we disembark watching as the bus drives back onto dry land. The old barge heaves a groan of relief as the bus's rear wheels bounce off the lowered ramp.

A further hour skirting the lake in our crammed bus and we pull into Copacabana where an all too familiar scene unravels.

Teenage accommodation touts surround us.

"¡Mas barato!" Dan tells them, asking for the cheapest accommodation.

We are led to a hotel, where we find two plait-haired women sitting at the front door in rocking chairs, knitting in the evening sun.

"Viente cinco," one says, not looking up from her clicking needles. "Twenty five, sweet. Bueno," Dan says, and walks inside.

We offload our gear and set out in search of a meal. The main street is blanketed in dust and we head for cleaner air down at the lake. A large St. Bernard dog joins us. Tiny shop fronts either side advertise boat trips while others sell t-shirts and caps. The dog cunningly leads us to one of the beachfront huts where an old lady wearing a frilly apron tosses it a bone and serves us up a fresh trout dinner.

"It's the highest navigable water in the world," Dan says, reading from his guidebook. I ponder this fact as the snowy peaks of the Andes are backlit by an iridescent orange sky that slowly fades to a deep blue.

Leaving the St. Bernard contentedly munching our leftovers, we make our way back up the hill in the dark, and a dreadlocked hippy girl stops us with a quiet but assertive voice.

"You want some grass?"

Through her stained teeth we can hear she has an American accent.

"Ten bolivianos," she continues.

"Why not?" I say, turning to Dan and shrugging.

Back in the hotel room, we roll a joint and bring it to the roof. We smoke it standing between the stiff washing hanging in the cold night air. The weed is dry and tasteless. It burns my throat. And our joint rapidly burns down like fire tinder in the cold night air. Back under the warmth of our thick blankets, we watch an episode of *Mr Bean* and pass out.

A heated argument in Spanish between two maids in the corridor outside our room wakes us. We head downstairs and across the road, where a bowler-hatted lady in an alpaca shawl brews coffee, scrambles eggs and heats beans. Sitting down at her plastic sheeted picnic bench, we are soothed by the morning quiet. The only sound in the cold morning air is that of her spoon clunking the tin mugs as she stirs the sugar into our coffee.

The sun grows hotter as we reach the halfway point up the flagstone stairs to the hill of crosses that overlooks the town. We encounter another lady in a bowler hat here; she is sitting on a short flight of cobbled steps outside her store, looking through a pair of binoculars. While her puffy skirt billows in the breeze, she stares intently into the binoculars at a football field across town.

"Her son's playing in a football match. That's my guess," Dan suggests.

I am dying of thirst, but I don't have the heart to bother her for a can of anything in case she misses her boy scoring a goal. I just hope the game will be over when we pass this spot on our way back down. We continue on, and I hope for a drink at the top of the hill.

At the top of the hill I momentarily forget my thirst, as it rewards us with spectacular views over the deep blue lake and Copacabana's sandy beach cove. There, stretching along the summit, stand a row of seven grey ornate crosses. Towering overhead, they serve as a place of worship for the many followers who make the pilgrimage here every year. And parallel to these crosses along the cliff's edge sits a row of sooty makeshift barbecues, fashioned from rocks and mostly unused, each one containing its own small pile of empty fizzy drink cans.

On the descent, the lady and her binoculars are nowhere to be seen.

"I'm gonna die of thirst soon if I don't get a drink inside me," Dan says, wheezing and bending over.

"Same," I reply, looking down at how far away the little town still appears to be.

Arriving at the base of the hill, our number one priority is quenching our thirst. Panting like dogs, we skirt the town making a bee-line for the edge of the lake, where we know we can sit and drink to our hearts' content. Sitting down with our bottles, we gulp them without speaking. The ice-cold Cokes instantly quash the burning sensation inside. Like an icy waterfall showering a cracked desert landscape, reviving it, soaking it and moistening its surface, the cool liquid does the trick. Twenty minutes later, now relaxed and wondering what to do next, we spy a blue and white wooden boat filling with passengers.

"What's that all about?" I think out loud, walking over to where the line starts.

A sandwich board advertises day trips to the Isla del Sol, an ancient Inca village situated on the island that sits in the middle of the lake.

"Keen?" I ask Dan, who's now caught up with me and drinking a second Coke.

"Might as well," he replies. "We got nothing else to do."

The boat putters across the calm lake and despite its leaky state delivers us safely to the other side. On the small island, we walk for an hour through dry landscape and come to a maze of roofless square white block walls and arches that look down on to the deep blue waters of Titicaca. Surrounded by terraced hills that were once cultivated by ancient tribes, the location commands stunning views in all directions. The loop track constructed of white stone stretches for miles and provides us with views of the lake: blue and shimmering like a mirror. And there: plaited women washing clothes on the rocks on one side. There: others wandering the burnt hills of sienna farmland collecting firewood. Dan and I pick our moment and leave the group behind us to score an extra twenty minutes, diverting off the designated track and sitting down behind a huge rock to smoke the remainder of the weed.

"This is a moment I'll remember," I remark, lighting up and staring out over the terraced green peninsulas and the deep blue lake.

"Fuck yeah," Dan agrees, taking the joint and pulling a deep drag while gazing out at the snow-capped mountain range in the distance.

The effects of the smoke hit us almost immediately and amplify the impact of our surroundings, sending my mind off to another place.

Until we are startled by voices. "The group's catching up with us, bro," I whisper to Dan. "I can see them over the brow of the hill."

Indeed, the group passes by in close range, just to the other side of the large rock where we've chosen to repose and enjoy our weed. Unaware we're behind the large rock, each one walks past, twitching their heads, obviously able to smell the joint but not sure of where it's coming from.

After another ten minutes of aimlessly gazing, Dan and I suck back our last few drags and return to the path where we walk unsteadily and stoned back to the boat.

"Looks like a checkpoint," Dan remarks, pointing to the yellow and black striped pole across the path up ahead. As we approach, we're stopped by a group of locals who ask for a small fee in order to proceed.

"Didn't sign up for this," I say to Dan, handing over the equivalent of around fifty cents to both groups. We are allowed to pass. And we quicken our pace, eager to get back to the boat now that we are feeling the combined effects of the marijuana and altitude. We hurry on, praying the boat hasn't already left.

We arrive just in time. The little boat is still tethered to the jetty in the cove below. The deckhand shoves us on board, and the engine grumbles to a start.

Back across the lake on the shore of Copacabana, another dinner of trout is accompanied by another perfect sunset. It doesn't get more beautiful than this: we're in awe of the day, the food, the lake, the island.

CHAPTER TWENTY-THREE
CUZCO

A new morning awaits. A new bus awaits.

The bus is as dirty as the last. The queue outside the large white and blue tiled church in the centre of town is as long as the last. The routine is starting to feel familiar.

But wait – there's something different this morning.

As I step up into the bus I'm hit with a strong smell that I can't quite place. It's somewhere between putrid and intriguing. I want to plug my nostrils, but I also can't help but seek it out. Soon my curiosity is answered.

There, in the front of the bus is a pair of old ladies – bowler hats, of course – who are steadily hacking something into chunks. The ladies wield their well-worn wooden-handled knives expertly, tossing the large pieces into an old twenty-litre plastic bucket. As I peer closer, I can tell what it is: half a cooked llama, pink, slimy, and squished vertically into the bucket. I watch, fascinated and also repelled, as the old ladies put handfuls of the smaller chunks of the meat – the ones they've just cut – into bags topped with a shred of oily cabbage and offer them around the bus for five soles.

The stench, combined with the heat, makes the trip unbearable but Dan and I partake nonetheless – and the meat tastes surprisingly good. We tuck in with gusto once we get past the smell – which we attribute as much to the half-rotten cabbage as the meat itself. But our enjoyment is short-lived when two European girls who settle in opposite us, their unimpressed looks indicating they may be about to throw up.

"You guys OK?" I ask them across the aisle.

Staring back with unhappy expressions and still looking ill, one of them answers, "Vee are vegetarian."

"Sorry," I reply, somewhat insincerely, popping another chunk of meat in my mouth.

The ladies and their bucket disembark at a cluster of houses leaving the smell to linger while the passengers suck their fingers clean before discarding their greasy bags under the seats.

We reach the border and follow the queue through a customs hut painted in the red and white bands of the Peruvian flag. We exit the other side onto new soil where a couple of energetic German lads join us while we sit on a kerb waiting to reboard.

"You guys were smoking de weed on de island?" the taller one says dressed in branded surf and skate gear with his chest puffed out like a peacock. We nod. His eyes light up and a greedy look appears on his face.

"Do you hef more?" he asks a little too enthusiastically.

Unknown to us at the time, these two turn out to be our sidekicks for the next two months. Mikal – the bloke who asks for the weed – projects what seems to me the typical high-strung German stiffness. He is tall with a general pointy-ness about him. His features are piercing against his dark curly hair. He wears only skate gear, with labels. Skate/surf guy's friend Jan was born from a German father and Moroccan mother, served in the military for two years after leaving school and, despite his military training, has a softer, gentler feel about him, with an approachable persona. He's a kind of beautiful guy: impeccably smooth head, tanned and shaved; manicured eyebrows; square jaw. His face is always lit by a genuine smile and he confidently takes everything in stride.

We settle in with our new companions, glad the stiff vegetarian girls have departed, glad for a couple of boys we can joke freely with.

Dry desert landscapes pass by outside the speeding bus. Cowboy-hatted men on bicycles ride along the edge of the highway, while families scatter coffee beans on sacks outside their homes to dry in the sun. The road north skirts the shore of Lake Titicaca, making two short stops in the dusty towns of Puno and Juliaca, before arriving at our new destination.

Cuzco is firmly on the tourist map, its streets are full of the un-mistakable sound of panpipes being played at every turn. Western restaurants and flash hotels in the central square Plaza de Armas outnumber local ones so much it's hard to avoid them. But we are diligent in our efforts and manage to find a hostel a little way out of town with a good selection of cheap local eateries to choose from. The neighbouring houses, like our hostel, are low and ramshackle, but back nearer the heart of town, Spanish buildings spring out of megalithic walls: the remains of the Inca temples and palaces destroyed by the Spanish conquerors.

Our hostel maid, Rosemery, is dim-witted and lazy – but incredibly stunning with plump lips, almond eyes and petite figure. I have to look twice every time I encounter this diminutive Peruvian beauty, with her long, soft hair that falls perfectly over her perfect shoulders and down her perfect, pert breasts.

"You like her, yes?" Jan asks me, patting my back. "She is very sexy." He beams a huge smile.

Dan starts a conversation that ends with Rosemery promising to take us out to her village where we can see her mother's guinea pig farm. I am overcome with romantic inclinations.

"That's the most random, man," I remark casually – secretly (or maybe obviously) relishing the thought of visiting such a place.

"Let's go to drink!" Mikal suggests excitedly.

"Can we eat first?" I suggest. "There's a place across the road."

The small restaurant is basically someone's kitchen that adjoins a cobbled courtyard. Chickens peck through the rubbish bins out the back and a football game plays on a small television inside.

"Pollo a la plancha para todos, por favor," Dan says, ordering us all grilled chicken.

The plates we're served are stacked high and we subsequently come to eat here every day during our stay. Beans, tortillas, a little salad and the chicken cost four soles each.

"This isn't even a dollar fifty," Dan says, delighted.

The town's nightlife seems pretty tame. We find the local disco and it's flashing neon lights. The place is empty but it does have complementary bowls of chopped fruit that sit on the bar.

"The guy just told me it's more busy here tomorrow," Jan tells us.

"Tomorrow is your birthday," Dan reminds me.

Sitting in the hostel foyer the next morning, I'm startled by a madman.

"HEEEY!" Mikal shouts, before running down the stairs and hugging me. "Happy fucking Birseday keevee!" he shouts, getting my Nationality wrong.

"So what shall we do for lunch? I mean it's your birthday and all!" Dan says as we sit in the hostel foyer.

"We haf to go make phone calls to Chermany, so vee see you later for drinking, yes?" Mikal says. He departs, followed by Jan. And with that, they are gone.

"Lunch for two then," I say, looking at Dan as they disappear up the street.

In the town centre sits the huge colonial plaza abloom with flower beds and dominated by two large cathedrals. Concrete arches span the streets leading out from the plaza, tilting uphill like giant launch ramps into the sky. Once a point where over 25,000 Inca roads converged, it's now a bustling centre of Quechuan women and children selling knitted finger puppets, cakes and tamales, as well as cut-price massages. Every day the pavements are lined with food stalls and the outdoor areas are filled with the sounds of pan pipes. Troupes of young girls skip through the wide cobbled streets, their elaborately made costumes inlaid with beads and shiny sequins, while alongside, young men in white shirts and black pants carry giant statues of the Virgin Mary on their shoulders. I wonder if these street parades are part of the school curriculum. They seem to be a daily occurrence in every place we visit.

There is a constant bustle to this place – it's festive and inviting. A place that feels quite optimistic. A good place to celebrate a birthday.

For my birthday lunch, Dan and I venture into new terrain. You only turn thirty-six once, after all.

There, a stall with street food unlike any we've tried before. Stacked on paper plates like little roasted trophies, shiny skinned with fur completely burnt off, piles of guinea pigs stare up at us, buck toothed with their two front legs poised just like those upright meerkats in the nature programmes.

"You down to try them?" I ask Dan, not sure what to expect.

"Fuck yeah," he replies, choosing his rodent.

A fat woman in her white butcher's cape places one of the animals on a board and, with one swift chop of her cleaver, halves it through the middle, exposing the innards and organs. This is placed on a paper plate and accompanied with a stack of hot chips. We find a table and study how the other patrons tackle their meals – how they crunch and chew at the rat like treats, swallowing every last morsel. We come to the conclusion that their guts are either made of steel or the bones are so small and torched that they are easily digestible. So I take my first fork full. I'm not averse to the taste or texture. I'm even pleasantly surprised.

"Tastes like chicken," Dan says, crunching his mouthful.

The street we follow after our noontime meal leads to the huge municipal markets, where we're greeted by a row of freshly severed pigs' heads that sit along a bench, their floppy ears framing their vacant stares. Ducking in and out of the various racks hanging from the ceiling through the narrow passageways, we arrive in a cluster of noisy women who chop and blend fruit into delicious juices.

"Definitely need one of these after that lunch," I say, looking at the colourful array of fruit stacked in clear tubes.

"Yeah, I still got bits of guinea pig in my teeth," Dan replies, picking at them with his fingernails.

Mikal's birthday falls in the same week as mine, and we decide to celebrate on the same evening. The night begins with two celebratory bottles of vodka in the hotel room before we hit the town. We then decide to return for the free fruit again at the neon blue bar, but as we enter the barman makes a cross with his fingers while hissing and standing in front of the dishes. The dishes, we see, are well stocked again, but now tightly sealed in cling film.

"No free!" the bartender shouts at us above the din of the music. "No touch."

"Shit!" Dan laughs. "It's for his cocktails!"

We all laugh, understanding now how we've unabashedly stolen the bar's cocktail decorations on previous occasions, marvelling at the tasty and nutritious snacks we assumed were put out for guests.

The night wears on. We enjoy drinks without fruit. A hideously ugly Peruvian woman takes a shine to me and we indulge in a disgusting display of slobbery kissing and groping as we balance half-on and half-off barstools. She sticks around for the free drinks I buy her and the drunker I become, the sexier she looks. It's obvious to everyone else that I am making absolutely no sense at all as I speak "Spanish" to her. In fact, it's only later that I realise I look and sound like all those other gringos I despise. I'm no different from them. Fact.

But I don't reach the point of no return, because we leave the neon blue bar and my Peruvian beauty. I'm not sure how we get from one bar to the next but the next memorable moment comes when I fall off a barstool in another club while the pumping sounds of a mega mix that plays the best two seconds of every popular song blares in the background. Pulling myself back up the stool, I am met by a mass of blurred faces – faces that have seen this familiar sight all too many times before.

Mikal slips away from us at some point. We have no idea where he goes or how long he's been missing. But hours later we stumble into him in another nightclub.

"Heeeeeeyyyy! Amigoooos!!!!" he embarrassingly shouts. He is singing and dancing (badly) with a middle-aged American. While standing on the bar.

Breaking away, I know that I can't stay up any longer. I stagger back through the narrow, walled streets, literally feeling my way home with my hands. When I enter the hostel foyer, I discover the owners are still up – they are blind drunk and having their own soirée in the foyer. Nothing to do but to join them when they pour me a shot of cheap, clear alcohol. They insist, after all. It's their establishment, after all. And it's my birthday.

Jan and Dan show up sometime later and partake in our home-base festivities until the early hours. But there is no sign of Mikal.

"He goes with the American girl!" Jan says, laughing.

I wake a few hours later, still in the foyer and fully clothed. My throbbing head is only made worse by little Rosemery – the maid, the beauty – casually vacuuming around me. Looking at my wrist to check the time, I discover my watch is no longer there – nor is it in any of my pockets.

"Fuck! That bitch stole it!" I exclaim under my breath, remembering the girl who had dragged me onto the dance floor before I'd become blurry and fallen from the stool. With only partial recollections of the night, I ask Dan if he remembers much.

"Nah, I was pretty pissed. You just got spiked, bro."

Dan is a little too nonchalant, as far as I'm concerned. But he's probably right. My head throbs, as does my heart, when Rosemery – bless her beautiful, round arse – vacuums past.

CHAPTER TWENTY-FOUR
MACHU PICCHU

Sipping on a coffee and still with a headache from hell, I'm struck with déjà vu. Mikal returns in the mid-morning light with a smile from ear to ear. Jan, now also in the kitchen, shakes his hand.

"Yes! You make sex wiz dee American?!" he asks in what we've come to call his 'Borat' accent. "She is so cool."

Mikal is silent, like a lovesick puppy and still smiling. At the time we have no reason to take his case so seriously, but later that day, while sitting in the plaza, we spot him and the girl hand in hand strolling together and kissing.

"Fuck he's got it bad, bro," Dan says, chuckling.

"I hope he doesn't bring her to Machu Picchu," I add. The dynamic of our group could be seriously threatened with a girl in the mix.

"Yeah, same," Dan replies. "We better go book that now if we're going tomorrow."

Meeting up with the Germans, we book our next few days away, choosing the cheaper of the options, which includes a long mini-van drive to a train that will take us to the town of Aguas Calientes deep in the foothills of the Andes.

"What about your new girlfriend?" Jan says, teasing Mikal.

"She's not my girlfriend!" He snaps back in a snotty tone. "And no. She's not coming, but guys! She is sooo cool!" he says broodingly and talking about her like we give a fuck.

We wake early, and surprisingly, Rosemery is already fossicking in the little kitchen, preparing breakfast. The coffee is burnt, as is the toast, but we appreciate her efforts and devour it quickly before heading out. Our mode of transport, a white Mercedes mini-van, fishtails its way up a road that ribbons along the side of the green slopes clinging to the Andes. The vehicle is erratically driven by our guide who seems a little too obsessed with constantly changing his CDs stored in a multi-sleeve wallet attached to his fold-down sun visor. His wrinkled brown face and long flat Inca nose is framed by a brightly coloured earflap beanie that hinders his peripheral vision, and he bobs his head excitedly to the loud reggaetón blasting from the speakers.

Jan, sitting in the passenger seat up front, takes charge. We are all relieved, considering the narrow width and badly maintained, winding white gravel road ahead. Jan expertly takes over the CD player for the next four hours. We all instinctively feel our chances of survival have greatly increased.

The driver stops in the tacky artisanal plaza in the tiny dirt-scorched town of Ullantaytambo for us to make purchases. Fluffy toys, cheap panpipes and Frisbees hang from the awnings of the market stalls that edge the central square, while traders beckon tourists with their car salesman smiles. Not in any desperate need for a stuffed toy toucan to accompany me to the ancient Inca ruins, I stand by the van and smoke a cigarette while the gaggle of bargain hunters use their five minutes wisely sifting through the tat at the stalls.

Spending that five minutes at the ruins of the giant stepped Inca tiers embedded in the surrounding hills of the fluffy toy market place would have been a far better option, but that's not going to bring in any money for the stall holders.

Our five minutes spent, we leave a cloud of dust behind and sink into the dense jungle, stopping two hours later in a small village where streets are laden with huge piles of bananas and mangos. I spot some cartons of 'Inca' brand cigarettes nestled in the tray of the 6-year-old selling them, their red and white cartons reminiscent of Marlboros. As I'd been smoking everyone else's for the last week – and, more importantly, because these were going for forty soles a packet – I splurge big time and shell out for ten packs, dividing them up between us. Everyone lights up.

"BLEEEARRGHH!!" They all cough at the same time. "What the fuck are these?"

I puff on mine in a prolonged manner, trying to prove my friends wrong. But they look at me hard. And I realise I'm not fooling them, or myself. I suck in deep, and the taste of sheep dung fills my lungs.

A few hours later the van pulls in to a dusty circular clearing among tropical trees with giant leaves. A dozen or so other mini-vans are also offloading their cargoes of eager travellers, all headed for a set of train tracks that start at the far edge of the clearing before disappearing off round a corner.

Walking down the overgrown line with around sixty other backpackers all jostling for pole position, we reach an old blue and yellow four-car train next to a line of low market stalls with a dirt path running between, no wider than a school ruler. We push our way up into a carriage and find a wall to lean against just as the links engage and the train pulls away with a shunt, jolting everyone backwards. Brushing past the row of market stalls, the train tilts down through the gorge through which the blue-green Urubamba river flows, every now and then revealing a glimpse of overgrown Inca masonry and the single, more adventurous backpacker walking the tracks.

The train terminates at Aguas Calientes. We stay aboard and let the initial rush of punters disembark the train.

The small town at the end of the line hidden in the foothills of the Andes was originally settled by farmers at the turn of the twentieth century, but now it caters for the hordes of tourists who visit the mystical Machu Picchu. We walk up through the new and old buildings that interlock and crowd each other, and cross an arched stone bridge spanning a fierce, freezing torrent of river that splits the town in two.

We soon arrive at a hostel. The façade is no more than a metre across but widens into a triangular shape as we enter. Bright orange walls adorn the interior and every room is an unorthodox shape. After setting down our bags, we're fed cheap pizza in a common room while being given a 'safety' briefing in broken English. All I understand is that the group will be leaving at 04:30am tomorrow, and that the return train leaves at 2pm sharp. Retiring to a bar with the others, we partake in a few cocktails of Pisco sour and hit the sack around 12.30am.

Four hours later and regretting the cocktails, we stumble outside and are greeted by a small dog. Dan and I, never able to resist a scruffy stray, feed it some pizza. It follows at our heels, walking down through the dark town and up through some scrub, where we reach the beginning of our climb.

"Deece is de first step of de climb. Inca steps," our guide tells us. "We have 1000 of deez to arrive at Machu Picchu." We sense he's trying to be encouraging when he says, "Some people do eet in one hour, some a little more, stick together and do not go too far ahead please."

The step he is standing on is no ordinary step. Each one is almost knee height, in fact, and we soon realise this near vertical climb will be a challenge, to say the least. In the pitch darkness our headlights – we always have them with us, we just haven't used them before – illuminate each and every one of these giant flagstones that weave their way, seemingly never-ending, up through the undergrowth. Most are knee-height, but some are as high as an average dining chair. At the halfway point, my knees are starting to show signs of defeat. I slow to a crawl while Dan and Jan speed off ahead to try and break the record.

The sounds of people chattering grows ever closer and I let out a triumphant sigh of relief when I reach the final 1000th stair.

"Fuck, bro, that was a dumb idea," Dan wheezes, slouched at the locked entrance gates and smoking a cigarette, the small dog asleep in his arm. "He started whining just past the halfway point so I had to carry him," he adds, taking a drag from his smoke.

I'm here, I think to myself, feeling triumphant and staring at the entrance. This is the lost city that I marvelled over as a kid in school. This moment is something I'll remember for a long time.

The gates are opened at 6am to the place that managed to keep its secret from the gold-hungry Spanish conquerors five centuries ago. Our sore knees carry us through a passport check and on to the deserted and silent misty ruins as the dawn light brightens. Standing on a spike of mountain made only for eagles, the ruins are linked by a saddle to another great sweep of mountains that dominate a labyrinth of gorges. Some of our group join the line up at the entrance of Huayna Picchu, a smaller site originally occupied by the high priest and his virgins and perched 360m higher on an almost perpendicular needle rock that seems to float off the edge like a magic carpet.

"Where's Jan?" I ask the group.

"He's probably met some girl," Dan mutters, setting the sleeping dog down under a tree.

"Only 200 people can go up." Mikal remarks, referring to the daily limit allowed up to Huayna Picchu. "Vere is he?!"

On passing through a second passport checkpoint, we climb a further series of sketchy steep flagstone steps that stick out of the side of the cliff face and lead upwards to the summit of Huayna Picchu. The views looking back over the giant mountain peaks poking into the atmosphere are stunning. The last ten minutes of this second climb are accomplished only by crawling on hands and knees over sheer faces of white stone. These large slabs provide great platforms to witness the first sunbeams slice through gaps in the mountains like bolts of gold to reveal new ranges of the Andes.

During the next hour, the clouds lift and I'm struck dumb by the labyrinth of roofless ruins and their white brick walls sprawling over the mountain below and dominating the centre of the valley. I've never seen anything like this. It's not like any of my boyhood imaginings. It's beyond anything I read about in my schoolbooks. The large birds that float in the air currents, dropping off into the valleys and deep gorges that surround the city, lend even more ambience to the place – and seem to emphasise just how incredible this feat of human construction and creative engineering really is.

Spending as much time as is physically possible up top without cutting into the exploration time of Machu Picchu below, we return to what is now a seething mess of tour groups speaking every language in the world and criss-crossing the place like leaf-cutter ants over the branches of a freshly fallen tree. Their tour guides usher them around, filling them with facts and figures. One of the strangest things we learn about is the story of the sacred stone, a large rock that the Incas tied to the sun, a rock that has recently been crushed to bits by equipment used for a TV beer commercial shot there.

Yes, you heard that right. A television commercial that ruined a rock *that the Incas tied to the sun.*

"You guys left me!" comes a cry from behind.

"Jan! What do you mean, we left *you*? You disappeared! What happened to you?!" I ask, looking at our friend's torn and stained clothes.

"I forgot my ID and vas not allowed to enter, so I vaited and climbed over zee wall behind zee hotel."

"Holy shit! Are you serious!?" we say, almost simultaneously.

Jan, not wanting to miss out on this wonder of the world, was not about to let a little thing like a missing ID deter him. So he had taken things in to his own hands and gone commando over the back fence of the hotel and up through the thick, snake-infested jungle foliage until he found the perimeter wall of the Inca city. Climbing up the stones and over the top, he landed at the feet of a security guard who promptly escorted him back through the site by the scruff of his neck and out of the entrance gates. After a lot of explaining and pleading from our guide, he was allowed back in. I will never forget the photo he showed us that he had taken for his family during his daring expedition: there he is, tangled in vines and the thick jungle undergrowth, smiling regardless.

"I thought I may die," he says in a serious tone. "I took dis photo in case anybody ever found my body and my parents vould know I vas happy."

I check my watch. "Fuck, it's 1.15!" I tell Dan. "We gotta get the train!"

Deciding that the quickest option will be to follow the road that snakes down the hillside into Aguas Calientes, we hot foot it out of there. We do not want to miss our return trip.

Grabbing our packs we'd stashed at the hostel, we arrive at the station in the nick of time: the whistle blows as we push our way onto the crowded carriage and the train jolts itself back in to the jungle.

The passengers are all wearing exhausted expressions on their faces and little is said during the ride back to the mini vans.

"Where are the Germans?" Dan asks me with a smile, knowing full well they've missed the train.

"NO!" I reply, smiling back at him. Those crazy Germans. We hope they'll at least catch the next train and avoid the snake-infested jungles on the way back down.

The Mercedes mini-van is waiting for us at the end of the line. Dan and I pile in, and I spend the following four hours asleep, my face buried in my pillow, which is fashioned from t-shirts and thermals.

Back in Cuzco, we seek dinner. The small family restaurant with the scuffed red tiled floor and rough wooden furniture seems to be missing the chicken that we saw eating out of the rubbish bins under the kitchen sink the week before.

I look down at the quarter section of bird on my plate, fried and lying now on a bed of rice, and I believe the mystery is solved. But I am far too famished to care, and I happily tuck into my meal.

A few hours later as dusk settles, Mikal and Jan arrive at the hostel, tired, grumpy and hungry.

"Fucking Scheister! Sixty dollars for a taxi!" Mikal blurts angrily, throwing his bag down and storming into his room. "Deez fucking Peruvians are criminals."

CHAPTER TWENTY-FIVE
AREQUIPA

The waiting hall of the Cuzco bus station is filled with old women sleeping on the floor, mountains of luggage surrounding them. Small televisions are strung up overhead with frayed twine; football games play on every screen. The ticket touts wail destinations at the top of their voices and battle with the football match commentary screaming from the TVs.

"¡¡¡ARI ARI ARI AREQUIPA!!! ¡¡¡LIMA LIMA LIMA LIMA LIMA!!!"

Jan shouts, joining in and imitating the touts, much to their amusement.

The bus arrives late, already full to the brim. We barely squeeze in, and are pushed further into our ill-fitting place by the fifteen or so street vendors shoving their way up and down the aisle selling food, socks, drinks and bibles.

We rumble out of the station, and a landscape resembling the surface of the moon passes by outside the window. It is mesmerising and the bus's wheezes and groans have a certain rhythm – broken by a television that falls from its bracket on the ceiling, smashing loudly in the aisle. Nobody seems too bothered by the disruption. I don't mind as the box was playing pop video DVDs at volume that distorted the already screechy voices even further.

At 3am I awake in my seat, frozen to the bone. I've been more or less crammed into the same position for six hours. I pull the curtain back, hoping to see something in the dark. My curiosity ends when my nose hits the half-inch of ice on the inside of the window. On my left, an old man in a poncho is holding a leash attached to a bleating lamb. The lamb, wrapped in a blanket, stares at me. The whole scene feels like something I might be dreaming. I pull the strings of my hood tight, leaving only my nostrils exposed, cross my arms and curl up in the foetal position. I close my eyes and shiver. I shiver the rest of the way there – three more long hours with ice to one side, a bleating, staring lamb to the other.

At our destination the following morning, man and lamb are nowhere to be seen. The pair have obviously disembarked somewhere in the wilderness during the early hours.

Arequipa is nestled at the foot of the snow-capped El misti volcano and is built of white tufa blocks cut from its slopes. Earthquakes have destroyed the place on a regular basis, yet each time the townspeople build their homes again, using the same material.

Following routine, we taxi to a hostel we've found in the guidebook, where inside we meet Picchi, the owner. An older, friendly fellow with a nervous excitement about him, he exudes a happy attitude as he shakes all of our hands.

"Welcome!" Picchi says in a booming voice, his rotund body shimmering like jelly as he shows us around his place. "I like a clean house and no parties, OK?" he adds, making his rules quite clear.

He asks us questions about our homes and travels; he's one of those people who has a tiny bit of knowledge of everything.

"Ah! New Zealandia!" he shouts when I tell him where we're from. "Many sheeps!"

Turning his attention to Jan and Mikal, who are eagerly awaiting to talk with him, he guesses their home country before they even have a chance to tell him.

"¡Bayern Munich futbol!" he cries with his hands in the air. "¡Bueno equipo!" There's no hiding his love for the sport. "You please make youselves at home," he says, sitting down in an armchair. "Mi casa es tu casa."

The rippling shake of what appears to be an earthquake jolts us suddenly from our quiet doze. Plates crash to the kitchen floor and I am brought to attention from my drowsy sleep. Dan falls straight to his elbow on the tiled balcony floor when the string that suspends his hammock snaps. We hold on to whatever thing is closest, whatever we can grab. Voices rise and fall. Car alarms scream. The building finally stops swaying and one by one the car alarms cease. All is silent again.

"It's just a welcome to Arequipa greeting," the maid says through gold teeth while she counts the guests outside on the street like children in a primary school fire drill.

In the afternoon, we are approached by an elderly fellow in the plaza wearing a crinkled maritime hat and one of those beige fishing vests covered in pockets.

"Hallo!" he chirps with raised right arm impersonating Hitler when Jan and Mikal tell him where they are from.

"Jesus! That's a bit off," I remark to Dan, slightly taken aback by his misplaced humour. The Germans don't seem to mind, however; they find the funny side of his bad joke and egg the old Peruvian man on even more. They are not fussed in the least when he goose steps in circles. I feel slight discomfort at this public jest, but Jan and Mikal seem to shrug it off. Maybe they're used to it, this overt mockery of a history that you just can't shake.

Turns out, the old man is employed by the town to guide tourists, so he directs us to a European café which turns out to be harder to find than our goose stepping guide has suggested. But Mikal insists on finding because he doesn't want to eat filthy street food.

"I vant some normal food!" he barks, walking in front of us, a little too fast, at a pace that resembles – dare I say it – a march. "No more pollo a la plancha, no more papas rellenas!"

"Fuck, he's a twat at times, eh, bro," I say to Dan under my breath.

"Mmm," he replies, shaking his head.

Little does Mikal know what's in store for him as he scoffs down a fancy sandwich in the café for more than double the price of a hearty local meal.

"It's so good, ja!" he says as he wolfs down the edges of his bread, spraying crumbs everywhere. "Zis is vaat I like!"

Later that evening, Mikal's stomach is giving him pains.

"Fuck! Scheisse!!" he moans. "Even dee normal food is shit here! Fucking Peru!"

"Let's leave tomorrow?" Jan suggests, trying to divert us all from

Mikal's rancorous complaining. Dan and I agree, and we hop into a taxi to secure our tickets at the main bus terminal. But we're soon informed that buses are being stoned on the city fringes in protest for indigenous groups who are being slaughtered in the Amazon in response to their resistance to government deforestation.

"We're stuck here! Scheisse!! Fucking Peru!" Mikal shouts, kicking off again.

"Ah, bro, it won't be for long," I reply, trying to assure him.

"These attacks last for a few days," Picchi tells us back at the hostel. "It's good luck!" he shouts from the kitchen.

"Why?" Jan asks, confused.

"¡Es pelea de toros mañana!" Picchi says, clapping his hands. "¡Vamos! ¡Bullfight!"

"Yes!" Jan says, his mood changing abruptly with this news. "Great! Zis is great!"

"Do the bulls die?" I ask Picchi, not keen on seeing the bloodshed.

"No, amigo!" he cries, with his hands in the air again. "¡Es toro a toro! – Bull against Bull!"

And so we're about to take a step deeper into a world of unknowns. Bull on bull? Never heard of this. But we're game. This is turning out to be a trip where we never say no.

"OK, my friends! Jump in!" Picchi beckons after breakfast the following morning. Two old green clapped-out Lada taxis await. We split up and jump in. They are driven by Picchi's mates, who whizz us to the outskirts of town and drop us in a sea of small Peruvian men in cowboy hats and candy floss sellers. We make our way into the stadium crowd, pushing our way up bleacher steps, hunting with children, women and ancient men for seats. The action has already begun. In the centre of the arena is a sea of dust, as giant bulls with backs taller than their handlers lock horns. The crowds cheer and hoot; the stadium noise is deafening. We don't go far when we find a spot with a great view – it seems crazy that no one has claimed it before. We make ourselves comfortable just as two bulls are unleashed on each other, butting heads and scuffing their hooves into the ground. The crowd erupts with cheers and claps, and we join in, as loud as everyone around us. But no sooner are we high-fiving each other at our good fortune – what a cultural *event* this is turning out to be – than we are sent running for our lives, jumping from our seats and scrambling to the back of the stands when one larger-than-life bull turns suddenly and, seemingly losing interest in his sparring partner, heads directly for us.

"That's why no one sat there!" Dan laughs. "I'm staying up here!"

"Me too," I agree, and Jan and Mikal join us in the higher stands too. "We were right next to the exit gate; they're trying to escape!"

The grand finale comes when El Gran Chapparal – a prize-winning bull of gigantic proportions – is led into the arena by two handlers. Everyone has been waiting for this. We, too, are on the edge of our very hard seats.

The large wooden gate swings open, revealing the silhouetted snorting monster. Golden rays beam over its back while the rest of its gigantic body blocks the setting sun like a steel curtain. The intensity of the crowd's energy startles the creature into a frenzy and, before it even gets five feet into the arena, it breaks free from its neck chain.

"Fuck! It's loose!" Dan shouts.

By this stage the whole crowd is in hysterics, laughing, clapping and making noise that can surely be heard for miles. Like the end of a Looney Tunes cartoon – I kid you not – the bull blasts through the open gates and charges off down the street at full speed towards town. Its owner, now shouting and flapping his arms like the sidekick cartoon character, chases after it. We are astounded at the speed with which this has all happened. There is no containing El Gran Chapparal. He leaves a cloud of dust and destruction in his wake, bellowing and head-butting parked cars as he makes his mad way into town.

CHAPTER TWENTY-SIX
LIMA

Picchi laughs the whole way home in the taxi. He is ecstatic that we've had such a good time.

"¡Muy bueno!" he bellows as we're dropped off at the hostel. "¡Buen dia!"

"¡Los buses, se puede pasar!" the maid tells us as we sit down in the lounge.

Dan translates for us, but by now I can actually understand a few phrases. Buses – easy, same: buses. Puede – able. That's all I need.

"The protests have stopped, we can get a bus!" I say, chuffed with my rough understanding.

"OK! We move tonight," Mikal says in his insistent manner, rushing to pack his bag. No one's in the mood for arguing, so the rest of us gather up our belongings too.

"OK, my friends!" Picchi says, hugging us one by one. "My brother has hostel in Lima, is in nice area, you stay there please?" He hands me a business card for his brother's hostel.

"Of course we will!" "Thank you so much for everything, Picchi!" We reply in sync before racing off to the terminal.

The buses are busier than usual due to the two-day strike, and the ticket lines stretch out the front doors. We wait for what seems like forever before we finally creep to our assigned bus and board our ride.

I sit up front on the top deck with my feet against the windscreen, while, one by one, the centre white lines of the Pan American highway are swallowed up by the darkness as they pass through the bus's headlight beams. We hurtle through the night towards Lima.

A few hours later, I wake as daybreak cracks on the horizon and lights up the landscape. At first we are in a coastal dust bowl of sand hills, but that quiet scenery eventually transforms into a sea of morning commuter traffic as we draw closer to the smog-filled capital of Peru.

For sixty days each year, Lima enjoys clear blue skies. The remaining days are permanently overcast, and mist and clouds are pushed in continuously by the Humboldt current.

We, of course, time our visit perfectly, arriving in thick fog. No sign of any of those sixty days of blue skies. There is zero possibility of splendid weather and our mood immediately sours.

"Shit timing as usual," Dan grumbles.

I don't say anything because he's right.

The city that's home to nine million people is a terrible eyesore for kilometre after kilometre as we pass through the outskirts. But gradually the swamp of development gives way to a more picturesque low-lying (sub)urban tranquillity, and we see what a beautiful town Lima must once have been, with ornate cathedrals and leafy plazas at every turn. The Miraflores district is made up of small blocks of spotless streets, expensive cars and high-heeled Peruvian beauties who strut the sidewalks, designer handbags swinging in rhythm from their shoulders.

Situated on one of these streets is Picchi's brother's hostel. The thin building is squashed between two larger ones that dominate it on either side. We're greeted by an old Dutch chap in a tweed suit. Resembling an historian emerging from the secret shelves of an ancient library in an Indiana Jones movie, he introduces himself while flicking the few single strands of grey hair that drape across his polished head.

"Where have you boys come from?" he asks us, trying to keep the strands of hair in place.

"Arequipa," replies Dan, rolling up a cigarette.

"Ahh. The white bricked buildings of Arequipa. Beautiful place. I teach in the university there."

"Cool, so what are you doing here?" Dan asks.

"Well, I teach here in Lima too, and also in Trujillo, one week a month in each."

"Cool job," I say, joining in the conversation.

"Yes," he says. "Travelling to each place keeps it fresh."

"You hef girlfriend?" Jan asks, changing the subject and with a cheeky grin on his face.

"Well…" the old guy starts. "There's the problem with these Peruvian girls – I just can't resist them."

Jan laughs. "Vat do you mean?"

"Well, you see, I have a girlfriend in each city and I need to decide which one I stay with." He looks somewhere between happy, like a boy with his hand in the candy jar, and a little ashamed.

"Hey don't be sad!" Jan consoles him. "Zis is a great place to be in your life!"

"Sly old bugger!" I comment to Dan outside while we smoke a cigarette.

"Yeah, lucky bastard." He exhales smoke into the night air.

We stay a while. At one point Picchi's brother is away on business and the hostel is minded by a small French girl who's staying in the city for a year on a study exchange.

"Let's have a drink," she says one sunny afternoon, pulling a bottle of vodka from the drawer in her desk. The music is turned up a notch and we make short work of the bottle over a few games of cards before turning in. Such is an afternoon on the outskirts of Lima.

But not every day is as lazy as that. Some days we go treasure hunting.

The following day we succumb to a boisterous taxi ride with electro music blaring, during which we barely miss a couple of pedestrians on street crossings. "Yaaa!!! zis is crazy!" Mikal screams, hanging out the window like a deranged baboon and waving his arms at people.

I sit watching him. It's bewildering, embarrassing and confusing all at once. His teenage screams only fuel the driver's recklessness and I'm relieved when we arrive unscathed at the black markets, a labyrinth of dark corridors and stalls offering all the latest electrical goods at rock-bottom prices. Famous on the gringo trail for bargains and all things invaluable to backpackers – mobile phones, digital cameras and their chargers, used walking shoes and waterproof clothing – these dingy alleyways contain everything you could ever need when on the road. And it's cheap. There's a reason for that, of course: all of the merchandise in the black market has been stolen from – who else? – backpackers.

We leave the markets empty handed but famished.

So we purchase our tickets for our next leg northbound and sit down at a small empty comedor for lunch. The owners, a solemn looking couple sitting at a table out front, spring to life as we approach and point at the specials listed on the chalkboard. One of the options is something called 'Hídago' – which sounds exotic and delicious, so I order it with visions of tasting something between eye fillet and a juicy lamb shank. The others order steak and while we wait, the young son of the couple rides in circles on his little blue bike in a matching shiny tracksuit. He seems excited to have our full attention. When I ask if I can take his photo, he strikes a series of bad boy poses while sitting on the bike – poses that would fit on any hip hop album cover of the nineties. Then he runs inside at the command of his mother. I worry I've offended the family; perhaps I've shown disrespect by asking to take photos. I feel like a typical gringo cad. Until the boy returns in his school uniform and a black blazer embossed with gold badges and small medals that would be more at home on the uniform of a king of an Arabian country.

"Toma foto, toma foto," his mother repeats, asking if I can take his picture again. Obliging, I snap a few off while they all strike poses looking at the camera intently, obviously expecting to see a Polaroid image magically appear from the bottom.

"¿Las fotos?" they ask, confused.

"Es digital," I try to explain.

But they all look at me like stunned mullets. Dan jumps in and explains the situation, telling them I'll return the following day with the photos. And then our food arrives.

I'm not served what I had in mind. It is large and brown and moves in an eerie way when I touch the plate.

"It's liver," Dan says. "And a fucking whole one at that! I couldn't remember what Hídago meant, but yeah, now I've seen it…" He tucks into his juicy steak.

"Fuck," I moan. I dig in as much as I can, knowing that if I don't I'm going to be starving for the whole bus ride.

The Peruvian criminals favour the art of robbing backpackers on night buses while they're sleeping – as Mikal discovers on the next overnight bus to Trujillo, further north. On arrival he finds that his passport, camera, iPod and money have all been swiped in the night from his bag – and the bag is still strapped to his leg! His enraged fit that ensues is priceless. Dan and I mask our smiles as we watch him search the bus and strut in circles, flailing his arms around the coach station car park like John Cleese in a Monty Python sketch, bad mouthing South Americans and stereotyping them – all of them thieves, all of them untrustworthy! – at the top of his voice.

"I'm just hoping none of them can understand his ranting," I whisper to Dan. "He's gonna need their help when he calms down."

We'd all been sound asleep and not noticed anything suspicious during the night. But I have other worries of my own, beyond the issue of the stolen money from the leg-purse. I'm now regretting the liver I ate for lunch. I lie down on my seat in the dark bus with an increasingly painful stomach, doubled over in pain, trying to focus on anything but the memory of the large, blubbery meat *that I ate all of*. Unable to stop, I squeeze out what I think is going to be a simple fart. But this manifests as a squirt of warm wet poo that fills my boxer shorts. My eyes pop open. What to do? For a few panicky seconds, I lie very still. Then I carefully manoeuver myself into an upright position, my arse cheeks clenched as tightly as possible, and make my way to the rear of the speeding bus with my knees locked together and my feet flailing outward at odd angles.

But bus toilets are not the best place to deal with a delicate situation, and generally speaking they are *sub-sub*-par when it comes to hygiene. But multiply the typically unclean public bus toilet by 1000, steal the toilet paper and the cistern lid, smash the faucet off the sink and break the flush button, and you get a fair picture of what I have to deal with. The thing that puzzles me the most are the random nuggets of faeces that end up in places nowhere near the toilet bowl. How these little shit drops get where they do is beyond me. I imagine a mother holding her child against her while pointing its arse cheeks outward towards the toilet, the fearless duo attempting to shoot said poo nuggets directly into the bowl. This, I reason, must be the method a poor mother must use to avoid contact with any piss splashed surfaces and also prevent the poor child from falling into the bowl. Taking in to consideration the breakneck speeds the drivers fly along at and the treacherous winding roads they swerve around, I almost laugh when I picture the mother looking more like she is having her first go on an anti-aircraft gun in a cyclone – *rat-rat-rat-tat-tat-tat-tat* – spraying the air with bullets in all directions. But this is no laughing matter. Nothing about this is funny, in fact. Not the shit already on the seat or the floor, and certainly not the shit in my underwear. I carefully get to work, cleaning myself with my underwear and throwing them away. But that's not the end of my ordeal, alas. No sooner do I accomplish the aforementioned task that I feel my gut wrench even more.

I spend the next two hours in this foul enclosure while my arse and mouth excrete a continuous jet of yellow slush.

I finally return to my seat and doze off into an uncomfortable sleep.

Back in the Trujillo bus station, Mikal begins to calm down, and we take a taxi to find a hotel. Checking in to a dive of a place, I crouch over the toilet bowl and continue with my now regularly-scheduled sick routine. The still fuming Mikal takes the others to file a police report about the robbery. On returning, they announce that we may as well keep heading north as Trujillo has little to offer and the nearest consulate for a passport replacement is in a small inland town three hours away called Piura.

"Did you shit yourself on zee bus?" Mikal asks me with a disgusted look on his face.

"Um, just a little," I answer sheepishly. "Why?"

"Why?! *WHY?!*" he says angrily, flailing his arms about. "Because I touched your shitty boxers when I was looking for my passport in ze toilet bin! Scheisse!!"

I can't help but smirk. Jan and Dan follow suit.

CHAPTER TWENTY-SEVEN
PIURA & MANCORA

"Let's gap it. This place is a dive." Dan slings his backpack over his shoulder and turns to leave.

"But how?" I reply, feeling bad about leaving without paying.

"Vee just valk out. Straight through zee front doors, don't say anysing," Jan says, following Dan.

And we do. We march in single file through the foyer at pace, then hightail it up the street and cram ourselves into a taxi that drops us at the terminal. The worst of my sickness is over, but my empty stomach still grumbles in pain while we sit in the rows of plastic seats bolted to the waiting room floor.

Across the road, a crowd surrounds a man. I can see them milling around through the grubby panes of glass in the bus terminal. We go outside to investigate and discover a street vendor with an overflowing pile of fake polyester football shirts spilling from a ripped cardboard box. Red and yellow shirts are scattered around the box, and the vendor is fending off would-be petty criminals intent on taking his loot. We soon see the urgency with which he is trying to offload the jerseys – a clear sign they're stolen property.

Jan and I bag us two each for ten soles.

"Dis is great!" Jan squeals with excitement, holding up his shirts.

When he turns back towards the vendor once more, he's gone.

"Look! Zey are all gone!" Jan says, wrapping his shirt round his neck and dashing back to the station.

I am left alone on the street, with only the ripped cardboard box. And my two shirts.

A six-hour bus ride up the dusty coast turns inland and lets us out at the small town of Piura. The streets are clogged with small yellow taxi cabs.

"¡Hostel barato, por favor!" Mikal barks at the driver, asking for a cheap hostel.

The driver collects his fare and drives for about a minute, then deposits us quickly before swerving back into traffic. We don't have time to argue.

"Fuck! We just got ripped!" Dan says angrily. "We could have walked that!"

From outside, the hostel we've been driven to looks like a brothel.

"Holy shit, it'd better be cheap," I say, walking inside.

"It's six bucks a night," Dan translates after talking to the fat guy wearing a stained vest at the front desk.

The first impression of our room is the door, hanging on a single hinge and letting out a screech as the bottom scrapes the tiled floor and the papier maché walls shudder when I jam it into its doorframe. Then there are the beds: musty and smelling like wet dogs. The TV snaps to life, surprisingly, with 100 channels – a huge luxury after three months, and something we make full use of in this little town of little interest.

Piura, we discover, has not much nightlife and only a few places worth exploring – but it's a necessary stop for Mikal's passport replacement and also, mainly foreigner free, gives us hope that we're away from the gringo trail.

The consulate the police in Trujillo advised Mikal to contact turns out to be the house of a very old German lady who used to work for the government in the nineties. Though, upon meeting her, I'm uncertain of what century that 'nineties' is from. She suggests he fill out the necessary forms and says she can process them in Lima for him, the only catch being she isn't leaving for two days and won't be back until the following week. The thought of spending six more days bored out of our minds here and worse, five nights collecting mould spores on our lungs in the musty hotel, drives us to seek an escape.

So we check out of 'Hotel Petri Dish' and take another three-hour bus northwest to the coast town of Mancora for a week, holing up there until the passport shows up.

White sand and rickety beach bars shaded by giant coconut trees surround the bus stop when we climb out in Mancora. We again fall for the old taxi trick when we hop into two auto rickshaws, which transport us about 500 metres to our bamboo hut dwellings and overcharge us for a distance we could have easily walked. Still, I don't want to complain too loudly as our new hostel is across from an idyllic beach.

Mikal overlooks the view, however. "Zeeze fucking Peruvians!" he grunts, kicking off again.

"Who cares?" Dan says, cupping his hands and lighting a cigarette. "Look at the view."

The view in question only works if you are facing outward. Inside, the place is another dump. Beginning with our grotesque host, an obese young Peruvian woman with a pair of giant unsupported sagging boobs hanging in her loose t-shirt, who grunts and throws a set of keys at us while pointing to a room at the rear of the courtyard. As she tosses the keys, we catch an unwanted peek of her fat roll that flops over the top of her baby blue cotton Lycra pants. These pants are clearly under a great deal of pressure holding in her flabby legs, legs that bring to mind the unfortunate image of condoms stuffed with sausage meat.

Two sagging double mattress beds cloaked in holey mosquito nets aren't exactly of the luxury beach condo we'd imagined, but the room is huge, the place is twenty soles a night and the beach is directly across the road.

So we settle in and spend the next four days mostly out of the room: sampling meat and fish cooked on the sizzling hot plates that line the dusty streets, guzzling rum and coconuts from strolling street vendors, and steering clear of the dead fish caught in clumps of netting strewn along the beach. One day, stepping gingerly around the discarded carcasses, I come upon a nearly new flip flop which has washed ashore – and, a few minutes later, I can't believe my luck as another one appears a little further up the beach. Both new and in good shape. Yes, they are different brands. Yes, they are both left feet. But I can't bring myself to throw them back, so I adopt them as my own, I strut the streets of Piura in my fine rubber footwear, but I'm rewarded with a nasty red sore between the first two toes of my right foot.

"Just spend a bit of money, bro," Dan remarks, seeing me rubbing my sore foot.

"That's rich coming from you," I snap back, knowing we need a break from each other.

Another rev-up in our room with a couple bottles of vodka kick-starts the afternoon of Jan's birthday and ensures we're in for another evening of cross-cultural faux-pas and ensuing embarrassment.

Nothing new for us, really.

What *is* new is the emergence of my bottled-up aggression. Alcohol has a way of releasing feelings and apparently I've been holding in intense anger since the robbery. Still in our small stuffy room, I suddenly let loose on Dan like a burst hydro dam.

"Why did you walk us into that gun?!" I scream. "You knew that area was dodgy! We could've been shot!"

I am shouting, red-faced and flapping like a headless chicken.

Dan takes my verbal attack well, remaining quiet as I carry on venting my anger and frustrations for the next few minutes.

"Look, man!" Jan says, stepping in. "It's over now, you hef to forget it. Zare is no point in diss."

Realising he's right, feeling calmer now, I let the heat of the moment die; we down a bottle of whiskey before wobbling into town.

At a local eatery, Dan slurs his way through chatting up one of the food hut owners, a toothless woman with her hair tied up in a bun on her head. She giggles like a schoolgirl while he feeds her love anecdotes and rocks back and forth in his plastic chair, barely managing to stay upright.

We drag him away and return to the hostel where there are now two smoking hot Peruvian girls lying in the grass out front. We persuade them to join us at the bar down the lane and walk arm in arm through the village. The girls drink like fish and eat like horses while expecting us to pay for everything. They definitely aren't part of our budget so, giving them the slip, we join a group of hippies in headbands playing instruments around a fire pit further down the beach. Their harmonious rhythms float over the flames and out to sea.

Now they say a true gentleman who knows how to play an accordion is only a true gentleman if he doesn't play it. The skinny Norwegian guy who wanders over with his wheezy squeezebox and a cheesy smile obviously wasn't at school that day. He quickly destroys the serenity by sitting down in the sand and presuming it's cool to join in with his ear-splitting wails, singlehandedly killing the tranquillity of the night. Most from the group – those people who had been sitting around enjoying each other's company all evening – get up and leave, heading off in different directions. Us included. Enough of accordion-boy. The mood is gone.

We stumble back towards our hostel, and halfway there I look up to see a speeding auto rickshaw fly out of the darkness and connect with Dan, sending him pirouetting into the air. As he soars across the street, the rickshaw drives off into the distance – I don't think it ever slowed down.

Dan lands with a thud. He doesn't seem to be moving.

"Holy shit! Are you OK?!" I shout as we all run over to him.

He groans a long "*fuuuuck*" and slowly gets to his feet, wincing.

"Let's get you back to the room, bro!" I insist, helping him as he limps the rest of the way.

Back in the light of our room we examine his bruised and battered body – and we see how hard he's been hit. Served with a dose of concussion, a grazed ribcage, bruised head and swollen lower leg, he's lucky to be standing. It crosses my mind that this is perhaps no accident. I wouldn't be surprised if this is connected to him getting sleazy with that woman in the eatery earlier.

Dan wakes in the morning with a sore body. "I need some weed," he groans. I roll him a joint that sends him to sleep for most of the day. On waking, he needs more so we hang around at the beach that evening until another tuk-tuk driver pulls over and offers up some. We agree and he says to wait while he goes to collect it. The whole scenario seems dodgy when, twenty minutes later, there is still no sign of him.

"Fuck this, I smell a rat," I say, turning to the others, who seem to want to wait a while longer. I return to the hostel alone.

An hour later they burst into the room, all trying to speak at the same time. "Whoa! Whoa!" I shout over them, trying to quiet them down. The dust settles a little before Mikal speaks.

"Deez fucking Peruvians!!" he says with a gloating tone. "Zee tuk-tuk driver comes with dee police!!"

"They threw me in the car and tried to plant weed on me," Dan says, beating Mikal to it.

"They were just trying to get money out of me, but I had nothing," Dan remarks.

"I knew it smelt dodgy," I say, looking at everyone. "But how'd you get free?" I am astonished – and grateful – that Dan has returned with the others.

"They didn't like the fact that I could speak Spanish and understand what they were saying to each other, so they threw me out a couple streets from the beach." He looks in bad shape, still sporting a swollen cheek from the previous night's collision.

Whether these two tuk tuk incidents were connected, we'll never know. But being as drunk as Dan was in a town as small as this is the kind of thing that gets you noticed – and I'd bet money they probably were.

In our small collective, the incident involving the tuk-tuk driver has raised Dan's status to something of royalty, and Jan and Mikal are in awe of his amazing ability to come out the other side of such situations virtually unscathed. As if pouring petrol on his already out-of-control fire, being bundled into a police car and living to tell the tale only skyrockets Jan's and Mikal's admiration for Dan. He thereafter earns the nickname 'President Dan'.

The name follows him wherever we go. And his reputation even precedes him. And it's usually proclaimed loudly, with great vigour, by his followers Jan and Mikal: "PRESIDENT DAN is here! Make way for ZEE PRESIDENT!"

Always the last to bed and last to wake up, Dan is the talk of every hostel we stay at and holds a crowd with his repetitious cuss-heavy stories in the courtyards of our dwellings most evenings. His ability to take over a whole bed, snore at an illegal decibel volume and sleep like he's dead has the Germans in stitches.

Simple phrases that Dan often uses now become the centre of attention. "Let's get a beer," he might casually say at noon on any given day, sending Mikal and Jan into a frenzy with their strong Borat accents. The theatricality of it all increases when they pretend to be servants granting his requests.

"My president vants beer, so vee shall drink beer," they announce in unison. "In my country vee haf beer fountains in ze local parks and free cigarettes for everyone! In my country we teach children to swear very much. Is nice."

They become devout followers of Dan in his make-believe country. But Dan, to his credit, is not very comfortable with this new attention, so he adopts a blasé attitude and tries to ignore the attentions of Mikal and Jan. Which only serves to solidify his status as fictional character *El Presidente*.

It's a bizarre turn of events. I am not in Dan's court, and I am not sure how to escape the madhouse.

PART II
GROUP DYNAMICS

PERU, ECUADOR, COLOMBIA, SAN BLAS, PANAMA, COSTA RICA, NICARAGUA

JULY, AUGUST, SEPTEMBER

CHAPTER TWENTY-EIGHT
GUAYAQUIL

Mikal's passport is ready.

Our week in Mancora has brought havoc to the beach town with President Dan's adventures, but all good things must end.

"Vee must go!" Mikal demands, returning to our cosy cabin from the bamboo framed post office, where he's received confirmation.

"Look, there's no bus until 1pm anyway, so just chill out," Dan grumbles from under his sheet. I look over to see his sheet is covered in streaks of pus and blood. His collision with the tuk tuk has left its mark, and the wounds have not been healing well. El Presidente is not as tough as he looks.

On Mikal's insistence, we go to the bus station early and arrive back in Piura later that evening.

A girl on a motorbike is sent by the old lady to fetch Mikal, and he hops on the back. They spin off, him clinging onto her small waist, helmetless. We are relieved when he returns unscathed.

"Crazy!" he shouts as the bike pulls up, flapping his passport at us.

"Put it away, mate." I think out loud: "Don't want that one stolen too."

We hastily plan our departure, jumping on a bus for the border town of Tumbes – the gateway to Ecuador.

Near the border, long lines of semi-trucks stretch nose to tail for miles along the highway verges, awaiting inspection from military police and customs officers.

"We're now travelling the cocaine route," I whisper to Dan, looking at the soldiers outside.

We clear Peruvian customs without a hitch, and the heavy military presence on the Ecuador side fills the air with tension. Officers board the bus and interrogate us individually, while outside, the bag holds are meticulously rummaged through by armed soldiers in desert storm camouflage.

The bus is finally allowed to continue and melts into the miles of yellow banana bunches hanging in the dense green plantations that flash by outside as the sun slips off the horizon behind the distant Pacific Ocean.

One by one the lights of Ecuador's Pacific capital, Guayaquil, blink on as dusk settles. Expecting the bus terminal to be in a state of disarray, we are surprised when we pull into a brand new edifice of mirrored glass and spotless marble floors, where the counters are all illuminated like an international airport. Shiny SUVs kitted out with bling trim and driven by teenagers arrive and leave, dropping and picking up passengers in the marked lay-by outside. We are astounded by how orderly the scene is.

We've selected our hostel from the guidebook. It's the cheapest, and nowhere near the city centre. So we ride in a taxi for what seems like hours. The tropical heat hangs in the high twenties even though it's late in the evening. We disembark in a dark alley and find our way to the reception area, which has a pleasant, clean smell about it. The rooms are tiny.

"Look at zeez!" Mikal shrieks, pointing at two pygmy marmosets hiding in the back of a small cage hung on the wall. "Gremlins! HaHa!" He pokes his finger through the bars as the little furry creatures shiver and stare at him with huge black eyes.

"You're scaring them. Leave them alone," I tell him, annoyed at his stupidity and tired from a long day.

"Ah! You! You relax!" he replies, ready to kick off.

Ignoring him, I bed down in our tiny dorm. The others do as well. No late-night partying tonight.

The city, we discover, is a bone-shaking one-hour bus ride from the hostel. It costs a mere twenty-five cents. The windows, scribed with tags, rattle in their frames as the sub-bass woofer speakers chained in the roof blast an incoherent mix of cumbia and rap music.

"That door's not shut properly," Dan mentions while we bounce around in our seats.

"I think that's the least of our worries," I answer, directing his attention to another broken window that clearly has a bullet hole through it.

Dan, still without a credit card that will work in an ATM, queues in the long line that stretches around the bank. Waiting for him, I notice a child on his bike riding in circles near a security guard who's smoking a cigarette. The AK47 that hangs from his arm directly lines up with the child's head, only a few feet away, every time it reaches its maximum point on its fulcrum of swing.

"Dude, check that out," I say to Mikal, pointing at the gun.

"Scheisse! I hope zee safety catch is on!" he replies, uninterested, before returning to his guidebook. I wish he wouldn't read that in public.

Dan finally emerges from the bank with currency, "Fucking stupid Kiwi bank," he mutters, referring to the mistake made by his bank when ordering his replacement card after the robbery in Buenos Aires. "I'm fucking over this shit."

"*You're* over it?!" I answer, making it quite clear that he's not the only one.

He stashes his money in his sock, and we make our way over to Cerro Santa Ana, the hill at the south of the boardwalk smothered from top to bottom in pastel-coloured dilapidated Lego brick shacks.

The path that leads to the summit winds its way up through narrow cobbled alleyways cutting through the barrios that cling to the hillside, while every fifty metres an armed security guard informs the previous one of our position via crackly walkie talkie.

The summit provides a view of the city stretching up the coast, and a giant window over the barrio that we've just climbed through, its rusty corrugated roofs weighed down with old tyres and cinder blocks – and the regularly posted security guards within it now making perfect sense.

We eat lunch under the solitary tree that grows out of the centre of the summit. Nearby are two more guards. Across from them, alone on a bench, is a belt with a pistol in its holster.

Mikal points. "Hey amigo! Is yours, yes?" he yells over to them.

"Si hombre, es mia," replies one.

"Can I try on?" Mikal asks.

The guard replies again with a laugh. "¡Si!"

Mikal picks up the belt and weapon, and the guards both spring to their feet with their hands outstretched, running towards us. The guard still wearing his holster draws his gun shouting "*¡DEJALA! ¡DEJALA!*" – telling Mikal to leave it and putting him in a headlock – while the other frantically radios for back-up. Almost instantly, five more officers arrive on the scene.

Clearly, there was a miscommunication when Mikal asked to pick up the weapons. I'm pretty sure the guard thought he heard something else when he nodded and smiled and said, "¡Si!"

We are all questioned and lectured. We are all told, repeatedly, how stupid we are.

"Thanks a lot, Mikal," Dan says. "Why the fuck did you think that would be OK?"

"Iss OK," he replies patronisingly. "Zey are just too stressed."

"Fuck me," Dan mumbles and walks off.

The descent is an uncomfortable one as each security guard we meet glares at us with stern disapproval, knowing full well the commotion we have caused at the top.

I know what they are thinking. *Los estupido gringos*.

I feel it, too.

Back down in the city centre, entering Simon Bolivar Park, we are greeted by a scene from Jurassic Park. Hundreds of giant orange and green iguanas, some as long as five feet, sprawl out lazily, sunbathing on the footpaths, while others dangle from the tree branches above the office workers who sit on the benches eating their lunches. Jan and Mikal are easily excited by anything so of course can't help themselves when prompted by such a scene. As if we've not had enough excitement for one day, they stupidly attempt to pick one up for a photo. Scared shitless and now suspended in the air with the two gooning Germans laughing at it, the lizard throws a fit, thrashing its tail and swiping its razor sharp claws. It violently wriggles free of Jan's grip, and lands at their feet on all fours. It then scurries off onto the lawn, leaving Jan with a deep scratch on his forearm.

I am, frankly, on the lizard's side and also quite shocked that Jan, who has been the tamer of our two companions so far, has gone to these lengths to get a photo.

"Scheisse!" Mikal says, inspecting the gash. "You need to wash zis!"

While the Germans wash the wound in a restaurant toilet, Dan and I sit down at a table and wait for them to join us. Dan orders four chicken soups and almost immediately they're set down in front of us.

"Two bucks! Sweet deal!" he says, tucking in to the delicious smelling meal. "So we're moving on tomorrow?" he adds, taking a break from his meal while Mikal and Jan pull up two chairs and dig into their bowls noisily.

"Yeah, there's not much else of interest here, is there?" I answer as I'm slurping my delicious broth.

"Holy fuck!" I shout with a fright. I dip my spoon into the bottom of my bowl. "What the fuck?!"

Two bloated pink feet float to the top of my soup.

"Eww! Eeets dee feet!" Mikal shrieks in disgust, pointing at my bowl.

The guy at the next table taps me on the shoulder. "¿No quieres?"

"Toma," Dan says, gladly spooning him the feet from our bowls.

He nods, delighted by his good fortune. He picks up the feet one by one and sucks the severed knuckles dry.

CHAPTER TWENTY-NINE
MONTANITA

The following day we travel a further two hours north around the Pacific coastline to the town of Montanita. The cheery little place is reminiscent in layout to Mancora back in Peru but far busier. Hammocks are strung throughout the two-storey hostel; the rooms are separated by colourfully painted cinder block walls. In the entrance, surrounded by trophies and leaning over his surfboard, vigorously waxing the base, is Jorgé, the owner. His bronzed skin, unkempt curly hair, chiselled jaw and perfectly sculpted muscles are too much for Jan, who instantly falls in love and spends the next week carrying a rental surfboard under his arm and hopelessly trying to catch a wave.

The beach is littered with seabirds pecking and tugging at the exposed organs of dead turtles and fish that have washed up with the tide, their giant shells smashed open by outboard propellers of careless fishermen. The protected Galapagos Islands and their rich and varied wildlife sit only a few hours out to sea, and yet what we've stumbled into here is far from how I've imagined this coastline. Indeed, our first impressions from our leisurely beach stroll are a far cry from the eco-friendly travel agent brochures that advertise this part of the world.

As we stroll along the sand the sound of an engine grows closer; I sense it's coming from behind. Looking over my shoulder, I see a large flatbed truck with wooden sidewalls approaching. The back of the vehicle is overloaded with fishermen and a huge boat that awkwardly overhangs the rear of the truck bed. The fishermen seem to be weighing it down so it doesn't tip off the back. *What an amazing photo*, I think, imagining the truck whizzing along the sand and backdropped against the deep blue ocean.

But before I can pull out my camera, Mikal lets out a squeal. "Hey! Hey! You guys!" he squawks, flapping his arms in the air.

The fishermen shout and the truck comes to a halt, while Mikal runs over to it. We follow. Before we or the fishermen can object,

Mikal is clambering his way up on to the back of the truck, bracing himself on the boat with one arm and flexing the bicep of his other.

"Take dee photo!! Take dee photo"! he orders with a military bark.

The fishermen smile, but Jan, Dan and I cringe with embarrasment while the photo is captured. We are already turned and walking back up the beach before Mikal alights the truck to join us once more.

Walking one of the village's five dirt lanes, I double-take as I spy a couple of familiar faces.

"Bro!" I say, tapping Dan's arm with the back of my hand. "It's the dudes from Uruguay!"

"¡Hola muchachos!" they shout, running over to us smiling. Dan engages them excitedly, learning they've travelled by bus for four days to enter in the surf contest that is happening this weekend.

"Now that's dedication," he says to me, sparking a cigarette.

Swallowing my pride, and itching to show them I've been trying to pick up the language, I stutter out a few sentences in Spanish. Their faces light up and they congratulate me on my progress. I can't help but smile, a little smugly. I let Dan continue, but my confidence has been boosted, and I manage to grasp most of what is said.

Meanwhile, Jan and Mikal have made the acquaintance of Frederik, a pale-complexioned, personable fellow with a crop of wavy blond hair who's staying in the hostel with his mother, visiting from Germany.

"He's teaching English at a school and living with a family in a jungle village northwest of Quito," Jan tells us before Frederik has time to speak.

"Yes, Jan is right," he says. "You guys would love the village and its people. Come and visit me out there."

It sounds like the perfect opportunity to get off the beaten track, so we exchange numbers and accept his invitation.

In the evenings, a row of cheap cocktail huts illuminated by twinkling golden bulbs line the dirt lane to the beach, the barmen desperately trying to draw in customers by spinning, juggling and flipping bottles to loud tacky chart music that blares from broken speakers. The once sleepy fishing village has been developed solely for the tourist trade and transformed into the world famous surfing beach that it now claims as its title. We spend our days watching heats of the surf contest from under the sea of rental parasols that shade the beach, and drinking into the early hours of the morning in the bars that come alive in the evenings.

The town's nightlife is dominated by several larger hostels that host huge discos in their open air courtyards, complete with giant foam machines, laser lights and swimming pools, overflowing with holidaying Ecuadorians and pissed-up gringos. Fully clothed and drenched from head to foot, they sing along to the auto-tuned chart music with arms waving. Swaying about in the illuminated water while spilling cheap fluorescent mixer drinks from their glasses, they look happy and not a little foolish. But the atmosphere is something Jan cannot pass up and spends most evenings in one or all of these many foam-filled party hostel courtyards. His newfound enthusiasm for his travelling lifestyle, with his surfing interest by day and his headlong dive into party life by night, results in a slight air of hostility between him and Mikal. It comes as no surprise when Jan decides to stay on for an extra week for more surf lessons – but we brace ourselves for the fallout, for the decision displeases Mikal immensely. Mikal sulks and fumes but has no choice but to continue on to Riobamba at the end of the week with the companionship of only Dan and me. We leave the scene, wondering just how long Mikal will last without his travel buddy.

I board the bus with Dan and a grumpy Mikal, find our seats and settle in for the next long ride, drifting off in a light snooze.

CHAPTER THIRTY
RIOBAMBA

I am aroused by the noise from a television. I open my eyes and feel something touching my shoulder. Turning to my left, I spy the round head of shiny black hair belonging to an old lady, who happens to have made herself comfortable in the seat next to mine and has found my shoulder to be a good head rest. Open-mouthed and away with the fairies, she snores through the violent film's gunfire, blasting loudly from the television screen overhead. For the next two hours, all the way to our change-over stop in Guayaquil, she continues to use me as a pillow. When we arrive, I'm forced to prise her head off me while the next passenger takes my place – and I watch as she resumes her comfortable position on the new shoulder in the seat next to her.

The terminal is busier than when we passed through a week before. I'm frustrated with Dan not wanting to ask about the next bus, probably due to the way I yap at him like a Chihuahua and knowing full well I'm not going to understand the answer I'm given, so I stubbornly approach a ticket office attendant. Pushing my way through the crowds, I arrive at the ticket booth where a long-faced docile-looking girl turns her head to look at me.

"¿Que bus va a Riobamba?" I ask her sheepishly.

Replying in incomprehensible rapid-fire Spanish, she tells me expertly where I need to go. I believe I've understood what she's said and unknowingly walk off in the opposite direction.

By this time Dan has since asked someone else and shouts at me across the hall to follow him, his stern tone making it quite clear that he's well over dealing with my impatient nature for the last four months. The tension between us is growing by the day, and it's only a matter of time before I spaz out again like I did back in Mancora. As compatible as we are travelling together, it's tough to live out of each other's pockets day in day out for such a long period of time. Considering our different backgrounds, we're actually not doing that bad. But even so, maybe it's time for a break.

Growing up in a busy town in southern England has shaped me with an energetic, some might say highly strung, opinionated and sarcastic nature, whereas Dan is a product of a small farming town in New Zealand's Northland, a place where childhoods are spent swimming in the ocean, riding quad bikes along the beach, chasing sheep and learning to smoke weed.

I wonder as I cross the bus terminal: *How much longer this can last before we follow Jan's and Mikal's decision to go our separate ways?*

I'm searching for that deep cultural experience while Dan is all about drinking, relaxing and socialising with whoever will join him. I get that what I'm searching for is what he experienced during his year in Argentina living with his ex-girlfriend's family, but right now his attitude is not helping my needs. We want different things out of this trip, and each stop makes that more and more clear.

But how will I survive without him?

Another relic of a bus groans its way out of the Guayaquil station and up to 2775 metres through watermelon, banana, cacao and coffee fields. We are engulfed in clouds. I'm starting to understand the need for the slogans that adorn the windscreens of these buses, their reassuring decaled claims working like prayer for the ascent. 'God is my guide' – as if that's a better bet than having faith in the driver and other road users.

The sun sets and we're dropped off in our new destination under the cover of darkness. A dim yellow streetlight lights the corner of a dodgy neighbourhood where a few mangy dogs wander across the street to us.

"Where are we?" Mikal says, looking around at the deserted streets that branch off from where we stand.

"I dunno," Dan says. "I don't like the feel of it."

It starts to rain.

Taking a seat under a tarp roof outside a comedor, we order hot chicken, fried plantain chips and corn cobs dipped in powdered cheese. They are cooked over a sizzling hotplate by a rotund grandma in a grease stained apron. We are the only customers.

"There's a taxi!" Mikal says, jumping up from his unfinished plate and flagging it down.

"For fuck's sake, Mikal! I haven't finished my food yet!" I bark over to him.

"Fuck zee food!" he shouts back. "If you want to be robbed here zat's fine, but I'm going."

"Come on," Dan says to me, grabbing a chicken leg from his plate and picking up his bag.

The driver takes us to a large hotel in the more built-up part of town. The building, a once grand structure, shows heavy signs of neglect. Its once ornate windowsills and guttering are now crumbling and rusty. The interior, with its high ceiling stud and large rooms, is all but an empty shell of what it must have been in years past. The four-poster beds and solid wood furniture have long been replaced with lumpy mattresses and cheap metal-framed chairs and tables.

We wake in our room of cracked walls and dim lighting and venture out under a sky resembling a pile of wet towels. We greet the misty cold morning with a coffee and empanada. As we munch our pastry pockets, a large group of indigenous wrinkly-faced women dressed in matching bright fuchsia shawls and black felt fedoras squeeze into the rear tray of a heavily dented pick-up truck. They are colourful and animated. I ask if I could take their photo. "NO!" comes the stern, gold-toothed reply accompanied by a dozen pairs of piercing eyes that burn through me.

Walking away sheepishly and disappointed, I'm glad I at least asked.

Riobamba, much like Salta in Argentina, is famous on the 'Gringo trail' for its mountaintop train ride. In contrast to Salta, here the attraction is taken a step further, as guests are able to ride on the roof. Ever since I was so sorely disappointed back in Argentina, when the train to the clouds was closed for repairs, I've been looking forward to this. I'm excited. I'm sure that riding on the roof in a mountaintop train will be a once-in-this-lifetime event.

We arrive at Riobamba's train station and find a note, handwritten in pen on a piece of lined paper torn from an exercise book, taped to the small green door:

No va el tren. Gracias.

We make enquiries in a nearby store, and learn that the train stopped running only two weeks prior to our arrival.

"Se corta la cabeza," the old shopkeeper says, making a chopping motion across his neck with his hand. "Una rama muy grande."

"Holy fuck," Dan says, translating for us. "Someone was decapitated by a branch."

The fort in Uruguay, the train to the clouds in Salta, San Pedro prison in La Paz and now the Riobamba roof ride: all highlights I've been so looking forward to, all dreams of this wayward traveller, now crushed one by one.

I am beyond annoyed. The sooner we leave this misty, drizzly cold-hearted town, the better. For once I agree with Mikal.

"Scheisse!" Mikal spits. "Zis fucking place is shit. Let's go to Baños."

"He's just pissed off that Jan dumped him," Dan remarks as we head for the bus after collecting our gear.

"Yeah, but three is better than two," I reply. I wonder if I should voice my concerns about our longer-term compatibility, but I too am at a low. But the hell with it. I say what's on my mind. "We need him. At least he keeps us from fighting. We just butt heads when it's just the two of us," I say, almost nervously.

Dan just nods, seemingly unaffected by what I'm saying.

CHAPTER THIRTY-ONE
BAÑOS

Staring at the sheet drizzle from the covered market in Riobamba with bellies full of *humitas*, a local dish of corn meal mash and chillies wrapped in leaves and cooked on a hotplate, we board another shitbox bus driven by a maniac screeching his way through the highlands. While bottle green mountain peaks flash by, seemingly floating on an ocean of clouds, we descend to 1800 metres and arrive in the misty town of Baños, surrounded picturesquely by verdant mountains. The domineering outline of Tungurahua appears, a giant active volcano that blew its top a couple of years ago and is now blanketed again in dark green forest.

Like Riobamba, the town is plagued by mist and drizzle, but the rooms of our well-kept hostel are cosily warm and dry. We dump our things and venture up the hill from our accommodation, following a steep track that winds up the side of Tungurahua, ending at a large kitsch statue of the Virgin Mary. Rewarding views look down in to the dark green basin of rooftops and the wide river of white water that meanders its way along the side of the town.

"Zis is better than shitty Riobamba," Mikal says, spoiling the moment.

"Gimme a ciggy, would ya?" I ask Dan, hoping it will calm the feelings that are churning just under my outwardly calm surface. I have not wanted to admit it – I was the one who said we needed him in our group, after all – but the angry German is annoying the hell out of me. If I dwell on it too much, like I do lying in my bed at night, or walking through the streets alone, I realise he's actually ruining my journey. This part of it anyway. I need out. I need to change pace. I need to get away from the angry German.

But I say nothing. I decide it's best to endure. He's harmless, after all. So we descend the hill and settle into our cosy accommodation, where we enquire about bus times to the giant waterfall outside of town and retire for a warm night's sleep.

Like a schoolboy piloting an imaginary jet fighter, the driver spins the wheel through his hands from left to right as the bus careens its way through the driving rain the following morning, alongside the gorge cut by the raging river. This angry torrent of water leads to the formidable waterfall Pailon del Diablo – The Devil's Whirlpool. The crazy bus driver pulls into a muddy lay-by and discharges us, and we make our way to a shed on the cliff's edge.

We step inside the shed, pay a small fee and wait where a rusty orange bucket poses as a small open-topped cable car. It hangs on a steel cable and waits to carry us across the gorge.

"Bro," Dan murmurs, obviously worried about the crossing after realising that this is what we'll be travelling in. But we are here to traverse the river, dammit, and traverse it we shall. After the disappointment of the train, I am not to be deterred. I step inside and the others follow.

Dan's doubts (and mine, though I won't openly show them) are intensified when a dozen schoolkids squeeze in with us just as we've committed to the ride across the gorge. To make matters even worse, they fidget while we wobble fifty metres across the flapping ribbon of white water down below – *far below*, in the bottom of the deep gorge.

"Calmase, calmase," Dan tells the kids, asking them to stop moving around. "Scheisse!" Mikal curses, hanging on for dear life.

By some miracle, we arrive safely on the other side and make our way through the mist to the waterfall's edge. The falls are colossal and explode with a thunderous boom as they crash into the giant rocky pool at the bottom. There are no signs, no guardrails. But there is a series of tiered balcony paths leading to outcrops that command stunning views of the green glacial waters. We stand on the edge of one such platform and are drenched head to foot as the water pours into the depths of the gorge below. For a moment everything goes grey. The noise is cacophonous. The clouds of water crash all around us – and I almost lose my balance. If I didn't get the thrill of riding on top of a train up through the mountains, this is another kind of exhilaration – and plenty, too.

"Let's get out of here!" Mikal shouts, climbing back out of the mist.

Further up the cliff face and out of the fog, we are confronted close-up by the wide deafening cascade of water that falls just inches away from the footpath's edge. The sheer volume of water rushing past is strong enough to rip an arm off. It's certainly powerful enough to pull you in, never to be seen again. I shudder. But we carry on – determined to see all there is to see. And as if all this wasn't enough, we crawl further up on hands and knees through a small tunnel in the rock. We are deafened by the thousands of tons of water crashing down above us. It is mind-boggling – and there are no guards, no chaperones. I wonder where the schoolkids are. I wonder if they come here all the time. I wonder how many people have fallen to their deaths. I scrape along on my knees, my hands red with cold. This is almost unreal. It's frightening – and exhilarating.

We emerge from the tunnel and find ourselves standing in a cave looking back into the violent roaring shaft of water from behind. I can barely hear Mikal as he shouts at me "*YAAAAAARRRGGGHHH!* One false move and we die!" He looks deranged – like he has a wasp in his pants.

Dan and I share a glance. I wonder about the wisdom of coming to such a place with Mikal, and I know Dan's thinking the same thing.

The reverse route is easier. We slide back down the tunnel and manage our way quickly down the worn path to ground level, soaked to the bone, but happy to still be alive. At the bottom, a small girl tending her barbecue warms up our saturated souls with hot plantains filled with cheese. We then make our way through fields of giant orchids where the air is heavily sweet with the scent of perfume and back to the rusty bucket cable car. One more dance with death again and we are back on the other side. There is no sign of the schoolkids.

The bus arrives on time but the road home is blocked by a severe earth slip, holding us up for two hours in our now sopping wet clothing. There's nothing to do but sit and wait, on the verge of freezing to death. Finally, a yellow gang of earth-moving machinery arrives and slowly scoops the road clear.

Back in Baños, squelching our way home from the bus station, we are just in time to see a Canadian girl try her luck with the primitive 'rope bungee swing' that hangs off the town's bridge, a highlight in the 'Things to do in Baños' guide. It's a simple set up: thick rope tied to the bridge's railing. The trick is to jump *out* rather than *off* in order to create an arc that swings you under the bridge with minimal leg-dislocating jerk. We have our doubts about the Canadian's potential to jump properly but we arrive too late to interfere or deter her. She's already negotiating with the men who run this top 'Thing to do in Baños'. We watch long enough to see she obviously does not understand the whole arc concept. We leave the Canadian screaming and entangled, dangling from the rope upside down with her arms flailing about. The proprietors of the medieval attraction, meanwhile, are desperately trying to calm her while heaving her back up to safety.

Now looking like a drowned rat, I spend ten minutes foolishly prancing around the reception in my wet clothes playing 'hairdryer charades'. The girl behind the desk finds this hilarious and I suspect she has known from the start what I am trying to say but is enjoying my show far too much to immediately oblige. Soon, however, she produces a hair dryer for me, and I beat a fast track to my room, anxious to get out of my freezing clothes.

In the room, I thaw out and apply the hair dryer to my sodden shoes. I am glad to slow down a bit, to relax our pace. I am glad to be warm and still. But Mikal's becoming fidgety and restless.

"Let's go to zee hot pool spas!" he says.

"Yeah, cool," I say agreeably, even though I'm just as glad to stop doing the tourist attractions for a day. "But I just need to dry my stuff first, bro." Secretly, I don't want to go at all – and I am so over Mikal's always demanding nature.

We go.

The roughly poured concrete pools resemble over-populated eel tanks. They are filled with squirming Ecuadoran families in bright shorts and bathing suits. We ease ourselves into the warm water, and even though I've been tired of being drenched all day, I have to admit that sitting in the natural hot water spring helps my muscles relax. I don't even mind the rain falling on my shoulders; this is a soothing end to a chilly, adventurous day. I sleep like a log. I think we all do.

On my morning stroll through the city streets next day, I pass an adult pig that's been slit through the belly lengthways, splayed out and nailed to a plank that leans upright against the wall outside a small butcher's shop. This is obviously a means to attempt would-be customers to enter and buy a cut of meat or two. The staring swine, perched atop his plank as he is at eye level, does little for my appetite. I can only feel a little sorry for it and the inhumane way it's being displayed here on the street. *No dignity in his death*, I think. No pork for me, at least today, I vow.

Continuing into town through the thick drizzle to buy a newspaper, I am disappointed when my lack of Spanish defeats me in the most basic of situations. I can't recall the word for newspaper, nor can I properly decline what I'm being sold. I return with a lined A5 school exercise book that I don't really need.

"What's that for?" Dan asks me on my return.

"Just something to make notes in," I snap back.

The failed morning paper mission is eating away at me as we pack and make ready to leave. I need to take more Spanish lessons. Either that, or brush up on my charades.

CHAPTER THIRTY-TWO
QUITO

This time we trundle along in a brightly painted 'collectivo' mini-van. We are packed in like sardines, with an enormous pile of luggage and fruit on the roof. Our van makes its way across the mountains to Quito, perched a further 1000m higher. When we alight at a terminal on the outskirts of the city, the calm drizzly streets of Baños are a distant memory: here we are sucked into a torrent of commuters, swept with the current down to a line of bus stands destined for the inner city. We jostle to stay upright, still loaded with our backpacks, and the doors of an extended bus hiss open as it stops at the kerbside. We are sucked in with the commuter current and find a space to stand in the mid-section bendy walled rubber area between the two ends of the serpentine vehicle. As we ease out of the station, a curly haired, broad-shouldered teenager wearing a holey woollen sweater in front of me presses his back against my chest. I know the bus is crammed full but the force he's applying is a bit much, pinning me between him and the pole I'm holding onto. Before I realise what's happening, I feel a hand rummaging in the side pocket of my trousers – obviously his accomplice. I push back with all my strength, sending the commuters around me spinning off in all directions and bouncing off the rubber walls. I quickly straighten up and look around, but the bus has already stopped and the curly haired lad and a girl in a striped t-shirt hop out fast and successfully disappear into the morning crowd – with the five-dollar note that was in my pocket.

Welcome to Quito.

Alighting the bus in the historic part of town, we check into our hostel, which is painted in a bright yellow hue and situated on the edge of a plaza where a fountain gushes and hundreds of pigeons waddle around on the ground.

"I have to email Jan and tell him to meet us here," Mikal says, leaving us to find the room and obviously eager to see his friend again when he arrives from Montanita.

That evening, we flick on the television and, watching the news, we are astounded at the shocking stories from the day. Bloody scenes from the city are on every channel: armed robberies gone wrong and gangs of drug traffickers face-down in the dirt with hands cable-tied. Not exactly a settling sight. Not exactly in alignment with the 'Visit Ecuador' posters in travel agents' offices back home.

A few hours later the door springs open accompanied by a familiar voice. "Hey! My President!"

Jan is glowing with a bronzed tan from his last two weeks in Montanita. Mikal jumps off of his bed and excitedly greets him and they gabble in German for the next twenty minutes as they catch up. Already we can tell that Mikal is in a much better mood. I am glad to have Jan back in our midst.

Mikal's new frame of mind now he's regrouped with Jan is such a contrast to the last week or so and that evening we are both restless and unable to sleep. We venture out into the city at midnight for a look around. And what could have been a very stupid decision ends up being a delightful encounter with a side of Quito I never imagined. The streets are now empty and rain soaked, reflecting the coloured lights that drape from the white walls of the old town's colonial buildings. We wander through the abandoned central park, filled by day with the buzz of infant shoe shiners and office workers chatting over lunch. The park is now silent and illuminated by the white glow of the fairy lights hanging from the trees that shelter its paths and walkways. It is enchanting – dare I say liberating.

Back in the hostel kitchen, we meet a stocky American guy who has also been wandering the streets, although his experience of Quito's nightlife has been slightly different to our fairy-tale jaunt. He tells us how he's been threatened by a dark figure in a doorway who demanded his belongings while aggressively swinging a bike chain, and how he switches up the situation by snatching the chain, beating the would-be mugger to the floor and taking *his* money and phone.

"That'll teach him for trying to mug me," he splutters while devouring the huge burger he's holding.

The following morning, Mikal heads off to meet some German friends flying into the country and I decide to spend some quiet time uploading a few photos. I've taken thousands of images with the replacement digital camera I purchased in BA, and I've been carrying them around all safely loaded onto several USB sticks. When I plug them into the hostel's computer, however, it appears they are all reading blank. I'm devastated. All my amazing pictures, all the memories captured, have been erased forever. Pissed off and now frantic, I head out to find a computer repair store in the hope that they will be able to shed some light on the subject. The busy mid-morning rush of the streets is disorientating. Positioned on every street corner is an armed soldier – a sight that doesn't particularly fill me with confidence. A lengthy language battle with the owner of a small stationary-*cum*-internet café results in a diagnosis but not a cure.

"Is virus," the small man tells me over his rectangular-framed glasses, "Lo siento, no puedo reparar," he adds, telling me he can't fix the problem.

According to him, the photos are still on the sticks but have a blocking virus that hides them from view. I was previously warned about internet cafes and their virus-riddled machines but ignored them. I have only myself to blame. Unfortunately for my friends and family in other parts of the world, this means I can't upload any more pictures for the duration of the trip.

During lunch, the two new friends of Mikal – the ones who've just flown in from Germany – join us.

"Yessss!" Mikal squeals with excitement as they arrive. Without introducing them, he yaps away in German seemingly getting them up to speed with who we are and what's been going on. When he switches back to English, it's with his characteristic angry tone.

"Zis fucking place!" he grumbles. "Never would dis happen in Chermany! Fucking assholes!"

"What his problem now?" Dan asks, while Mikal switches again back to German and shouts at the one wearing glasses.

"Manfred," Jan says quietly, pointing at the one he's shouting at. "He brings new camera for him, but it's already stolen."

"Karma's a bitch, eh?" Dan mumbles with a huge smirk on his face. Mikal has returned to his animated conversation in German with his new friends, so Dan turns to me more directly and says, "I can almost hear him now, firing his orders down the phone at the poor guy: *'You mast git ze top model! Ze best one!! I will not use inferior camera!'*"

I laugh quietly at Dan's impression.

Mikal goes on with his litany of complaints, and we continue our lunch. The atmosphere between us and the new arrivals is uncomfortable, to say the least.

To ease the awkwardness that Mikal has created, we take the new guys to a gigantic Metal statue of the Virgin Mary, which sits on the summit of El Panecillo and watches over the city. The hill is similar in geography to the Cerro Santa Ana in Guayaquil with its slopes carpeted in shanty neighbourhoods.

When we arrive, the taxi driver gives us his best sales pitch. "Es muy peligroso a bajar caminando hombres." He says it's only a ten-minute walk down but warns that there's a slight possibility of being robbed due to the lack of security guards. But by now we are savvy travellers – we won't be fooled by a taxi driver's ruse for more cash. As if he could guard us properly anyway – he's short, and old, and he doesn't look much of a fighter. No, we're fed up with stories from cabbies trying to make a buck, so we send him on his way and spend a half hour or so on the summit gazing up at the gigantic tin woman, discussing how many bolts she has holding her together. The city surrounding us below is massive and stretches off into the distance as far as the eye can see.

"Surely this is the biggest so far?" I question out loud.

"Nah." Dan replies, once again quashing my enthusiasm. "We just got a good view up here compared to the others."

Ignoring the warning from the taxi driver, we descend through the narrow alleys of the barrio that separate the summit from the city below. And soon the tension grows as we approach every blind corner.

"Maybe that taxi driver had a point." I can't help but feel vulnerable. We are definitely in an area where we don't belong.

Pastel-shaded walls support low, corrugated iron roofs that jut out at head height and force us to crouch as we make our way through the alleys.

"There's six of us, bro. Chill out," Dan says, failing to reassure me.

Eventually we reach the bottom unscathed and the air of relief is palpable. No one says it but we all know full well that the walk could have taken a turn for the worse.

Thrusting into the sky above the buildings that surround it on the opposite side of the city stand the steeples of the Basilica of the National Vow, the largest neo-gothic basilica in the new world, adorned with gargoyles of all descriptions that peer down googly-eyed with tongues hanging out, carved from a gun metal grey stone. The main steeple can be accessed by a vertical iron ladder that climbs up through a series of platforms of a precariously rusty looking mesh. At the top of the ladder one comes to a level where various graffiti-scribed ancient stone windows cast amazing views out over the city. Other views can be enjoyed up in the church rafters, where, hanging thirty metres up in the roof pitch of the main church, is a flimsy, single-beamed, hand-railed walkway that looks down into the vast hollow of the building and all its grandeur.

Thus we conquer two tourist venues in one day at opposing ends of this huge city. And so we reward our efforts, naturally, with two bottles of rum in our room. Fully boozed and raring to hit the town, we hail a taxi that takes us to a packed nightclub where a long line of mini-skirted and slick-haired party-goers wait to gain entry. The club begins to fill up, and a short Colombian girl in glasses dances like her life depends on it, smiling at everyone, spinning and flailing her arms around giving off strong signals that she is 'well up for it'. Dan zones in on her, shimmying onto the dance floor and ruffling his feathers, parading around like a peacock in heat, performing what can only be described as his mating dance.

"Zee President! He is dancing king!" Jan shouts, loving what he's seeing.

And Dan's moves, believe it or not, impress the girl, and they spend the next hour or so performing their mating rituals while we drink at the bar. When we leave, Dan stays on, cross-eyed and still flapping around like a chicken with his dance partner, who is now doing the same.

Dan's not in his bed the next morning. I am nursing a throbbing hangover, and I don't care much to wonder about when he's coming back.

"My president has found his queen," Jan squawks, happy that the next time we see Dan, he'll have a new story to tell.

But when I arrive back at the hostel after breakfast and see he's still not there, I begin to worry. By 4pm we still haven't heard from him or received replies to our numerous Facebook messages and emails. Quito is not exactly the safest place (especially at night) and thoughts of phoning Dan's dad in New Zealand with some terrible story involving details of how to organise his body to be sent home feed my paranoia. By now my stress levels are reaching boiling point and I'm fuming at the inconsiderate bastard for not having contacted us to let us know he is still alive.

"Let's wait until dark and zen vee can phone police," Jan suggests, trying to calm me down and now also worried at how long Dan has been gone. What Jan can't know is that his support makes my fears even more intense: if the always joking, always boisterous Jan, who seems to take nothing seriously, is showing signs of concern, we've got something real to worry over.

"OK," I say. "I guess that's all we can do…wait." I am feeling rattled.

At 8pm my nerves are shattered but then I receive a blasé email message from Dan, saying that he's just finished eating at the girl's apartment and will be home shortly.

This incident brings to light the question of my independence and how little I now have, invisibly handcuffed to Dan and his couldn't-care-less attitude and, more annoyingly, his fluent Spanish. His twenty-four hour disappearance affects me greatly: I desperately want to learn Spanish now, so I can remove myself from this debilitating dependent state.

I am trapped. I'm starting to think more seriously about how I can separate from Dan and survive alone on this foreign continent, but for the meantime I am going to have to stick with him to survive.

I am miserable, and I am trapped.

"Zee president is alive! Zees is great!" Jan says with delight as Dan shows up, freshly shaven and smelling of girl's soap.

"Fuck you, man!" I blurt out uncontrollably and killing Jan's humour. "I was fucking worried sick about you, bro, and you didn't even have the decency to call."

"I only woke up a few hours ago, bro," he replies. "We didn't get home till nine o'clock this morning."

"Whatever," I bark back, angrily heading off to the room. I'm fuming at the whole scenario, but at the same time can't help but feel relieved that my best friend is still alive.

CHAPTER THIRTY-THREE
QUITO CONTINUED

I've noticed a barber shop in the small plaza outside the hostel and, waking before the others, decide to go and try out my Spanish. A tiny man in the doorway leads me in to a seat.

"¿De que estilo?" he asks, querying the style I'm after.

"Todo grado uno con este, por favor," I say pointing at his shaver.

Grade one: passed – and the old man changes the attachment and begins to cut off my scruffy mop. He understood! I'm elated and a deluded confidence washes over me. For the following fifteen minutes it takes him to buzz my hair, I rattle off as much as I can ask, hoping he's game to listen to my bastardisation of his language. He 'si's' and 'no's' at appropriate intervals and I think he's vaguely understood some of the things I've told him.

When he's done, he removes my cape, patting me on the back as if he feels sorry for me.

"Un dolar" he says, holding out his hand.

I pay and leave hairless and delusional, thinking I've actually had a coherent conversation with a local.

Our whole group, new Germans and all, venture out to the equator line attraction by bus. Tall wooden poles wrapped in pampas grass stand proudly in an area outside a straw roofed adobe construction. Inside its hemp clothed walls, moth-ravaged leopard and snake skins drape limply over any available surface, while various stuffed jungle animals, including a jaguar, a six-metre anaconda and a jar containing a 'penis fish' are proudly displayed. These little critters are found in the Amazon and it's advised not to urinate while swimming as they (as the name suggests) like to swim up into the eye of the penis. Just thinking about this brings tears to my eyes as I wonder how the hell these things manage to get up there: they are the size of a small cricket.

Manfred, the new German addition to our group, has an air about him that I'm finding annoying. I don't like his attitude. I don't like his beady little eyes behind his round spectacles. Unfair as it is, all I can conjure are images of a Gestapo officer every time I look at him. His know-it-all approach to just about everything wears thin fast. Backed up by Mikal, who is incidentally ecstatic to have a new sidekick, Manfred conceitedly insists on embarrassing and proving the guide wrong when he demonstrates water flowing round a basin anti clockwise on the south side of the equator line and the opposite on the north.

"It's a lie!" he snorts, demanding the guide pour the water into the opposite side of the basin to prove his theory of it being a trick.

The guide glares at him. The guide is just a guy doing his job.

Manfred tries to grab the bucket and pour the water in. "It's a lie!" he repeats, still trying to prove his point.

"Dick," Dan mumbles, sparking a cigarette.

I am still blanking Dan for his dumbass move the previous day and night, but I can't help but chuckle quietly – and agree wholeheartedly with his assessment of our new travel companion.

I feel for our poor guide. Because, even if his demonstration doesn't work entirely, due to the sinks being only a metre from each side of the imaginary line, it still doesn't warrant being picked apart in front of the tour group.

Something comes over me. I know that I can't travel with these guys much longer. Their combined energy is too much for me. I'm here to experience Latin American culture, not German opinions of it.

But I'm not free of them yet. The following morning, we sit in smog outside a bakery with bags packed. Two old men pull up in a dented Nissan micro van with its sliding door ajar and one headlight hanging out like those 'eye hanging out' joke spectacles. The driver and his mate are dressed in ill-fitting suits and splutter at us through gumming grins.

"¡Adelante! ¡Cuandoquieras! ¡Ocho! ¡Ocho!"

Eight bucks to go anywhere is too hard to refuse, and, much to the disapproval of Mikal, we stuff our backpacks and ourselves into the tiny van. The hilarity that follows is like something from the 1970s

British comedy series, *The Benny Hill Show*.

They speed and swerve around the city streets in third gear at 4,000 revs, laughing and honking the horn, playing the stereo at full volume and throwing us around in the rear of the tiny van. Eventually we arrive at a deserted bus station on the opposite side of the city. But it's closed, and by the looks of it we can tell it's been closed at least a few months.

"Zis is not zee bus station!" Mikal squeals at them, starting to turn red. Dan translates in a more relaxed manner.

"¡Si, Si, es el terminal!" the old codgers reply, their toothless grins trying to reassure.

"But it's not the one we want!" Dan explains.

They smile, laugh and drop us back at the bakery where we got in an hour before. Driving away, still smiling and eight dollars better off, they disappear into the river of honking traffic, waving us goodbye and leaving a cloud of black exhaust smoke. We wave back.

"Did that really just happen?" I ask the others, confused.

We hail a taxi.

CHAPTER THIRTY-FOUR
MINDO

Manfred stays in Quito. Dan and I can't help but be happy – not only about his staying there, but about the reason why. It seems like a classic case of instant karma: the ever-knowing, ever-talking, ever-sure-of-himself Manfred has been taken down by a stomach virus. We figure he's been cursed by the guide at the Equator attraction. We can only hope.

An hour or so after mingling into the crowds at Quito's northern bus station, we are once again bumping along a dirt road lined with vine-strangled trees. Giant butterflies flutter through the branches of the trees that flash by as the midday heat grows increasingly unbearable. Our route takes us to the tiny jungle town of Pachijal where Frederik – the chap we met back in Montanita – has invited us to stay. But first we stop for the night in a small town about halfway there – Mindo. Sitting on the bus in front of us are two caramel-skinned native girls. Jan and I smile and start a conversation. Their command of the English language is limited, and our Spanish is non-existent as always, but we are both persistent and patient, and we manage to score a place to sleep in Mindo, where the local girls live.

We climb out of the bus with them into a blinding afternoon at the intersection of a small dusty plaza. They lead us, their long dark hair swishing behind them, to a hostel owned by their brother. The village high street looks like an old Wild West town with its dirt road and wooden balconied facades sheltering old beaten up pick-up trucks. The truck beds overflow with freshwater crabs, crayfish and pineapples. The song of tropical birds surrounds us as the jungle quietly creeps around the edges of the village. The hostel sits on the bank of a wide river that courses its way through the forest. As its current carries the water right past us, colourful birds take flight and skim its glistening fast-moving surface for food. The rear balcony, shrouded in exotic bright flowers and more giant butterflies, is lined with comfy hammocks where we while away a few hours with the Germans. Peta, who arrived with Manfred and is now our new travelling companion (inherited awkwardly when we left Manfred behind), has been quietly existing in the background ever since he showed up in Quito. This is partly due to the fact that the battle of egos between Jan, Mikal and Manfred has not allowed any room for another personality – the poor guy's not really had a chance to fit in. So we choose a hammock each, and lie back and deepen his acquaintance.

He turns out to be quite personable. A tall, handsome and muscular blond fellow, he could be mistaken for another, well, tall, handsome, muscly German. But he's studying for his doctorate, and his priority is to find some work in a Colombian hospital once we arrive there. I instantly like him far more than Manfred – though that's not hard to do.

"I'd like to see whatever you guys are going to on the way," he tells us in good English. "But my main goal is for the work experience."

We venture out as dusk settles, strolling the length of this main strip, joining the townsfolk who shuffle along under the twinkling lights of the street stalls that house glowing barbecues sizzling with meat.

Memories are all the more vivid in these smaller places with no tourists or obvious attractions. Walking through the quiet streets of the picturesque Mindo, I feel acutely how big this planet is – and how small we all are as individuals, our daily lives and worries insignificant in the grand scale of things. We could be a million miles from anywhere. We *are* a million miles from anywhere. And yet, these lives here thrive, far from typical commercial concerns, with only butterfly wings beating and the jungle river flowing at the centre of life. I'm beginning to loosen up. If we are respectful towards the people we meet and take a keen interest in their worlds then we can only feel educated and enriched by these chance encounters.

One such memorable encounter happens the next day, when Dan and I go for a little wander across the wooden bridge that spans the bubbling river rushing through the gorge. We follow a narrow dirt road past a makeshift goalpost in a field of long grass to a dead end, where we come upon a lady hanging out her washing. She smiles a hello, and then surprises us when she tells her kids to put their shoes on, show the gringos the waterfall and bring back some bananas.

Our ten-year-old guide shakes our hands and picks up a long-bladed machete from the porch. Leading us into thick undergrowth of giant leaves, the 'ting!' of his knife neatly trims back a path that draws us deeper into the jungle. In matching blue Wellington boots, his younger brother and sister join, hacking their own way through the dense foliage with smaller blades. They regroup with us and offer a handful of bright red berries, similar in size and appearance to the raspberry.

"Mora," the girl squeaks, eating some. She rolls some into my palm.

They have a sweet but tart taste and hang plentifully from the bushy shrubs on our walk. The two younger kids watch in apprehension as we try the fruit, waiting for our reaction to the taste, and look pleased as our faces glow with pleasure and approval.

A further ten minutes of chopping and the bush thins out, revealing their little secret waterfall. The frothing white river has cleared a path through the jungle and is banked with smooth grey pebbles; the whole clearing is swarming with giant butterflies of every colour imaginable. For twenty minutes we soak in the sounds of the birdlife singing in the trees until the eldest boy shouts over to us.

"¡OK, vamos!" he says, before disappearing into a hole in the undergrowth, closely followed by his younger siblings. Catching up with them under the dark canopy of the jungle proves difficult, but Dan and I scramble through the brush and come to them in a clearing where they are chopping down a huge pod of bananas. The elder boy heaves them onto his shoulders and leads us back to the house. Waiting at the door, his mother greets her children and relieves the boy of the weighty pod and drags it inside, while the two youngest kick off their boots, wave goodbye and follow her inside.

We don't even have a chance to thank them.

CHAPTER THIRTY-FIVE
PEDRO VICENTE MALDONADO

The next bus stirs memories of the more questionable transport we've ridden thus far. An uncomfortable silence hangs over us as the vehicle rattles its way deeper and deeper into the jungle until, as if out of nowhere, a remote, dusty market town springs up around us. Brightly coloured banners and bunting flags hang between buildings while assertive vendors barter with shoppers that overcrowd the market stalls that line the wide street.

"Get to that little street over there!" Dan shouts across a sea of heads balancing bowls of food.

Clawing our way through the chaos, we take rest at a bench table shaded by a black tarp. An old lady brings five glass bottles of Coke, beaded with cold condensation. One by one, she clicks off their caps with a key ring bottle opener. Cooled by the cold liquid gushing down our throats, we slump in our seats.

A short local man climbs the broken steps to the shack and enters the kitchen with a wriggling plastic bag. He hands it to a woman who is washing potatoes. She opens the top of the bag and, with a cluck and a flap, a chicken pops out. Holding it firmly, the woman takes a small worn knife from her pinny and slits its throat expertly. The blood that pours from its neck gushes in to a bucket. The smile on the woman's face as she kills the bird in her bloody hands is priceless. She is obviously pleased she has an audience for her slaughter show. She knows she has deft hands. "Scheisse!" Mikal squeaks squeamishly.

"I'm going to find Frederik," he says, somewhat freaked out by the woman's display and heads in the direction of the school.

Mikal and Peta turn up an hour later on the back of a pick-up truck driven by a man in a fedora. Frederik jumps off the back and welcomes us with a giant smile.

"Hey, guys! You made it!" he shouts, looking genuinely stoked that we've come to see him.

Mikal, ever polite, shouts, "Vee haf to hang a door at zee school! Vait here!" They disappear down the street in the truck.

"For fuck's sake" I remark to the others, now completely over waiting for him in the heat of the day.

Dan leans in close and, still sipping his Coke through a straw, says conspiratorially, "We gotta ditch these dudes soon."

We fill the following hour devouring the chicken that has been bled dry, quartered, fried and served on paper plates with rice and salsa.

The others finally meet up with us and we walk to the house where Frederik is staying. The comings and goings of this little place in the middle of nowhere are quite remarkable. Shop fronts display TV sets and modern clothing while horses draw carts carrying fruit and produce. The posters stapled to various trees and poles around town tell us there's a 7pm – 7am house curfew. We have never been in a town with a curfew like this. We ask Frederik, a little concerned.

"There's lots of vigilante gang activity during the night here, and innocent people out after dark have been caught in the crossfire," he says, "so it's best to stay inside." He's smiling as he delivers this warning.

I'm not. I feel more than slightly vulnerable and am not keen to stick around, but it's not like we have any other choice.

"Can vee rent a truck to take us tonight?" Mikal asks, also not wanting to stay.

"I think maybe it's too expensive?" Frederik says, unsure of how much we are willing to pay.

Jan, who has been quiet and keeping to himself all day, joins in. "Vee try to rent a truck." He too is obviously worried by the posters.

The accommodation options are really scarce, so we ask around and hire an open-back wood-framed 4x4 truck for $35. Piling it high with our bags, and standing in the wooden cage on the rear of our vehicle, we head off rattling through the dark jungle. Giant bugs in the night air bounce off our faces and we barely miss a couple of oncoming trucks on a bumpy unsealed road winding its way to the tiny village of Pachijal. Two rough hours later, the truck begins to descend, circling the twinkling bulbs of the dimly lit village as it clings to the narrow road that hugs the steep cliffside.

"How many people live here?" I shout to Frederik, holding on as the truck sways us back and forth.

"Only 500!" he calls back.

The truck slows to a crawl as we enter the village, squeezing between the houses on a rocky trail. Frederik directs the driver to the dirt driveway of a single-storeyed yellow house where we are hugged and greeted by a plump Afro-Caribbean woman with big white teeth and friendly eyes.

"This is Martha, my friends," he says. "You can stay here." Frederik gives Martha a big hug.

"Ima goin' Quito for da weekend," Martha tells us in a loud Caribbean accent, and wearing an even louder orange t-shirt. "But you can stay for as long as you want!" She smiles with her shiny white teeth, and clapping her hands in glee. We instantly feel welcomed – her warm hospitality after only meeting us for mere minutes is comforting and reassuring, and we bed down in the silent night air and fall into a deep sleep.

CHAPTER THIRTY-SIX
PACHIJAL

The little village is cloaked in a steam of morning humidity, and surrounded by slopes of banana, sugar cane and coffee plantations. We depart our small yellow house and walk through the eerily quiet streets looking for Frederik. Workers peer down from the slopes while they pick coffee. Shirtless, oil smudged and tinkering on an old motorbike in a front yard surrounded by a few local kids, our host, apart from his white skin and blond hair, really does look like he belongs here.

"Hey!" he greets us, with that happy smile. "You are hungry, yes?!"

"Very hungry!" we reply in unison.

"Great! Let's go!" He claps his hands together and wipes the grease from them. A few doors down and looking over a grass volleyball court with straw-roofed concrete shelters stands an adobe structure housing a large wooden table with a few hammocks strung from the roof beams. Owned by a friendly woman and her two beautiful, almond-eyed, golden-skinned daughters, it's one of two places in town to buy cooked meals. The hammocks are all occupied by babies and small children, gently swinging. We sit.

"Hi, girls!" Frederik calls to them in Spanish through the beaded doorway to the kitchen. "These are my friends and they would like to try your delicious cooking."

An old man leading a mule loaded with two milk churns passes by, tipping his hat. "Buenas, bienvenidos," he mumbles, soft and welcoming.

"We've timewarped," I say to Dan, happy we actually made the effort to come this far. I think back to the churn we held on the pickup truck back in Argentina. It seems so long ago.

Our plates are brought to the table piled high with fried plantain, eggs, refried beans and warm tortillas. We tuck in while Frederik explains the adventure he has planned for us.

"The kids want to take you to a waterfall," he tells us excitedly. "We will be gone all day."

"Is the trail steep or rocky?" I ask him, shoving some more breakfast in my mouth.

"The trail is very wet," he replies with a snigger, raising his mug of coffee to hide his mischievous smile. "It rained all last week, you'll see."

We return to his homestay house after breakfast, where we find the kids eagerly waiting in the garden with their machetes. They lead us to the edge of the village where an earth-moving machine is repairing the track washed away by the rains. Wading into the middle of a river, Frederik looks back.

"You see! It's very wet!" he calls, laughing.

Wading waist deep for three hours upstream, we are mesmerised by giant electric-blue butterflies and hummingbirds that hover among the creeper-looped branches at the river's edge. Nelson, the oldest of the kids, cuts sugar cane to chew on and chops slits in the thick stems of bamboo, filling our bottles with crisp cool water. A faint rumble of water grows louder the farther we climb and finally reveals itself in all its glory, glinting in the sunlight. A towering white shaft of crystal clear fresh water cascades into a perfectly round turquoise pool enveloped on all sides by overhanging rock faces veiled in thick green moss and vines. An abundance of giant blue butterflies play with the plummeting water, fluttering in as close as possible, only to be thrown out from the force of the airstreams it creates. Cooling the prickly heat, we spend an invigorating and refreshing hour wallowing in the pool and boost our energy for the return trip. There is nothing that could disturb this idyllic scene, surrounded as we are by nature's bounty.

Well, almost nothing.

During this peaceful moment in a place where time has seemingly stood still, Mikal and Jan insist on flexing their muscles, bare-chested, while growling loudly at the waterfall and posing for photos.

"What the fuck are they on?" Dan says before diving back in to the pool.

The children who have brought us here look at them momentarily with stupefied gazes and shake their heads.

Muddy, exhausted and drenched, we arrive back at the village at dusk, to the wafting aroma of fresh baked bread emanating from a small blue wooden house perched on stilts.

"¡La Panaderia! ¡Se hace dulces!" shout the kids in unison, running through the gate and up the front stairs.

Following the children into the hut, we are greeted by a plump couple, sprinkled in a light dusting of flour and surrounded by wooden shelves of sweet bread twists and iced buns. The local bakery! We fill a bag with the freshly baked goods, hand over some money and stroll over to the volleyball court to eat our feast.

A group of teenagers punch a ball to each other over the volley net while others congregate under a straw roof at the edge of the court and giggle, watching us eat our bread.

"Tonight is party night!" Frederik tells us, clapping his hands together with a smile. "The school is celebrating its 100 year anniversary!" He jumps up and down like an excited child.

Back at our yellow house, we wash away the mud and sweat of the day in rainwater from large buckets situated in the rear garden.

"OK, let's go!, Paaaarrrtyyy!" Mikal booms.

"We need something to drink, Fred," Dan says.

"Yeeeesss!" Jan interrupts. "My president must have much alcohol! In my country my president Dan always have drink with party."

The drink of choice in this town is 'Cania', sold by the kitchen where we've been eating for the last few days. Cania is the village version of moonshine, an 80-proof distilled sugar cane juice. Served in recycled plastic Coke bottles, it smells like petrol and stings the eyes.

"Holy fuck!" Jan squeals as his eyes start to water. "It's too strong!"

"Haha!" Frederik laughs. "You need Coke or lemonade with it!"

We prepare ourselves by mixing the soda with the fire juice, and skull back a few mouthfuls before going to the dirt yard of the tiny school. Parents and kids of all ages mingle in the yard and a small platform set up at the back of the main hall provides a stage for the cultural songs and dances performed by students dressed in shimmering skirts. Burgundy strips of silk hang from their waistlines and string bikini tops provide a support for triangles of paper that drape down over their brown bellies.

We find ourselves next to a moustached local called Mario. We offer a swig of the Cania juice to him – it seems the neighbourly thing to do – but he chuckles and turns his nose up, refusing to touch the stuff. He swigs beer instead. Adjusting his ivory handled pistol in his belt, he puts an arm round my shoulder and spends the rest of the evening trying to persuade me to buy the wreck sitting at the edge of the schoolyard. I can only think of the gun in his belt and how drunk he'll be later.

The dilapidated micro chicken bus is riddled with rust and long grass grows around and out of the flat tyres. Mario gives me a complete tour. Miraculously, when he turns the key it starts with a rattle and engulfs the surrounding area in a cloud of black smoke.

"¡OK! ¡Vamos a la playa!" he shouts, pretending to drive us to the beach as we climb in. We have a pretend tour of Mario's favourite places, all the while sipping our local concoction, Mario sticking with his beer.

The moonshine leaves us with cracking headaches the next morning, and we leave Mikal in bed and dip into Peta's medical journals searching for his newly contracted symptoms, which he swears amount to dengue fever. The others and I are positive it's solely a bout of food poisoning, but the placebo effect is in full swing as Mikal comforts his aching body with the books.

"See you later on, Mikal" Frederik calls out. "Youll be fine later, trust me!"

Giant bunches of ripe bananas litter the trail that we walk en route to Frederik's friend Rodrigo's place – a stilted house on the banks of a wild river that can only be reached by crossing a crude but effective bridge made of three wobbly ropes and split bamboo stems. We twist, jerk and hold on for dear life traversing the raging rapids below.

After our introductions, Rodrigo introduces us to his prize fighting cockerels. The two huge birds stand hooded on a rope perch and wobble back and forth, trying to keep their balance. Transferring them to his arm, he takes them down carefully and pulls off the hoods. He then attaches little tie-on gloves that cover their claws, preventing them from harming each other. Passing one to Frederik, he steps back a few feet.

"¡¿Listo, amigo?!" he asks him, making sure he's ready to drop when he commands.

"Si. ¡Listo!" Frederik replies.

Simultaneously they let go and the birds cluck and lunge at each other erratically in a frenzy of feathers. It is a sight to behold. I don't quite know where to stand, as feathers fly and beaks snap. But the show's over as soon as it began – they are expertly caught and put back and all is suddenly quiet again.

When they fight for real in the ring, each cock gets one razor steel spur about half the length of a ball point pen, which is tied on the back of his claw just below the drumstick. The gamblers scream and shout waiting to see which rooster survives. Clouds of feathers fill the air during a fight that only lasts a few seconds. As a visual spectacle, it resembles someone slashing a feather pillow with a knife.

After re-hooding the roosters, Rodrigo leads us down to the river's edge. Thigh deep in fast flowing water, we tread lightly over smooth pebbles on the river bed, following Rodrigo and his young daughter through a tunnel of dense vegetation which they trim with machetes. The air once again is filled with giant butterflies that float within reach, proudly flaunting the blues and purples of their wings. In little more than an hour, we reach an area where giant brown spiders crawl over huge sandstone boulders that enclose a small box canyon. The water flowing over the sandstone riverbed is an almost cyan shade of blue. I'm astounded by the things I could not imagine before.

We launch ourselves into the icy cold water; the invigorating tingle shocks the senses and revitalises us after the long walk. As the sun beams through the canopy onto the white rocks of this natural untouched beauty, the only thing missing is Indiana Jones swinging across the river chased by poison tipped arrows from the blow pipes of a long lost tribe.

Wading back downstream to Rodrigo's, we say our farewells and make our way back to Pachijal, collecting a banana pod each en route.

The hospitality we've recently been shown is changing me for the better. These experiences that take place off the beaten track, in settings far away from the typical gringo trail, are really starting to have an effect on my perceptions of the trip. I can't quite pinpoint it, but I know I'm changing. With every flitting butterfly, with every dip into a cold river current, I feel my own view, and my own sense of my place in the world, shift. These people, fuelled by the excitement of showing us their lives and skills and way of life – so cherished by them – have no idea how they are changing us. But when they quench our thirsts with water from a bamboo stem, or feed us with the right part of a sugar cane, or take precious time out to show us – complete strangers – their prized roosters…well, it matters.

Their time matters. Their energy matters. They matter.

CHAPTER THIRTY-SEVEN
CIELO VERDE

Our last morning in Pachijal is spent over a simple but luxurious breakfast made all the more memorable by the almond-eyed daughters gliding around the kitchen.

"If you want an adventure, this is where you'll get it," Frederik assures us over breakfast, describing the even smaller village of Cielo Verde another two hours deeper into the jungle. "There's a direct bus from there to Quito every morning too."

"It's far too early to be returning to civilisation just yet," I say in a persuasive tone.

We discuss it and agree that none of us is ready to get back to bigger towns – not yet. We're up for Frederik's recommendation so we pack up and wait for the bus outside the kitchen. Frederik waves us goodbye and jumps on the back of a motorcycle bound for Vicente Maldonado.

"The Ranchero will be here soon!" he shouts as the motorbike fires up and speeds off.

A few minutes later the rumbling noise of a diesel engine echoes through the village and turns into our lane. Noisily making its way towards us is a 4x4 flatbed truck with a colourfully painted yellow, white and red ornate wood-framed box. In it are seven rows of church pew bench seats, neatly arranged and secured for passengers. It's already full so we climb on the roof and cushion ourselves amongst our backpacks. Holding on to the side rails, riding with the rice sacks and beans, we pass through the landscape veiled in thick jungle from which tall palm trees reach for the clouds.

In amongst the dense vegetation, groups of cinder block and adobe houses appear at the sides of the road from time to time. I catch the eye of a pretty local girl swinging in a hammock on the porch of one of these dwellings and wave. She smiles wide, a gold tooth glinting in the sunlight. Seconds later a guy appears through the coffee sack curtain hanging in the doorway behind her. Angrily, he shouts something at me with a machete in his hand. I pray the bus isn't going to stop anytime soon and avert my stare. The bus, fortunately, continues on its path, and my fears reside as we rumble off down the road in a cloud of dust.

"Haha!" Jan chuckles, seeing what just happened. "He vants to kill you!"

We bounce around on the top of the vehicle and duck under low-lying branches for another half hour, when we're deposited at a fork with no sign of any civilisation whatsoever.

"¡Cielo Verde!" shouts the driver in the direction of the roof.

"That's us!" Mikal squeals, throwing his bag off.

Quickly climbing down the back ladder, we follow an old man and lady who have also disembarked from the seats below. At the bottom of a wet overgrown mud track, we reach a high gorge with a rusty bucket cable car hanging from a frayed thick steel wire. I remember the orange cable car at Pailon del Diablo and realise how safe it was in comparison to what's before me.

"Holy shit!" Dan says, peering over the edge. "That things not gonna hold our weight."

The old couple confidently pull themselves across in the rusty crate. We gawk. But having no other choice, and seeing the example set by the village locals, Dan and I climb aboard. Somehow we've been silently selected as the first of our group to go. No one – not a single one of the five of us – believes this monstrosity is going to stay in the air. The mere weight of our backpacks not centred correctly on the floor creates a back and forth swing and scares us shitless. Dan and I settle into uncomfortable positions, straddling the centreline of the floor to stabilise us. With every tug of the wire, the fast flowing white water below comes into view. Thoughts of slipping out of the open ended bucket now become a growing reality.

Our lives hang literally in the balance.

"Stay still!" Dan barks, doing all the pulling, to propel the bucket along.

"I'm trying to!" I snap back, holding on for dear life while fifty metres below the river rushes over jagged rocks.

We arrive on the other side, surviving the dangling death trap, and then watch as Jan and Mikal winch the crate back across the gorge, load themselves and begin their crossing, leaving Peta to make his way across last and alone. The bucket creaks with the same sketchy traversing sway as ours and eventually we are all on the opposite cliff, and finally let out a collective and audible exhale.

A red mud trail leads us another forty-five minutes uphill through a slippery path in the ever-growing humidity. Not a word is said between us as we pant in the heat. We finally reach the rambling edge of a village, where we come to wooden-planked houses – if you can call them that. The cracks in the planked walled structures are big enough to see through into the simply furnished dirt floored living rooms and kitchens of these dwellings.

It is an eerily isolated place. We truly have stepped back in time.

We spy what must be the bus Frederik mentioned in a puddly side street – there is a huge 'Quito' sign on the front, as well as the ubiquitous 'In god we trust' stickers across the top of the windscreen. I for one am glad that our exit strategy involves a bus driver who trusts in The Good Lord – anything's better than going back across the gorge.

We continue into the village to enquire how we go about riding the bus to the city. The village's main green is a muddy volleyball court with a limp strip of knotted mesh connecting two poles fashioned from branches as a net. Alongside this green stands a little wooden store selling Chiclets, bottles of fizzy drink and chunks of ice that prevent a huge chest freezer from closing.

"¿A que hora va el bus chica?" Dan asks the shop girl, hoping to get information about the bus departure.

"Todos los dias a las 4:30 en la manana," she replies, directing us to the house where we'd seen the bus parked.

We knock on the door – a door we only find after walking around the large bus parked outside – and it creaks open to reveal Miguel, the driver, a shirtless short fellow with a pencil-thin moustache and a round shiny belly emerging proudly from the top band of his track pants. Looking us up and down with a pair of friendly eyes, he informs Dan that his bus leaves at 4am and that for $4 dollars each his wife will cook us dinner and we can share the bunk beds with his children.

Suddenly, Mikal, who has beat the fever but is still complaining about mosquitoes and generally not wanting to be in the jungle, whips out a $50 dollar note and flaps it at Miguel, screaming, "TELL HIM DAN! I hef fifty dollars for him to take us to Quito now! We have to get out of zis shit hole!"

I am beyond mortified. "Dude! Shut the fuck up!" I shout, as if I'm telling a naughty child off.

I'm not the only one who's shocked and disgusted by his behaviour. The others agree while Miguel, shaking his head, shuffles back inside.

Dan, who rarely gets angry about anything, loses it and takes Mikal to one side. "How fucking dare you wave money like that and demand such things! You're embarrassing all of us. WE go when the BUS goes, and THAT is tomorrow morning!!"

Mikal, now looking like his head is going to explode, is pacing like a mad man. "You stupid lazy Keevee! TELL HIM! TELL HIM!!" he fires back like a spoilt child.

Dan looks at him with distain. "Prick," he says, turning and walking away.

The situation, now rather awkward, is the turning point of a downward spiral in the group's dynamics and the defining moment – the moment that eventually splits us up.

Escaping the bad atmosphere, we return to the village field and challenge the locals to a muddy game of volleyball where I end up being the main source of entertainment for them. They laugh hysterically as I slip and slide in the puddles, trying to hit the ball over the net, landing on my arse and covering myself from head to toe in dark brown mud.

Returning to Miguel's, I enter the kitchen and am startled by a rodent the size of a large cat sitting on the bench eating food scraps.

"Tranquilo, tranquilo, jajaja, es una Capaybara," Miguel informs me, laughing at my reaction. "Es mascota."

I'm not so glad to meet his pet, but there is little room for disagreement – we've already shown enough disrespect to our kind host. We share a prayer followed by a delicious meal of chicken, rice and beans with his family while sitting on the black fake leather arm chairs in the lounge, its walls adorned with kitschy trinkets and pictures of Miguel's boxing-gloved brother who, he boasts proudly, is a force to be reckoned with on the local circuit. Grabbing a couple of photos from an old shoebox, Miguel insists we accept the photos of his children that he passes to us for good luck on our travels. I try to refuse, not wanting to take away something so precious, but he insists. I gratefully accept.

The night comes to a close and we squeeze onto the thin foam mattresses with the kids.

"AGH!" Swat! "AGH!" Swat! "Deez fucking mosquitoes!! I hate zis place." While Mikal complains, slapping the bugs that only seem to be interested in him, we hold back sniggers and sink off to sleep with Miguel's children snuggling up with us in their single beds.

In what seems like moments later, we're woken at 4am by the bus coughing to a start and climb aboard, half-dressed. We pull on boots and button up shirts and hop aboard. It rumbles its way up and down the uneven dirt road, the headlights cutting through the thick layer of dark jungle ahead. Stopping regularly at the clusters of cinder block buildings that skirt the road, it is soon stuffed to the seams with passengers heading into their jobs in the city. If Mikal had had his way yesterday, chartering the bus with his tantrum, these people would've been denied their right to travel to work.

To say I feel ashamed to be associated with this guy doesn't even come close. This is a place where we have been taken in like family, shown so much warmth and hospitality – and where the people have proudly shared with us their secret little part of the world. My memory of this village is sullied by Mikal's rude outburst and offensive behaviour. But I carry the photo of Miguel's young kids, and I hope it will bring me the luck he promises. I reach for it in my pocket and smile. I carry far more memories from this place, memories that run deeper than an angry German and his selfish demands.

CHAPTER THIRTY-EIGHT
OTAVALO

We plan to stay in Quito for only one night. We check back into the same hostel in order to wash some clothes and link back up with Manfred, now recovered from his illness.

The atmosphere in the group is sour. Dan and I keep a wide berth from them and get our own room.

The early morning bus going north to Otavalo arrives during the off-peak season. Countrywide famous for its artisanal artefacts and perched in the mountains, the town thrives on the tourist trade, selling everything from hand-woven hammocks to cellphone covers. The market town's misty cobbled streets are relatively quiet and this seems like a perfect place to put our feet up for a couple of days and recharge our batteries. Our group, now ⅔ Deutsch, is simply too large, with too many German minds wanting to do too many German things. At least we split up for room accommodation, offering some relief from the constant banter between Mikal and Manfred. The two of them are now bunking with Peta, while Jan – who, on his own, is more tolerable – is sharing the room with Dan and me.

Mikal and his minions dump their bags in their room and race into town for fear of missing out on something – anything – while the three of us pick a three bed room, lie back and flick on the television. After the non-stop jungle expedition, I'm content just to watch films for a couple of days in a nice hotel room, maybe do some more laundry and re-organise my pack. Mikal and his new friends, on the other hand, appear to have insatiable appetites for tourist trap day trips, and book an excursion to a leather shoe and straw fedora hat village the next day.

Snuggled in warm beds with a thick drizzle falling outside, we flick on the remote and spend a relaxing day in the comfortable warmth of our room. Late afternoon falls upon us and our peace is shattered when the others return.

"HEEEEY!" leers Mikal through a gloating smile with a newly purchased hat on his head. "It vas soo great!"

To me, they look like a barbershop trio. "Nice matching hats," I say sarcastically.

"So great, yes?" Manfred replies, obviously not sensing my tone. They leave our room and we burst into laughter before settling back into our television marathon. I bump into them in their silly little hats having breakfast in a café the next morning. Not wanting to be rude, I join them for a coffee. The atmosphere is a little tense and Mikal, as usual, starts complaining in a raised voice that his eggs have come out before his bacon and that this would never happen in Germany. Manfred adjusts his spectacles and sniggers.

Well, fuck off back there then, I think to myself. I wish I hadn't joined them. I finish my coffee and leave, now absolutely certain that it's time to split.

CHAPTER THIRTY-NINE
IPIALES

Crossing the Tulcan border between Ecuador and Colombia is slightly more complex than the border transits we've previously experienced. Bus number one leaves from Otavalo to another hectic terminal in Ibarra, followed by a bus number two from Ibarra to Tulcan where we are stamped out of Ecuador but still five miles short of our destination. What remains is a peculiar stretch of no-man's land that we only traverse after haggling with the driver of an old Dodge pick-up, who drives a little too fast and makes no attempt to avoid the bumps in the unpaved potholed road. We sit atop our bags, trying to soften the impact.

"Allá," the driver mutters unenthusiastically. "Colombia." He points in the direction of a yellow, blue and red metal sign that spans the road, reading 'Bienvenidos a Colombia'.

We pay him and climb out, stretching our legs and rubbing our arses. Walking under the huge sign, I'm confused as to why there is no passport control point. The usual suspects congregate at the sidelines, eyeing our bags and fanning wads of bank notes encouragingly in hopes of swindling us with bad exchange rates.

Still walking, I'm sure we've covered far too much ground without being stamped in yet. Wherever we are, it's unsettling and we feel exposed: we've checked out of one place but we've not arrived in the next.

"We gotta go back," Dan says, turning on his heels and not waiting for an answer.

Back at the Bienvenidos sign, a row of crumbling ticket booths stand on a concrete plinth. It appears to be border customs. As we approach the building, I'm not surprised we completely missed it: it looks more like a derelict stadium entrance than an international border checkpoint.

A long wait inside the condemned building ensues, where we are heckled by a group of open-shirted taxi drivers who follow us out once we're stamped in. The ambience has once again changed, as it does through every border; this time, seemingly for the better. The Colombian people project a more open and less inhibited vibe than their reserved Ecuadoran cousins.

"¡Hola amigos! ¡¡¿A donde va?!!" chirps the overly friendly taxi driver, with fingers adorned in gold rings asking us where we want to go.

"Ipiales, por favor," we reply in unison.

We screech to a stop outside our taxi driver's recommendation.

"¡¡Aquí estamos!!" he announces, telling us we've arrived. Unfolding our bodies from his dilapidated car, we find ourselves looking at a crusty little hotel where a lady stands in the doorway sporting a swirly bouffant hairdo.

"How long you stay?" says the woman, who I can't help but think would be more suited behind the bar of any East End pub in London.

"Um, solo una noche," I reply.

"¡No!" she says, disappointed. "¡Tienen que ver la virgen!"

"We have to see the Virgin?" I think out loud.

"Sounds promising," Dan jokes.

She tries her best to persuade us to stay for an extra night and visit the incredibly long-titled El Santuario de la Virgen del Rosario de las Lejas, a huge white-bricked spiky cathedral built between 1916 and 1949 on the impossible cliff face of a densely bushed gorge, connected only by a double-arched bridge. As marvellous as it sounds, we're only staying the night and not in the least bit interested in any sightseeing – thanks to the increasingly bad dynamics of our group, which our bouffanted hostess could not know. So we decline her sales pitch, sink into the lumpy beds in our room upstairs and find a channel on the ageing TV that plays non-stop mega mix music videos. Not as inspirational as *la virgen* – but all we are up for tonight.

My first encounter with a local outside our hostel is with a scary-looking silver-toothed thug who approaches me with open arms in Ipiales' main plaza the next morning.

"¡Amigooo!" he shouts excitedly across the road, running over and embracing me, prattling on about how we'd been in Quito prison together.

I am confused. I'm pretty sure I've not been in Quito prison. But I go along with his rant, scared that if I disagree I'll offend him. I pat my pockets afterwards, but there seems to be nothing missing; perhaps my doppelganger is living behind bars in a South American prison? I wonder if this is an omen for what's to follow in our Columbian adventure. I am not generally superstitious, but I hope we've not made a grave mistake by refusing to visit the grand virgin on the gorge.

We depart the hotel and our friendly hostess, and we hike with our bags down through the grey neighbourhood to the bus station, exchanging *holas* with a bunch of happy little kids clinging to the fence inside their school. They are clearly excited to interact with us. Lugging our bags through this dusty town with no real idea of where we're going, I think of these kids and how they'll probably end up never leaving here. I walk on and reflect that perhaps they have the better deal. I wonder how it would be to teach in one of these schools. My mind wanders to Frederik, and how content and fulfilled he was back in Pachijal, teaching in the school and learning Spanish along the way. Maybe one day I can do the same. At the moment, bus after bus travel is starting to look monotonous and meaningless. I am not entirely sure anymore why we're even doing this. Are we learning anything as we go? Will I be able to differentiate one small town from the next once I'm back in my world? What will I take from the constant movement of this trip, other than a strengthened palate and a formidable stomach.

The bus crawls out of the terminal and in to the Andean foothills. Looking out of the window in to the green jungle, I see masked armed soldiers sporadically nestled in the bushes at the side of the road; the route is littered with military roadblocks. This is cocaine country; along with many other densely forested areas in Colombia, the FARC guerrillas are at war with the government forces. And soon we come face-to-face with what is the reality of travel in Colombia.

Less than an hour after we leave Ipiales the bus comes to a halt and four soldiers in camouflage board.

"¡¡¡¡Baja hombres BAJA!!!!" they bellow, walking up the aisle while their automatic rifles clink against the metal seat backs.

All the men are ordered to step off the bus, while the women are instructed to stay on. We're told to spread our legs and put our hands above our heads, palms against the bus while we are frisked and our passports are checked. After twenty minutes of frightening interrogation and digging through our bags and pockets, we're allowed back on board. Soon we are chugging our way through the mountainous jungle highlands for another two hours – but we sense the soldiers lurking in the undergrowth, and I wonder about the decision we've made to come here.

And sure enough, my fears are confirmed when at the next road block we come into closer contact with the patrols. This checkpoint is much more heavily guarded, black and white striped sentry boxes on either side of the road and groups of soldiers leaning against trees, smoking cigarettes with a casual but threatening air. One climbs aboard and, from the doorway, without even looking at anyone else, points at me sitting towards the back and tells me to follow him. The Germans and Dan share troubled glances but there's not a lot they can do. I get up, squeezing through the aisle packed with Colombians, who I sense are also fearing for me, and follow him around the back of the vehicle, where he demands my passport with a loud bark.

"¡Documentos!" He opens his hand out.

Surveying me critically, he conducts an interrogation in Spanish: why am I wearing camouflage army pants, and why is an Englishman travelling with Kiwis and Germans in Colombia. Although I'm getting most of what he's saying, my Spanish isn't good enough to answer his questions and I watch as his face contorts into an angry shape, frustrated by my silence. Just when I think I'm truly fucked, the bus ticket guy appears, obviously aware that I'm not going to be able to talk myself out of this one, and assists with some pretty rough translation.

The guard flicks through the pages and stops on my New Zealand residency permit. This only adds more confusion and he commands the bus assistant to explain what it means. Finally managing to work through the translation and explain that I'm just a simple traveller, that I have no business here, that my companions are not business associates but rather a random collection of ragtag travellers as well, he gestures my passport towards me. Relieved, I stretch my arm out to grab it, but he pulls it back and glares at me, taunting. There's nothing to do but wait while he stares me straight in the eye for what seems like forever. Confused and now sweating, I try not to look scared, but I am seriously about to piss myself. I think back to this morning's encounter with the market man who insisted we shared jail time together, and now more than ever I realise I really do not want to know what the inside of a Colombian jail looks like.

I hope I'm not shaking too much. But obviously, I am. I'm fucking terrified.

The armed guard bursts into laughter, slaps the passport in my palm and flicks me away in the direction of the bus door with the backside of his hand like an unwanted insect on his lapel.

CHAPTER FORTY
POPAYÁN

The Germans have pre-booked a hostel owned by a fellow countryman in the town of Popayán. It's a UNESCO world heritage site, a picturesque grid of streets made up of low-roofed whitewashed buildings capped with terracotta tiles. The hostel, despite the backdrop, is not so picturesque.

"I'm too tired to look for something else," I say to Dan.

"Yeah, same," he replies, and we reluctantly follow them in.

Manfred instantly feels right at home; the place has a very German feel about it, down to the dark-stained wood-panelled walls and black leather chairs that make me feel quite hemmed in but seem to offer a warm welcome to our travelling companions. And Klaus, the grumpy pot-bellied owner, reinforces my already unfair first impression, looking down a big nose sitting between his chubby cheeks and inspecting us while his fat thumbs stretch the braces holding up his brown corduroy pants. I swear he looks like he's just walked out of the garden gnome collection. I can barely contain my laughter when he speaks.

"You must read de rulebook and agree to de terms before you can stay."

His tone is suitably parental. A long list of *dos* but mostly *don'ts* are covered in his 'Guide to being German', ranging from curfew time to the appropriate manner and place for footwear removal. Seriously: there is a rule about which room our shoes must be taken off in before entering the house, not a simple *Please remove your muddy shoes before entering*. I am sure we'll be tested on the rules the next day, so I try to pay attention, all the while avoiding eye contact with Dan. Mikal and co however are standing there smiling at everything he says like they've found a cherished, long-lost family member. I feel myself cringing.

One night will be sufficient torture, I am sure. Manfred and Peta are now in the command of Mikal who decides they will be going their own way tomorrow and that maybe we'll meet up in Bogotá in a few weeks. I for one couldn't care less if that happens or not.

"I'm going wiz de Kivis," Jan tells Mikal, surprising us and, judging by Mikal's face, him too.

"Ah, yes!" he snaps at Jan. "Zis ees no problem." He looks for reassurance from his team, but receives little more than an 'OK' from Manfred and Peta.

Mikal, no longer in need of our company and up at the crack of dawn, whisks Manfred and Peta off to another tourist trap known as the Coffee Village. A few hours later Jan, Dan and I head off to find breakfast before catching our bus to Cali. With those guys out of our hair, and feeling our Little Bavaria accommodation may have cheated us out of a genuine Colombian experience in Popayán, we head to the edge of town and the rickety wooden labyrinth of the markets. We weave our way through the puddles and horse-drawn carts, and, stooping to avoid the sharp edges of the low corrugated roofs, we enter an orange steel-framed prefab building. Bubbling pots, steaming coffee and sizzling hotplates surround us. This feels like authentic Popayán. Our only problem is choosing where we're going to eat.

We select a blue-tiled bench in a clutter of steamy kitchen cubicles and order an Arepa breakfast: a thick pancake, made of corn and fried, accompanied by an egg. As we chew I feel eyes on us. The other proprietors of the nearby food stalls shoot jealous stares, and we feel guilty for not having large enough stomachs to buy something from everyone. We stuff ourselves and then leave when we can hold no more, averting our eyes as we go. Washing down the Arepas with a piping hot sweet coffee, we leave the racket and clutter of the building and navigate the muddy lane of puddles back in to the town.

Later that day, we leave for Cali. The next bus is bound northwest. The road between Popayán and Cali is sprinkled with the occasional small town, swathed in unbearable heat and engulfed by jungle that creeps over rooftops in an effort to reclaim what was once undergrowth. The bus arrives in one of these and I can sense, even from the bus windows, the prominent Afro/Caribbean feel of this place. The town is called Santander. The main street is clogged with foot traffic coming and going and alive with a riot of colour and a hum of noise. From inside the bus, I watch as a constant flow of human traffic flows past and there, to the right, an ancient wood-panelled bus is loaded way past a safe limit. Towering piles of bicycles, tyres, flour sacks, and anything else that will fit in the gaps are strapped down to the roof with frayed twine. Among all this chaos I spot a hive of activity across the road where a guy sits on his motorcycle in the shade of a tree. A steady stream of people approach him and hand him money, exchanging it for something I can't quite make out. As we pull away and pass by, my vantage point improves, and I see from above how he's handing out little bags of what looks like cocaine.

CHAPTER FORTY-ONE
CALI

We arrive from Santander into Cali's hectic terminal. With the heat baking the day to a crisp, a busy hum blankets the station as we make our way outside. Countless beat-up yellow taxis cough exhaust fumes while their pushy drivers fight for our business, loudly calling to us – "¡Ándale, muchachos!" – to jump in.

Now travelling as three, we squeeze into a late-80s Oldsmobile cab that barges into the busy traffic. The driver fits the description of the other taxi driver who drove us from the border to Ipiales. Staring at us in the rear view mirror, he has the same somewhat shifty look and cocky air about him. Although this guy, in contrast, is dressed to impress in a pink collared shirt and huge shiny watch on his wrist that he taps on his open window to the beat of the cumbia music blasting from the stereo. I turn to look out of the rear window in an effort to stop catching eyes with him in the mirror, and I see the stack of unsecured backpacks in the open boot – and there's mine, at the top of the pile, bouncing around like it's going to be thrown into the road behind us every time we hit a bump.

"¡Todo bien! ¡Tranquilo!" the taxi driver calls back from his seat, as if to reassure me. I keep my eyes glued to my pack, twisting my neck an uncomfortable 180 degrees until we reach our destination.

The cocky driver overcharges us and disappears before we have a chance to check if the hostel has vacancies.

"No hay," a small man tells us through a crack in his door. Fingering through the guidebook for other accommodation, we find an alternative a few blocks over. The place has a good vibe – a far cry from the 1940s-era German décor of Mikal's choosing. Tropical plants take up a fair amount of the space and a large spa pool sits sunken in the blue-tiled floor of the patio area. The owner, a tall, well-built German man, sits behind his desk in the main foyer. Yes, another German – but not of the garden gnome variety. He's married to a Colombian girl, and he's of a kind nature. We instantly take a liking to him, and decide that everything about this place beats the rule-oriented confines of the hostel in Popayán.

The weather is fantastic; a balmy year-round average temperature of 25 Celsius persuades us to spend a week here. Spanish lessons are advertised. I seize the opportunity and sign up for ten hours. My friendly teacher Leandro, a smartly dressed student with neatly combed dark hair, slots in two hours with me at the hostel each morning before he heads off to university. His limited English vocabulary works in my favour and his kind and patient nature while I stutter through sentences is more than reassuring.

During a morning class, Leandro stops when a beautiful olive-skinned girl arrives and drops her giant, loaded backpack at reception. We are distracted beyond words as she signs in and disappears off to a dorm. Later, she joins our group and quickly picks up the rules of Yanif, a card game introduced to us by an Israeli couple, whereby the players start with five cards and try to reduce their hands down to zero – the first one without cards declared the winner. Her name is Katya. Her humour, soft smile and personable nature are a welcome addition, and she decides to travel along with us for the next month or so. Katya is gorgeous, with long dark hair tied up in a bun, but she doesn't draw attention to herself, and she even fades in to the background against the women of Cali. They are all beautiful, each one more supermodel-perfect than the previous. Dreamy. Desirable and alluring: heavenly curves swaying as they sashay down the narrow streets, perky breasts desperately trying to escape from their tight fitting business suits that shimmer in the warm sunlight.

The main drag of the Zona Rosa – Avenida 6 – comes alive at night with neon-lit dens, their dance floors full of the goddess women gyrating curvaceous bodies to loud rumba and salsa music. For a week, we spend every night wandering this strip and drinking at various bars while beams of disco lights spin around the rooms blinding us. A small price to pay for the show, I reason.

The street outside is a different story. Hookers loiter, smoking cigarettes and bantering with prospective customers, while the homeless sift through bins and beg for money. One is particularly persistent. A short, dirty creature, wears only what I can describe as underwear fashioned from an equally filthy bath towel. He squawks at us, tugging at our clothes with his greasy hands and asking for money. He targets us every evening. I try to focus on the glamour and glitz of my single-minded focus, but he's always there, at the night's dirty edge.

Countless games of Yanif are played during our stay in Cali and virtually everyone who passes through the hostel has a go.

"Ello everybody! Wot's that game then?"

We look up to see a short, ebony-skinned guy smiling at us.

"I'm Harry, how are ya?" he continues in an urban London accent. "What's that game you playing then?" he repeats.

"It's called Yanif," Katya replies with a sultry smile that beckons him to sit next to her.

Obliging and squeezing onto the bench beside her, Dan passes the guy five cards across the table.

"Where you from?" I ask him, offering him the bottle of rum that's being shared.

"Well, I'm Nigerian but I live in Reading in the UK."

"No shit!" I blurt out, surprised. "That's where I'm from! All this way and I meet someone from the same place!"

"Oh, yeah?" he replies, seemingly far less surprised at the fact than I am. He picks his cards up and studies them. "I've just come out of the Amazon."

"Fuck, seriously?" Katya says.

"Yeah, we were staying in an eco-lodge," he says. "Quite a posh little place, all the mod cons and that."

Trying not to show what little interest I have in these types of excursions, I engage him further. "So what did you do out there?"

"Well, we had these organised group day trips, cruising along the river in a flash boat – they let us feed the monkeys and that."

I am sorry I asked. Our new card player relates his story for the entire game, telling his soul-less experience to a table of travellers who are clearly on smaller budgets and, more importantly, eager to finish the card game. A half hour later, we are still deep in the game and he's still droning on, enamoured of his own tale, when two more guys show up – and thankfully interrupt.

"Do you have any weed?" the taller one asks.

Slightly taken aback by his bluntness, but intrigued by his nature, we welcome him at the table along with his friend.

"I'm Elias," he says, introducing himself.

"Yeah, and I'm Ariel," his shorter friend adds, also sitting down.

We learn a little more about the newest members of our card group. Elias and Ariel come from well-off backgrounds, and they originally met while studying at a prestigious college in the US, and are taking a three-week break. Elias, hailing from Caracas in Venezuela, looks more Arabian. Tall, dark-skinned and with a bearded face, he divulges stories of how every member in his family has been kidnapped at some stage during his lifetime and held for ransom.

"I'm from Panama," Ariel tells us from the other end of the table. "And I'm glad! Caracas is gnarly."

We all laugh but he grows serious and repeats, "Caracas is gnarly."

"So you'd advise against going there?" I ask him, now worried about our loose plans of visiting there after Colombia.

"Well…," he begins with a wry smile. "Let's just say that Hugo has openly given the green light via national TV broadcasts that it's OK to steal from gringos."

He means the President, Hugo Chavez, of course. He means that Hugo is extremely anti-USA and that visitors are getting the brunt of his hostility directed at them. I'm not keen to try explaining to would-be muggers there that I'm actually *English*, as I'm not sure it'll sway their original intentions.

"So anyway," Elias backtracks in his American accent, "about that weed…"

"We haven't had any since Peru," Dan tells him in a defeated tone.

"Well, if you can round up 20,000 pesos between you – that's about 11 dollars – I'm sure I can go get us some."

We are slightly reluctant, due to only knowing him for five minutes, but we shrug and give him the money anyway.

"I'll be back in half hour," he says, disappearing out the front door.

Several card games later, Elias returns. Putting his hand down his shorts, he pulls a large plastic shopping bag out – and it's stuffed full of weed. The other hand produces a small bag of white powder from his front jeans pocket.

Waving the coke baggy in the air, Elias explains. "The guy was bagging a huge shipment when I arrived, and had no change for the 20,000 bill, so gave me this! All this for eleven bucks! Not bad, eh?!" he exclaims with a laugh.

"But how?! Where?!" we all ask simultaneously. We are astonished.

"There's a little street hobo who took me to a hooker that got a cab with me to the dealer's place in a neighbourhood that's well off-limits to white dudes."

"How'd you know to ask a street bum about drugs?" Dan asks.

"They always know." he says confidently.

"Surely not the little grubby guy?" I say to Dan.

"On Avenida 6 – short guy, wearing a towel?" I ask.

Elias grins. "Yup! How d'you know?"

My afternoons are spent studying the Spanish I've learnt in the mornings and getting stoned off the coke-laced joints with the guys in the gorgeous weather around the city. One afternoon involves a trip to the zoo with Elias and Ariel. The entertainment provided by two-toed sloths, huge crocodiles, giant fruit bats, screeching monkeys and the most incredible butterfly compound, all amplified by cricket song, are further boosted by the high of the numerous joints we've demolished. Rolling yet another one, we smoke it in the car park and walk back through the palm tree-lined fringes of the city to the hostel as the rush takes hold.

We arrive at the hostel to find Dan, Katya and Jan back from a waterslide park and are already warming up with a round of Yanif.

"So how was it?" Elias asks Jan.

Giggling, he looks over to Dan and bursts into laughter.

"What?! What?!" we ask inquisitively and laugh along with him.

"Well, zee tubes for zee water slides were for two people so Dan had to join up wiz different little kids! My president is zee greatest!" he laughs, gripping Dan on the shoulder. "In my country, we love zee children."

I'm hungry from the weed smoking but feel confined, and frustrated that I'm still lacking confidence to go out alone. I ask the others if they need to eat but the answer is no. I need to face my fear. I venture out into the darkness to get some food.

"Where you going?" the receptionist worriedly asks me. "It's not safe to go alone."

"I'm hungry, just going to the supermarket," I reply, trying to sound not nearly as scared as I am. She urges me to stay, but I am determined. I make my way alone to the main street but soon get lost in my thoughts and find myself in a maze of dimly lit backstreets. I put my head down and try not to look scared. I walk at a hurried pace. I'm relieved when I see, finally, an illuminated beer sign hanging above a door up ahead. I quicken my pace and arrive at an entrance below it leading to a small grocery store. Walking its few aisles and scanning the dusty shelves, I discover they are all half-empty and hold a limited range of anything edible. The round lady at the till gives me a look that clearly tells me she's unable to speak English, so I point at the last dried-out empanada limply perched in the warming tray and mutter a quiet "Por favor."

The return journey is no better. The streets feel darker and meaner. Now absolutely shitting myself, I retrace my steps back through the darkness. I pass under the dim orange glow of the street lamps and soak up my mouth's remaining moisture with the dry pastry. The sight of the hostel entrance is a relief and I smile at the receptionist when I am safe inside.

The dry empanada sticks in my throat and keeps me from uttering *Buenas noches*.

CHAPTER FORTY-TWO
CALI CONTINUED

Although Cali's weather is glorious, the extreme divide between rich and poor is noticeable wherever we go. The modern mall complex just a few blocks away from where we are staying is a prime example. Designer stores and perfume shops display items in their windows that even I find over-priced. These are surely only for a clientele of drug barons and dentists. The outside perimeter of the complex is surrounded by pushy Jamaican guys hiding behind sunglasses and gold teeth hawking fake name-brand cologne, jewellery and sports gear. As we approach the mall, there's nowhere to hide. They pounce on us.

"¡Hombre! ¡Amigoooo!! Look, look!" they tout, twisting their forearms back and forth showing us the string of shiny watches covering them. I haven't owned a watch since the nightclub theft in Cuzco, so just to shut the guy up, I pick a 'TAG' branded one.

"Twenty pesos!" he demands, through his silver grill of teeth.

"Ten," I haggle.

"Aiii, Hooombrrrreee," he fires back, rolling his r's and laughing. "¡¡Es de buen calidad, twenty!!"

Sure. Great quality. I know he's lying but I am loving the barter. We settle on fifteen and I escape with my new wrist piece, feeling like I've bagged myself a bargain. I wear it proudly inside the mall while window-shopping. A swing tag reads $120 for a Colombia football shirt. The shirt is authentic, but no comparison to the knock offs being sold outside. I leave empty handed, happy with my shiny new watch. Pleased with my bartering skills, I feel my new purchase has made up for the previous night's mission that ended with the pathetic empanada. I'm aware it's going to be a long road to becoming fluent in Spanish and not something I can master in five mornings at the hostel kitchen table, but I'm quietly pleased with my progress all the same. Pushing open the hostel door, I feel something click on my wrist. Looking down, the strap pin of my shiny new watch pings out and I watch in horror as it slips from my arm in slow motion before exploding into tiny pieces on the floor.

That afternoon we find ourselves being interviewed for an educational pro-Colombia kids' TV show by a young presenter, a girl by the name of Joanna who comes to the hostel with a two-man TV crew. Sitting outside the entrance of the hostel, she prompts us to tell the camera how much we love Colombia and what an awesome place it would be to live in. We end up with a Friday night invitation.

"Come to the bar where I work," she says after the interview.

"Hey, that sounds great, and it's zee President's birthday too!" Jan replies.

Friday evening arrives and the dance floor is alive with the gyrating hips of curvy Cali girls while the bar area is stuffed to bursting with university students, all waving notes desperate to get the attention of the staff. I spot Joanna working, but she's far too busy to notice us.

Since we landed in Chile over five months ago Dan has been focused on celebrating his birthday here in Colombia. Our time in Peru was cut short, in fact, for this sole purpose. In light of this, it comes as a great disappointment when, halfway through the evening, the guest of honour informs he's going back to the hostel to sleep. What brought this on, I never find out, but the fact that Katya left a half hour before could have pushed him to thinking that he was in with a chance with her. Never mind – his loss as the evening's just getting going, as far as we can tell. Harry, Jan and I meet some random but lively local uni students who want to continue partying when the bar closes, and we relocate the party to a small side street.

"I got weed at the hostel, I'll go get it!" I announce and run back to grab the bag. Elias' haul of weed is something we need to get rid of before moving on. Entering the dorm, hoping to catch Dan and Katya in bed together, I'm disappointed when I find them both passed out in separate bunks.

Back on the side street we smoke a stream of endless joints while the girls dance to the salsa blaring from the car stereo. *Dan would love this*, I think to myself.

Two headlight beams blind us as a car turns the corner at the end of the lane. The kids frantically hide their beer and weed thinking it's a cop car. As the vehicle slowly creeps towards us, the sound of bumping gangster rap can be heard. What is now a giant black SUV crawls next to us and a guy in a striped polo shirt leans from the window looking straight at Harry.

"Hey, nigger," he whispers, sneering as he passes by.

Before I can stop him, Harry loses it.

"Oi! Fuck you!" he shouts. "Get out the car and say it again!" He has his arms outstretched. The brake lights of the SUV brighten as it slows to a halt, followed by the white reverse lights engaging as it starts to travel backwards. Gulping and now feeling a little worried, we appear frozen in place. A hand appears out of the window, mimicking a gun shooting at Harry's head, and then the car speeds away and they disappear into the night.

"Come on, man, let's get out of here," I tell Harry, dragging him away while he curses and fumes. "Gracias guys!" I shout back to the kids, leaving them to dance the night away.

Back in the bright lights of Avenida 6, we stop at an empanada stall. Two tall slim hookers dressed in what I can only describe as latex bikini skirts and bras wobble precariously on block high heels.

"Heeellooo, sexy man. Oooo, sexy man, you love me? You love me?" one says in very bad English while stroking my face and fluttering her long fake eyelashes that stick out of sky-blue eyelids. Before I can answer, she grabs my head, pulls my face in and licks it with her wet tongue and big fat lips while cupping my balls and massaging them through her fingers. Looking over at Harry, I see he's being subjected to the same treatment. We share a worried look. Thinking quickly, we make out we have no money. They are undeterred and lead us to a park bench. They don't seem fazed at all by our lack of coin; they pull a couple of bottles of pure Aguadiente alcohol from their handbags. Sharing the booze with us, they ask for useful English phrases they can apply to their trade. I try to assist but can only think about where their mouths have been as we all sip the neat alcohol from the same bottle.

CHAPTER FORTY-THREE
BOGOTÁ

We rise in the early afternoon with Aguardiente hangovers and in no state to sort our bus tickets to Bogotá. There are still four large bags of weed stashed in the dorm and Elias has since left. But we can't take it with us for fear of being caught with it.

"Just stuff it under the mattresses, bro," Dan suggests. "Someone will be stoked to find it!"

I do as he says, putting one under each bunk before we make our way slowly to the station.

Ignoring the warnings about the recent spate of armed hold ups on the overnight bus routes, and heavily swayed by how cheap the tickets are, we decide to take the risk.

We load our beaten up backpacks into the belly of the bus, and it leaves the alienating concrete sprawl of Cali and heads north diving back into the deep green undulating wilderness. My allocated seat is next to a stout man in his fifties wearing a well-worn baseball cap and drinking an aromatic coffee from a Styrofoam cup.

"¿Como esta usted?" I test my Spanish.

He smiles excitedly and keeps me awake for the following two hours with a barrage of facts about his life. The Spanish lessons are starting to sink in, I can tell: by the time he has exhausted himself asleep, I know all of the fruits that grow in Colombia, the full history and geography of the country, and that his daughter is studying in Argentina, his nephew is working in England and he has a new TV in his house which is surrounded by miniature model motorbikes. His animated narrative is illustrated by a fuzzy photo on his tiny mobile phone screen.

While he and his conversation have captured me, Dan has assumed his usual position across the aisle. Like a slug dolloped with salt, he curls into an uncomfortably contorted twist of hairy arms and legs. He is not silent like a slug, however: he lets out a staggered series of loud piglet snores. Next to him sits an indigenous girl, dribbling on his shoulder and placing her baby, comfortably cradled among his hairy limbs, in a blanket.

Underneath dawn's heavy grey skies, we pass through windswept high-rise concrete estates that tower over the empty streets on the outskirts of the capital. Crisp packets and plastic bags blow around in the wind alongside the bus as we blast through the barren landscape. The city limits gradually fill with people on bicycles. Soon, hundreds of families ride alongside the bus. "Es Ciclovia," says my new friend in the seat beside me, now awake. He tells me it's a Sunday morning bike ride everyone gets involved in. This sight warms me, it's not expected after hearing of Bogotá's dangerous reputation. Seeing families enjoying weekend recreation together calms my anxiety somewhat.

A long row of yellow taxis outside the terminal all queue in orderly fashion while their drivers lean against their vehicles smoking cigarettes and chatting. The fares are a standard set rate to avoid competition and argument but the prices however are almost double to what we've previously paid. We decline and walk away.

A cry from behind of "¡Oye! ¡Venga!" turns our heads and a lone driver offers us a slightly cheaper fare. This turns the other drivers around him rabid, and is reminiscent of the dog fight scene all those months ago in Salta. We creep away while the rabble of old men shouting at each other with their hands in the air gains heat. We take the cab at the front of the line, paying full fare.

The driver sets us down in the heart of the city and we stand around our pile of backpacks surrounded by tall office blocks.

"¿A donde quieren ir?" a small gentleman in a tweed flat cap asks, inquiring as to where we want to go.

"Candelaria, por favor," Katya answers, telling him the name of the suburb our hostel is located in. The man shares a confusing reply of directions and Katya leads us off up a cobbled lane towards our new home.

As we traipse through the city, the surrounding area becomes more rundown, and we enter an old and crumbling but colourfully decorated neighbourhood. Candelaria, it turns out, is a maze of narrow streets and alleyways that are patrolled by the military due to its proximity to one of the city's slum areas. As such, it's yet another city quarter that seems prime for hostel owners. We've seen this all through Latin America: find a city slum and you'll find a dozen cheap hostels. Its walls and garage doors are plastered in graffiti and tagging.

The blue wooden entrance door creaks open and we are met by a cute receptionist.

"Hi, I'm Nikita, come in, guys," she says in a British accent.

Flicking through the guest book at reception is a soldier.

"Don't worry," Nikita assures us. "It's normal. They come and check our guest book twice a week due to the big numbers of overstayers who get caught up with cocaine."

"Really?" I exclaim, mesmerised by her eyes and perfect teeth.

"They bounce between hostels avoiding deportation."

The hostel is homely and inviting. I spot a cozy DVD room full of cushions while out back an open fire adorns one corner of the courtyard. Our dorm is spotless. Each bunk is made of solid timber beams and loaded with wool blankets. All these attributes are a warm comfort, considering the cold drizzly weather that's beginning to settle.

El Museo de Oro, Bogotá's gold museum, displays an extraordinary selection of pre-Hispanic gold, the biggest in the world. Modern lighting illuminates its remarkable collection of over 55,000 intricately crafted pieces. Worshipped gods and animals of gold perch inside spotless glass cabinets. The museum is located a short walk from a glass bubble cable car that transports sightseers up Cerro Monserrate, the large mountain that looms over the plateau at 3152m.

The glass sphere cable car drags us up the hillside and reveals the city below us as we leave the tree line that surrounds the base of the hill.

We rise higher and higher, the vast concrete jungle of modern day filling the view, trapped in a bowl encircled by giant mountains. It's breathtaking in its own way – and I'm glad we have a secure cable car and not the rusty bucket we used to hand-haul ourselves across the gorge back in Cielo Verde, Ecuador.

We alight at the summit and shuffle out into the sunlight with the slow-moving crowds of families, following the main path lined with trinket stores selling inflatable Power Ranger dolls and candy floss.

"Let's go this way," Dan suggests, breaking away to try and find the other side of the ridge.

Passing through a network of old rusty stalls where a few stray dogs lie scratching themselves and wholly disinterested in us, we reach a path that drops downhill through pine trees and out on to a ridge with a view looking into the dark green Andes towards the East. We choose a spot to sit down and enjoy the peaceful view. A couple of skinny grey horses wander in through the trees and lazily munch away on the long green grass. We lie back against the trees, far away from the chaos and crowds that scurry around snapping photos on the other side of the hill.

Back on the other side of the ridge, Dan and I somehow lose each other when I use the bathroom. Less than a couple of minutes later I return to find him nowhere in sight. I do a quick search and give up – no choice but to make my way down alone. I'm not relishing the thought of this, remembering distinctly that the route back into the city is a hotspot for theft and muggings. I sigh, silently cursing Dan for wandering off.

I step into the cable car and descend down the side of the hill. Different conversations run simultaneously as we drop towards the base, none too dissimilar to ones I might hear back home. From what I can make out, two middle-aged women are discussing price rises in their local supermarket and a couple of kids argue over a game on a mobile phone. I'm hoping these people are walking into the city; I'll stick close to them to avoid being a target for the thieves I've read about in the guide. At the bottom we spill out of the glass globe – and they squash themselves into a taxi and speed off towards the city.

Great, I think to myself.

The path that follows the street into downtown is littered with people the whole way – which reassures me a great deal. I'm even happier when I'm sucked into the lunchtime rush of university students. Ecstatic that I've got this far alive, I again test my new level of Spanish in a school supply store: I purchase a retractable pencil. And it's exactly what I intended to purchase. I exit with what I'd actually gone in for, and I procure it with no charades.

I walk the rest of the way back to Candelaria with a satisfied smile on my face and a new pencil in my pocket.

Dan is already back at the hostel when I arrive. He's smoking a joint by the fire out back with a short American guy.

"Dude! What's up?! We were worried about you!" the American guy says in his American way – as if we've met already.

"Where'd you go?" Dan adds, blowing a plume of weed smoke into the flickering flames.

"Nowhere!" I exclaim, confused. "I came out of the chapel and you'd gone."

"Oh, I just went and took a piss and came back and couldn't find you so I gapped it," he replies nonchalantly.

"Anyway, you're both here now!" the American guy interrupts in a lazy California surfer accent. "I'm Brian. Let's get stoned!"

The log-filled brazier turns out to be a regular meeting place during the cold drizzly week in Bogotá. Whenever we need a warm-up, we escape the climate with good company in the courtyard. Sometimes we watch DVDs in the cosy hostel; other times we sit and talk. It's a good week overall, and our down time recharges our batteries.

"Who's hungry?" Jan announces after returning with Katya from a day of walking.

"Yeah! Me!" Nikita shouts from the kitchen. "There's an Arepa stall down the street!" she says, putting on her coat and leading Jan out by his arm.

"See you soon!" she shouts with a wave. Twenty minutes later, there's a banging on the entrance door.

"Let us in! Let us in!! Quickly!!" comes Nikita's cry from outside.

Rushing to the door and pulling back the bolt, she jumps in, followed by Jan with his flip flops in his hands.

"What the fuck happened to you guys?!" Brian asks, startled.

"Shut the door!! *Now!*" barks Nikita, swinging it closed and sliding the bolt back across.

"Holy shit!" says Jan, trembling a little. "Zere was a guy viz a knife in zee dark doorway. I bashed it from his hand and ran barefoot all zee way back." He tries to regain his breath.

"He chased us back," Nikita adds also out of breath and exhilarated.

"Well, dudes," Brian pipes up. "Time to get stoned!"

Jan is clearly shaken by his experience with the mugger, but he is happy to be staying on in Bogotá due to the arrival of his fiancée from Germany in a few days. Yes, *fiancée*. We had no idea he was engaged until a month after meeting him, back in Montanita, Ecuador, where he'd stayed on to surf. He hadn't really mentioned her much, except when he'd disappear to phone her back in Germany every week or so. And I could never quite make out the meaning of the flirtation with Katya. But he seems genuinely happy about the prospect of his long-time romantic interest arriving to join the party – so we're happy for him, too.

I've come to appreciate Jan more and more, and it's a shame to be saying goodbye. His upbeat energy was at first slightly annoying, but since he arrived as a package with the *way* more irritating Mikal, his own tendencies to annoy have been considerably muted. In fact, he has single-handedly come to make our group happier, and more balanced. He's an excellent travel companion, and his company quickly grew on us.

But it's also time to move on so we will bid him farewell – but not before partying with him one last time.

Colombians don't need an excuse for a street party; they just have them, all the time, and every weekend seems to be another celebration of Saint This or That's day. Nikita invites us to join one. The jam-packed, music-filled, flag-lined streets that surround the hostel celebrate Bogotá's 471st anniversary with gusto. There are street food stalls, bands playing under professionally lit stages on every corner and joyous crowds of happy Colombians dancing the night away. These celebrations are a testament to the liberated attitude of the youth of this country – it's as if there's not a care in the world. Despite my worries over our safety as we drove into Bogotá, and even with Jan's near-mugging, I feel a sense of warmth towards this place. There's a peace during the street festival, a positive energy that seems a far cry from the atrocities associated with the internal conflict and drug trade of years gone by. This particular carefree air and positivity, however, seems to only be projected by the youth. The military presence and continuous news feed of violence is almost wholly ignored by the younger generation, now far more in touch with the rest of the world than their elders were at their age.

Still hungover and with bags packed after a lazy day smoking up with Brian in the courtyard and watching DVDs in the cosy cushion room, we head out to the terminal in the late afternoon light. We turn a corner and come to the main plaza and are startled to see it full of military police marching outside the court buildings, their white helmets lined up in neat rows, their guns strapped diagonally across their backs. This plaza was once the scene of a siege in 1985 by the now defunct M19 guerrilla group that resulted in 120 deaths on both sides. The city's huge military presence has been felt everywhere we've been during the past week, but even so it is surprising to come to them in formation like this.

We continue on and I reminisce fondly of our week here: rain, gold, the American, Nikita and the brazier. A young guy in blue running straight towards me breaks my thought. Before I can jump out of the way, he holds his hand up for me to 'high five' it. Obliging, I'm confused why he's approached me. He points at his hat and chants, "¡Millionarios!"

I'm wearing the same hat as him. A Bogotá Millionarios football team hat.

It takes some getting used to for any newcomer, this place they call Bogotá.

CHAPTER FORTY-FOUR
MEDELLÍN

The bus travels overnight from Bogotá, and we're hit with Medellín's morning heat as we squeeze into a small Japanese car doubling as a taxi cab. Our timing couldn't have been worse as the city's week-long annual flower festival has finished the day before our arrival – which means all of the hostels we try are fully booked. This unfortunately means we have no other choice but to try the party hostel advertised in our guidebook that we've been so desperate to avoid.

"There is new skate bowl near my sister house," the desk guy excitedly tells us, seeing our skateboards strapped to our packs when we enter reception. "You watch desk for ten minutes and I take your friend on my bike!" he says to me, pointing at Dan and already kick-starting his motorcycle.

"Back soon! I hope?" Dan calls back at us, clinging to the guy as they speed off down the road helmetless.

And just like that, we're left in charge of a hostel reception desk.

"Let's see if there's any coffee," Katya says, walking towards the kitchen area.

"But what about the desk? I'm supposed to watch it."

"Pff… come on," she replies, not even looking back. "It's 8am on a Sunday."

A percolator sits steaming on the worktop, but has been emptied of its contents and not switched off, while several lifeless figures shuffle around the kitchen and fire us unfriendly glances. One is making a mess of smearing butter and jam onto a half-browned piece of toast, while another rummages in the cutlery drawer trying to find a spoon for his bowl of cornflakes. The lounge area is just as depressing. More barefooted zombies lie sunken into the white leather couches, watching the violent horror film *Hostel* at full volume on the giant flat screen TV that hangs on the wall. *Oh, the irony*, I think.

Outside, at the rear of the building, a portable radio bounces salsa music around the walls of an empty swimming pool. A group of local women stand in the deep end, laughing between themselves as they trowel cement into cracks in the walls. Next to the pool is a straw-roofed bar where more flat screen TVs hang between the huge Union Jack and Irish flags that adorn the walls. This grotty little area, we later find out, is situated below our dorm and unfortunately plays football games on Sky TV from 10am to the early hours every day.

The dorm upstairs resembles one of those ship containers, run aground and spilling its contents all over the beach. The size of Grand Central station, it houses over twenty bunks surrounded by the contents of exploded backpacks spewing out into the middle of the room. The beds are still occupied by snoring backpackers tangled in the sheets while their arse cracks on full show munch on their underwear.

This establishment, a stalwart of the gringo trail, is a self-contained, fully serviced tourist attraction in its own right.

"I've bin 'ere for two weeks an' only bin out once for some fags cuz the machine was empty in 'ere," a lanky grey-faced lad tells me. "Wos the point if you've got everyfink right 'ere? Iss too hot to be walkin' around an' that anyway." He wipes his nose on his sleeve.

Taking all this into account, it comes as no surprise that the two Irish guys we met in Mendoza back in April have been residing here for over a month. Looking worse for wear and drinking beers for breakfast, neither of them remembers me from the hostel back in Argentina. Craig, the previous owner of the spotty penis, has obviously cured his problem as he is now dating the daughter of the family who owns the place.

"We're gun-ter set up a bar hurr in Medellín," he tells me through teeth that have got a hell of lot blacker since our last meeting. "Oi ain't going back to Ireland, oi love it hurr," he adds, boasting that they're the perfect couple to run such a business (*if she survives the STD he's now probably passed on*, I think – *and providing he doesn't drink all the stock, which is highly likely*).

Dan returns from his jaunt to the skate park with a windblown clump of hair. "Bro, it's mean!" he says convincingly. "It's practically brand new!"

So we escape the hostel with Katya in tow, retracing the route of Dan's motorbike ride on foot and following a main highway leading to a park. In the centre of it sits a brightly painted series of concrete bowls. Giant murals of parrots, dolphins and flowers decorate the bowl's surfaces while shirtless BMX bikers and skateboarders fly in and out of the curves. Jumping on my board, I take a turn and manage to carve my way in and back out of the bowls without pushing once, while Katya stands at the top happily snapping photos.

Losing control of my skateboard at one point, I watch as it flies out of a bowl and travels through the air heading at an unsafe velocity in the direction of a fat guy clutching a pump-action shotgun in one hand and a Rottweiler in the other. The board lands close to where he's sitting and startles the dog, and the man springs to his feet, tugging on the leash attached to his wrist.

"Venga hombre, tranquilo," the man tries to assure me, telling me to grab my board while snapping back on the dog leash and seating it.

I approach slowly and he asks where I'm from.

"¿De donde son ustedes?" he nods to all three of us, and since he's got both a weapon and a dog, we oblige.

"Nnnnueva Zelanda, y ella es de Suecia," I answer, stammering and shit scared of the dog who is now eyeballing me like it wants to rip my throat out.

"Vos y sus amigos. ¿Les gusta el porro?" he asks, curious to know whether we like weed and holding up a large joint between his thumb and forefinger.

I expect a repeat interrogation scenario from the bus road blocks back in the south of Colombia, so I carefully assess before answering. His offer startles me but I beckon the others over to join. Katya and Dan translate what he's telling them while we share his joint.

"He's the skate park security guard," Dan says.

"Is that really necessary?" Katya asks in Spanish.

"Si, chica. Esa parte es muy peligroso," he answers, exhaling and confirming that it's a dangerous part of the city.

Now pleasantly stoned, we return to the hostel tired, but unscathed. Various football games play on the TVs in the bar area, watched by the zombies. Katya calls a contact she's been given by an old university acquaintance back in Sweden and after a long conversation she arranges to meet him the next day.

"So who's the guy?" I ask her when she hangs up.

"A friend of a friend in Sweden," she says, shrugging her shoulders, as if to say that she knows him as well as we do.

Tagging along with her the next morning, we walk a couple of blocks to the train station. Round women in sun visors block the sidewalk with ice-cold chilly bins full of Coca-Cola while others sell cheap mobile phone cards. This scene out front is no different to any other train or bus station we've been to, but on entering through the sliding doors we step into another world. Tidily dressed cleaners mop the shiny polished concrete platforms, and digital screens that hang from the ceiling inform passengers of times and destinations. The rails hiss and a spotless air train glides to a halt alongside the platform. We board a train and sit down in clean seats and are soon whisked along the elevated rails into the heart of the city and to the university, where we are to meet the guy outside the entrance gates.

Standing in the archway in a wrinkled plaid wool shirt and jeans with a head of long dark hair that reaches halfway down his back is David.

"Hi, guys, how are you?" he asks us, hugging Katya and shaking hands with Dan and me.

"Good thanks," we answer as crowds of university students pass us.

"Do you have your passports?" he further asks.

"Yeah, how come?" Dan replies.

"You'll need them to get in to the university."

We enter a small black and white striped sentry box and show the guard our passports. He glances over them quickly and lets us pass. Wandering through corridors and across leafy courtyards with students rushing to their next classes, we soon find ourselves on the sports field. Like a scene from *Dazed and Confused*, it's dotted with drugged up students: hazes of weed smoke and students sitting under the large trees rolling up joints while others snort lines of coke off Frisbees. A school security officer patrols the perimeter of the field but seems to be deliberately turning a blind eye to the goings on around him.

"How much do you want?" David asks, presuming we want to buy some weed.

"Just enough for the next couple of days really," Dan says.

David holds out his hand – "Twenty is good" – and heads over to a group of students sitting under a tree with the note I've coughed up. In no time he returns with a small clear bag of what looks like very dried out weed. We leave the campus – *yes, that was university* – and follow him down a maze of backstreets that will lead to the hill that looks over the city. En route we stop at his favourite restaurant and he insists we order the Sopa de frijoles. A pretty waitress brings us three bowls of a thick, dark red soup and sets them down on the table with a dish of chillies. The bean soup is delicious, and we all savour the taste sipping it slowly while a tele-novela plays on the old television set hung on the wall with twine. We devour the last few spoonfuls of its silky texture, bursting with rich flavour and spices, and then continue our walk with contented bellies. A few blocks on we pass a black armoured van freshly smothered in exploded paint bombs.

"It's just come from a protest in the city," David informs us as we stare at it. "They happen all the time."

Crossing a busy roundabout with a huge yellow steel centrepiece of cogs and wires built by students of the university we've just visited, we begin to climb the grassy slopes of the hill. Halfway up David stops and sits down, urging us to roll up some of the weed we've bought. Tall pine trees grow out of the long green grass where we lie, and the joint is lit and passed around before we continue on up the incline. It's a surreal feeling and I'm glad we are in his company – sure that, if alone, we'd be arrested for choosing the wrong place to do such things. When we finally reach the top, we're greeted by the blue sky ablaze with hundreds of colourful kites dipping in and out of the airstreams, backdropped by the sprawling city which is encircled by the red-roofed Comuna slums that cling to the hills.

Suddenly, an errant kite dips and threatens to crash. It catches my eye and I dash after it heroically – only to land, with it, in a tangle of prickle bush. Passing the remains of the kite back to the grateful mother and child, I spend the next few hours plucking a line of long sharp thorns from my arm.

Dan chuckles, enjoying my pain.

Back down in the city, it seems the old buildings are slowly making way for tall beautiful modern architecture that slot themselves in between the existing edifices. I think back to Santiago, all those months ago. A perfect example is the strange Plaza de Cisneros and its 300 poles of varying heights, some as high as seventy-eight feet, that fill the sky like branchless trees. Such renovation efforts can be seen across the city, many of these funded by the money of the now deceased cocaine king Pablo Escobar. Smiling children kick off their shoes and dance in the water jets that shoot up vertically from the sandstone ground in front of the glass museum building while pedestrians cool themselves from the spiky heat through strategically placed mist sprays in the modern parks that burst with bright tropical flowers.

Dominating the sun-drenched main plaza are a series of tall chubby polished figures of bronze, sculpted by the artist Botero and backdropped by a giant cathedral constructed of brown and cream chequered bricks. Another of his figures sits on a concrete plinth in Parque San Antonio a few blocks away. The large 'Bird of Peace' sits buckled, twisted and destroyed, ripped apart by a FARC rebel bomb that exploded in 1995, killing twelve people and spraying many others with pieces of flying shrapnel. Another reminder that, despite the people of Colombia being the happiest I've met since the journey began, they've endured an extremely violent history.

Leaving the plaza to find somewhere to eat, we stop at a pedestrian crossing. A jolly old fellow takes a shine to Katya and insists on taking us to his favourite comedor. Her good level of Spanish and her gorgeous looks and beautiful smile seem to magnetise locals, and today is no exception. Finding a spot on one side of the stainless steel bar benches that run parallel with each other through the lunch spot, we eat a delicious hearty two-course meal of meaty goodness, accompanied by a fresh juice. The slurping sounds that surround us and the look of joy in the old man's face as he watches us enjoy our huge plates of food – all for under two dollars – is heart-warming, and a sure sign that he's brought us somewhere special.

David guides us back to the station and waits with us until the train arrives. Thanking him for showing us around, we board and watch as he disappears down the flight of stairs and back into the crowds of the city.

The hostel is in full swing on our return and our mood from the pleasant day strolling the city is soon washed away. Shirtless loud-mouthed louts talk in raised voices, while the disco lights in the straw-roofed bar beam across the flat screen televisions playing British football games. Hungry from all of our walking and keen to escape the noise, Dan and I take a stroll to a local kiosk that serves empanadas. As we approach it, a motorbike screeches up behind, startling us. Two policemen dismount the bike and approach us in haste.

"You smoke marijuana! We smell!" they say, interrogating us, sniffing our fingers and accusing us of smoking a joint. We haven't smoked since earlier with David, so we know full well they are trying to scam us. With no notes in our pockets (apart from the loose change for our empanadas), it soon becomes apparent they've picked the wrong gringos to try and extort money from. We know it – and they soon realise it. So our evening ends with a lecture, the police telling us not to wander the street at night before speeding away empty-handed.

CHAPTER FORTY-FIVE
CARTAGENA

Riding Medellín's air train one last time, we are carried silently to the bus station across town, gliding above the rooftops while we seal up our backpacks, ready for the next leg.

Three seats remain on the overnight bus so we purchase our tickets and make our way down to the waiting area. The absence of Jan has been noticeable since leaving him in Bogotá but Katya's presence has alleviated the problems between Dan and me and helped make a memorable stop in Medellín. Without Katya, I'm not sure how things could have turned out – she adds a much-needed balance that we just don't achieve as a twosome.

The spotless upper floor of the station is soon forgotten as we plonk our bags down on the greasy lower platform in front of a long line of giant buses with their loud warming engines filling the airspace.

We sleep the whole ride and arrive on the outskirts of Cartagena twelve hours later, where the bus comes to a halt in a dusty car park, the only building a half-white, half-blue concrete toilet block.

When we step off, the intense heat immediately hits us. And it's a shock after the cooler climate of Bogotá.

"Fuck!" Dan exclaims, desperately trying to take some layers off. "It's roasting!"

The thermals and puffa jackets we've wrapped ourselves in during the bus's air-conditioned deep-freeze climate are now complete overkill. "I've gotta take some clothes off before we get in another car!" I say, joining Dan and Katya as we do a fast striptease before we're cooked alive in the 40-degree heat.

A taxi skids to a halt. "¿A donde va?" the driver shouts, with his arm hanging out, tapping his hand on the door to the blare of his radio. He whisks us away through low-slung paint-flaked neighbourhoods reminiscent of Jamaican shantytowns.

Situated in one of the colourful but decomposing colonial Spanish streets, our hostel's faded blue façade sits squeezed between two grocery stores where fruit and vegetables spill out onto the pavement. The hostel's interior is cramped, with very little ventilation, squeaky beds and wobbly ceiling fans that circulate hot air. We spend no time organizing our bags and beds and step back out into the unknown to explore.

The narrow streets hang heavy with heat and are a hum of activity. African women loosely dressed in brightly coloured cotton throws walk at a snail's pace, balancing wicker baskets on their heads, while young boys ride ancient bicycles that carry fresh warm bakery goods on racks bolted to the handlebars. The intersections of these streets are particularly busy, with prostitutes standing and joking with policemen while shifty silver-toothed adolescents openly peddle weed and cocaine.

At the water's edge, the original walled fort town has been lovingly restored. Splashed in a brand new coat of paint, the oranges, yellows and light blue shades mask what once would have been a derelict and destitute area of the city; now, there's a sea of boutique jewellery stores and tat shops that peddle their wares within its high-walled perimeter and lure in tourists among the narrow lanes.

Dan, not one to miss a chat, is lured in by two guys Katya and I ignore as we pass by. Looking back after realising he's no longer with us, we see him arguing while the men raise their arms and shout back at him.

"For fuck's sake," I think out loud. "I fucking knew he'd stop."

As we turn to start walking back to him he shouts something at the men and walks at pace in our direction.

"Fucking idiots," he says when he catches up with us holding an ice cream. "10,000 pesos for a fucking ice cream."

Holding back the giggles, I try to help the situation. "Dude, it's only $4.50," I say.

But I know – we all know – that an ice cream really should only be 25c, possibly 50c in a tourist area like this.

Browsing through the scraps of paper that hang from the notice board at the hostel, I'm startled by someone calling my name. Turning my head, I see Peta standing in the doorway.

"Hey!" he says, looking around. "I made it!"

"Hey man!" I shake his hand. "Where did you come from?"

"I've been in Salento," he answers. "It's a small coffee town in the mountains."

"You wanna go here?" I ask him, pointing at a mini-van trip advertised on the hostel notice board.

"Sounds good," he replies, then leans in conspiratorially. "I need to be away from those two." He is referring, of course, to Mikal and Manfred. I am glad to hear they are still a few days away from re-joining us.

A small mini-van follows the coast road, passing blocks of tall white modern condos. "Apartamentos del familia Pablo," the driver calls out as we drive by. These regal buildings nestle in the hillside, reminders of the riches Pablo Escobar once controlled.

The winding road finally leads to a dusty car park where at the edge stands El Totumo – a mini volcano with a bottomless crater of warm mud at the top. It is accessed from a rickety wooden staircase gripping the side of the tall pointy dirt cone. Our group climbs to the summit and we submerge ourselves into an overcrowded bath of gloop, sliding in to the warm brown treacle between the other bathers. Suspended up to our necks like dinosaurs in a tar pit, we wallow for an hour or so before partaking in what I regard as the highlight of the tour: the beautiful girls who wash you off in the lake at the bottom for a dollar. Scooping up clods of the gloop from the lake bed, I smear more of it on me when mine isn't paying attention. I'm enjoying being washed by this girl. She laughs and rolls her eyes making me feel dumb for doing such a thing.

Returning to Cartagena, we watch from the van windows as miniature monkeys scuttle along the roof tops and swing in the trees of the little park.

"So what happened with Mikal then?" I ask Peta, curious as to why he's arrived alone.

"Ah, it's nothing," he answers diplomatically. "I just need a break."

CHAPTER FORTY-SIX
ISLA BARU

A poster in the hostel advertises an island called Isla Baru. It shows turquoise waters and white sand where dark-skinned Caribbean girls walk the shoreline balancing baskets of exotic fruits on their heads.

"We need to go here," Dan and Peta tell me, already decided.

So we board a small ferry down at the port, and are given yellow life vests for our safety. We slip alongside the naval fortress that once protected the city before sailing out into the sparkling ocean – and soon we leave the modern skyline of Boca Grande behind us. There isn't an empty seat on the vessel that's bursting at the seams with daytripping Cartagenans all decked out in stylish beach attire and ready to soak up the Caribbean island's alluring charm. Looking around me, I suddenly realise how much I stand out: I seem to be parading as a surf shop window display mannequin dressed by an over-excited teenager. And I instantly become self-conscious of my choice of garments. But in my defence, it must be said that, during this whole trip, I've only owned five t-shirts, a puffa vest, a rain coat and pants, the camo pants I bought in Argentina, various holey thermals and the ensemble that's about to unravel. The fire engine-red board shorts constructed from a plastic tarpaulin type material and emblazoned with giant Rip Curl logos that I'd scored for a bargain six dollars back in Mancora now seem like a remarkably bad idea. Paired with a white t-shirt, they'd perhaps not be noticed, but I've unwittingly dressed myself like a blind person in an assortment of eye-burning colours. A fake Colombian football shirt of an equally un-breathable bright yellow material clashes with an electric blue Bogota football cap, some cheap aviator shades and a pair of green flip flops that Dan made me buy after I'd found the mismatched ones back in Mancora.

What I was thinking when I had dressed myself this morning, god only knows, but this is to be my outfit for the remainder of the trip. And it is a trip that extends from a single night to eight.

Unbeknownst to us, the ferry makes a stop halfway at a smaller island clustered with straw-roofed huts. Disembarking, we're hassled by hordes of African shrimp sellers. "¡Camarónes! ¡Camarónes Camarónes muchachos!" they cry, rolling their r's and walking alongside us persistently while shoving their nets of squirming pink shrimp in our faces.

"Jesus, these guys won't let up!" I say to Dan, annoyed at the smell and edging away from them.

Fortunately they're only allowed so far and we're ushered through a gate into a marine sanctuary, where a couple of sad looking dolphins swim around in an enclosed area of ocean while the ferry passengers take photos. I leave the enclosure first, saddened by the spectacle but also forgetting about the shrimp men outside. Like flies to shit, they buzz around me again as I make a dash for the ferry.

The passengers reboard and the boat pulls away. I breathe a sigh of relief as the shrimp men retire to the shade of the coconut trees. No sooner has the island disappeared from view, another appears up ahead. A wooden jetty juts out from a white sand beach stretching as far as the eye can see in either direction. Palm trees sway lazily above a collection of straw roofs set out in rows. The white sand glistens.

"*This* is the Caribbean!" Katya remarks, smiling and stepping up on to the jetty among the droves of other passengers.

I scrunch the sand between my toes. It feels good to be here, good to be away from the city. Several huts offering accommodation line the beach and we choose one at the far end away from the crowd. Our new home consists of six hammocks under a straw roof – which sound delightfully romantic at first but I soon discover that sleeping in a hammock is both an art and an acquired skill. Only after two uncomfortable, fidgety nights of very little sleep, swinging like a pig caught in a snare trap, I learn lying diagonally across the length of the hammock is going to work best. The small wooden kitchen bench area is posted in front of the owner's quarters where he prepares our meals. This whole set-up sits about fifteen metres from the tepid, gently lapping, turquoise waves of the Caribbean. Our mornings are peaceful. Girls offer us fried corn cakes, shrimps and mangos from the baskets on their heads. We are living in the travel agent poster from the hostel.

The weekend arrives and the ferry dumps a writhing mess of daytrippers off at the jetty who set up stripy umbrellas and beach towels at a safe distance from us. We watch as they enter the water and are slowly carried down the shoreline with the current. Our serene ocean view is now a splashing and screaming mess of kids.

"I knew it was too good to be true," Dan comments on our first day, disappointed that our spot of paradise is so disturbed.

"No, I think all these people will go home on the ferry this evening," Peta offers. "It's just the weekend crowd,"

Three scantily clad women in silk sarongs appear from the crowd of beach goers and approach our hut.

"Hola," one says, smiling and taking her bowl from her head. "Masajes, masajes. Viente minutos tres dòlar."

"Three bucks for a twenty-minute massage," Dan translates, excitedly jumping up from his chair and lying on his belly in the sand pointing at his back. "¡Si, Si, por favor!"

I join him, and we both spend the next twenty minutes being caressed and rubbed by the girls' slippery hands while staring off out to sea, swathed in the scent of coconut oil.

"Anovva free bucks will get you an 'an job," comes a British sounding voice from above.

Standing over us is a pasty guy in his early twenties wearing a Manchester United bucket hat. "Not really wurf it tho – she weren't nat good."

Before we can reply – or tell him we don't need to hear more – he continues: "I came too quick."

"That's not really her fault, bro," Dave replies, bursting into laughter.

"Yeah, whatever, mate," the guy says before leaving.

"What a freak!" Katya laughs.

Just like Peta predicted, the ferry fills up and leaves the beach empty, save for a few crisp packets floating in the surf and the odd Coke can in the sand.

"I told you so," he says contentedly. "Now this is all ours."

And so we while away the days playing cards with Peta, staring at Katya in her bikini, swimming in the calm sea and drinking rum from coconuts. We watch from our hammocks as the military patrol the beach, regularly checking for weed smokers. We manage to avoid the patrols, following the example of our shifty Colombian cook, who spends his nights smoking copious amounts of the stuff, drinking rum and singing to himself in the shadows behind our hut. We know from watching his movements that smoking weed during the day will land us in a heap of trouble. Beyond that, we don't learn a whole lot from him. He's a filthy little man with the nature of an ex-con still on the run, and his moods swing like changes in the wind. We fear him a little, and mock him. Mostly, we find him rather sad. Each evening he scuttles up to us from his den behind the kitchen.

"I have dee cheekin or dee feesh," he repeats every single night, offering us our meat options and rubbing his hands together with dollar signs in his eyes.

We try to avoid him wherever possible. His only friends are an army of crabs that shuffle in at dusk and nip any rogue toe that wiggles under the table. There's also an undernourished cow that thinks it's fine to bump its way through our hammocks swishing its tail while we sleep.

On our final night, I'm woken by the swishing cow's tail in my face. The stars are shimmering on the water and I need the toilet, so I cautiously make my way to where we've been going for the past week. Not so much a cleanly maintained toilet block, but more of a series of granite caves in the coral rock face twenty metres behind the huts. The grey entrances are adorned by a thick layer of upside-down fruit bats hanging from their roofs. It takes some getting used to, and we've trained ourselves to go within daylight hours. A night mission for a poo is exactly that – a mission. I tear a few leaves from a bush and approach a cave entrance hoping not to disturb the bats. Piles of shit-smeared toilet paper lie in wait like landmines scattered randomly underfoot, and hundreds of crabs scurry across my path. Fearing for my unprotected nut sack being nipped by a claw or, worse, losing my balance and having to peel off the used, shitty toilet paper that's stuck to me, I quickly squat where I am, clean myself with the leaves and carefully run back to the hammock.

CHAPTER FORTY-SEVEN
CARTAGENA REVISITED

We stretch our stay to eight days, but the time finally arrives when we must return to the mainland. Not a word is shared as we wait solemnly at the jetty for the ferry. The palm trees sway along the white shoreline and finally disappear as we float away, and I wonder if I'll ever visit the island again – and how it will change in the future. With the hypnotic hum of the boat's engine, my mind wanders off into a reflective state, thinking back on all the places we've left behind and how different they'll be if we ever get to return to them. Progress, as slow as it is in this part of the world, is still apparent, though it occurs subtly in some places. Even more than progress – because sometimes I'm not sure it can be called that at all – is change. I wonder almost every day what a place like this will look like in another ten, twenty, thirty years.

Our previous hostel in Cartagena is full.

"Let's upgrade," I say, putting it to the others.

"There's a new one around the corner with a rooftop bar," Katya suggests, and I can tell by the way she's looking at us that she hopes we'll agree. We don't say no to Katya. I wonder if she knows it's actually physically impossible for us to say no to her.

The spotless yellow courtyard, blue swimming pool and white porcelain bathrooms of the newly opened hostel are bliss after a week of washing in the sea and shitting in the bat caves. Although a few extra dollars than we're used to, everybody seems quite content with a little extra luxury. The receptionist hands us each a set of fresh white sheets.

I make my bed with the crisp sheets in the spotless dorm and head to the bathroom for a clean up. "Ahh," I exhale, as the hot water jets wash away the beach grime and salty crust. I lather up a creamy bar of soap and smother myself.

And then…

"Holy fucking shit!" I shout in pain.

A burning sensation bites into my arse crack. Washing off the soap, I gently dab the area dry and twist in ways new to me in order to see the affected area in the mirror. It's bad. It's really bad. Red, raw and inflamed. Dressing myself, I'm baffled by what could have caused such a painful rash down there. Then it dawns on me. Although I've succeeded in dodging the piles of shit in and around the bat caves, I'm starting to doubt my choice in leaves that I wiped that last shit with on the island.

"That's it!" I say to myself, relieved but still in pain. "Poison leaves!"

It is both a relief and a misery to know what causes my discomfort. I'm glad it's something organic, at least – and not something contracted from a fouled toilet facility in the middle of paradise. But the butt crack agony continues for several more days while we search for a vessel to transport us to Panama – and for an ointment to sooth the poison jungle rash.

Back at the hostel, Jan and his newly arrived fiancée have caught up with us from Bogotá.

"Hi, I'm Linda," she greets us with a smile, showing off a perfect set of teeth. Cute, fair haired and stunning eyes; I'd expect no less, knowing Jan.

"Lovely to meet you," Dan says. "Jan has talked about you a lot."

Jan fires me a grateful look, knowing full well he's spoken very little of her.

"That's good," she replies, looking at Jan with what appears to be suspicious eyes, with Katya standing maybe a little too close to him.

My happiness at their arrival is soon changed when Mikal and Manfred appear behind them.

"Oh, hey, guys," I remark, in a tone that clearly shows how little interest I have in them re-joining us.

"Hi," they say, looking down their noses at me and pushing past, making a beeline for the Coke machine. Peta fires me a look that clearly says he's not overly excited about them arriving either.

The narrow roads that crisscross the old town where we are staying all lead to small plazas, most of which are centred around a church of colonial Catholic design. These urban spaces, though lazy and deserted during the heat of the day, become a hive of activity in the evenings. Orange streetlights illuminate families in rocking chairs that block the sidewalks while portable radios push happy melodies of salsa and cumbia music through open windows and out into the streets.

The plaza situated closest to our hostel is alive with children playing and chasing each other while the crumbling concrete benches are occupied by teenage couples locked in each other's arms, whispering sweet nothings. Our group now reunited, we purchase a few beers from the store and park ourselves up in the plaza to catch up from where we left off in Popayán. Mikal brags about how much he enjoyed his trip to Salento; he regales us with minute details from being shown the coffee farms. Peta fills me in with the real story.

"He was being himself again," Peta recalls, leaning in to tell me quietly about the trip. "Too loud in such a quiet village."

"What happened?" I ask, waiting and hoping for some juicy gossip.

"Well, he was talking to some girls for too long and some local guys didn't like it. The family we stayed with said it's probably best to leave."

Before I have a chance to laugh, I'm startled when a petrified cat runs through the plaza with two tin cans tied to its tail that clatter and bounce off the road, making more noise the more it tries to shake them off. It's closely followed by a group of laughing kids, who disappear after it into the darkness down another street across the plaza. As the shrieks of the kids fade into the distance they're replaced by shouting and screaming. Turning our heads, we see two young women fighting each other, pulling hair and throwing punches, down another street nearby. The fight is a vicious one and neither of the girls is ready to back down. We watch dumbfounded as clumps of hair are pulled out and blouses are ripped, baring plump breasts supported in frilly bras that bounce around while the two women scratch and kick each other. Eventually they tire and disappear back into their houses and the humid still night air becomes quiet again. Such is life in urban Colombia.

The evening signifies the end of the road with our whole group. Jan and Linda are retreading our footsteps and heading over to Isla Baru while Peta also bids us farewell. He won't be making the Caribbean crossing and has found a voluntary placement in a hospital in Medellín where he'll gain valuable points for the doctorate he's studying for in Germany. Mikal and Manfred will be heading to Central America but are staying on in Cartagena for a few days in a hostel in a different area of the city so we won't be seeing them again. As for Katya, she's bound east for Santa Marta before ending her trip in Caracas, Venezuela.

After almost three months of travelling as a group with the people we've met along the way, Dan and I will once more be back to two. I'm hoping we can get along without our previous companions. Security in numbers, they say. In our case, the extra people have provided great help – even if they didn't know it – in diffusing our frustrations with each other. Now, it's up to us to make it work.

At least my arse has stopped itching.

CHAPTER FORTY-EIGHT
CAPTAIN FRITZ

The Pan-American Highway vanishes in the north of Colombia, swallowed by a vast thick jungle known as the Darien gap, a dense forest controlled by drug cartels and the FARC rebel forces with an almost impenetrable access to Panama. Although it *is* possible to get through, we opt for the more expensive and far safer choice of sailing with an able captain and ship across the Caribbean to the Panamanian east coast. A leaflet on the hostel notice board advertises a large catamaran that makes the trip regularly, though the price of $270 US each seems a tad extreme.

"We can find cheaper," Dan assures me. "Let's go down to the marina and talk to some captains."

Tall masts gently creak and sway with the tide that swells under the wooden jetties and gangplanks. We search among the moored boats in the marina, looking for someone who can take us to Panama.

"Hey!" Dan calls out to two fishermen who appear from the back of a boat carrying a fish bin of live crabs. "¿Ustedes saben alguien que tiene barca para Panama?" He is sure he can find a boat willing to take us.

The fishermen advise us that captains who do provide the service advertise on the hostel notice boards in the city. We leave, relinquishing our efforts at the dock to pick up where we left off at the hostel pin board.

Fort San Felipe once guarded the city from the countless pirates that sailed the seas, eager to get their hands on the gold and silver the Spanish were mining from the Americas. Defeated by the captain hunt at the marina, a visit to this fort is in order. A long wide path leads uphill to its arched entrance and the naturally air-conditioned temperature shuts down the intense heat of the day as we enter the cool musky interior of sandstone rooms. Climbing a flight of narrow stairs in the cool depths of the castle, we are glad for the respite from the midday heat. But at the top we are once again blinded by the harsh light of day and thrown into the sun's rays as we step out onto the roof.

Gun battlements and crumbling turrets surround us. Giant corroding cannons sit lifeless on rusty wheels, poking out through the slits in the curtain walls and aimed at the shiny skyscrapers of Boca Grande that now occupy the skyline. We inspect the cannons and the walls, and head back down into the depths of the fort, descending into the basement. A vast, confusing labyrinth of low-roofed tunnels constructed of cobbled red bricks sit underneath the fort. Claustrophobic, waterlogged and dark, they are not for the faint of heart. We pull out our head torches and follow the passages past where the lights end and into the unknown.

It crosses my mind to wonder why the hell we're doing this and what we expect to achieve or find down here – when suddenly we're knee deep in cold water. "It stinks!" I shout, turning around and ushering Dan back the way we came. The smell of stagnant seawater we've stirred is putrid.

He illuminates the tunnel with his head torch. The roof is just inches above our heads. With soaked feet squelching and our hands feeling along the mossy wet walls, we thankfully emerge into a lit passageway where a small flight of steps leads up to the light of day. Our pointless mission goes unmentioned.

We leave the fort and reach the bottom of the entrance path, where a group of pushy sunglass salesmen swarm around us and block our exit.

"¡Gafas, amigo! ¡Gafas baratas! ¡Compre! ¡Compre!" they say persuasively, trying to put sunglasses on our heads. I'm instantly taken back to the hustling of the watch salesmen outside the supermarket in Cali, and I take charge, buying a pair for a mere five bucks. I'm pleased that this solves the problem, quite instantly, and sends them all running to pounce on their next victims.

Back at the hostel, a few other travellers are sitting in the common room. A shirtless old leathery-skinned man with a tan like burnt toast and a pot belly hanging over his shorts enters and greets us.

"Hi guys!" he says in a thick Austrian accent. "I hear you want to go to Panama?"

"Well, yeah, we do," I begin. "But we can't find a captain, and the Fritz the Cat boat that's advertised on the board is too expensive."

I can tell by the look he gives me that he must be the captain of the boat.

"Before you start sinking my price is too much," he says in his humourous European accent, "I haf to tell you some sings."

He speaks in a fatherly tone. His safety briefing is smattered with sexist jokes and, although I am slightly taken aback by his humour, his confidence and maritime experience is swaying me to go with him, and I think Dan feels the same way.

"Just last veek, three guys who had sailed vis an inexperienced captain had to pull zair own mutiny," he tells us. "Zee guy was drunk zee whole time and got zem lost at sea."

"So what happened?" a young blonde girl asks from her seat in the corner of the room.

"Zee guys had no choice but to tie him up and sail zee boat back here," he says, shaking his head. "All for a few dollars less, ven zey could have sailed in comfort vis me." Fritz sells his trip, beyond his assurances of experience and safety, with promises of fresh fruit, fish and a diving trip with some of the Kuna people that inhabit the San Blas islands en route.

"I'm in," Dan says.

"Me too," I agree.

"I vill see you here at 11am tomorrow," Fritz tells us. "Bring $270.00 and your passports so zat I can get our supplies and your documents stamped out by immigration. "Vee sail zee day after tomorrow."

CHAPTER FORTY-NINE
CARTAGENA CONTINUED

"I need cash for myself as well as the $270 for Fritz," I say to Dan over coffee and fruit at the hostel the next morning.

"So?" he grunts moodily, not having smoked his morning ciggy yet.

"Well, it means I'm gonna be running the gauntlet from the bank with five hundred bucks, and the route back to here isn't exactly the nice part of town."

"Not much we can do about it really though," he replies, slurping from his mug. "We'll be fine."

Walking to the bank in the stifling heat, I'm extra observant of the people we pass, trying to figure out which ones to avoid once I'm loaded with cash and making the return walk. Although I've pulled money out in every country so far, it's never been an amount as big as this and paranoid thoughts race through my mind. Three women sat behind their street stalls under low slung tarp shades smile at us. *Do they know we're going to the bank and are they going to set up a trap for us on our way back?* I think to myself. *What about those guys hanging out in the park chatting? Will they ambush us on our return route? So many tourists probably make this route to the bank.*

"Bro, are you OK?" Dan asks me, breaking my thoughts and interrupting my far-away stare.

The security guard at the door of the large air-conditioned bank asks us to take off our hats and sunglasses and points to a row of seats, much like a doctor's waiting room. We sit down quietly and wait our turn until a teller becomes available and we both go up together to draw our money.

"¿Cuánto quieres?" she asks, wanting to know the amount.

"Cinquenta," I burst out before Dan can speak.

"Quinientos," he corrects me.

"!¿Cuanto?!" she asks, in a surprised tone.

Dan explains about the boat trip.

"Ahh, OK," she says, handing us back our passports. Counting out the cash in front of us raises my paranoia. I can't help but wonder who's going to be waiting for us outside. Stepping out of the bank, I survey the area like a hawk but nothing seems untoward. "For fuck's sake," Dan says, now becoming annoyed at my bullshit. "Come on."

The return route is peppered with potential muggers and Dan's pace quickens. My paranoia has spooked him. I grip the envelope in my pocket the whole time.

"Halloo effrybody, so glad you could make eet!" Fritz says, still shirtless and counting the wad of notes we've just given him. "OK, vee'll meet at the marina at 10am tomorrow. You'll have no problem finding me: you cannot miss my beautiful catamaran."

Travellers of all shapes and sizes pass through the hostel during the afternoon while we watch from the comfort of our hammocks. Some check in, some check out, while others stop by to visit friends. As the sun sets, the rooftop bar of the hostel opens and our last evening in South America begins.

A longhaired English guy orders a beer and introduces himself. "Rupert." He tells us, shaking our hands. The bar commands amazing views of the Fort we had visited yesterday and is now floodlit in an orange glow.

"Alright, fellas? How's things?" he politely asks in a posh accent.

"Yeah, not bad," Dan replies.

"Yeah, good," I add. "It's our last night in South America."

"You fellas will be keen on a few lines of coke then?" He speaks with an insistent tone.

Downstairs in his room, he chops up four rails of a yellow / green looking powder.

"You sure that's coke?" I ask him.

"That's what the guy that sold it to me said," he replies nonchalantly, rolling up a Colombian bank note. "It seems to do the trick."

Vacuuming a couple of the lines up through the bill, I wait for the desired effect – but all it leaves me with is a headache, a sting in my nasal passage similar to what I'd experienced on my arse after the poisonous leaf incident and a dick that is terribly hard to find when I go to take a piss. Standing over the toilet and looking down at my penis, I am rather surprised to find that it closely resembles a roasted cashew nut.

Hitting the streets with a stinging buzz from Rupert's 'coke', we pass the doorways where the prostitutes lurk. "Hey baby, hey gringo baby," they whisper at us as we walk by.

I have a good chunk of money hidden in my shoe and wonder if I've got the balls to use it with one of these women on the way home. It is my last night in South America, after all. The night is a failure of empty nightclubs and headaches from Rupert's powder and my efforts to pull a local girl are pathetic. Even the doorways where those voluptuous ladies previously stood with their wares on display are now all empty. And so, I arrive at the hostel feeling miserable, frustrated and defeated.

But, ever the optimist, I chuckle as I drift off to sleep picturing how ridiculous I would've looked with my pants down standing in front of a woman laughing at my little shrivelled cashew nut.

CHAPTER FIFTY
FRITZ THE CAT

Our final breakfast in South America is of the usual standard that is included in the price of the room and only slightly varies in choice from country to country. Starting off our trip in Santiago, we had been served the pancakes accompanied by strawberry jam and coffee every morning (there was even a gluten-free option). This admittedly became a little boring after five days but looking back now I reckon it was probably one of the better breakfasts on our whole continental journey. Argentina and Uruguay would serve coffee, tea and generally bread rolls, butter, and jam, with a pot of Dulce de Leche, a caramel type spread that's part of the national diet / heritage. A sweet treat, yes, but not substantial enough to satisfy the morning hunger for more than a couple of hours. As a rule, breakfast wasn't included in the price of our lodgings throughout Bolivia, but considering that a generous plate of beans, eggs, tortillas, a juice and the odd wafer-thin slice of steak, would cost no more than a dollar, we had the opportunity to hunt out a different street eatery daily and in turn delivered memorable experiences. How fondly I look back and recall the old toothless man in the tin shack place in Coroico. Peru and Ecuador usually included our morning meal in the price, but even there we mostly opted to hunt out a street stall where the food would be hot, fried and tasty, rather than fighting for the milk to drench the already stale cornflakes and slurp weak filter coffee. And topping our trip is Colombia's food, which is, in one word, hearty. The breakfasts of Arepas, served with beans and eggs, would keep us going until early afternoon. The heat of the day was strong enough to quash the most ferocious of appetites but the huge lunches, like the one we ate with the old man in Medellín, were sufficient to fill even the fattest blimp to bursting.

Thus, after polishing off a rainbow of succulent fruits at the café across the street, I sit back and enjoy my last breakfast: an Arepa, placed in front of me with a fried egg on top. I chew slowly, savouring it and washing the last remnants down with a sweet piping hot coffee. Dan does the same, only I can't tell if he's enjoying his meal half as much as I am. He seems to be in a hurry to go.

We bid farewell to our hostel and take our leave. I feel change in the air. With packs on backs again and moving on for what feels like the millionth time, Dan and I trudge down to the marina and head over to the others who've signed up for Fritz's passage, already sitting at the edge of the berth.

They are as follows:
    Alina, posh English girl, 19.
    Kevin, Kiwi dentist, 28.
    Dave and Kate, Australian honeymooners, late 20s.
    Teren, Egyptian gynecologist, 21.
    Richard, Australian student, 21.
    Martin, recently redundant Dutch nuclear physicist, 26.
    Julian, South African student, 22.
    And Dan and me.

The thirty-two-foot catamaran bobs at the dock. 'Fritz the cat' is written along the bow next to a picture of Felix the cat. Hanging nets are stuffed to bulging with fruit and vegetables and several chilly bins sit on the deck full of beer and meat. Fritz clambers over the vessel checking lines and hatches, readying to set sail.

The voyage begins when Fritz unties the thick line from the berth, and we drift out into the current. On our way out of the harbour, we pass a group of dark-skinned shirtless locals paddling dugout canoes in slow motion while surrounding them in the bay are multi-million-dollar super yachts anchored by the dozens, swaying gently from side to side.

And so, we leave Cartagena for the last time and sail into the sparkling sea, the mirrored buildings of Boca Grande and the anchored yachts in the bay gradually disappearing in the wake behind us.

The initial scramble by some of the group to pick the best beds is all wasted energy, as the nets spanning the front of the cat quickly become the most popular spot to sleep to avoid the hot claustrophobic cabins below deck. They also provide a great place to lie down in the shade of the sail while the ocean spray cools from below. Fritz's first mate, the thin boy we watched preparing the boat for sail, introduces himself as Jason, and balances his time between smoking weed, prepping meal ingredients and staring at the girls in their bikinis.

"¡Propina! ¡Propina!" he asks daily with his hand out, harassing for loose change, only to be denied again and again.

This has no effect whatsoever on deterring him; he persistently asks each day during the week at sea.

The stern of the cat is home to a sheltered dining table; this is also where Fritz sits in his customised captain's chair and controls the helm. Countless card games are played over animated conversations. At first, the chatter is friendly and full of genuine interest, but it slowly changes in tone as the days go by. Fritz must know these scenarios, and even the conversations, from memory by now, after thirteen years of ferrying travellers between the two countries.

The first person who undergoes a visible change is Richard, a scruffy Australian who has decided to take a break from his friends; they've chartered a similar boat but Richard needs space.

"They were doing my head in, and the boat they went in wasn't as nice as this one," he says, scratching his beard. His happy outlook changes, however, soon after leaving when he loses a petty argument with Kevin the dentist – who happens to be from New Zealand. Kiwis and Australians have been at odds since their countries have had Europeans staring across the Tasman at each other – and will be until the world's end. Richard's argument with Kevin is a classic example of the Aussie-Kiwi conflict.

"The Aussies are gonna take it," Richard says, aggressively.

"I think you'll find that you're wrong, mate," Kevin replies calmly, seemingly perceptive about his approach to the argument – taking in how the relaxed way he is going about badgering his opponent is only winding the younger Richard up more.

The heated discussion continues for some time – and ruins their afternoon when Richard storms off to the other end of the cat and sulks for the rest of the day.

Of course, the topic at hand is a Rugby League game being played today back in New Zealand – what else could get these two so riled?

"Well, I don't know about you guys," Alina pipes up, with her bushy blonde hair blowing in the breeze. "But I think rugby's a bit of a stupid game anyway." She drapes her bikini-clad figure across the back rail of the dining area.

Although lovely to look at, Alina is a tad precious. With a plummy accent that only comes from a posh British upbringing, she consistently verifies this every time she opens her mouth.

Between them, Fritz and Jason do an amazing job with the meals and our first dinner served is a succulent barbecued steak accompanied by rice and white beans.

"Zis is your last red meat for a week," Fritz says, chewing on his lump of steak. "Seafood from now on!"

During the nights while Fritz sleeps we are all assigned an hour of watch to look out for any boats that may obstruct our course. The most difficult part of this task is waking up the person after finishing your own stint. My shift occurs from 3am to 4am and I'm woken for this by Alina tugging on my arm. Sitting out over the front as the lightning storms off to the east flash and light up the huge starry sky, I watch my feet dangling over the waves, phosphorescence trailing behind. I listen to the engine humming below deck as the cat's hulls slice through the water with a hobbyhorse motion, bobbing front to back. Flying fish skim above the surface with a flutter, travelling for over fifty metres before plunging back into the sea, the unlucky ones landing with a slap on deck every once in a while as they miscalculate their flight. At the end of my hour, I return below. I'm fortunate I don't have the task of waking Dan to take over from me, especially after the experience of trying to get him up back in Buenos Aires when we were late for the ferry to Uruguay.

"Teren! Teren!" I whisper. "Your turn, mate."

Teren groans and slips down from his bunk and heads up to keep watch. But I'm unable to sleep, so I keep him company during his shift on deck.

"So what brings you here?" I ask him, curious of his story.

"I'm studying gynaecology in the UK, and got a work experience placement in a hospital in Ecuador." He pauses. "That's all over now though, so I'm having a holiday for a couple of months."

"Cool, man." I reply, interested to know more. "How was the hospital in Ecuador? Did you have to treat any nasty cases?"

"Yep," he says with a grimace. "The ones from the jungle all think that god will help them and refuse to take the pills that are prescribed. This one chick had the worst puss infected wound down there and still took her priest's word over ours that god would heal her pain and that the pills were evil." He sighs, then continues. "It's hopeless trying with some of them."

Leaving him at the bow, I lie back in the net and drift off to sleep.

Waking the next morning, we're surprised to see a large billed bird with huge grey, webbed feet standing on the deck surveying us. Surrounded by the pecked remains of the flying fish that never made it across the boat during the night, he looks content, not bothered one bit by our presence.

"Hey!" Fritz shouts, raising his hands in the air. "It's a booby!"

"A what?!" we all ask, giggling. "It's a grey-footed booby. He's lost." Fritz points off to the East. "He's on his way to Venezuela. He'll be tired."

Two days into our voyage and Dan's cheek has inflated to the size of a balloon. It's his rotten tooth – one he's ignored for the past two weeks. It has now come to bite him on the arse. Or, the gum.

"Haf yer go' anyfin vat can help?" he asks Kevin, sounding like Quasimodo and hoping the dentist will have a solution to his pain.

"Alcohol will help keep any infection at bay," says Kevin. "That's all I can suggest, mate." Then he adds, seriously: "It will need to be attended to when we reach Panama. I'd say it'd be best to just get it pulled."

"I'm gonna drink as much rum as I can and hopefully it'll ease",

Dan decides confidently. I roll my eyes, not sure he's really much of a self-treating patient. But sure enough, the swelling does reduce over the next few days while his head swims in alcohol.

The booby, meanwhile, sticks around for another night, gobbling up any food scraps we throw his way but always keeping a safe distance from us. The following morning he's nowhere to be found, obviously back on course for Venezuela and humming on a refuelled engine.

CHAPTER FIFTY-ONE
SAN BLAS

Just off the southeast coast of Panama, tall coconut palms sprout from a collection of idyllic Caribbean islands known as the Archipelago de San Blas. Ringed with white sand and surrounded by turquoise water, they are postcard perfect. Anchoring just offshore from an uninhabited island, we dive from the boat and feel the Caribbean's cool refreshing water for the first time since being at sea. Crystal clear water provides an amazing view below the surface as brightly-coloured fish dart all around us, the white sand seabed just metres below. The coconut palms bend out over the shoreline and cast large areas of welcoming shade with their giant leaves.

"Let's walk around the island!" Alina suggests excitedly.

"What's the name of this island?!" I call over to Fritz, who's untangling the wire of a fishing rod.

"Fritz Island!" he says jokingly. "No names, zey just islands." He doesn't look up, still focusing on the tangled fishing wire.

"Lunch vill be ready ven you get back!"

The island is of a long thin shape, much like a cucumber, and looking through the trees and vines that grow from its middle, it's easy to see the beach on the other side. Reaching the end and following the shoreline around, we are met with a sight that instantly transforms this idyllic place – a place we believed to be so different from the polluted cities that we've travelled through. A bubbly foam, off-white in colour with a disturbing brownish tinge, froths back and forth in the lapping waves while plastic drink bottles with their labels torn off lie embedded in the sand.

"Ewww!" Alina shrieks as she navigates her way through the petrol cans, frayed rope and other discarded bits of boat debris that litter the tiny beach.

"Fuck, this is bad, bro," Dan says, tip-toeing through the trash and opening the door of an old microwave oven in the sand.

We circumnavigate the island and swim back to the cat and find Fritz, who is frying up a box fish that he's caught with a spear gun.

"Ahh! Here dey are! My passengers!" he shouts, serving up the fish in a sauce he's concocted from onions and white wine. "Sit down! Let's eat!"

During lunch I get to know Julian, the South African, a little more. "I'm mid-way through my studies," he begins. "Yeah, really just here for the diving, although I'm open to anything else of particular interest that comes along. I'd like to see some Mayan stuff in Guatemala," he adds in a blasé manner while sinking a beer.

The discussion changes to the rubbish washed up around the other side of the island, when the splutter of an outboard motor interrupts us. A thin, dark-skinned man wearing a tatty sailor's cap floats up alongside us in a dugout canoe, and, reaching up with his long bony fingers, pulls himself aboard.

"Alfonso!" Fritz says, greeting him and shaking his hand. "How are you, my friend?!"

"Hola, hola, everything good," Alfonso replies, looking at the girls in their bikinis.

The indigenous Kuna tribe, a short statured race, own and inhabit these islands. I remember a picture in my guidebook showing a woman with painted face, gold jewellery and arms and legs wrapped in orange beads. Judging by Alfonso's board shorts and old polo shirt, I'm guessing the men aren't so worried about tradition. Their main source of food is from the ocean, namely king crabs and lobster. They've developed a useful skill for procuring their meals: able to dive down to depths of twenty metres while holding their breath, they forage the ocean to put food on the family table. In light of this skill, the Panamanian government has banned them from using oxygen tanks; this is done to protect the marine life, since, aided with any form of breathing apparatus, fisherman would soon eradicate all sea life from the depths of the ocean that surround these islands. Intermarrying with other races is heavily frowned upon amongst the Kuna, in order to preserve their culture. Their ramshackle villages sit on cane stilts constructed from bamboo, palm leaves and jungle creepers.

Every coconut that falls on the islands is their property. The captains of all the charter boats have good relations with them, bartering rice and other goods from the mainland countries of Colombia and Panama.

"I have some customers for you!" Fritz says, turning to us. "Who wants to catch some king crabs with Alfonso!? Five bucks each and you get to keep everything you bring back."

The honeymooning couple and Alina stay behind with Fritz while the rest of us squeeze into the wooden log canoe. "Here!" Fritz shouts, tossing masks and snorkels into the already jam-packed boat. The ocean becomes dangerously close to spilling over the sides and sinking us. Unperturbed by this, Alfonso fires up the outboard and we lurch forward and out to sea, holding on to our hats.

"Alla!" Alfonso yells over the din of the motor, pointing at a pile of bamboo sticks in the bottom of the boat.

We pick them up and untangle the fishing wire loops at the end. On inspection, they seem to be some sort of pulley lasso

"¡Para las Jaibas!" Alfonso shouts.

"For the crabs!" Martin translates, adjusting his glasses. "Crab lassos!"

Twenty minutes of gasoline fumes and waves crashing over the sides of the canoe, and we arrive, it seems, at the place to dive for king crab. The engine slows to a putter before shutting down, leaving us bobbing in silence. Looking around, I see we are in the middle of nowhere: there's nothing in any direction but horizon.

Alfonso urges us to slip backwards off the boat's edge and into the water. I spit into my mask and clear it with sea water. I pull on my fins. Dan and I clumsily clunk off the side, bashing our legs as we tip off the edge and plunge backward in to the ocean – which means we miss the palaver behind us regarding the others leaving the vessel. When I land in the water, I am stunned – not so much by the salt water stinging my arse rash still lingering from last week but by a whole world of stingray, trumpet fish, barracuda and other curious-looking fluorescent sea creatures swimming through the rays of light in a whirlwind of colour. Where I don't see fish there are coral of oranges, greens, yellows and every single shade of blue imaginable, all reflecting under the surface as the sunlight cuts through the deep water like laser beams. The sheer size of the coral formations and their multitudes of colours is something I have never seen before. The wonders of the underwater Caribbean take my breath away.

We glide along the surface, looking below us and periodically diving down to look more closely at fish and coral. Then the coral floor beneath us suddenly gives way to sheer cliffs that fall away to a dark bottomless abyss, while countless crevasses disappear behind walls of kelp, silently swaying in the underwater currents. Everyone in the group manages to submerge a few metres, but reaching that depth is hard work for us novices and by the time we even spot a crab it's time to resurface for air. Large schools of silver fish curiously swim around us as we search for the crabs with our lassos at the ready.

There are plenty of crabs, it turns out – but our efforts prove worthless to their cunning escapes. They hide in cracks and caves that are impossible to hook them out of. We watch as Alfonso scoops them out with ease, darting in and out of holes way below us like a merman, noosing six crabs and a couple of lobsters. Resurfacing for the last time near the skiff, I pull myself out and back into daylight, closely followed by the others and Alfonso with his haul.

"¡OK! ¡Vamos!" he cries, ripping the start cord and twisting the canoe around sharply in the direction of where we came. We all dry out in the sun before we reach the catamaran, where Fritz is waiting to help unload Alfonso's haul.

Dan cracks open a box of beers, while Fritz drops the shellfish into a pot of boiling water.

This life at sea is a life I could get used to.

CHAPTER FIFTY-TWO
THE CARIBBEAN

The movement of the boat wakes me. Up on deck, the sun is shining, as is Fritz, guiding us through a patch of dangerous reefs. Off to the starboard side, a lifeless yacht sits awkwardly on a lean in shallow water. "French!" Fritz calls out, pointing at the empty wreck with its mast at a forty-five-degree angle to the horizon. "Zeese expensive mistakes can only be airlifted out by military helicopter, which very rarely happens," he adds.

These statistics are all too familiar to the Kuna, who, like piranha devouring a carcass, waste no time at all and strip such vessels of any valuable materials within hours of the owners being rescued. An abandoned ship is a ghost ship in no time in these parts.

A small Navy dinghy pulls up to the cat and Fritz jumps aboard.

"I still haf your passports so I am taking zem to be stamped into Panama. See you soon," he says, clutching a leather satchel and waving as the dinghy turns around and zooms back to the Island leaving a frothy wake behind it.

"So what's your story, Martin?" I ask the Dutch guy who I haven't really got to know yet. We're sitting at the table, amicably sipping coffee. Some of us are sleeping below; some are reading on the trampoline. It's a quiet morning while we await Fritz's return.

"What do you mean, my story?" he asks me with a puzzled look.

"Well, what do you do for work?" I ask him. "I mean I know you love to dive and you spoke of being in Honduras before, but how do you travel so much?"

"Ah, well I was working for a nuclear testing centre in France and they were offering large severance pay outs for anybody who wanted to leave."

"Wow," I reply, intrigued. "Like nuclear weapons?"

"Mmm, I can't really say," he says, sheepishly. "Something like that."

The conversation is interrupted by Fritz, who arrives with our stamped passports. We pull up anchor and sail a little further north until dusk, where we drop anchor for the night between two heavily populated islands and sit down for our final dinner on board. Filling a huge pot with the remaining crab and lobster meat from our jaunt the day before, Fritz conjures up a thoroughly delicious chowder while the quiet hum of hymns in the village church sail through the night air. My mind drifts. The shiny white vessel we've arrived on feels like a spaceship compared to the scene unravelling around us and soon I'm daydreaming, conjuring images of Han Solo and Chewy setting The Millenium Falcon down in a forest habited by furry Ewoks. Except there are no ewoks here, only topless women in little wooden canoes who skate by us on the shimmering water, their silouettes illuminated by the stars and the twinkling lights of the two islands. Overcrowded shanty huts jostle for space and spill out over the shoreline on the two islands while the rumble of small petrol generators powers the village lights.

A man slows his log canoe with an oar and floats up alongside, handing us his mobile phone and charger. Without saying a word, he purses his lips and points them at the power point on the boat.

"A mobile phone! I've seen it all now!" Teren giggles as he takes the phone and plugs it in to the wall.

He says what I'm thinking. These islands feel like a step back in time, on the one hand – hand-carved dugout canoes as transport, shellfish-diving the means of sustenance – and yet, there is a distinct tell of the ways in which the Kuna engage and adopt the ways of the outside world. They trade enthusiastically; they punt with oars fashioned from any old plank but rely on petrol to power their necessary generators; the women dress traditionally tribal while the men wear polo shirts and stay in communication via mobile phone.

I am not quite ready to leave the Caribbean: one week skirting the edge of this island world is not enough. But the passports have been stamped and our money only pays for a week of chowder and hospitality.

Fritz makes a game of handing out our passports, trying to guess the owner of each one but a look of worry appears on his face as he realises that Dave and Kate are left empty-handed. Fritz's usual happy-go-lucky expression changes to the look of a stunned mullet. Rummaging in his holdall, he pulls out the two passports, still unstamped.

"Zeese ver in another envelope, FUCK!" he curses himself. "How could I be so stupid!?" Then he adds, steaming as he exhales, "Vee vill haf to go back in zee morning to der customs island – Scheisse!"

I'm reminded of Mikal.

Fritz retires to his quarters, mumbling to himself and rubbing his head while the rest of us, slightly dulled by his outburst, finish off the game of cards and head down into the claustrophobic cabin bunks as a heavy rain sets in. The constant bobbing motion inside the tiny sleeping capsules is all too much for Teren, who, minutes after closing his eyes, makes a dash for the top deck, firing a blast of projectile vomit over the side and into the waves.

I wake early after a fitful and sweaty night of sleep, and slip out of my bunk and poke my head up out of the hatch. The bad weather has broken and an overcast sky hangs in the air. The cat is moving fast.

"Vee are making good time, friends!" Fritz shouts from the cockpit, already en route back to the Lighthouse Island. "Should only be another half hour to zee customs and zen four hours to zee Panama coast and my Panamanian love."

He's referring to his girlfriend – the *other* girlfriend, that is, who obviously has no idea of the one he has in Cartagena. We arrive at the first customs island again and he jumps into the outboard and gurgles off in a froth of ocean. Good as his word, he's back on the cat after stamping the other passports, and we catch a strong tail wind that takes us towards our destination.

"OK, my boy!" Fritz howls at the cat as its sails fill with wind. "Let's catch up zat time!"

Before long we're skirting the thick overhanging jungle of the

Panamanian coastline. The dense green foliage thins out and muddy embankments curve inland away from the ocean, revealing a cluster of small motorboats that bob in the waves waiting for us.

Letting the cat's main anchor drop and closing all the windows and hatches, we transfer our belongings to one of the smaller boats which transports us to an old wooden jetty. Before we can even set foot on dry land, a small crowd of old women surround the top of the jetty's ladder and offer us mangoes, bananas and cold cans of Coke that they balance in plastic bowls on their heads.

"¡Espera! ¡Espera!" Fritz shouts at them, telling them to wait and shooing them back with his hands so we are able to breathe. Dropping my bag in the scorching heat, I buy a Coke and a couple of bananas and wait with the others on a bench outside a concrete building block at the edge of a disused dirt airstrip. Cutting a dusty brown gash through the thick jungle, its verges are littered with oil drums and the abandoned rusting wrecks of various light aircraft. These neglected metal birds with broken propellers and doors ripped off sit lifeless on flat tyres while the jungle slowly grows up around them.

"Zis place was a very busy airstrip in zee eighties," Fritz says, seeing our interest in the plane wrecks. "At least two planes a week to and from Miami. Zee drug runners used it mostly, more cocaine zan I ever saw… Ah, zose were zee days. Hello Central America."

He smiles with a far-off stare, thinking back to a more carefree and, dare I say, higher time in his life.

CHAPTER FIFTY-THREE
PANAMA CITY

Two jeeps appear from the jungle and pull up outside the concrete building where Fritz wards off the locals, again shooing them away with long arm sweeps and telling them that the jeeps are here for him and his passengers.

"Hurry!" he yells, pushing us through the small crowd and into the claustrophobic 4x4s. The oppressive heat increases as the dirt track is swallowed by dense foliage. The jeeps twist viciously from side to side as they tackle eroded trenches that threaten to swallow us whole. On several occasions, ocelots appear up ahead before vanishing back into the undergrowth.

Meerkats dart from the thick foliage, stopping mid-way across the dusty white track to check us out as we speed past.

"Pull over! Pull over!" Teren pleads insistently. Scrambling out, he bends over and throws up at the side of the jeep. Our blistering hot two hours rumbling along in the vehicle are a little too much like his experience in the boat's cabin: life in motion isn't agreeing with him or his equilibrium. He wipes his mouth on his sleeve and climbs back in, sitting green-faced and silent for the remainder of the ride.

Culture shock. The city is beyond imagining after our week at sea. Massive McDonalds and Coke billboards sprout above rooftops, battling for prime skyline positions, while SUVs and shiny sports cars fill the streets. In complete contrast to this and far below the skyline attractions, homeless families huddling on sheets of cardboard beg for food outside run-down storefronts. The jeeps pull over in a busy lay-by on the city's fringe and we assume guarded positions while we withdraw cash from an ATM in a bulletproof glass booth on the sidewalk.

"This is all a bit much, isn't it?" Alina asks, her iPod in her hand in full show.

"Just a precaution," Fritz answers. "You never know. OK, guys!"

He continues once we've procured our cash. "Zis is where I leave you. Thank you very much and I hope to see you all again sometime."

"Thank YOU, Fritz!" we all say, shaking his hand one by one.

"Just remember!" he adds, "If anyone at the hostel vants to sail, you guys tell them that Fritz the Cat is zee best! See you!" With that, he vanishes into a taxi with only a small sports holdall and disappears into the clogged traffic.

The five-story hostel in the old town of Casco Viejo has seen better days, much like the run-down neighbourhood that surrounds it. The four-storey wooden building, reminiscent of a Wild West saloon on a Hollywood film set, has a rickety balcony on every level where backpackers lounge around smoking cigarettes and drinking cold beers.

Dan and I grab a cold beer and join the balcony dwellers. It's time to talk about the rest of our trip, and do a little planning, now that we've reached Panama.

"There's no way we're gonna make it to New York by land, man," I tell him. "We just don't have enough time."

"Yeah," he replies, sipping his ice-cold beer. "I wanna find somewhere and hole up for a while anyway."

"OK, I'm gonna check out some flights then," I suggest. "I'll be back in a bit."

Sitting down at a computer I search for some options for flights to New York. It's mid-August and our flights to Europe leave on the 22nd of December, giving us four months. We want at least a week in New York and a month each in Mexico and Guatemala, leaving us just shy of a couple of months to play with. Knowing that Dan will be fine with whatever I book online, so long as he doesn't have to get up and put down his beer, I pay for two tickets from Mexico City to New York on the 14th December, giving us eight days in total in the Big Apple.

"Yep, sounds good, bro." Dan seems uninterested when I tell him the exciting news. He seems wholly unaware that this booking has just saved our trip from disaster. When it comes to planning, we are never on the same page. Dan would've quite happily flown by the seat of his pants until realising at the last minute that he was still on a beach in Mexico but his flight to Europe left from New York that evening – whereas I'm thinking about this in Panama, four months before that day when Dan would've come to the shocking realisation that would interrupt his snoozing under an umbrella in Acupulco.

While the view from the hostel's front balconies is of the giant half-moon bay backdropped by a long row of skyscrapers that stretch along the peninsula and glint in the orange sunsets, the rear balcony reveals another side of Panama's inner grime. A dilapidated block of flats is situated just across the back fence and mark the start of the 'red zone' – the city slums. Hostel guests sit on the balcony chatting, sipping lattes and eating pizza just metres away from lines of sad-looking washing hanging from makeshift clotheslines while lifeless characters shuffle back and forth along the rusty railing balconies that stretch the length of the building.

Panama City's tourist draw card is without doubt the Canal, and the obligatory trip to visit it is arranged by Martin, the Dutch guy from the boat. A blue taxi covered in rusty dents pulls up outside the hostel and weaves its way through the minefield of holes that riddle the narrow lanes. The old town's grid layout is similar to that of Potosí in Bolivia where the narrow cobbled streets were shadowed by rotten balconies that hang over them, waiting patiently to break off and disintegrate below in a cloud of termite-infested sawdust. En route, we are suddenly stopped by a police roadblock. They ask for our passports, which we hand out through the window obligingly.

"What was all that about?" Martin asks in Spanish as we drive away after the check.

"No es nada grave hombre, es un atajo," the taxi driver says, informing us that he's taken a short cut. I'm starting to worry as we pass through sky-high slums of concrete flats. On either side of our rumbling vehicle, grass and weeds sprout from cracks in the streets. *Did they think there's a chance we might not make it through?* I wonder to myself, watching the lost souls roam the open areas between the buildings like scenes from the *Day of the Dead* zombie movies. I do not want my last moments to be spent in Zombieland of backstreet Panama City.

I'm not the only one.

"Where are we?" Dan asks the driver, clearly disturbed as much as I am by the scenes out of the window.

"Es atajo, la zona rosa," he replies again, repeating that it's a short cut through the red zone.

Eventually, we arrive at the Canal in one piece. We scramble out of the taxi with haste, and we enter a building and climb a flight of stairs to a reception desk where a young man charges us an exorbitant entry fee. It's always the case with these 'world' attractions – and usually they are the most boring. Give me a 70c entrance fee to the 'Devils whirlpool' waterfall – complete with missing apostrophe – any day, where there's at least something exciting to experience, even with the risk of injury (or worse).

Behind him is a pair of sliding doors that open for us and lead to a glass-walled viewing room, which leads out to a balcony. From up here we can see the vast canal stretching north – and, surprisingly, a little west – through the countryside towards the Caribbean Sea. Directly underneath us, two colossal container ships queue while another is raised to their level within the giant Miraflores lock system.

How the locks raise one of these behemoths sixteen metres in a mere twenty minutes through its system is incredible to witness. Even so, after a few minutes I'm bored shitless and can't wait to leave. I've built up the idea of the Panama Canal in my mind over years, and more so in the months leading up to our arrival in this city. But now that we're here, something has dulled. Maybe it's the disparity between the highrises and the slums; maybe it's the glass-walled distance we experience between us and the real action below. Maybe I've sat too many times on balconies sipping lattes while real life happens around me – but I can't be sure of that because at the moment, I'd rather be sipping a latte than standing with my hands in my pockets, pacing and waiting for a ship to move sixteen metres vertically. Whatever the case, the view from here does little to inspire me. I'm more of a street-vendor kind of guy, I reckon.

"Can you take us into the city?" Martin asks our next taxi driver in Spanish, stressing that we don't want to pass through the red zone again. The city street we're dropped at is overflowing with the comings and goings of pedestrians. Busy sidewalks parade racks full of used clothing that clog the flow of foot traffic while cars honk at each other in the street. This is more like it; this is the world I can relate to.

Ducking into a small food bar, we see the choices on the wall have a very American theme to them. Burgers and hot dogs are advertised as well as milkshakes and sandwiches, the only available local dish being coconut rice and black beans.

"Nice!" Martin says. Biting into his toast, he sends cheese oozing down his chin.

Back at the hostel, Teren and I grab a beer and sit down in the bar. The guests occupying it are an indication of what's to come. We seem to have shaken off the beer swilling, football-mad English sect. Perhaps they end their trips or U-turn back towards Buenos Aires once they reach Colombia. Either way, there's no sign of them anymore. What we have here is American all the way.

"OH MY GAAAAAAD!" blurts a short guy in an orange singlet clutching a beer. "They have McDonalds here, duuudes!" He's talking to a group of spring break students. "I was getting so tired of that slop the locals eat," he continues.

Sitting at the bar, listening to this drivel and unable to hear myself think, I share a worried glance with Teren and realise the Brits of South America have been replaced by the even more obnoxious, younger and louder American version.

CHAPTER FIFTY-FOUR
BOCAS DEL TORO

A long-haired, olive skinned Israeli chap joins us at the bar.

"This is Raan," Teren says, introducing him to me.

Shaking his hand, I'm taken aback by the amount of woven travel bracelets he has tied around his wrist. He seems to notice my interest in them, he comments, "One for each place I have been."

He leans back on his stool and lifts both feet in the air. "These too," he adds, revealing a whole lot more tied around his ankles and hanging above a pair of Jesus creeper sandals.

Teren and his new mate engage in a similar phlegmy language that kept us awake all those months back in Santiago while Martin, Dan and I sip cold beers staring over the bay.

Teren switches back to English and informs us that Raan will join us for a week or so.

"The more the merrier," I say. I'm quite glad for the new energy – even though I'm still trying to figure out why anyone would need that many woven bracelets attached to them.

"Where have you been before Panama?" I ask Raan, a little worried how long the answer may take.

"Here," he says, pulling a photo from his wallet.

"HOLY SHIT! – Is that you?!" I say, shocked.

Two curly-haired guys – Raan and a friend, I presume – kneel blindfolded in the dirt with hands tied while masked men in camouflage stand over them, pointing automatic rifles at their heads.

"Yes, it's me," he replies proudly.

I am stunned, speechless. He breaks into laughter and explains.

Having been singled out and pulled from a bus in Colombia's mountains by FARC soldiers, he and his friend fear for their lives. The armed rebels surround them and lead them over to the open boot of the car that has blocked the road in front of the bus. Peering into the open boot, they see it's full of machine guns. The soldiers explain they've just received their weapons from an arms dealer in Venezuela.

"They knew of our military training – it's compulsory after finishing school in Israel," Raan tells us. "So they wanted us to show them how to dismantle and reassemble their guns!"

"Fucking hell!" I exclaim, astonished.

"So what about the photo?" I ask, worried where this story will lead. "Why did they tie you up?"

"Haha!" he answers, smiling. "We said we would help them if we could get a photo like this." He laughs. "It's cool, huh?"

I am not so sure it's as cool as he thinks it is. More like fucking weird. Who poses like that? Nutty bastards, that's who. People a little too in love with military weaponry, that's who. People a little too in love with themselves, that's who. I make a mental note that we are now friends with a guy who knows something about such things – for better or worse.

And so we travel as five, with our new crazy Israeli in tow.

We take a taxi to the next overcrowded bus station that ferries passengers north. Dragging our packs through a modern food court in the mall that sits in the middle of the terminal, we throw them into the hold of the beast belching black smoke that's going to the Caribbean islands of Bocas del Toro. Volcanic green landscape flashes by and we're dumped two hours later in a small town that lies at the edge of the ocean. The torn red canopy of our small motorboat flaps in the wind as we skim across the sparkling water to Isla Colon. In the sweltering heat, we are greeted by a stoned group of Rastafarians congregating by the jetty on tatty beach cruiser bikes with dogs in tow.

"Heeey, brother, I got good weed, good coke, pura pura, cheap, cheap," they offer, while herding us with their bicycles like sheep from the jetty to a hostel.

Nicknamed 'The Roach Pit', our new abode is run by two American girls in their early twenties. Dayna, a skinny girl from New York, is involved romantically with one of the owners. She's been left in charge of the place while he's away on business, while her friend

Leslie flaunts her gigantic breasts that are bursting out of the tiny t-shirt that tries but fails to hold them in place. Typical of American youth, they giggle at me, infatuated with my British accent.

"Oh, hello, how do you *doo?*" they ask, attempting to emulate a plummy British sound. "Your guys's accent is *sooo* adorable!" they add, embarrassingly.

Cockroaches scuttle around the weather boarded interior walls that are riddled with woodworm. The small shady balcony at the top of the creaky stairs fits two couches, a coffee table and a hammock. Commandeering this area, we occupy it for the majority of the following week, smoking joints and playing rounds of Yanif.

"We need to at least venture somewhere," I suggest strongly, mid-way through the week. "Let's take those bikes out for a spin."

The others somewhat reluctantly agree and with rough directions from Dayna to a place called Rat Beach, we wobble along on a deserted dirt road for twenty minutes on bikes that should have been thrown away years ago. I think of the bike ride to the skate park in Montevideo and appreciate what I'm now pedalling. Arriving at our destination, I can see why it earned its name. The shore resembles an abandoned recycling plant where piles of discarded boat trash and plastic bottles litter the beach.

"The currents must push all the shit around this side like that island in the San Blas," Martin says, pointing at a pile of seaweed and rubbish. "LOOK!"

We turn our heads to see two large rats scurrying across the sand. They move fast and disappear into a pile of trash. There's a reason they call this Rat Beach.

"Yanif and a joint?" Teren asks before any of us have even dismounted our bikes.

We ride home. It seems the balcony is the best place to be.

The main attractions of this cluster of islands are the aqua bars, with their square jetties that stick out into the water, creating natural swimming pools. Hordes of American students flock here in the holidays to frolic and drink in the evenings to their hearts' content. We partake in this paradisiacal pub life for the last few evenings and climax on our final night. Priming ourselves before hitting the nightlife, we're juiced and ready.

No sooner than setting foot in the bar, we're pushed in the water by a group of muscle-flexing frat boys. Martin and Dan both surface without their glasses. The drinks flow as does the sexual liberation. Teren swims over to a trampoline pontoon with an African-American girl, and they strip naked and fuck while being cheered on by the partygoers drinking at the bar. Raan holds a staff member from behind by her tits as they gyrate on the dance floor. Martin, Dan and I, by comparison, engage in far more innocent – even tame – activity. We are still in the water, and we spend our time, not necessarily by choice, flirting and groping – only mildly – the assortment of American students who frolic in the shallows with us.

Next morning, I wake with a killer headache, and I have no recollection of leaving the bar or how I got back. Martin and Dan have it much worse, as they are squinting like moles in the early morning sun. We return to the bar by boat and dive blind for their missing spectacles. Martin's have been swept away by the tide and are nowhere to be found, but the sheer weight of the copper coil holding Dan's pair together sinks them to the bottom like a lead balloon, anchoring them in the sand. Not only does this please Dan immensely – he now has a new story to add to his list for his drunken late-night hostel lectures. And another photo: one more of the electrical coil that holds together his glasses and has brought them back to him. I can imagine what Jan would say: *"Zee President is ze greatest! He has ze lucky glasss, always coming back like zee – how do you Keevees say? – boomerang!"*

CHAPTER FIFTY-FIVE
SIXAOLA

We're haemorrhaging money here on the islands.

We keep hearing from other travellers how cheap it is to stay in Nicaragua, so we discuss moving on and making only a short stop in Costa Rica. Teren and Raan are having too much fun in Bocas; they want to stay for a few more days. Which leaves Dan and me to carry on together. I've failed to feel any kind of cultural draw here in Panama; the westernised ways are no different to any Californian town I already know. I'm sure following a less trodden route would have changed that, but again, we've all too easily been sucked back onto the gringo trail for the past week or so. The mindless drunk fest that surrounds these islands has got the better of Dan and me. I worry my liver will shut down from all the abuse it's had in an intense short week, feeling the unhealthiest I've been on the trip so far after days spent constantly either drunk or stoned. I'm glad to be moving on.

Another small boat whisks us away from the islands to the mainland. As we skim across the water I reflect on the past week. Great company, not a care in the world, but shadowed by an excess of weed and alcohol.

The bus drives through the green northern back country. Through a chain link fence I watch forklift trucks carry giant crates of bananas to a container ship emblazoned with a Chiquita logo. Rusty shells of old American motorcars and farming machinery lie strewn across the land on the other side of the fence.

The bus drops us at a small concrete building at the end of a one-lane bridge. Spanning a dry riverbed, the bridge's side beams are pieced together from triangular sections creating two large half-hexagonal arcs.

"The bus will meet us on the other side," Martin says as if he's done this before. "You want a juice? I'm dying of thirst," he adds, seeing me sticking my tongue out spotting an old lady with an icebox.

We agree and hold our place in the border crossing line. The old lady, dressed in a flowery apron, drops a handful of lemons into a tube that she caps before turning a handle and producing a stream of yellow juice that fills a bucket.

"¿Heilo?" she says.

Martin greedily eyes the ice. "Si, por favor."

We watch her fill three plastic bags with the fresh lemon, glistening ice cubes and a straw. Martin joins us back in line and everyone shuffles forward while we quench our thirsts with the cold juice. In single file outside the shabby border patrol hut, one by one, our faces are matched with passport and identity card photos as we pass the dark hole in the wall. We survive the scrutiny, pick up our bags and follow the others.

A wrinkly-skinned mother with a long ponytail of dark hair leads a small boy by the hand ahead of us and a feeling of déjà vu comes over me. We are in no-man's land again, those narrow strips of uncertainty between two high barbed wire fences where the rules of neither the country you've left nor the one you're about to enter apply. It's a rush, in a way. And also unsettling.

The first encounter with a new country is both scary and exciting. In this case our no-man's land is a walk across a bridge – an obvious symbol, and one that holds all the more weight due to its rickety and questionable state. I look down through the oversized gaps between the planks to the dry riverbed far below. Will we make it to the other side? We'll only know once we get there.

To walk forward but have no idea what's round the corner, to wonder what's to come: this is why I love this year of travel. I most enjoy the moments when the greatest mystery is how one foot in front of the other will lead to something else. Not the skyscraper landscapes of the grand city centres, or the gargantuan symbol of human achievement that is the mighty Panama Canal. The simplest sights such as this woman and her boy, walking through a border crossing just in front of us, become a meaningful point of focus: another photo that can tell a colourful story. We know where we've been but not where we're about to set foot.

At the other end of the bridge, we glide through Costa Rican customs without a hitch; our bus, parked up and surrounded by soldiers, is not experiencing the same ease with the rite of passage.

CHAPTER FIFTY-SIX
SAN JOSE

A semi-truck carrying 300 kilos of cocaine inside Virgin Mary statues has been busted the day before, raising the security level at the border. The entry into Costa Rica is crawling with military and drug enforcement agents, creating a watertight seal between Panama and Costa Rica. Long lines of traffic and pedestrians queue for hours in the beating sun while camouflaged soldiers meticulously search every single vehicle and bag several times before being allowed to enter.

The bus driver kills the engine and subsequently the air-conditioning. The stifling heat is made even worse by the fact that we're prohibited from getting off while we wait. Four very long, tense hours later, we are once again rumbling through acres of banana plantations. The outskirts of San Jose slowly grow up around us and we are dropped, eventually, in a graffitied, war-torn street outside the terminal.

"¿Por que no vamos a entrar el terminal?" Martin asks the driver, enquiring as to why we are not driving into the terminal.

"No hay espacio amigo, aqui no mas," he replies: No room inside – this is the end of the line.

The bus pulls away and disappears around a corner, leaving us standing in what now is a deserted street.

"Where the fuck are we?" Dan says, looking worried.

"I need to take a piss, watch my bags," Martin replies, walking over to an alley to urinate.

A white, nondescript car creeps to a halt next to us and the boot springs open.

"Taxi?" says the shifty-looking character, with a hint of hesitation in his voice.

"Si, gracias," Dan replies, throwing his bag in the boot.

"What the fuck are you doing?" Martin asks us, furious on his return.

"Getting a taxi; this area's dodgy," I say, throwing my bag in as well.

Martin blinks. "Come on, guys, think about it." His voice is stern and steady. "Taxi drivers who take tourists directly to a loaded gun a few blocks away? This isn't a legit cab."

We turn to peer at the driver and his now nervous body language. Maybe Martin has a valid point.

We pull our backpacks from the boot.

The driver doesn't complain. He doesn't say a word. He knows what we're thinking and departs quickly.

"Come on," Martin barks, and leads us to the taxi stand at the front of the terminal.

A far superior taxi delivers us safely to our new abode. A high-walled perimeter of spiralling razor wire surrounds the accommodation. On the contrary, the interior is built around a shimmering blue swimming pool area and straw-roofed bar.

"What's up?" says a short American guy in a yellow t-shirt and shorts. "I'm Brad. Where did you guys come from?"

"Straight from Bocas del Toro. We're just staying for a night or two." Dan answers. "How is this city? It seems pretty dodgy."

"Dude," Brad starts, "I was robbed yesterday at gunpoint ten yards from the front door."

"WHAT?!" we say in unison – and in shock.

"Yeah, a car pulled up outside and a dude got out waving a gun," he says, seemingly unperturbed. "They got my wallet."

"Fucking hell," I exhale. "The sooner we're out of here the better."

"I got off lightly, man," he says. "There were two Swedish girls here yesterday – they flew home last night."

"What happened to them?!" we ask, expecting the worst.

"They jumped in an unmarked taxi at Managua airport in Nicaragua."

"And?" Martin asks, nodding at us with a knowing look.

"A couple of dudes jump in the taxi a few blocks from the airport and the girls were kidnapped."

"No fucking way!" I exclaim, looking at Martin, who now has a smug 'I told you so' smirk growing on his face.

"Yeah, they were held in a room and tied up for two days while their credit cards were rinsed dry of all their money in different ATMs all over the city."

"That's some gnarly shit, man," Dan says, lighting a cigarette.

"Dude," Brad adds. "If that wasn't enough, they were then dropped on the city outskirts in the middle of the night in only their underwear."

The Westernised culture of Panama that I found so uninspiring doesn't seem so bad now. These stories shake me up pretty good, and I'm getting the feeling that Central America is going to be a hostile place.

Hungry and with no other choice but to leave the barbed wire walls of the hostel, we make our way into downtown. The city feels dangerous. The deserted lonely streets drag up images of the neighbourhood surrounding the Boca football stadium back in April and heighten my fears. Weeds grow from the cracks in its pavements while the faces of the people we pass all wear faraway glassy stares. A man blocks the sidewalk up ahead, not in a menacing way but frightening nonetheless. Lying upside down in a heap on the front steps of a doorway, he is motionless, and his foot dangles limply off the kerb. We expect to see the dried blood from a gunshot wound as we step over him, and we hesitate, wondering what we ought to do. His snores, however, prove he's just another casualty of a hard night on the drink.

We walk the streets like an elite pack of commandos, covering each other from all angles in anticipation of attack before stumbling on a fried chicken shop. It's not dissimilar to a greasy café you could find on the streets of England. We empty the rotisserie cabinet, quickly pay and regroup as commandos, moving swiftly back to the safety of the hostel.

An overweight black girl is sitting by the pool.

"Hey y'all," she greets us in a fidgety manner. "Whur y'all from?" Her thick Southern drawl is musical and sing-songy.

"New Zealand," I say. "And what about you?"

"European, huh?"

I decide not to challenge her geographic intelligence.

"I'm from Dallas, I'ma jus takin' a liddle break from ma boyfriend and ma *bay*bee," she explains, her eyes huge and dilated. "I jus wawnt some peace an' quiet, but I ain't slept fo' days."

"What have you been doing here?" I ask her.

"Weeelll, I been inside the hostel for two weeks an' ain't slept in days," she says, repeating herself. "Ya'll want one o' deeze?" She pulls out a container of blue capsules.

"Thanks! Don't mind if I do!" Dan says, stepping in and grabbing a couple.

Up in our dorm room, I'm starting to freak out.

"Where the fuck are we?" I ask the other two. "The city's a war zone and the hostel's deserted apart from the crack head chick and the dude with the 'Holidays in hell' stories."

"I just need some glasses and we can move on," Martin says, still squinting like a mole. "Let's go to the mall and order the lenses now."

We make our way on foot to the mall a few blocks away in the opposite direction of the city – where the scenes are slightly less daunting. Condo-style houses sit among manicured palm trees behind spiked fences, while modern cars pass through their security coded gates. Although we are still supremely wary of our surroundings, our commando configuration isn't necessary in the leafy suburb we walk through. This leafy suburb delivers us to the mall in one piece and we wait while Martin orders a new pair of spectacles.

"They'll be ready tomorrow," he tells us. "I'll get a taxi back here before we go to the terminal."

Surprisingly, the lenses are ready the next day, as promised. Except they are not the correct prescription. We have swung by the mall on our way to the bus stop. The taxi's waiting outside.

"Well," he says, resigned. "I don't wanna wait around any longer so these will have to do." He is still squinting as he shakes our hands on the terminal forecourt and jumps into a bus bound for the east coast of Nicaragua.

Our travels with Martin have been easy and relaxed, but he is off with his own agenda now, bound for the Corn Islands and a few weeks of diving. I'm glad our paths crossed, he was a pleasure to travel with.

The shiny Tica bus at Stand 19 waits patiently as it fills with passengers, a sign in the front windscreen reading 'Managua'. It looks surprisingly orderly and secure. But that is not our bus. Our bus, also bound for Managua, is a different story: a dirty grey beast, idling at Stand 17 with a plume of black smoke belching noisily from its guts.

Banana plantations pass by. Mile after mile until we finally arrive at the border crossing. Passport control is a far simpler procedure than what we'd experienced coming into Costa Rica but I'm stung by another unforeseen border experience.

"Good rate! Good rate!" says a friendly, smartly dressed man with a jet-black mop of slicked hair. Holding a thick wad of Nicaraguan córdobas wrapped in an elastic band, he yaps at me like a Chihuahua confusing my already tired state with rapid-fire Spanish and flicking the wad of bills in my face. I decline, but he won't give in and conjures up some currency conversion multiplications on a school calculator that he pulls from his pocket. He is determined to exchange my money, and I have a feeling he won't let me go. I lean in and eye the number of notes he's offering to exchange for my US $75, and I see he can only be short-changing himself, so I make the deal with him and continue standing in line while he moves on.

We reboard the bus after passport control. I double-check the money again.

"No!" I mumble to myself as the checkpoint disappears in the distance. "Fucking arsehole!"

The guy saw me coming, and has exchanged me US $25 worth of córdobas and pocketed $50 for himself.

Feeling cheated and foolish after falling for such an obvious scam, I'm absolutely fine with leaving this country behind. I close my eyes as I reflect back on my own personal view of this country – a place I would never have known exists, apart from the lush green and abundant wildlife package tour posters I've seen in travel agent windows in pretty cities.

Some tourists have that view, sure. Those tourists get whisked in shiny rental vans straight from the airport to their gated beach resorts, armed with cases of sunscreen and dollars for overpriced cocktails. Tourists who have no clue about the Costa Rica that I've just experienced.

The charm of South America is but a distant memory. The whistle of panpipes and the clean mountain air of the Andes have been replaced with chart music and scorched low-lying banana plantations, McDonald's and Coca-Cola billboards sprouting at every turn. We've been floating from hostel to hostel on the wave that is the gringo trail since our time in Panama City, and I'm now having serious thoughts as to why I'm really here and if it's all worth it. Central America so far has left a bad taste in my mouth and a feeling that I don't belong and shouldn't be here.

I keep thinking back to the Dallas girl in the hostel. *Ya'll want one o' deeze?*

The phrase 'America's backyard' that I've heard so frequently is beginning to make more sense. But it's not the manicured backyard from feature films or commercials. It feels a lot like America's dumping ground.

CHAPTER FIFTY-SEVEN
MANAGUA

Driving from the Costa Rican side of the border into no-man's land feels like we've entered the gates of hell: the infernal heat is unbearable. Gangs of flies buzz around the skinny stray dogs that wander across the road at the Nicaraguan checkpoint. Sniffing around plastic bags of cheese-stuffed tortillas that lie stacked on neatly folded tea towels at the kerbside, they're shooed away by dark-skinned, high-cheekboned women.

"¿Cuánto vale?" I ask one of the squatting girls, enquiring of the price.

"Diez," she says, smiling up at me with eyes like pools of onyx and holding up the tortilla, drowning in sour cream in a clear plastic bag.

"Thirty-five cents!" I say to Dan, and buy three.

This sends the other women into a frenzy; they now focus all their energy on Dan.

"Si, uno cada uno," he tells them, evenly distributing his money between the three women surrounding him.

Back on the bus I open my passport to see an inky stamp much like the ones I received from Bolivian customs. Outside, the tortilla sellers enthusiastically wave us goodbye from the kerb.

"I have a good feeling about this place," I say to Dan, as we pull away from the border.

"Yeah, cheap is good," he mumbles before dozing off.

We pass by the stunning bottle-green landscape of Ometepe Island out in the middle of Lake Nicaragua, wispy clouds gently kissing its giant volcanic peaks, and I'm overcome with a contented feeling I've not had since the hospitality of Pachijal in Ecuador.

A clutter of dilapidated hostels and cheap comedors surround the bus terminal in the heart of Managua's sketchy Martha Quezada neighbourhood. More stray dogs, clearly undernourished, wander the streets, balding fur coats stretched over skeletal frames. We again disembark into unknown territory and are followed by two also underfed but friendly local lads in baggy basketball vests. We quicken our pace but are not sure in which direction we are supposed to head.

One of the lads shouts out to us. "Hey! My friends! You smoke, my friends?" They discreetly shake a bag of dry weed.

"Um, no thanks," I reply, paranoid they're part of a set up by corrupt police.

"OK, maybe later," he says, not giving up. "Where you stay?" He is still walking with us.

"No se," Dan says, shrugging his shoulders.

"Don Julio, my friend," the kid offers. "Good hospedaje. Venga, venga, I show you."

They lead us around the side of the terminal, and we step into a spacious lobby where the boys collect a small commission from the owner for bringing us here and disappear out the door. The large downstairs is an open area with rooms running along a second floor balcony. The open area has literally been smeared in a coat of bright yellow paint. Nothing has escaped the brush: the hinges, any small windows, every door handle, even an ancient spluttering air-conditioning unit spitting cold air. It's a lumpy custard interior that is strangely welcoming.

"¿Tienes habitación por una noche?" Dan asks the owner, who sits behind the desk in a rocking chair fanning himself with a banana leaf.

"Si," the fat guy answers, not bothering to look up. "Ciento viente cinco, cada uno."

"Five bucks each," Dan says to me, roughly translating the 125 córdoba. "Sweet."

In the comedor across the road from our dwelling, I furiously battle with the saltshaker that refuses to part with the congealed lump it retains inside its glass tube. Soon our razor-thin steaks are brought over to us, resident flies swarming as they make their way from the kitchen to our table. We can see the flurry and buzz of commotion hovering around our plates en route. And as if that's not enough to make me question the meal we're about to eat, I see, just as our steaks are dropped onto the plastic cloth that's stapled to the table, a furry brown rat scuttle up the peeling wall, its pink tail disappearing into a hole in the ceiling. I glance at the woman who's brought our food with a dumbfounded look, not knowing if I should believe what I just saw. She laughs, bearing a full set of gold teeth, and wobbles off back into the kitchen.

"Holy shit! Was that for real?!" I say to Dan, still shocked.

"Yep, that was a giant rat, bro," he says, digging into his chewy steak.

The sweltering late afternoon humidity is slowing us down like lead weights as we return across the street to Hotel Custard. The two boys from earlier are waiting outside.

"So you wan' smoke, my friend?" they ask again.

"OK, just a little," Dan says and hands them the equivalent of a dollar.

"You like, is good, adios!" they say before vanishing down an alley.

Rolling up in front of the fuzzy TV in our room, we spark it up and puff away on the dried-out joint, blowing smoke out the broken window in the back wall before sinking into the marshmallow mattresses. The ticking noise of the ceiling fan sends us to sleep.

Breakfast: another fly fight at the comedor. But it's sustenance that we need; soon after we walk, terrified, through six blocks to a mall that we're told has an ATM. Our journey takes us past a maze of desolate, crumbling side streets. The lack of people around is worrying and assuring all at the same time. I try to reassure myself that, if crime happens mostly at night, then perhaps all those desperate muggers I've heard about – the ones who will 'shoot you for your tortillas' – are asleep right now.

My watch reads 10:30am. I don't feel any safer, not really.

We glance left and right, down each one of those streets, and see every vertical surface sprayed with bad graffiti and the Sandinista Front initials, FSLN. I'm feeling well out of my comfort zone. Even so, each block we walk, the more scared I become. I'm glad we've taken the main thoroughfare route. Miraculously, we make it to the mall and stop to smoke a calming cigarette before entering.

"No te vas a sentar allá!! Te vas a caer!!!" shouts an armed security guard, pointing at me and referring to the wall I'm sitting on, at the top of a set of stairs. It's an odd juxtaposition of detail: getting told off for sitting on a wall, just after we've arrived here through un-patrolled streets. A trifle over the top, I'd say, but seeing the automatic rifle swinging from his arm, I don't question his decision or authority. I jump down.

The building is air-conditioned and like a walk-in freezer compared to the temperature outside. Searching the three levels, we find the ATM and Dan uses my card to withdraw enough money to get him a bus ticket, food and a couple of taxi rides in the city.

Apart from the few shop employees in the mall, the place is empty. It feels like a mass exodus has taken place and the city has been deserted. It feels like something's amiss. It feels surreal. Desperate but not threatening, calm but uneasy.

"I don't wanna be carrying around more than I have to," Dan says, not wanting to be robbed with a large amount of cash on him.

"No chance of that!" I say nervously, trying to make light of how I am feeling with such an absence of human life here.

"These are dollars though. You need córdobas, no?" I say, confused.

"The ATMs all give dollars that need to be changed to córdobas with the currency guys on the street," he says confidently. "I read it in the guidebook."

Directly behind the mall is a hill that looks over the city, and the home of the twisted remains of the Presidential Palace. A small sentry hut stands at the foot of the road leading to the summit and a guard calls us over as we try to walk past.

"Veinte córdoba, cada uno," he says, asking for an entrance fee of twenty córdobas each.

"This wasn't in the guidebook," Dan says to me. "It says it's free."

"He's got an AK47, give him the eighty cents," I say under my breath.

Bent and buckled, the former palace sits defeated and broken like a half-demolished multi-storey car park. Exposed steel reinforcing rods twist and protrude out of decayed levels of floor sections, and large cracks riddle the framework. The view of Managua is swathed in a haze of unbearable heat and backdropped by the giant brown polluted lake of the same name. A view that reveals the utter destruction reaped by the huge earthquake that flattened the city a day before Christmas in 1972: a cracked hollow cathedral off to the right; whole city blocks of empty lots, lying dormant for decades; high-rise shells plastered in graffiti with giant trees growing from their gnarled and ghostly frames. The quake was a mere 6.2 on the Richter scale but the epicentre was only five kilometres deep, and directly under the city, leaving 5,000 dead, 20,000 injured and 250,000 homeless. Even standing here today, so many years later, we can see the destruction. The emptiness is palpable. The lots that were destroyed were never to be built on again, due to the hundreds of fault lines lying directly below the surface. Plus, the rescue aid money was stolen and pocketed by the government.

The ruined palace is now home to a museum that tells the brutal stories of its time as a government-run prison housing the Sandinista soldiers captured during the Revolution. Again, we're confronted with a strange contrast of image and sound; this time it's not delivered by the barking instructions of a security guard against the desolate backdrop of the lawless landscape, but rather a noisy bunch of day-tripping school children. Their excited laughter reaches us across the courtyard as they climb in and out of old US school buses and play around the memorial statues and tanks. Somehow, the view from where we stand, just inside the museum, makes the atrocities carried out here less than three decades ago hard to comprehend. Amidst the chaos outside, I see a boy, no more than ten years old, swinging off the neglected tank. His face beams a massive smile as he monkeys himself across its flaking horizontal gun barrel. I smile, and then the warmth I feel from watching him is immediately turned to a shiver as the guide explains that splitting the foot between a soldier's toes with a machete was one of the most effective forms of torture carried out during the civil war.

There is something surreal about the whole scene: for these kids, this is their history, their trauma. These kids live with the violence of everyday existence, the gun relics mere playground items. *How do they live with it,* I wonder. I have the feeling I'll be the one who can't shake it once I leave.

Back at the bottom of the hill, a moneychanger is standing outside the mall.

"Do you think he's legit?" I ask Dan.

"Only one way to find out," he says, walking over to him.

Pulling a wad of notes out of one of the many pockets adorning his beige fisherman's vest, the money changer punches in the exchange rate and passes Dan the córdoba notes.

"Yep, seems to be sweet," Dan says. "His commission is tiny."

As soon as we've finished our exchange, a taxi pulls up and the driver motions adamantly.

"¡Adelante! ¡Adelante! No caminar por fa. ¡Taxi mas seguro!" He seems rather insistent that we get in, stressing that we need to be guided around and it's not a safe place for foreigners to be walking the streets. As he takes us into the old downtown area, I think back to the kidnap story of the Swedish girls in this very city, and now realise how stupid we've been to just jump in like we did. My mind races. Are his accomplices waiting around the corner, ready to pounce, or was wandering the streets like sitting ducks more dangerous? Especially as Dan is now loaded with his recent withdrawal.

Five minutes into the ride, I've had time to study the driver's kind face, the rosary beads hanging from his rearview mirror and the photos of his children stuck to the dashboard. I settle down. I breathe. I think we're going to be alright. As he drives us down the deserted scorched streets he's relishing his role as an incredibly informative sightseeing guide.

"Es de la Revolución," he says, referring to the war as we pass a giant bronze statue of a Sandinista soldier pointing his AK47 to the sky. "Y este amigos, es pueblo de plastico," he says, pointing left to a long wall of black tarpaulin, blue twine and sticks that hold together the makeshift plastic tent village that covers around four square blocks. This is the home for hundreds of people who were poisoned by pesticides on a government-run banana plantation and are all too sick to work. The government, however, has been denying these claims for over ten years, washing their hands of the problem and leaving these people to fend for themselves, penniless and suffering in silence in their plastic tarp village.

It must take years to learn these streets, a confusing mess of roads and unsigned disorientating lanes riddled with potholes. The lanes crisscross each other erratically, while rusty yellow-painted traffic lights stand at intersections, their red, orange and green bulbs fizzled out years ago. The taxi parks up outside the old plaza where the aforementioned derelict cathedral stands, eerily burnt out and stained. It's missing one of its bell towers and is riddled with gaping cracks in its cement. A ghostly wind whistles through its innards, swaying the empty hammocks of the homeless who occupy it. A silence befalls this area, seemingly abandoned for over thirty years.

Across the plaza the mood changes. Tall fluted concrete columns line the pristine white front of the new Presidential Palace, the one that replaced its destroyed predecessor up on the hill, while the white and blue national flags on its roof proudly flaps in the sweltering tropical heat. Suddenly, the silence is broken by the beat of three ex-Russian military helicopters that appear in the distant sky and fly directly overhead, casting shadows across the plaza floor. As the whirr of the chopper blades fade, a small barefooted boy in torn clothing and hair matted with dirt approaches and gives me a winged insect that he's made from a leaf. When I offer him some loose change he refuses and skips away, contented that I like the gift.

Standing in the middle of the plaza looking at the gift with a lump in my throat, I'm speechless and humbled. After the negative events of Panama and Costa Rica and my anxiety around wanting to integrate into somewhere meaningful on this trip, I think I've found the place I've been looking for.

CHAPTER FIFTY-EIGHT
LEÓN

"¡OYE! ¡OYE! ¡OYE!" The pack of silver-toothed, hungry touts surround and tug at us like wolves as we walk into Mercado Israel Lewites bus terminal, one of Managua's four bus stations.

We shake them off and weave through the chaotic mess, narrowly avoiding being backed over and squashed. The chaos is complicated by decorations that adorn the groaning gas-guzzlers. It's hard to tell a flashing indicator from a string of Christmas lights draped across the bumper, and brake lights can be easily confused by the dozens of blinking Jesus statuettes cable-tied to the back. We wait on a bench while the eager queue of people fight to be first aboard, thrilled at the idea of a jolting, hot, dust-choked two-hour trip. When we finally board, we find the now overloaded wreck has exactly two seats left near the back.

"Bro! We scored!" I triumphantly say to Dan.

Squeezing into the seat, I come to realise why it's vacant. Perched uncomfortably and directly over the rear wheel arch, it ensures our knees stay firmly up around our ears for the ride. Our bags are dumped at the rear door as we settle in for the ride and bid the hustle bustle of Managua goodbye.

After what seems like an eternity in the intense heat, our arses sticking to the boiling vinyl bus seats, two men dressed as clowns tell us that this bus doesn't actually go in to León and that we've already passed the turn off.

"¡Parate! ¡Parate!" they shout down the aisle to the driver, ordering him to pull over. The back door flies open and we climb down while our bags are thrown out at the side of the road. Coughing and engulfed in a blanket of black exhaust smoke as the bus pulls away from the lay-by, we look at each other, more than a little surprised at how quickly we've been deposited on the side of the road. In the middle of nowhere.

A beat-up taxi appears through the thinning cloud.

"¡¿León?!" shouts the driver.

"¡Sí!" we reply desperately, running over to him, eager to be somewhere less vulnerable.

We throw our bags in the boot, and the creaky cab rattles its way through a maze of cobbled streets and into the city centre.

My impressions of a place always begin with the route I take into it, and the images that flash by as we enter León feed my excitement. Soon we arrive in the centre: a busy little market town where light traffic cohabits with ox-drawn carts plodding through low-terraced streets, some houses painted in bright hues while others reveal eroding mud walls of adobe horizontal stick construction. These sunburnt buildings show decades of neglect. And they are all built around the largest cathedral in Central America.

We choose a hostel from the guidebook, and the taxi drops us outside and charges us virtually nothing. The narrow street where we'll live for the next few days is home to a few buffet-style restaurants serving cheap Nicaraguan food, four hostels, three internet shops and six second-hand clothing stores. The hostels are all featured in the guidebook but each caters to differing types of traveller. Our choice is equipped with a bar and a tiny pool that, at any given time of the day, is filled with guests desperate to cool off in the dry heat. Parked outside is an ex-military Mercedes truck that ferries people on day trips to and from Cerro Negro, a black volcanic hill where thrillseekers can slide down its sides in orange boiler suits on top of wooden snowboards. Across the street is a more civilised hostel and one which we should have probably checked into instead. A pool table and bar where locals congregate is surrounded by an airy, open courtyard, alive with gecko-filled trees and a series of cool, shaded dorm rooms out the back.

"Let's move over there after our last paid night here," Dan says, popping the top off of his cold glistening beer while staring at the hostel across the street.

As the story goes, León's giant cathedral was a mistake. The plans were accidentally switched in the 1700s with the smaller cathedral in Lima,

Peru that was being built at the same time. Although its discoloured mouldy grey walls are in dire need of a high-pressure water blasting, this colossal giant has stood the test of time, surviving lightning storms, earthquakes, hurricanes and the bombing raids of the revolution.

The city was at one time the capital of Nicaragua. It's also the birthplace of the famous poet Rueben Darío; the house where he lived and wrote his famous poems, open to the public, has been preserved exactly as it was the day he died. On top of all this rich history, the city is of course steeped in the revolution's history – and is most famous for its role in serving as a vital base for the Sandinista soldiers during the revolution. As well as toppling the government from power and overthrowing the dictatorship that had brought the country to its knees, they managed to decrease illiteracy amongst the poor by 70% within a year in the makeshift schools they ran in the mountains.

I am intrigued to learn more of this fascinating history. So is Dan.

Across the main plaza that sits in front of the giant cathedral is a grey, two-storey building. The window openings on the second floor are boarded up; the openings on the ground floor are without glass panes, and with open wooden shutters. A torn red and black flag flaps pathetically from a pole that juts out from the exterior wall. I've seen this flag before. In those deserted streets of Managua but in graffiti form: the FSLN flag. At the top of a small set of semi-circular steps is a thin, old man in tatty clothing with an eye patch and a walking stick.

"Ven, ven hombres," he beckons to us, pointing at an equally tatty sandwich board.

The sign reads 'Museo de la Revolución'.

"Come on," Dan says, starting up the steps.

The old guy, now smiling, turns slowly as if he's in great pain and leads us in to a room where a few more malnourished old men sit, each one sporting a type of long-ago acquired injury. A missing leg, a permanent facial scar, one arm. *Veterans,* I think to myself. The eye-patched man leads us around the walls of photographs, explaining loudly in Spanish the story of the war and how it was won.

"Are you getting any of this?" Dan asks me while the old guy carries on passionately at the top of his voice.

"Kind of," I answer, lying through my teeth.

"Glad YOU are, bro," he replies.

I can't understand a word of it. The passion the guy is putting into his story is intense, poking at the photos with his walking stick and almost yelling when he comes to a point he wants us to remember. Finally the tour finishes and we gladly donate coins with gratitude.

"Holy shit. That was intense," I say, descending the four front steps on to the street. Dan pauses on the top stair and lights a ciggy.

"Mental," he says, blowing out a plume of grey smoke.

Although coming away with few of the facts and figures Mr Eyepatch has divulged, the essence of what a massive part these guys and the town of León played during that turbulent time is apparent.

We smoke on the steps. I shiver. We light another.

The town is begging me to stay. Dan and I need a break from each other anyway and I am overcome by the feeling that the place might just offer exactly what I've been looking for. Is it the gentle rhythm of the town and its people? The passion of the old veterans in the museum, or the fact that we haven't been ripped off yet? I'm still not sure, but I'm feeling genuinely comfortable about where we are for the first time in a long time.

The following morning I head out into the grid of narrow streets to find a language school. A small sandwich board stands outside an open door, offering one-on-one lessons, so I enter to find out more.

"Hi, sit down. I'm Roberto," says a well-dressed man in perfect English. Nicaraguan without doubt, but obviously well-educated. "How can I help you today?"

I explain my plight to him, and he suggests I start with a couple of twenty-hour weeks – and that I stay with a local family to help me with my Spanish.

"I think you should stay with this family," he suggests, pointing at the house across the street. "They are close to the school and they also speak English."

"I really want a full immersion, if that's possible," I say, not content with his suggestion. "Which family speaks no English and lives the furthest away from the school?"

Maybe it's a foolish idea, but I am committed to making a full go of this.

"Hmm," Roberto thinks a moment. "OK, I have the family for you. I will pick you up from your hostel on Sunday morning at 10."

"Great!" I reply, chuffed with myself for going through with it. Walking back to the hostel, I'm excited about what lies ahead. *Holy shit,* I think to myself. *I've done it.*

"So, how did you get on?" Dan asks, already sipping a beer at the bar, even though its only 10.30am.

"I move in on Sunday."

"Whoa, really?" he says, obviously thrown that I've actually gone ahead with the idea.

"Yeah, they live about eight blocks from the centre and don't speak English."

"Haha! Fucking hell, I'd love to be a fly on the wall!" he says, imagining the frustrations I'm going to face trying to communicate.

"Fuck off, man – at least I'm trying," I snap back at him, with a bruised ego.

"Nah, you'll be sweet, bro," he answers congenially. "'Bout time you got a handle on it. I can't believe you've put up with my shit for this long."

CHAPTER FIFTY-NINE
LAS PEÑITAS

The small fishing village of Las Peñitas is situated on the shore of the Pacific and about twenty-five minutes from León by bus.

"It's my last weekend as a hostel hopper, we should go stay at the beach," I suggest over beers one night in our León hostel.

"Yeah, I'm keen," Dan agrees, and adds, "I got an email from Teren today too. He's arriving today; he'll be into it."

Meanwhile, life at the hostel has brought new people into our lives. A couple of girls from New York arrive and we get to know them over drinks. Kim, a waiflike creature who's been studying Spanish in Guatemala, and Shannon, her African friend, jump at the idea.

"Hell yeah, we wanna go to the beach!" they say excitedly when we mention our plan for a two-day excursion.

"Look who's here?!" Dan says, pointing at the door.

Standing in the entrance with his aviator shades perched up on his afro is Teren.

"I made it! What's up, fellas?!" he says, hugging us and ordering a beer before his bag leaves his back.

"Not much, bro," Dan says. "And don't bother checking in your bag," he adds. "You're coming to the beach with us."

For twenty córdobas, any taxi will go to the tiny bus terminal and market known as El Mercadito in the Subtiava neighbourhood that lies to the west of León and runs an hourly service out to the beach. A mangy dog chews its way through a rubbish sack at the front of the bus yard and slow-moving market shoppers shuffle around the stalls while we wait patiently in the sauna heat of the bus's interior for it to fill with passengers.

The bus follows a dusty dry road stopping every minute along the way to pick up and set down passengers and eventually takes a right turn on to a dirt lane that skirts the ocean. Empty shells of hotels pass by the window: victims to the fierce tides continuously battering this stretch of the Pacific coast. Those that are just a few feet further back are still occupied and stand strong. The bus performs a U-turn at the end of the road in the village of Poneloya and follows it back along the shore before crossing the road we'd come in on from Subtiava. Continuing further down a new stretch of the coast road, we reach Las Peñitas. Similar to Poneloya, the dwellings here are half washed-out ruins and half left standing. Our hostel, still intact, is located a dangerous ten metres from the high tide mark.

Gangs of cute but pushy children walk the beach with necklaces and googly-eyed miniature animals made from superglue and shells. When they approach, the trick is to outright refuse and shoo them away, as buying anything from one of these little critters ignites a shit storm. My first experience of these little hustlers occurs while I'm sitting in the dining area just before dinner – and ends with one punching the other one in his eye for making a sale first.

Over dinner, Teren gets to work on Shannon, using his smooth talking and romantic mind games to lure her in. It's all a little too reminiscent of Bocas in Panama and the trampoline pontoon romp – I only hope they find a more secluded place to carry out their night of passion if she succumbs to his ways. I don't think I can watch such a performance twice in one year.

The deafening sound of the crashing high tide waves serve as an excellent muffler for the squeaking bunk that Teren and Shannon are putting through its paces as they pump each other like randy teenagers. So distracting is their rhythmic movement that I think nothing of the breaking waves, encroaching on the fragile shoreline.

The next morning we see just how close they were.

I wake to a whole lot of commotion outside and draw back the curtain to see a chain gang passing sand bags through the destroyed dining area.

"Holy fuck!" I shout in the direction of the others still sleeping behind me. "Check this out!"

The sand bags are being passed along the chain and then stacked on top of each other to create a sea wall – a last-ditch effort to protect what is left of the place. The Pacific has risen up during the night and like a giant claw has dragged half of the grounds out to sea. Our hostel's eating area and its two-storey straw roof are now collapsed at one end and embedded in the sand.

"No way!" Teren says, jumping out of bed and staring at what I'm watching. "We were just sat there, like, twelve hours ago!"

The tables, chairs and large block of concrete steps that were there yesterday have vanished entirely.

PART III
GOING IT ALONE

NICARAGUA, EL SALVADOR,
GUATEMALA, MEXICO

OCTOBER, NOVEMBER, DECEMBER

CHAPTER SIXTY
FAMILIA

I leave the others at the beach at Las Peñitas and return to León solo, checking back into the hostel for one last night. I'm slightly jealous of the others (especially Dan) who are staying at the beach for the next few days, but I have to do this for myself and break free from the monotonous routine of backpacker life.

The next morning I am nervous, anxious and wondering what the hell I've let myself in for, and, waiting for Roberto to collect me, a thousand thoughts race through my mind. *What if the family don't give a shit about me and just want the money? Will they even talk to me or show any interest in helping me with my Spanish? And who's my teacher going to be? I haven't been in a learning environment for over fifteen years.*

I stub out my cigarette, and realise I've smoked close to a whole pack of the things while talking to a young girl who has recently arrived from Honduras.

"I really like those tattoos on your arms," I comment. "Are they Henna or real ones?"

"Haha," she snorts, "These aren't tattoos!" She rubs the brown lines on her arms. "They're the trails left by a type of worm parasite that infected some food I ate in El Salvador. The worm travels through veins just under the skin, feeding on blood and passing it through its body, depositing waste as it goes, thus creating these lines."

"Fucking hell!" I remark. "So what happens now?" I am shocked by the calm way in which she's explaining her malady.

"Oh, it's no real drama," she says, unperturbed. "As disgusting as it sounds, the doctor told me that the worm will eventually die, the lines will disappear and there are no side effects."

She walks off and I snap back into reality. My nerves are shot. Never have I felt like I'm taking such a huge step, the thought of living with a totally foreign family I can't communicate with now scaring the shit out of me.

Roberto arrives in a taxi. "Everything OK?"

"Yep, I'm good," I answer, softly and unconvincingly. I am sure he can sense my nervousness.

Block by block, the neighbourhood becomes more rundown and a far cry from the tourist-friendly centre of town we left just moments ago. We pull up outside a heavily barred house where he introduces me to a lady standing on her doorstep. Malena, a pretty, trim figure of around forty with a gap between her two front teeth, and her daughter, Malenita, greet Roberto and say a few words I don't understand.

Shyly, she greets me. "Hola, soy Malena y es mi hija, Malenita."

"She is a little shy at first, but just you wait, my friend," Roberto says to me with a smile. "She's just a little wary after hosting so many foreign students. Some can be quite a handful, you know. OK, hasta mañana." And with that he is gone.

The house is immaculately clean and has a shiny tiled floor that you can see your face in. Lived in by the family for over seventy years, it is well maintained, and loved. The collected photos and memorabilia of siblings past and present adorn every wall and horizontal surface. Statues of the Virgin Mary sit in every room, including the largest one in an illuminated glass box in the garden. The shrine of Mary and her outstretched arms stands at around four feet tall, positioned against the exterior wall of my room.

My detached purple cinderblock cube is built in the middle of the yard, with the odd brick left out here and there for ventilation. A forty-watt light bulb hangs from the ceiling and winks regularly as León deals with its daily electricity shortage. At the rear of the brick structure is a shower cubicle. The cube within the cube has a steel pipe sticking out of one wall and a stopcock tap below it to control the icy cold jet of over-chlorinated water that shoots from it. Images of disinfecting hose-downs described in various books I've read involving South American prisons and the foreigners locked up there for drug smuggling immediately come to mind.

I unpack my bag for the first time in six months and transfer the contents into the handle-less set of drawers. Apart from the stack of football shirts I've collected, I'm travelling with virtually nothing and haven't even noticed or cared. I've never been a person focussed on material goods, but my current lack of personal possessions has taken that to a whole new level. Sliding my now empty backpack under the bed, I feel an optimism sweep over me. Suddenly, I feel a sense of freedom.

I venture back into the house to see what's happening. Malena's cousin, Nelly, a slim girl with distinct indigenous features, is standing in the kitchen with a green parrot perched on her shoulder nibbling a brazil nut.

"Nelly, este hombre es Da... Darra... Dara...," she stutters, trying to pronounce my name. "¡Darío!" she cries, satisfied that she's found a substitute for a name she simply cannot pronounce.

"Hola," Nelly replies in a soft voice. "Me nam Nelly," she adds, trying her best to speak English.

Clapping her hands, Malena gets up from her seat and starts rummaging around in a broom cupboard. Without saying a word, she carries a box of brushes while Nelly follows her with two large sealed buckets out to the front veranda. I follow them and pick up a brush and dip it into one of the buckets.

"¡No! ¡No! ¡No te vas a ayudar!" they cry, both flapping their arms, telling me I can't help.

I assume that their resistance is because I'm the home stay guest; it's not customary to be helping with things such as painting. But my insistence wins them over. Which I'm glad about because what else am I going to do? Sit by and watch?

I climb up a ladder with my brush and paint pail to reach a higher place on the front wall of the house, and they again shout at me.

"¡No tocar las cables Darío!"

I've picked up the word 'cable' in that sentence – so I look up and see the concern: above me is a bare tangle of wires sticking from the wall – the cables that supply electricity to the house. I put two and two together. I move away from the cables, now mindful to avoid a high voltage zapping. *Dan would* love *these for a photo,* I think to myself.

And so we continue with the painting for a while. Malena turns the stereo on inside the house, sending a volume of reggaetón tunes out into the street. She then reappears with three glasses of dark rum.

"¡Toma! ¡Toma, Darío!" she says, handing me up a glass, now swaying to the music.

Applying a coat of black paint to the bars that protect the windows, I laugh at the tiled floor below me that's slowly becoming splashed with paint. The girls, now covered from head to toe, obviously don't realise the paint is dripping from their brushes. Nelly picks up on this and fires a smirk.

"¡Oye!" she says to Malena, laughing. "¡Es rierse de nosotros! ¡Malo!" I can tell she's informed Malena that I'm laughing at them and their messy brushwork. I laugh too, feeling like I'm making headway with this family.

We continue with our work until it's too dark to see and clear up the mess before going inside. In helping them with such a simple task, I've won their trust and broken the ice between us, and, sitting down on my bed, my anxiety and nerves from earlier have all but vanished. I've overcome what I've been putting off for so long.

I'm snapped out of my dreamy state of self-satisfaction when Malena calls me inside to eat. This will be the next challenge: sharing a meal.

Plastic bags of tacos in sour cream, similar to the ones we'd eaten at the border, are placed on plates on the dining table. Sitting at the table is a large, pock-cheeked man who stinks of rum.

"¡Raphael!" Malena says, addressing the man. "Es Darío, estudiante."

Before we can be properly introduced, the thump of little feet can be heard descending the wooden spiral staircase.

"Malenita, es Darío," Malena says. "Venga." – 'Come.'

No more than ten years old and dressed in a Miley Cirus t-shirt and jeans, the girl shyly approaches. She then sees her Dad.

"¡Hola Papi!" she shouts excitedly, hugging him tight and looking at me.

"Mi hija," Raphael says, ruffling her hair. "¿Como estas, niña?"

"Bien, bien," she replies before running off back upstairs.

Redirecting his attention to me, Raphael shakes my hand. "Mucho gusto hombre. ¿Como te llamas?"

He slurs, stinking of alcohol and asking my name, even though Malena has already introduced me seconds before.

"Me llamo Darío," I say, timidly trying out my Spanish.

"Ah," he says, relating my new name to León's famous poet. "Como Rueben Darío." He seems satisfied. "Que bueno nombre, chele."

The word 'chele' is something I come to hear very often, and at first feels derogatory, but after hearing it used as commonplace as it is, it's meant more endearingly. Slang for white person, it's basically an anagram of the word 'Leche' – milk, and refers to the pasty colour of the skin compared to the caramel brown of the Nicaraguan people.

Raphael invites me out to the front porch for a shot of rum. Sitting down, I can feel what's coming as he puts his massive arm round me.

"¿Te crees en Jesús Cristo, chele?" he asks me, questioning my stand on religion and blowing a cloud of rum-soaked breath into my face. Not of the religious persuasion, but wanting to make things easy, I decide a little white lie won't hurt. So I tell him that I do. This pleases him immensely, and he puts his other hand on my leg, squeezing my inner thigh with his chubby fingers. When he leans in towards me, I'm not sure if he's going to bite my ear off or kiss me.

"Hey, muchacho, you like girls?" he asks in bad English with a smile and a wink.

"Si," I reply, now a little scared.

"OK," he says in a stern tone, seemingly happy that I'm not gay. "Aquí en Nicaragua, nos tenemos las mujeres mas bonitas del mundo."

I am glad the conversation has shifted to more comfortable ground, as he tells me of the beautiful girls here.

"Si," I reply, trying desperately to widen the gap between our faces.

He then blindsides me with his next comment. "Nelly, she need good man, that girl, but you no touch Malena, OK?"

Whoa, I think to myself.

"No! No!" I answer quickly. "Of course not."

"OK, bueno, chele." He smiles and releases his grip on my leg.

I sit with him on the veranda like a stunned mullet while he leers and whistles at young girls who pass in the street. He insists I help him finish the bottle of rum.

CHAPTER SIXTY-ONE
LIFE IN LEÓN

I have opted for the 8am – midday slot at school. I wake at 7am to Malena's voice.

"¡Desayuno, Darío!" she calls, informing me my breakfast is ready.

Nelly is already up and applying black eyeliner in the kitchen, while a plate of eggs, beans and tortillas are waiting for me at my place at the table.

"¿Quieres caminar conmigo?" Nelly asks.

Trying to think quickly and decipher what she's just said, I fail and run her sentence back and forth, slowly breaking it down. I know that 'caminar' means to walk, so I'm presuming that she's asking me to accompany her to work.

"Sí, OK," I say, hoping it's the correct reaction.

The house is situated in the San José suburb of León where its narrow, cracked sidewalks that line the potholed streets are paved with slippery bathroom tiles. Careful not to slip, we pass one shop after the next as squeaky roller doors are wound up and iron bars covering windows are removed for the day of trading. As we reach the block before the church, Nelly waves me goodbye and crosses through a plaza under a line of jocote trees towards her shop. The dense foliage of these trees harbours tropical birds that twitch and shudder the branches with a deafening din. I am amazed by the sheer volume of the things hiding in there. I continue on, the various market stalls that pop up around the main cathedral are already set up and waiting for the day to start.

"Tarjetas postales, chele," an old wrinkled woman says, approaching me and presenting a basket of postcards depicting scenes from the revolution. "Para comprar, chele," she adds.

Hmm, I think to myself. *'Comprar' is the word for 'buy'.*

"¿Cuánto vale?" I blurt out, asking how much with a phrase from my limited Spanish.

"Cinco, mi amor," she replies, holding her hand out.

Five córdoba, I think to myself. *That's twenty cents, more or less.*

"OK, cinco, por favor." I want five of them. From the look on her face, I just made her day.

"Gracias, gracias, mi amor." She beams a giant grin up at me that adds to her wrinkle count as I turn and continue on.

Conducting these interactions alone, as mundane as they are, satisfies me intensely.

"¡Buenos dias, Darren!" Roberto greets me. "Your teacher is not here yet, but here is some coffee." He points at a shiny plunger and a stack of plastic cups. I nervously pour myself one.

Six tables sit around the edge of the school's courtyard. I take a seat with a feeling I've not had since starting high school twenty years ago.

Two other students sit down in the courtyard and I reciprocate their waves without getting up. I'm not interested in chit-chat.

"Darren, this is Eva." Roberto introduces me and plugs in a fan for us. "I will bring you some test papers to complete, so we can figure out what we should work on with you."

"Hola. ¿Como está?" Eva says, shaking my hand and putting her bag down. This Mestizo girl standing in front of me has divine caramel-coloured skin and mesmerising brown eyes. She also happens to be my teacher, so I check myself and behave like a good schoolboy.

"Hola," I say sheepishly, not wanting to make a fool of myself by trying to say anything else.

Our morning begins with getting to know each other and filling in the test sheets that Roberto brings us. Eva has a good grasp of English and after only five minutes or so can tell that she's going to need to use it a lot with me.

Studying child psychology in university and raising two daughters under five, it's a wonder she finds time to teach in the school. Her wages are the sole income for her family, apart from the donations from her mother-in-law, who regularly drip-feeds a small amount of cash through her son, Eva's husband.

I would like to say I gleaned all that in her native language on my first day – but the truth is she told me a little about herself in English, and Roberto filled in the rest.

Malena is on the couch when I return from morning lessons – drinking rum with a friend. "¡Darío! ¡Darío!" she calls, pointing at my lunch on the kitchen table.

"Y entonces Darío, la escuela. ¿Cómo está?" she asks from across the room.

I run her question though my head. Escuela – school. ¿Como está? – how is it?

"¡Bien, gracias!" I reply, tucking in to my plate, tearing the warm tortillas apart and making little fish tacos. We awkwardly try to have a conversation while I eat before her patience wears thin and she continues in Spanish with her friend and the rum.

I decide to make a point of doing at least three hours of homework every afternoon; if I'm really going to make a dent in this language, I'm going to need to study hard. Malenita is usually home in the afternoons and always keen to play in the garden. She's a great help to my learning process and, at seven years old, well ahead of me with her Spanish. But it's still easier for me than trying to talk with adults. By helping her with her English homework, I contribute something to her learning, and we gradually form a bond. Being with her is good for me, and this kind of learning is a break from homework.

The following day, Eva seems suspicious when I tell her about my flash lunch – the fish, the tortillas, the special care around the food.

"No es normal." She seems puzzled. "What have you done there? Students don't usually get meals like that."

"Well, I helped to paint their house on the first day I moved in," I tell her, offering up a reason.

"Haha," she says. "¡Por *eso*!"

CHAPTER SIXTY-TWO
STAYING PUT

Eva and I openly talk about a range of topics during lessons; the learning environment is comfortable, and we are able to laugh and joke while staying within the curriculum that Roberto has structured and set in place. She opens up about her problems at home.

"My husband, he's very lazy," she begins. "He studied politics, but cannot get a job because of his hatred for the government we have at this time. He supports the other party, but they are small and have no jobs."

Not wanting to get too deep into her personal life, I suggest we go for an outside-the-classroom excursion. My desire to integrate as much as possible with the culture and people of León leads me to try a little shopping. Entering shops has been a daunting experience for me, especially as Dan and I have always chosen the more local places. Now I feel I'm ready to give it a go in León.

When Eva says yes, I am excited.

My confidence grows with my native escort and teacher; perusing the shelves is a more relaxed experience. Heads turn as we wander the aisles – and Eva now feels watched, too, as the other patrons want to know why we're together.

"Would you like to meet my daughters, Florencia and Dani?" she asks one day. "We can go to my mother-in-law's house during the morning break and say hi."

"I would love to!" I can only assume our outing to the shops has increased her confidence in me, and I relish the thought of being with another family of such a different culture to the one I was brought up in.

"We're going to go for a walk in the town," Eva tells Roberto, as we pass him in the foyer of the school. "I think it will be good for him to learn some of León's history."

"OK, no problem," Roberto answers without looking up from his computer screen.

The walking pace of a Nicaraguan is approximately ten times slower than what I'm used to. Nicaraguans don't walk; they shuffle, they crawl at a snail's pace. Perhaps it's to conserve energy in the baking hot sun. I find myself tailgating people on the tiny sidewalks in my unnecessary haste. Eva constantly tells me to slow up.

"Can you walk on the road?" she asks me, as we turn a corner in the town centre.

"Why?" I ask her, puzzled. "You want me to get run over?"

"No, of course not," she says seriously. "You're too tall and we're almost the same level when you're down there." She points at the gutter.

Great. I'm to walk in the gutter.

But what she says is true. I am not even six feet, but I tower over Nicaraguans, who, much like the rest of Central Americans, are by and large a lot shorter in stature than someone with European genes. By now I've grown accustomed to standing in a crowd like a tall mushroom sticking out of a patch of short grass, to looking down on round heads of shiny black hair.

So I stay on the road for the rest of the way – *do as the teacher says, Darío.*

We arrive at Grandma's house. A large grill of vertical bars covers an open window through which Eva calls. "¡Mariella! ¡Soy yo!"

The thick wooden door creaks open and we enter into a room where shelves of books stretch to the ceiling and two rocking chairs stand on a red tiled floor.

"¡Mamá! ¡Mamá!" cries a small girl as she runs in and hugs Eva around the top of her legs.

Without even being introduced, I immediately fall in love with this child. A kind-faced, miniature version of Eva, she looks up at me conspicuously with bright eyes.

"Es Darío," Eva introduces me. "Mi Alumna." She turns to me. "Darío, mi hija, Florencia."

"Hola," I say in a soft voice, bending down and shaking her little hand.

"Hola, Darío," she replies in the cutest squeaky little voice. "¿Es como Rueben Darío?" she adds. A tune from the television in the other room interrupts us and Florencia runs off and jumps in a hammock hanging from the ceiling.

"Dora the Explorer," Eva says. "¡Ella la encanta!"

My mind clicks into break-down mode. 'Encantar' is to like very much.

Through a doorway I see a tiny baby wrapped up and in a hammock. *Must be Dani, the new addition,* I think to myself. And I'm once again baffled at how it's possible to work, teach and care for a family on a pittance.

There's a grunt from the living room.

"¡Carlos!" Eva snaps. "Es Darío, mi alumna."

The balding man sitting on the plush couch in the other room twists his flabby neck and stares at me. "Buenas dias," he grunts, uninterested.

Fat, unemployed and lazy, Carlos spends his days watching TV. He is at the beck and call of his mother, who is constantly at odds with Eva. If this isn't bad enough, he also has two kids from a previous marriage who now live in the US with their mother and are sent down to stay once a year during the school holidays. They are visiting now, so I make the pleasure of their acquaintance, too: they sit at the dining table, rudely sniggering like spoilt brats when their meagre lunch is placed in front of them.

"I'm paying for that," Eva whispers to me, "And look at the thanks they give."

At first I'd thought Eva had embellished her stories of home, that her whining is mostly boredom, especially since the new baby was an unexpected addition to a family already under financial strain. But after meeting her husband – if you can call our brief exchange a 'meeting' – I am filled with sympathy. And I'm won over by her positive attitude to push on, to stay strong and keep a brave face for her children. Something here begins to chip away at my First World way of thinking. I think more and more about our easy everyday life back home, and how insignificant the things we complain about really are. I am feeling something change inside – and it's not from just learning the language a little, but from the view I have into everyday life in a place I'd never dreamed of seeing or living in. I feel a shift in how I look at – and act in – the world.

"¡Hola Darío!"

I'm greeted by Malena at the front door as she sells cellphone credit to a customer. The red 'Claro' and 'Tigo' logos that hang from the front wall next to where she stands inform people it's a place to buy such things.

"¡Hola!" I reply feeling welcomed and push through the louvered saloon doors in to the kitchen where Nelly is sat at the dining table crying.

"¿Que paso, Nelly?" I ask her.

"Su pájaro se fue," Malena answers, informing me that her parrot has flown away. "No es buena mascota."

Not a good pet – it almost makes me laugh, but I see she is distraught.

"Era salváje y de los árboles del Merced," she continues, adding that it was a wild parrot from the Jocote trees next to the Merced church that I walk past in the mornings.

I invite her to the movies, feeling sorry for her and hoping to cheer her up.

"OK, si, gracias." She looks slightly cheerier, while Malena shoots a raised eyebrow at me from the kitchen.

The little theatre is the only place in town with air-conditioning, and at three dollars a film is a pretty cheap way of cooling down in the sweltering tropical heat. We choose the comedy *The Hangover*. It provides suitable entertainment and sends us walking home giggling. It's not a film I would choose to watch again, but over the course of my stay, I end up watching it three more times: the air-conditioned relief of the theatre lures me in, and the only other option is *Alvin and the Chipmunks 3*.

With daily morning sessions at school, an unspoken feeling begins to surface between Eva and me. It happens quickly, in our first week of lessons. All I can think about is being alone with her. I am in a quandary. *She's married and we're from very different cultures,* I tell myself in an effort to stop my desire. Besides, I know I'm walking a fine line: if I overstep, I could go and fuck everything up; our friendship and my lessons would be in ruins. On the other hand, I can't overlook her meticulous attention to make-up and clothing – and I am not imagining the little indicators that she's thinking of me too. I know I should distance myself from the situation. I know I should worry about her fat slobby husband and any retribution he might take against me. But I become lost in my fantasy of getting it on with my Spanish teacher. I can't help myself.

I book another week of lessons.

Friday comes around quickly. I haven't seen Dan for five days, so I walk down to the hostel. But I'm shocked when the reception guy tells me he's no longer there. *What the fuck?* I think to myself. How could he just leave without saying goodbye? My paranoia kicks in and I start to wonder if he's gapped it because I left him on his own. I guess he really didn't want me to break away for my language course after all.

"Yo!" I hear a voice from across the street. "I'm over here now!"

Dan shouts from the opened-walled bar of the other hostel that we'd talked about moving to when we first arrived in León.

"Fuck! I thought you'd left!" I say, relieved and hugging him.

"Nah, no chance of that, bro!" he assures me. "It's so fucking cheap to stay here. This is exactly what I've been after the whole time."

Dan is in his element: drinking all day and playing pool with the Nicaraguan locals who hang out at the hostel, Dan is happy. He's in no rush to move on, and now that we live across town from each other, all the tension between us seems to have dissolved. Having a beer with him is once again enjoyable.

"So what have you been up to?"

"Absolutely fuck all, bro." He smiles contentedly.

CHAPTER SIXTY-THREE
LEÓN VIEJO

The ruins of León Viejo, situated on the northeastern shore of Lake Managua and founded by the Spanish in 1524, is the original site of León before being abandoned after the 1610 earthquake. Gradually buried by frequent eruptions from the volcano, Momotombo, until its discovery in 1967, it's a humble site in comparison to others such as Tikal in Guatemala. Even so, an impressive majority of the town's foundations are still intact.

"If you can pay the gas money, maybe Carlos will take us in the truck," Eva suggests, adding that it's a great opportunity for Florencia to see the ruins for the first time.

"Yeah, maybe Dan would like to come," I say, thinking out loud.

"OK," she agrees. "Then it's better for price too. I will ask this afternoon and we can go on Thursday morning?"

When I ask Dan to join us later that day, he immediately agrees. "Yeah, I should probably see something of interest. Furthest I've been since we arrived is the beach."

Thursday rolls around and Carlos and Eva pull up at the kerb outside the school in a brown, dented, late-model Toyota pick-up truck. Embarrassingly, Dan still hasn't arrived and I'm beginning to wish I'd never invited him in the first place. He shows up ten minutes late and it is clear he has crawled out of bed moments ago. He stinks of beer.

"Bro, I took those blue pills last night," he says.

"The ones the girl in the San José hostel gave you?" I ask.

"Yup. They knocked me out." He rubs his head.

We squeeze into the back with the overly excited Florencia and her cousin Eduardo, who's also joining us for the trip. I'm pretty excited about experiencing a day trip with real locals.

At the petrol stop, Carlos gets out and starts filling the tank.

"I think it will be around 300 córdoba," Eva says, turning round to us in the back.

"I didn't bring my wallet," Dan remarks, looking at me.

"What?!" I snap at him furiously. "Dude, we can't expect them to pay the gas. It's like half a week's wages." I am fuming at his stupidity.

"Can't you just pay it and I'll pay you back? It's no big deal," he says in his oh-so-familiar blasé tone.

"No! I can't," I reply. "I've only brought 200!"

Eva overhears and takes a 100-córdoba bill from her purse and begrudgingly adds it to my cash.

"I'll bring you the money to school tomorrow," I assure her, "Dan will get it out when we get back." I fire him a pissed-off glare.

The car park at the entrance to the ancient ruins is jam-packed with old American school buses full of children. From the top opening of the bus windows flutters an almost continuous stream of chocolate bar wrappers and plastic bags that float through the air and end up entangled in the surrounding bushes. Nicaragua has not come to terms with its enormous litter problem. The school children have arrived, presumably, to learn about their history – but they are blithely trashing the existing space they live in, with no regard for the future. It is mind-boggling for someone coming from a place where the three Rs – renew, reuse, recycle – is drilled into us from a young age, where school trips are organised just for beach clean-up. This country has a long way to go in changing how the people discard their unwanted rubbish.

A dirt path leads to the area that was once the town's plaza where a pink and beige monument depicting a Cacique figure stands. This muscular chief represents the Chorotega people who farmed and lived peacefully on the land before the Spanish conquerors invaded. This site marks the place where a horrific mass murder of eighteen indigenous people was carried out by mad dogs in a closed-off arena, while the Spanish watched, cheering. The monument is a gruesome reminder, complete with a ferocious dog biting on the chief's leg. But the locals view it as a commemoration of the indigenous people's resistance to the Spanish conquerors. I am disturbed by the monument itself: it represents savagery and cruelty in the extreme. Of course, it's just one more example in a long and brutal tradition of one people conquering another. Such plazas form the centre of every town, every city, marking the frequent scenes of horror – from modern regimes, too. Dismemberment, disembowelling, decapitation. Tearing apart by horses, sawing in half, burning. These are just some of the ways humans have inflicted destruction on other humans.

I seem to be the only one moved by this violent history and the images it conjures. The schoolchildren squeal and kick cans in the parking lot. Florencia and Eduardo have found a hicoro tree and are throwing the hard green pods that grow from its trunk at each other. Dan also seems rather bored and chain-smokes with a far-off stare in his eyes. I reckon he's dreaming of cold beer and the pool back at the hostel.

I'm pulled back to the present when Florencia calls to me. "¡Hombros! ¡Hombros Darío!" she says, indicating that she wants to sit up on my shoulders. Obliging, I lift her up and run around the grounds pretending to be a horse until I can no longer stand the heat, and setting her down she runs back to her mother who's now staring at the pointy cone of the volcano and the small waves that lap at its muddy shoreline. Eva breaks her stare across the water and suggests we visit Carlos' great-grandmother in the adjacent town of La Paz Centro.

We come to a ramshackle settlement of colourful adobe houses, where a lingering scent of burning plastic floats in the air as the townsfolk sit in rocking chairs dissolving their household rubbish on bonfires. The old lady we're visiting is 104 years old, wheelchair-bound, practically blind and under full-time care. She's without doubt the oldest person I've ever met and probably ever will. The family spends a fleeting moment with her over glasses of juice.

No doubt she has lived a very clean life to get to such an age.

And yet – Nicaragua seems a country on the verge of destroying itself with all its rubbish. We drive away with the black smoke from discarded plastic pluming into the air. I marvel again at the idea of living to 104.

Driving home, Florencia, picks a 50 Cent song on her mum's phone and recites it word for word in an American gangster accent. Sitting next to her, I can't decide if it's hilarious or disturbing that this American rapper is so familiar to someone so young and innocent.

Hoes, bitches and weed – these topics carry us down the road. I hum along.

CHAPTER SIXTY-FOUR
THE WATERBED

Dan and I sit with a beer. We've returned to his hostel to get the gas money he owes Eva. "You like her, eh?" he says to me, swigging from his bottle. "She's real cute."

"Nah, I don't like her like that," I reply, unconvincingly. "We're just good friends."

He knows I'm lying. "You like her."

Back at the house, a thin, rat-faced builder is clambering about on my roof, fixing on new sheets of corrugated iron.

"Es Cesar," Malena tells me from the back of the garden where she's hanging out washing. "Se reparar el techo. He fix roof."

"Hola Cesar," I greet him, waving up.

"Buenas," he says, wiping the sweat from his brow before climbing down and bumming a cigarette from me.

Next day, I feel sheepish when I arrive at lessons. "Here you go," I say to Eva, handing her Dan's gas money. "I'm sorry about that."

"Gracias," she says, looking happy to see me. "You were very quiet yesterday."

"I'm nervous trying to speak Spanish when Dan is around," I explain. "He has this thing about always correcting me."

"I thought so," she agrees.

"We are going to Las Peñitas for a day this weekend," she says. "Carlos has a house there. Would you like to come?"

"Yes of course!" I answer, always keen for an adventure.

At the end of the week, I find myself once more in the back of the brown pick-up truck, tickling Florencia while Carlos and Eva talk in the front. My grasp of Spanish is definitely improving as I'm able to understand so much more of other people's conversations and I'm speaking the language (albeit a bastardised version) more than I am English now. Carlos is saying something about preparing the house to try and sell it and Eva is disagreeing with him, telling him he should keep it for when the children grow up.

Understanding key snippets of sentences gives me such a sense of achievement. I've come a long way since feeling left out of the Bolivian card games up in the salt flats.

The twisted concrete structure sits a block back from the beach and, although cute and positioned on a sizable plot, is in dire need of repair. A large crack runs down both walls in the centre of the house and the two rooms are full of old furniture covered in cobwebs.

"It has leaks in the roof that we need to fix," Eva says, pointing at the terracotta roof tiles above us where light leaks in and casts beams across the dusty air of the interior. I think of Cesar climbing around on my roof back in León. While Carlos surveys the house and then leaves to return to the city, the two girls and I head across the road to get some lunch in a beach bar and settle in for the afternoon. Florencia runs into the sand and starts digging a hole.

"¡Darío! ¡Darío!" she calls, beckoning me to join her.

But I'm not ready to go dig in the sand. I'm enjoying my drink with Eva too much. We are sitting at the table, looking out to sea, the tension between us palpable. We talk about the clouds. We talk about the sea. We talk about Florencia. We don't talk about our feelings for each other. Our situations are so different. This is her home, her world. I only live in it fleetingly and superficially, at best. I want to touch her, to reach across the tension. But it would be selfish to make an advance on her and then leave in a few weeks. It would be far too easy for me to leave, and for me to leave her behind. As the sun glints on the water, I imagine the pieces her life might be in if I shattered what little stability she has achieved.

"¡Darío! ¡Darío!" Florencia shouts again. "¡Vamos a nadar!"

I make to get up and swim.

"Oye, con mucho cuidar por fa," Eva tells me sternly, warning me of the dangerous rips.

"¡Dame la mano!" I say to Florencia, grabbing her hand as we enter into the water.

The waves are ferocious and the undercurrents unbelievably

strong. Holding on to this small child is harder than I'd imagined. A big wave nails us, and her hand slips from mine. For a split second I watch as she's sucked away from me in the strong rip between the fierce waves, but I lunge and lock on to her arm. I fight my way back in, collapsing on the beach but glad she's with me.

"¡Yo te dije!" Eva says, angry that I did not heed her warning. "It's dangerous!"

"OK, OK, lo siento," I apologise, drying us off in the shade of the grass umbrella.

We wait for the bus in awkward silence. I feel bad I let Eva down. I feel a fondness for Florencia like I've not felt before. Bumbling along on our return bus ride, I realise how attached I am to them, how much I love spending time in their company. There's a real bond between me and Florencia, and I think it's bringing Eva and me even closer together.

Which makes me both happy and confused.

Darkness falls and we part ways taking separate taxis back to León from the Subtiava suburb terminal. Exiting the taxi in León's centre, I'm startled to hear my name shouted from across the busy intersection. Malena and Nelly stand outside a taco stand waving their arms and beckoning me over with big smiles.

"¡¿Quieres tacos, Darío?!" Malena asks as I reach them.

"¡Si! ¡Por favor!" I say, now famished.

We walk back to the house. With Nelly and Malena I'm happy – but not confused as I am with Eva. My relations with Eva are far more complex than the platonic ones with the family. Our easy conversations create a connection I've been dreaming about for the past six months. Our chatter gets easier by the day, now that I'm fully immersed in the language.

"What did Raphael say when you first met him?" Malena curiously asks me in Spanish while we munch on our tacos.

Speaking slowly and trying not to fumble my words, I recall the moment as best I can, explaining how he'd grabbed my leg and warned me off her.

"¡Dios mio!" she exclaims. "¡Que hombre!" She laughs and puts her hand on my shoulder in sympathy. She shakes her head when I elaborate about our porch chat, and his advice-slash-warning.

"What's the deal with him?" I ask her in Spanish.

"Ah, we've been apart for a long time," she explains. "He got too violent when he drank, so I kicked him out. He still lives up the street with his mother and just won't let go."

I meet Dan later on for a beer at his hostel, and he tells me of his plans to leave in the next few days for Guatemala.

"It's even cheaper up there," he says, lighting a cigarette. "I'm gonna go to Estelí first, then up there. The girls from New York – the ones who came along on the weekend in Las Peñitas, you know? – also want to leave, so they're joining up with me."

I nod. I don't say a word. This means that I'll finally be here in León alone – a scary but exciting thought.

As Dan and I finish our beer, the heavens open and the city is deluged by a storm of epic proportions. As if a giant bucket is emptied from above, water fills the roads within minutes. A fork of lightning strikes a power plant and leaves half the city in darkness. I wait it out at Dan's hostel. When the rain finally ceases, I walk home precariously and fully aware of how slippery those bathroom tiles are that pave the sidewalks. I sit on the side of my bed and hear a splashing sound. I stand and sit again. More splashing. I lie back to a squelching noise. Squish, squish. It's a waterbed.

I lower my head between my legs and see my mattress is completely water-logged and dripping into a huge puddle on the tiled floor. I don't want to cause a fuss, so finding my head torch, I unravel my roll mat and fashion a pillow from a handful of underwear and socks. From the bottom of my backpack, I pull my sleeping bag out and bed down in the corner of the room in the only dry spot.

Cesar has been on my roof all week. Between smoking all my cigarettes and disappearing for hours on end to the hardware store, only five houses down the street, he has banged nails through the sheet metal into the roof joists. He has done this with great vigour. There are many new nails in my roof, and many new holes. None of them have been sealed.

An incident such as this would result in Cesar's termination of employment and a sincere apology anywhere else, but my story the following morning has Malena in tears of laughter.

"Ai Ai Ai, Darío, Darío, Darío," she cackles, chuckling and making light of the situation before phoning Cesar to bring a tube of silicone sealant over.

CHAPTER SIXTY-FIVE
HOLY COMMUNION

September is a month of almost constant celebration in León. The sounds of fireworks exploding above fill the air. They commemorate one or another saint or religious event daily. When I say *daily*, I mean beginning at 4am daily and then sporadically throughout the day; and when I say *fireworks*, I mean deafening air bombs that explode with an ear-splitting crack without warning.

Unperturbed by these surprise explosions and determined to get a better handle on the Spanish language, I book in another six weeks of school. Studying intensively alone in my room after lessons in the afternoons, I am pushing myself every day. My brain is tired by the time dinner rolls around but I'm beginning to understand more and more and the rapport I have with Malena and the family is building my confidence in speaking in the native tongue.

"Cuando sueñes el idioma, vos la tiene," Malena says, one evening at dinner.

'When you dream in Spanish, you're there.'

Our street outside the house is like any other in León. The scent of warm tortillas wafting fragrant on the hot breeze can be smelt several times a day. The most common types being sold are either plain tortillas or 'rellenos' – the stuffed version, usually full of pork or chicken and a selection of vegetables and rice. Wrapped in tea towels, the tortilla stacks sit in bowls that balance on the heads of the women shouting into the sky, making everyone aware they have stock to sell. They choose the quiet periods in the day and shuffle through the slow hum of the streets mid-morning and afternoon.

As well as these regular local passers-by, a colourful spectrum of pedestrians also roams the streets, especially a bizarre duo of two brothers: tall and lanky and both with heads of natty unwashed hair, they clear a wide path through the other pedestrians sharing the sidewalk. One wears nothing apart from a mini skirt created from plastic bottles hanging off a string belt around his waist while the other wanders completely naked.

"¡Muy grande Darío!" shouts Malena, crying with laughter and pointing at the dick swinging between the naked brother's legs as he shuffles up the street. She laughs harder when she sees my reaction. "Ai Darío," she continues in a sympathetic voice. "Es normal aquí, no te preocupes."

Not to worry: this is *normal*. Later, at school, Eva explains that Nicaragua cannot afford to run institutions such as mental homes – and that sights like this are a common part of everyday life. The country has been in tatters since the revolution and the people have become immune to these harsh realities.

Tomorrow celebrates Malenita's First Communion. An important part of the Catholic culture, this religious ceremony involves children usually of around eight years, all smartly dressed in suits and white wedding dresses – a celebration of the child's first reception of the Holy Eucharist. For me, it's an utterly foreign concept. I grew up in a family not particularly devoted when it came to attending church. For me, this was a cultural experience sure to be extraordinary.

"Can I join you in church tomorrow?" I ask Malena. Her startled expression reveals she is clearly shocked by my request. But she smiles, nods.

The house has an air of activity the following morning as Malena, already dressed in a tight but elegant red satin dress prepares Malenita for her big day, fixing her hair, adjusting her in the white dress and helping her with the lace gloves and veil that she'll be wearing. It's a lot of material; it's a lot of frill. I wonder if my only partly unwrinkled slacks will do. I watch as Malenita meticulously tucks herself and the dress into the back seat, paying a great deal of attention to keeping it from dragging on the ground. I climb in after, worried I may sit too close, or crush some of the delicate flowers on the hem. I try to keep a safe distance, but we're squeezed together. I am relieved when we arrive, only minutes later, outside the church, where a group of parents and children all stand in anticipation of the big day.

I sit alone, just off to the side of chattering families. Soon quiet falls and I can tell from the change in mood that things are about to begin. There's a serious air in the church. I'm sweating – but I figure the kids are sweating more, in all that lace and finery.

The interior of the church is spectacular. Dark wooden fittings and walls painted white, with tall stained glass windows on all sides. The heavy door we came through remains open so a slight breeze enters the already cool interior. There are twenty or so hardwood pews on either side. The walls are decorated from top to bottom with glittering gold and silver, the grandeur of it shimmering impressively behind the pulpit. It's very ornate inside – not what I expected at all. Wonderfully elegant flower displays adorn the various pedestals that bookend each pew.

Soon the ceremony begins. We're asked to stand as the procession begins. I rise with the congregation. I stick out like a windsock. Being the tallest and only non-Nicaraguan among the churchgoers, I tower over the congregation. I hear whispers all around, but I have no idea what they are saying – and I think it rude to draw any more attention to myself by asking. Later, I find out the whispers revolve around whether or not I'm Malena's new partner.

As the organ pipes up, the children follow the priest down the centre aisle to the front of the church. I am mesmerised as eight boys and girls dressed in their fancy attire are taken through a ritual of speeches and blessings. But my pleasure ends when the high-pitched priest wails psalms from the Bible. This seems to go on forever, and I'm beginning to regret asking if I could attend. But it ends quite abruptly, and before I can grasp what's happening, the children run off to a side room of the church. The atmosphere shifts dramatically as balloons and cake take centre stage in the same side room and a Mariachi band play their brass instruments off to the side while the children, now armed with sticks, smash the shit out of a huge piñata swan that hangs from a roof truss. The large papier maché bird hangs on for as long as possible until a final whack rips its guts open and spills a pile of sweets all over the floor. This sends the kids into a frenzy as they all dive on the spoils and swim around on the ground fighting over it. I can imagine the horror on my mother's face if I were to swim around in a smart suit she'd paid for but the parents of these children don't bat an eyelid as if it's part of the process.

The party back at the house shifts the mood further. The deafening volume of cumbia music, plus festive streamers and balloons, fill the lounge while children juiced up on fizzy drink run around and dance like wind-up toys. The mothers are more subdued and sit chatting and laughing but as the night goes on, they too begin to loosen up and migrate to the dance floor. Being one of the only three males in the house, I am encouraged – no, forced – to dance with every one of them. I oblige, of course. It's no tribulation. But I am born with British genes, cursed with possessing not one rhythmic bone in my body. I spend the evening under a disco ball, twirled around by 50-year-old women half my height with moves that make me feel like I'm made of stiff cardboard.

Afterward, I help Malena with the clean-up. I clear dishes while she climbs a ladder to unhook the decorations from the ceiling. I come through the kitchen door to see her looking unbalanced on the chair she's teetering on, and I rush to steady her. My hands grip her firm hips. As she turns around on the chair, she bends down and pushes her plump cleavage into my face. *Just an accident*, I think. I keep my hands steadying her hips and take her weight so I can lower her. But before her feet touch the floor she wraps her legs around my middle. I'm shocked – stunned, even. She lunges in and kisses me. I hold onto her firmly and carry her, still wrapped around me, to the dining table – I sense she's not ready to let go.

We kiss for a while, drenched in sweat and panting for breath.

And then, we pull away from each other, and come to our senses. We sneak off, wordless, to our separate rooms.

Swinging in my hammock, surrounded by the torn decorations and carnage of the night before, I gaze around to see the house is an untidy mess.

We barely speak. I'm content that I've finally had some kind of sexual encounter but also like I've betrayed the code of ethics. Malena, I feel, also shares my thoughts. In one short night, the atmosphere has shifted: now everything is slightly uncomfortable. And I don't foresee the awkward feeling between us changing.

It's time to move on.

CHAPTER SIXTY-SIX
SAN SEBASTIÁN

I return to the hostel for an evening of music. Dan has since gone to Guatemala, making me officially solo for the first time since April. But I'm not solo for long: I meet a guy at a music gig in the hostel looking for a flatmate. Trent, a British fellow who reminds me of the height-challenged British '70s comedian Ronnie Corbett, has found a house for rent in the San Sebastián neighbourhood on the other side of town.

"How much is the place?" I ask him, hoping for the right answer.

"It's $100US each per month including power and water!" he shouts over the noisy band playing. "It's not flash but it's a good price for your own space."

"I'm in!" I shout back, confirming with a chink of our beer bottles.

Sitting down at the kitchen table the following morning, I break the news to Malena. Her face drops and I feel like crying. After showing me such warmth and hospitality, she's not ready to say goodbye to me. I couldn't feel any worse — I feel I'm letting them down somehow.

But it's definitely the time for a change of scene and I have to stick to my plan.

"¿Cuándo?" she asks solemnly, referring to my departure.

"Este es la última semana contigo," I reply, telling her this is my last week.

I meet Trent at the hostel, and we head down to the new house to meet the landlord for the finalities.

"Here she is!" Trent says in a very British way, pointing at the place.

Behind the parasite-tufted bombed ruins of San Sebastián Cathedral, overgrown and littered with drink cans, used toilet paper and piles of human shit, we come to a Spanish ruin. Half the cobbles in the narrow lane's surface are missing and a mangy grey horse tied by a rope to a cinderblock contentedly munches on the grass that grows out of the front wall. The edifice is painted in a shade of burnt orange and has a tall arched, double entrance door made of hardwood.

"¡Hola muchachos!" says a short guy in a pinstripe shirt. "¿Habla español?"

"¡Si, bastante!" Trent answers.

"OK, OK, bueno. Soy Rodrigo, ¿Y ustedes?" he says, asking our names.

"El es Trent, soy Darío," I answer.

"Ah, como Rueben Darío," he replies, predictably.

He opens the security bars and unlocks the door, and Trent and I walk into a high studded room with a pitched roof of clay tiles and a white porcelain tiled floor. Two rocking chairs sit alone in the vast space that leads to what looks like the kitchen area. A solid wooden table stands at one end of the back room while a low hung stainless steel sink is bolted to the rear wall.

"Whoa!" I yell, as a giant iguana the size of a small cat suddenly appears from behind the fridge and runs up the wall to a hole in the roof.

"No te preocupes, chele, es normal," our host assures us, referring to the lizard and telling us not worry.

He leads us through to the backyard, where we find three rooms next to each other in a line along one wall slathered in the same orange paint. Unfurnished, apart from guardless fans and rusty beds that have seen better days, they are divided by walls that finish a few feet from the ceiling – making any privacy virtually impossible. Tropical plants grow wild in the garden planters and a papaya tree hangs heavy with fruit.

"¿Es papaya?" Trent asks.

"¡Si, chele!" Rodrigo confirms, cutting one down. Taking a knife from his pocket, he cuts a slit down each seam of the fruit's skin and places it on the edge of the planter box. "Manana good," he tells us. "Hoy la leche no es bueno."

"What's he saying?" I ask Trent, who's listening intently. "The milk is bad in them, and we have to bleed them like this for a day before we eat them." Trent raises his little Ronnie Corbett eyebrows.

Rodrigo interrupts, "El techo tiene una fuga." He points at the roof. "Solo un poco de agua cuando hay llueve."

"Eh?" I ask again, turning to Trent.

"Part of the roof leaks a bit when it rains."

I think back to rat face Cesar the builder and my waterbed.

The neighbouring streets and buildings, I soon learn, are riddled with bullet holes. This particular area of León has suffered significantly due to its close proximity to the National Guard headquarters that was eventually stormed by the Sandinistas. Now that I've relocated to a new neighbourhood, I'm disoriented again – I have to learn once more where I should and shouldn't go. Roberto offers reassurance; he insists the area is safe. My confidence is somewhat restored, and I feel a new surge of independence. My walk to school each morning offers a refreshing change of scene to the busy straight road that I grew accustomed to as I walked from Malena's into the centre of town. Here, the streets are narrow and the buildings bleed history: unrepaired damage is everywhere, walls showing their scars from the revolution. Bullet holes that surround any window openings.

The quiet street that runs uphill alongside the neglected hospital opens out into a mess of colour, strong odours and noise. Plump women in frilly aprons sit on stools surrounded by blocks of white cheese and bunches of plantains in all their yellows shouting in fierce competition with each other while the traffic of buses and motorbikes clogs the square with a choking cloud of grey smoke.

Settling in to the new accommodation, Trent and I haggle with a guy at the markets and get a couple of good quality hammocks for US $10 each to hang in the lounge. Rodrigo brings an old radio round for us to use and the space starts to look lived in. Lying down in the hammock for the first time and staring into the rafters, I gaze and imagine life in my new surroundings: not as cheery, perhaps, as life with Malena and Malenita, but just as real.

I close my eyes and put my arms behind my head. I gently sway, contented. I feel good here.

A drip falls on my head.

"Is it raining?" I call out to Trent, somewhere out back. My eyes are still closed and the gentle sway still soothes.

"No way!" he shouts back.

I open my eyes and wipe the drip away. My fingers are smeared in a brown liquid. Directly above me are two jet black eyes looking down from the middle of a furry brown rat-like face.

I don't feel so good anymore.

"A massive bat!" I shout to Trent, swinging out of the hammock. "It's fucking shitting on my head!" Jumping up, I flick a tea towel upwards in its direction but it stands its ground, unperturbed.

"I think it's been living here a lot longer than us, mate," Trent says. "Just leave it." He sniggers at the smeared shit on my head.

"But what if it bites?" I ask him, not taking my eyes off the thing.

As if to punctuate my sentence – to show me who's in control here – the bat drops a pile of shit on the floor, leaves the rafter and swoops around the room in a circling motion, just missing our heads.

"Jesus!" I shout. "It's trying to attack us!"

Trent just looks at me and walks into the kitchen. "It's a fruit bat. It lives here, and it's not leaving," he says, making a sandwich.

After a few days, the furry creature's presence is something I get accustomed to, and we learn its routine, flying out through the back entrance at dusk, resuming its upside-down position on the same rafter before we wake in the mornings.

One morning, I push open the doors to the lounge.

"Shit! We left these closed all night!" I shout to Trent. "Check this out!"

The bat, that's had no way of escaping all night, has left a trail of shit all over the room.

"Oops," Trent remarks, ducking as the flying rat angrily swoops down from the roof and disappears into the garden.

Filling a bucket to clean up the shit, I tug on the kitchen tap – and it pulls away from the wall, sending a jet of water across the room and soaking us.

"Find the stopcock! Find the stopcock!" I shout to Trent, while trying – but failing – to block the jet that's drenching everything.

Trent tracks it down out on the street outside and shuts it off, but his efforts are all too late. We are up to our ankles in a diluted mix of water and Bat shit.

The week only gets worse for Trent.

I spend a couple of evenings alone in my rocking chair on the sidewalk at the front of the house, and I begin to wonder where he is. I know he's been seeing a local girl so maybe he's staying at hers. On the third day he emerges from his room, looking withdrawn and lifeless.

"What happened to you?" I ask him, dragging his chair outside next to mine and shocked at his appearance.

"I think I got bit by a mosquito that was carrying dengue fever," he replies, sitting down wearily and blowing his nose.

"Why didn't you say something?" I ask him, confused.

"Dude," he begins. "I couldn't even open my eyes the first day and what with the painful itchy rash all over my body and the hallucinogenic dreams it was giving me, I figured it was best to just stay out of your way."

"Jesus, Trent, I could have helped you," I say, feeling like I've let him down.

"The only thing you can do is take paracetamol tablets and drink lots of water; there's no cure as such. It's all good, man, nearly gone now." He rocks back in his chair.

But he's still weak and absent for the following few days, leaving me with a pretty boring week of evenings, my only company being the fruit bat, a hummingbird that flits around draining the papaya flowers of their nectar and the giant lizard, who continues to dart from behind the fridge when I least expect it.

CHAPTER SIXTY-SEVEN
THE RETURN OF JAN

Eva possesses a good level of English but will only use it when I am having a hard time understanding. During classes she reads my every expression; I try, unsuccessfully, to lie. She looks right through me when I tell her I understand what she's saying. Whenever she senses I'm having trouble, usually by my blank expression, she wiggles her fingers next to her head and makes a 'fsssssss' noise, indicating that my brain is short-circuiting. Today, I seem to be especially muddled.

"OK," she says, closing her book. "We go for a walk."

Shuffling along at Nicaraguan pace, with me on the road and her up on the sidewalk, Eva looks down at the litter that fills the gutter. Discarded ice cream wrappers and shrink-sealed water bags block the drains.

"These dogs are far skinnier in comparison to the mutts of other countries," I remark, trying to change the subject as we pass one sniffing the litter.

"Siiii, Nicaragua es el mas pobre de America Central."

And it's true: Nicaragua is the poorest in Central America. Even the dogs live a meagre existence.

Eva shares the story of the Russian circus that toured Nicaragua in the mid '90s. "While they were in town," she starts. "The majority of the dogs mysteriously disappeared from the streets."

"How come?" I ask, fearing the answer.

"The lions were hungry," she answers. "Free food."

The situation with Eva's husband becomes more intense when she receives an irate call from a woman in Managua claiming that he is also the father of her child. Eva doesn't believe it but still, it's a blow. Later, she confirms what the woman had said – and that the child in question was Florencia's 'cousin' Eduardo, who had come on the trip to León Viejo with us. I feel so sorry for Eva, and my feelings of endearment are becoming more complicated. Every time she confides in me, I feel us growing closer. Now that I'm living in my own space, all I need is an innocent reason to invite her over. I think of this constantly. I am torn about whether this is the right or wrong thing to do. But the pull is magnetic. And so, when she complains of sore shoulders and back, I offer a massage. She declines – three times. But the fourth time she complains, she agrees to a visit, and we arrange for the upcoming Friday when Trent will be in Managua extending his visa.

At 1pm there's a knock on the door and there she is, standing in my lane, looking more beautiful than ever.

"It's going to be my first massage," she tells me, looking a little worried.

"It will be fine, you'll feel much better and relaxed afterward," I assure her, hoping my desires are hidden from my facial expression. "Sit down here."

I point to a plastic seat in the garden. Standing behind her and exposing her shoulders, I slowly begin to rub in some baby oil and she scoops her thick long black hair up into a bunch. After ten minutes, her neck is loose and she's very relaxed. Bringing my head down to her level, I whisper in her ear. "Would you like me to work a little further down your back?"

"Mmm," she replies and we move into my room.

She lies on my bed facedown. I squat over her and undo her bra strap from behind. I caress and knead her shoulders. I wonder if I should advance down her back, or if I should let this go. I don't want to stop, but I can't be sure what she wants. Maybe this is, after all, just a massage.

In one swift motion, she grabs my hand and turns over, pulling me in. Our eyes meet and our lips join. The first kiss is pure passion, hunger. We spend the next two hours entwined in each other. Our tongues dance together like ribbons tangling in the wind, her curiosity insatiable, and her inexperience a turn-on.

Not just a massage, then.

Exhausted and lying on the bed, we stare at each other, a feeling between us that something special just happened.

"No quiero mas," she tells me as she goes to leave, stating unconvincingly she doesn't want any more. Paying no attention, I take her in my arms and kiss her. I slide the strap of her dress down her shoulder, slowly, and that's all it takes. We're back in my room to repeat the whole scene again.

During the next two weeks, we spend our daily walks in my room.

"We're going to study the historic buildings of the town," Eva tells Roberto daily, without waiting for his approval. He nods, approving of my deep interest in local history.

Successfully extending his Central American visa in Managua, and after bouncing back from the dengue incident, Trent is eager to move north and the balmy evenings sipping cold beers in our rocking chairs on the street outside the house are nearing an end.

"Let's do something before you go," I suggest. "There's a baseball game on today – what d'you reckon?"

"Yeah, something different sounds good."

Baseball is Nicaragua's national game and the fanatics who follow it rival the excited crowds of the soccer world. Joining these crowds for the León vs. Managua game at the war-torn stadium on the edge of town, we line up to buy tickets at a hole on the outside of the stadium wall. I sense many eyes among the spectators' queue on us, valuing perhaps our worth, and am glad I've only brought the equivalent of four dollars and dressed in my usual hobo fashion.

"Mas sencillo, chele," says the ticket seller with a frown as he hands me back my 100-córdoba bill.

"¿Sencillo?" I say to Trent. "Is it sold out? What does he mean?"

"The note's too big; he has no change. It's slang." Trent pays for us both with a smaller note.

The crowd's view is from a covered semi-circular concrete stand that sits at the pitcher end of the field. The opposing team is kept at a safe distance on the other side of a chain link fence that reaches all the way to the roof.

Portly old women in frilly aprons pace the perimeter carrying plastic bowls balanced on their heads. "¡Quesiiiiiiiillos! ¡Quesiiiiiillos!" they wail continuously, referring to the cheese-stuffed tortillas swimming in cream they're offering up.

Recently, I can sense how my Spanish is becoming more fluent. I love being in the crowd, the smell of those tortillas, the rush of the crowd. More and more, *I get by in Spanish*. I even *wake up* in Spanish some days. Just as Malena said, I have been waking in the mornings realising I've been dreaming Spanish. This pleases me immensely and pushes my confidence even further with everyday interactions.

But sometimes I still get things wrong.

If being the only two foreigners at the game isn't enough, after half an hour of cheering on León among a rabid crowd that jump and scream at a deafening volume, we realise we're in the wrong stands.

"I wondered about the funny looks," Trent says, laughing. I come to the realisation that even with my grip on Spanish, I'll always be a gringo.

The fenced in supporters behind the pitcher that we stupidly thought were the Managua fans are in fact the León crowd, but luckily our surrounding Managuans are too busy laughing at us to be angry that we're cheering on the opposing team. Estupidos gringos.

Now that Trent is leaving I need to find someone else for the room at the house. This proves to be easy; the first person I ask at school is interested. Christina, a pale-complexioned Italian girl with a bob of dark hair, is planning to stay in León for sixth months. She quickly agrees.

"Is perfect!" she says, walking onto the tiled floor of the lounge and looking up into the rafters. "I will take it."

Luckily, the bat is out today and, worried she'll change her mind, I fail to mention that it lives with us too.

I receive a surprise email from Jan to say he'll be stopping through on his way to Mexico and a day or so later catch up with him for an evening during his short stay.

"HEEEY!" he greets me at his hostel. "And where is zee president?"

"Ah, he left for Guatemala last week, man – you just missed him."

"No, zees is not great!" he says, disappointed. "But YOU! Look at zees!" he says putting his arm around me. "Zees is your place, Darren. You are so comfortable here, no?"

"Yeah, it's pretty cool, man, I like it a lot." I am proud of myself for going it alone.

"You have a girl here, I know eet!" Jan adds, putting his arm around me again.

I grin but keep mum.

Jan is determined to soak up at least three weeks of Mexico's beach life before he flies home, so he only stays a night before moving on. He's made his way from Colombia via the dangerous Darién gap, chartering a small boat from a little town called Turbo that skirted the dense jungle via mangrove estuaries, before eventually landing on Panamanian soil. To say I'm jealous of his adventure is an understatement and only wish I had his courage and personable and calm manner in dealing with potentially risky situations.

"How about Katya and Mikal and the other Germans?" I ask, curiously, wondering where they've all ended up.

"Mikal is OK. He will see me in Mexico," Jan says. "Vee have zee same plane home; he is zere now viz his bruzzer."

"And what about Katya?"

"I sink she is already in Sweden again," he says. "But she had some trouble in Santa Marta in Colombia."

"What happened?" I ask, worried.

"Ah, it's not serious, man," he says, assuring me. "Zee police got her for smoking weed on zee beach. Zey took her to an ATM and made her give zem 300 Euros."

"Shit," I say, feeling sorry for her.

"I sink she vaz more upset by zee sings zey said zey would do to her if she didn't pay zan losing zee money. Assholes."

We spend the remainder of the evening in Jan's hostel where, unaware at first, I end up translating between the friendly owner and Jan the whole time.

"You!!!" Jan says with glee and gripping my shoulder. "You have great Spanish now!"

He's right, I think to myself, now overly chuffed. It's actually not that bad. I've been able to mediate for these two without even realising it. The night comes to a close and we say our final farewell. I walk back to the house, revelling in this new language I'm finally grasping.

"Vee see us again, I know it," Jan says, confidently.

"OK, Jan, we'll make it happen," I agree, and disappear into the dark night of León's streets.

Jan was right: this isn't the last time I see him. Two years later I find myself in a tiny village in the north of Germany at his wedding to the woman we'd met in Colombia.

CHAPTER SIXTY-EIGHT
PROFESSOR HUGO

I have a new teacher. His name is Hugo. He is a short man who appears on our first day of lessons in a loose polo shirt, battered baseball cap and ironed dress pants with shortened hems that meet comfortably at the top of his tan suede walking boots.

Eva and I have decided she can no longer be my teacher. Our lessons these days amount to little more than petting and flirting and we both have a suspicion that Roberto may be noticing our affections.

"Buenos dias, Darren." Hugo pronounces my real name perfectly.

The features of his thin brown face show signs of a long but interesting life and I'm looking forward to finding out about it. A neatly combed dark wisp of hair resting on his shiny bald head curls in the breeze of the electric fan behind him.

"Sentate," he says, leading me into a plastic chair at our desk with the palm of his open hand. "Vamos a empezar." Time to begin. He speaks through his thick but neatly trimmed bushy moustache.

Pulling a thick leather-bound book from his bag, Hugo places it on the table. "Aquí tenemos un buen libro," he says with an animated expression, opening the cover.

The book, *A History of Nicaragua*, is our go-to reference for our classes and an incredible source of information. Turning the pages and peering at me over the top of his square-framed reading glasses, Hugo stops.

"El terremoto de 1972," he says, referring to Managua's earthquake three decades ago.

"Did you know anyone in it?"

"Si." He replies, looking me in the eyes, "Yo."

"You?!" I blurt out, loudly enough to make heads turn at the other tables.

"Si," he answers, before switching to English. "I was living in apartment with other student friends in city."

"Wow," I say softly, wanting him to tell me everything.

"The quake struck in night and we have big party," he recounts, thinking back. "Lots of drinking."

I wait like an impatient child for his story to unfold.

"The buildings make shake. Muy fuerte. I try wake up many other people in room before I jump from first floor window to the street." He hesitates, shakes his head. "Only four of us make it. I lost good friends that day."

"I'm so sorry, Hugo," I say.

"It's OK, Darren." He sips a cup of water. "The aftermath was worse."

Wandering the streets, not sure in which direction to turn and unable to stay upright with the violent quake tearing up the asphalt and downing buildings all around, Hugo and his friends came face to face with a fireball heading towards them.

"Una chica," he says with his head in his hands.

He's either a damn good actor or this is just dragging up bad memories, I think to myself as he tells the painful story of a girl trapped alive under a telegraph pole in the path of the fire.

"We try lift the pole off her body but not possible. There was no way she would survive the fire."

"What did you do?" I ask him, now on the edge of my seat.

"The most terrible thing," he mumbles, putting his head in his hands. "I took out my pistol and shot her in head." He adds, so quiet I can barely hear, "Better than burning alive."

During the next three weeks with Hugo, he pulls me into another world. His life is at times shocking, and always fascinating. His colourful life captures me and takes me on a ride I'll never forget. His gripping stories of his previous life as a sniper, enduring seven years of unbearable conditions in the heat and torrential rains of the Nicaraguan forests, are like scenes from a blockbuster movie.

"Pitchouf!" He describes the sound of a bullet piercing a skull and the head jolting in its helmet.

"Contras putas," he snarls, talking of the opposing Honduran rebels.

"We would take everything from them as they lay there dead," he tells me in Spanish, clearly egged on by my interest in his tales. "Their food, weapons, jewellery, clothes and ammunition – everything!"

Hugo is a well-known figure in León. He's greeted in the street wherever he goes. He's heavily involved in the town's mayoral committee. And I soon learn that his poetry is famous throughout Nicaragua. My teacher, it turns out, is a well-respected man who has endured an existence that I will never experience, and one that I grow to respect and admire beyond words. Besides being a sniper and a poet, he also has a sense of humour to carry his sometimes serious stories. His humour is edgy, crass. And it's fuelled more by mine. During classes, we are sometimes raucous and disruptive. Other people stare. But I don't worry, because I assume the respected Hugo can take the lead.

"Hay muchos hipopotamos aqui en Nicaragua," he says with a cackle, slapping his thigh and referring to the larger women.

I can only guess that his humour comes from a hard place – his has not been an easy life, and the levity Hugo brings to his everyday observations seems to balance the otherwise difficult stories he shares. His heavy involvement in the pre-revolution protests against the Somoza dictatorship resulted in inhumane punishments. Once, he was chained by the feet in a concrete tube, forced to stay there six weeks, up to his neck in mud and sewer waste; he was slid two trays of cockroach-infested rice a day.

"I was in hospital with major organ problems for a year after," he says without flinching.

The more I listen, the more Hugo digs into his past. Many of his horrific stories come from the seven years he served as a soldier for Carlos Fonsecas' revolutionary Sandinista movement (FSLN). One of these stories made world headline news, and involved Hugo's battalion and a US cargo plane they shot down over the jungle. After hiking for two days, they found the aircraft wreckage with only one surviving crewmember, a man by the name of Eugene Hasenfus. He was sleeping in a hammock he'd made from his parachute, suffering from a broken arm and early stages of malaria. The plane was carrying guns and money to Honduran rebels being trained to fight the revolutionary Sandinista soldiers, and the whole incident had heavy connections to the Iran-Contra scandal of the time. A black book of phone numbers found by Hugo's troop linking the operation to a US airbase in El Salvador proved all of this. For three weeks, Eugene was held at their camp due to heavy rains that prevented any aircraft transporting him to Managua. During this time, Hugo helped him win his battle with malaria. When the weather finally broke, Eugene was flown out but not before thanking Hugo for nursing him and more so, for sparing his life; he urged him to contact him if there was anything he could ever do in return. Twenty years later, a crate of Spanish medical books arrived on Hugo's doorstep, after he had remembered Eugene's offer and written to him, asking if there was any way he could help him with the costs of sending his daughter to medical school. This clearly was a touching moment for Hugo, and was the defining factor in his daughter gaining her nursing papers and working in Matagalpa's hospital in the northern highlands of the country.

But if I am learning a lot from Hugo about the history of his country, I am also finding great enjoyment in the days we spend together, during both lessons and after-school tours through town. The latter are usually filled with jokes and mischief. Sometimes they are a more personal tour through Hugo's life. On the celebrated Day of the Dead, we go to the Guadalupe district where thousands of pink and teal crosses sprout from the colossal graveyard.

"Aqui es," Hugo indicates, sweeping his hand across the area of his grandparents' gravestones. They are barely visible through the overgrown foliage that grows around them. We clear the weeds and sit in silence while countless other families shuffle through the cemetery, placing flowers at their deceased loved ones' tombstones.

"Muy tranquilo, gracias por accompanarme," he says calmly, taking in a deep breath and thanking me for joining him.

My fortune in meeting this man has been a defining factor in not only my trip but also my life. I realise even as we roam the streets that this powerful man will have a lasting impact on me. It's impossible to meet someone like Hugo and not reassess your own life. At least, that's the case for me. My view of the concepts of happiness and fear, of the ease of some challenges and the seeming insurmountability of others, changes immeasurably during the months I spend in León. The hardships he experienced make even more of an impact on me because of the calm manner in which he retells his stories. The way he takes his suffering in his stride, the way he shares his life with such pride.

I listen with deep admiration.

CHAPTER SIXTY-NINE
LAS PEÑITAS BY NIGHT

Christina and I are like ships that pass in the night. She has settled into Trent's old room, but I hardly ever see her. When I do, she complains about the iguana and how it's a dangerous lizard that should be caught and put in the wild. I'm praying she never looks up in the rafters when the fruit bat's at home.

Meanwhile, Eva leads her busy life and our meetings have all but ceased.

I'm starting to feel alone. Or, I'm starting to feel ready to be even more alone. Which it is, I can't quite tell. But it may be time to move on.

I'm definitely feeling a need for change. The longer I reside in León, the more comfortable I feel but also the lonelier. This is a place I can settle into, and certainly a place where I am learning a lot. But I am without any familiar friends, and in time that fact begins to weigh on me. Overnight, León becomes a very lonely place.

An escape from this loneliness comes in the form of an offer from Eva after a brief coffee with her in town.

"You can use beach house if you like?"

"I would love that!" I say, jumping at the chance. "Maybe I can take Hugo and Christina?"

"Si, is no problem. I get key from Carlos and you can go this weekend."

I put the idea to Hugo and Christina, and they too are excited for a night away at the beach.

The hot sticky bus carries us out to Las Peñitas where we find a beachside bar and cool off with a Granadita, a delicious mix of coconut water, orange juice and rum – a classic Nicaraguan drink. The waves slowly take on the pink colour of the sky while crashing on the beach as we sip the cool drinks from straws. Hugo is interested in Christina's

Italian heritage and asks question after question. It seems he knows a lot about the history in general, and Mussollini specifically. His knowledge of dictatorships is vast and, I reckon, fed by his experiences during President Somoza's reign and his years spent fighting him with the FSLN.

Baked fish plates are placed in front of us and we tuck in while the sun sets over the crashing waves.

I buy a bottle of rum in a tiny store on the way back to the beach house, and we settle under the veranda in the yard, passing the bottle around while the stars become ever brighter in the giant sky. The silence is incredible. The whole village is asleep, and much like the more off track places I have been, the inhabitants live by the sun, up at the crack of dawn and sleeping the moment it becomes dark. We continue with the Italian history conversation until a swarm of ferocious mosquitoes attacks.

"Aaiii!!" Christina yells out, slapping her arms and legs.

Even Hugo and his native blood shields no escape from their attacks.

Fleeing inside the house, we take cover but this is no deterrent whatsoever to the insects.

"¡¡¡No hay ventanas!!!" I say, realising the holes in the walls have no glass and the insect screens are torn from the foliage that grows through them.

"¡¡Es como película de horror!!" Christina wails, still slapping her bare skin and now hopping around like she's a Scottish sword dancer while spraying the whole can of her insect repellent aerosol.

I can't help but smirk at her comment. Horror film – haha. But she's got a point. And if the mozzies don't kill us, I'm pretty certain we'll die from choking on the cloud of insect spray she's now blanketed the room with. We wrap ourselves up in sleeping bags and spend the hot night unable to sleep from the constant buzzing, *oh the buzzing*, that awful high-pitched hum swirling all around us, so close and with the critters just aching to find somewhere to sink their stings into. We are all sweating profusely in the tropical night heat, with only our mouths showing for air to protect us from the blood-thirsty creatures' bites. We get little sleep.

At day break we are up and out of there quick smart and wait for the first bus. The village dirt track is already alive with locals, fishermen pulling boats down to the shore and women walking with intent, balancing bowls on their heads. Christina has a huge swelled cheek that didn't escape the attack of the mozzies and now looks a little too much like Quasimodo. She is distraught.

"Espero que no tengo dengue," she whines, claiming she may have dengue fever and growing increasingly annoying to listen to.

She'd be a great girlfriend for Mikal, I think to myself, remembering how he regularly whined and how similar it felt.

"¡¡¡Terriiiible!!!" Hugo repeats as we rumble back to León.

So much for a relaxed night away.

Back at the house in León, I brew a coffee on the stove, drag the rocking chair out front and settle in for another riveting morning of watching the mangy horse tied up opposite as it chews dry tufts of grass. Suddenly its head jolts up as a loud, clattering sound approaches. The sound is familiar to me, a sound that moments later turns the corner and is upon us. A lanky, long-haired teenager scoots past on a skateboard not fit for human use, both ends completely ground away and the wheels so worn it's incredible he's able to propel himself along. The thing is a disgrace to skateboarding. My board has been strapped to the side of my backpack, sheathed in a cut off sweat pant leg since I last used it in the colorful concrete bowls in Medellín, Colombia. The thing is weighing me down and of little use in these pot holed lanes of Central America – a First World skater's problem of course but I figure the enjoyment this teen will get out of it will far surpass any I will see in the following months. So the next morning, I flag him down as he passes.

"¡OYE! ¡CHICO! ¡VENGA!" I call out to him, beckoning him over. He's startled at first, scared even – almost like he's in trouble, but he flicks his board into his hand and cautiously approaches me across the cobbled street.

"Espera aquí," I say calmly, telling him to wait before running inside to fetch the board from my room. I'm more excited than him right now.

He's still there when I return. "Por favor, tomala," I tell him, handing him the board and telling him to take it.

"¿Por qué?" he asks, almost bewildered as to what's happening. He runs the palm of his boney brown hand across the shiny smooth paint of the board. His fingernails are long and dirty. He lightly drags them across the paint, before spinning a wheel with his skeletal fingers.

"Ya no lo quiero," I answer, telling him I don't want it anymore.

The guy can't believe what I'm saying, he can't grasp the fact that I'm gifting him the board. "¡Gracias, gracias!" he says finally, timidly and shaking like a child.

I shake his hand before he skates off still using his shitty piece of driftwood, waving, with my near new set up under his arm. The following morning, I'm back in my chair on the sidewalk, sipping my coffee when he turns the corner with a new spring in his push and a huge smile on his face as he punts along on my board. He gives a hearty wave as he speeds by and I wave back. *Skateboarding – The gift that keeps on giving*, I think to myself. I'm happy to be rid of my board, but happier that I've just given this guy the chance to take his skating to the next level.

Dragging my chair inside, I lock up the house and stroll to the square in town where a young woman joins me at my bench. Her name is Elisa. I've seen her before, hanging around with the artisanal guys in the main plaza. She seems a kind-natured girl, of caramel skin and a curvaceous body. I admire her plump round breasts, large brown eyes and pronounced cheekbones – traits inherent to indigenous Nicaraguans, and ones that never fail to entice me. She surprises me when she strokes my leg gently with her tiny hands.

"Let's go to bar," she says. "You buy me drink."

Bored out of my mind and desperate for company, I agree. Maybe this girl will help alleviate that desperation. My mind flits briefly to Eva, but I've not seen her all week and her interest in me has waned. So I enter a dark bar with Elisa, and moments later we're drinking beers.

"I love your skin," Elisa tells me as we sit with a beer in the small bar. "So soft."

We toss back our beers and leave for my place. Elisa makes herself right at home, swinging in my hammock like she belongs there.

She beckons me over.

I call out for Christina, making sure she's not home. Elisa reaches for me, pulls me into her, her smooth legs dangling from the hammock. She grabs me by the belt, unzips my shorts and plunges her hand in my pants expertly. I lift her out of the hammock and lead her to my room. We squirm around together in the sweltering midday heat. I hear the front door shut. Christina is home. The interruption breaks the mood and we swiftly get dressed and leave while she's in the bathroom.

"¿Como fue? Jaja," barks one of the artisanal guys when I return to the plaza. They are sniggering. They want to know how she was.

"What d'you mean?" I answer in Spanish, surprised that they already know what we've been up to.

"She likes cheles," says another in broken English, laughing. "You not the first!"

I laugh with them, trying not to show how embarrassed I feel. Once I've stayed long enough to share the joke, I walk away quickly, grimacing at the knowledge that this is a familiar scene to them.

León's humidity regularly reaches an unbearable level this time of year, and to call this season autumn is quite frankly a joke. The air is so heavy it's impossible to move without breaking a sweat. The thought of an autumn breeze is tantalising. Hitting boiling point one afternoon while Eva and I are having a beer, our peace is split in two by deafening thunder claps that set off car alarms while forked lightning bolts illuminate the sky for miles around.

"¡Muy fuerte!" Eva says, holding her hands in the air.

Moments later the city's power is taken down after a spiked lance of lightning sends a direct hit into the main bank of power generators.

Within twenty minutes the streets are over a foot deep in water. Children on their way home from school laugh and splash in the torrential rain, body surfing down the streets on squares of corrugated iron and plywood that have been ripped from the roofs by the ferocious gusts of wind. Some kids swim in their uniforms, oblivious to the damage the storm is causing all around them. Eva and I wait for the storm to ease and then part ways. I head over to Malena's place to say hi. Parked outside the house is an old model Toyota car that's been hand-painted in a bizarre shade of blue. The brush marks on the panels are only upstaged in their bad taste by the silver clip-on wheel covers.

"¡Chele!" Raphael shouts from the front porch. "¿Te gusta mi carro?" He clearly loves his car, nodding to the blue pile of shit parked at the kerb.

Not wanting to offend him, I lie. "Si, me gusta mucho. Que bueno."

"Darío," he continues, with those pocked cheeks of his, again leaning in way too close. "Es carro de China." He is completely wrong about the car's origin. "Pero no Chinandega, chele, es de China – el pais."

I am amused that he thinks I might confuse China with the small town of Chinadega thirty kilometres northwest of León, but I'm in a generous mood and do not want to correct him about the car's Japanese origin. So I nod my head and agree with his spiel. Malena appears at the door.

"¿Todo bien entre nos?" she asks me, inquiring if I'm alright after what happened between us.

"Si," I answer – and this is no lie. I'm glad that Raphael hasn't got a clue what she actually means.

"Malenita y vos, ven a mi casa para cena antes de saliré," I say, inviting her and Malenita for dinner before I leave. "¡Ai! ¡Darío!" she yelps. "¡Tu español es bueno!"

"Gracias," I thank her, blushing.

"¡¿Puedes cocinar?!" she asks me, surprised I can cook, being a man and all. "¡No quiero frijoles o tortillas por fa!" Malena laughs, specifying her desire to have something other than beans or tortilla.

"¡JAJA! ¡Por sopuesto!" 'Of course!' I am not sure what I will cook, but I walk home with a feeling of happiness, ecstatic about the seamless Spanish conversation we've just had.

CHAPTER SEVENTY
ADÍOS LEÓN

The following morning, the only remnants of the storm are a few blocked drains and clumps of plastic litter that have been dragged by the current and now dot the streets. Sitting at my usual spot in the square, I watch as the slow beat of the town goes about its daily routine.

My stay in León is drawing to a close. Soon, these quiet rhythms of my days will be replaced with the hustle bustle of bus terminals and change. I anticipate I'll get back into the pace of moving every few days. First step: I book my bus ticket to Guatemala.

"Este bus, viente cinco, o este, cincuenta," the woman in the ticket office offers, presenting my two options. The cheaper ticket is a three-day chicken bus for $25 dollars; the second option is a sleeker-looking 'Tica bus' for $50 with an overnight stop in San Salvador. I go with the latter.

My last outing with Eva and Florencia involves taking them to the ice cream shop. I watch as Florencia slides down the plastic tube in the play area. I can't help but feel sad as Eva and I meet eyes but don't speak; we both know that there's no telling when I'll return.

"¿Cuándo regreses?" says Florencia, bouncing towards us for ice cream.

Leave it to a kid to ask the question Eva and I both are avoiding. Florencia wants a real answer about my return to León.

"Mas pronto que antes, niña," I reply, holding back a tear and telling her sooner rather than later.

"Mamá?" she asks, looking up at her. "¿Eres triste?"

Is mama sad? I do not want to know the answer. But before I can change topics, Eva answers, "Un poquito, niña."

She sends Florencia back to the play area. And I'm sad, too.

Although our time spent together became less and less during my stay in León, Eva has shared a little part of her life with me. It's an emotional goodbye for so many reasons.

We finish our ice cream in silence and I drop Florencia at school. I choke back the tears in my eyes; I promise her that I'll be back some day.

"¡Adios, Darío!" she cries – and disappears into the sea of blue and white uniforms that swarm the inner courtyard.

Eva desperately wants us to be together just one last time. We catch a taxi to my house – but we drive straight past when we see Christina and her friends hanging outside smoking cigarettes. Eva tells the driver to take us to Fundecí, a small suburb on the outskirts of town where her mother lives, explaining to me in English that we can be together there as her mother's at work. I pay the driver, and he smirks at me in his rear view mirror. A pretty petite Nicaraguan girl and a tall white gringo disappearing into a dilapidated block of flats can only mean one thing here in this neighbourhood. I wince a little as I recall my encounter with Elisa, the girl who favours gringos. But this is different; this is *Eva*. I don't need to explain to the cabbie.

I slam the door and follow Eva up the steps.

We climb three flights of a rusty metal staircase to reach a tiny flat. We are greeted by two small mangy grey dogs, the red ribbons tied on their heads contrasting with the matted dreads that hang around their wet eyes and mouths and the saliva that glistens and hangs from their chins. They yap furiously and bite at my legs, but Eva shoos them away, locks them outside on the tiny balcony and throws a table cloth over her mum's bed.

She says her mum will be home in an hour. She says we'll have to be quick.

Looking back on our secret rendezvous, I now realise what a bunch of serious trouble I could wind up getting myself into with this woman. She comes from a strict culture with strict religious beliefs. She has a husband who could do me bodily harm – even if he is thus far oblivious to our trysts. More than that, I realise that all this could result in some very serious consequences for her, as she will have to live with whatever happens next, while I saunter off on my travels like nothing ever happened. I am full of melancholy as I watch Eva arrange the bed cover and begin to undress. I worry that our last time together may be ruined by my bad mood – and my own worry and guilt.

But my worries are quickly forgotten as she pushes me on to the bed and straddles me, whipping open my belt while unzipping my fly and rummaging in my boxers.

Our last session is not disappointing.

We linger a while, wrapped in sweat and a sweet exhaustion, when I suddenly remember Eva's mother. I spring off the bed.

"¡Tenemos que ir!" I say frantically, telling her we have to leave.

Neither of us is sure how long we've been there, and we quickly fold up the tablecloth before hurrying back to town.

We part at the school before Florencia finishes. I promise I'll write whenever I get the chance. We are unable to kiss or hug goodbye – the chance of rumour is far too great. We keep a respectable distance between us as we say our last goodbyes. I have a lump in my throat as I turn and head back to my house, alone.

That evening, I prepare a meal for Malena and her daughter. I want to show my appreciation for all she's done for me. I decide to try my hand at something British; I've marinated beef all night in red wine, and now I'm slow-cooking a beef stew.

Their faces after the first fork full are priceless. First, intrigue, then surprise – and finally, joy. Clearly they are impressed by the foreign but delicious tastes.

"You are the first man I've ever met who can cook," Malena tells me in Spanish. "¡Es muy rico!" She beams her approval.

The meal is my thanks to both daughter and mother, for including me in so much of their family life, for everything they've done for me.

They leave in a taxi – and this marks the end of my stay in León.

Next morning, I wake and dress, and leave my key on the kitchen bench. I walk out into the dark morning. My bag is reloaded with all my belongings. I am hoping a taxi will drive past. After a few minutes one rumbles up and drops me at the gas station on the edge of town where the Tica bus will leave for El Salvador.

And there, sitting alone on a kerb at 5am in the middle of

Nicaragua waiting for a bus that might or might not show up, it hits me. I am about as far from life in a sleepy suburb of Auckland as I can get. I am eight months out of that life; I am a universe away. A moment of clarity comes over me. Simple lifestyles, strong family values, laughter and deep, heartfelt smiles – these are the memories I'll forever associate with León. This is the life I have grown accustomed to. This is a life to cherish. Life has been a challenge here, yes – but the experiences and hospitality that I've enjoyed over the last few months have been life changing, of that I'm sure. I can only feel upset to be leaving it all behind, but deep down know that it won't be long before I return.

As the gas station slowly comes alive, bright headlights alert me to two huge buses pulling into the lay-by at the edge of the Pan-American highway. One bus is heading to Tegucigalpa in Honduras, the other to Guatemala City via San Salvador.

I feel melancholy, dejected and like I'm leaving a family behind. But I also have a growing independence welling in my chest, a sense that my time in León has brought me further in my travels than I may have imagined. I am armed with a confidence I lacked three months ago. I am sad to leave, but I am ready.

I board the bus to Guatemala City.

CHAPTER SEVENTY-ONE
SAN SALVADOR

The bus is practically empty. I nervously do a head count – six passengers. We glide through the border; the soldiers check our passports and our fees are all collected in no time at all. We cut through vast green lowlands of southern Honduras. The giant blue skies are flecked with wispy white clouds while tall green volcanic cones fill the north horizon during the two hours it takes us to reach the next border.

Among the six passengers is a young honeymooning couple from Australia whom I easily befriend. I hope to disembark with them, once we reach San Salvador. Something about heading into this city with such a badass reputation leads me to desire company. They are coming from a resort on the Nicaraguan coast, and they are also staying the night at a hotel in San Salvador before they switch buses bound for the Caribbean in Belize.

The next border serves to reinforce the media portrayal of Gangland El Salvador. Countless soldiers dressed in dark green camouflage and black balaclavas outnumber civilians by at least five to one. Patrolling the frontier and searching vehicles, they interrogate passengers one by one. But we're still a small group, so we manage to avoid a lot of the hassle I have anticipated, and pass through unscathed.

More lush green hills and volcanic cones carpeted in coffee plantations paint a picturesque scene – a scene that changes all too quickly. Makeshift stalls of corrugated iron lean against the smog-stained streets of San Salvador. When the bus stops at a hotel on the fringe of the city, I rise from my seat with the Australian couple and start for the front of the bus.

"¿Que haces, amigo?" the bus attendant asks me as I follow my new friends.

"Voy a quedar en el hotel," I reply, telling him I'm staying the night.

"Este hotel, no," he says, indicating that it's not this one. "Su hotel es poco mas lejos." My final destination is a little further.

So I say goodbye to my potential new friends and return to my seat. Now I am the only foreigner on the bus; I watch from the window as the Australian couple wheel their suitcases into the hotel. The bus creeps back into the traffic.

I am alone. And I am now entering one of the world's most dangerous cities.

The bus crawls at a snail's pace through heavy traffic blocking the choking streets. We arrive in a rundown area and drive through a pair of giant metal gates into a razor-wired, high-walled compound. The passengers disembark and are directed through a doorway across the parking bay, where a series of floors resembling a prison block stand. Above the small reception desk a peeling sign reads 'Welcome to The Tica bus hotel' and I'm handed a key with a huge wooden block attached to it, similar to those keys used for petrol station restrooms. Reaching the third floor via a flight of metal stairs flaking white paint, I push the key into the room lock. But the door clicks open; it's already ajar. I step into the room. It's small, cramped and has a musty aroma.

I secure all of my valuables in the bottom of my backpack and shove it under the bed, locking my wobbly door as best I can as I head outside. At the entrance downstairs is a security guard in shiny boots and holding a well-worn shotgun. Now confident with my Spanish and that an official guy with a gun is a good guy to know in a neighbourhood like this, I casually joke with him and make small talk for half an hour or so.

"So we are near the old city centre?" I ask him in Spanish, hoping he'll have some tips.

"Si, pero no te vas solo, chele, es peligroso." He confirms what I feared: it's dangerous and not safe to explore.

"Have you ever used that?" I ask him in Spanish, pointing at his gun.

"Not for this job, my friend," he says. "But yes, I shot a guy in the stomach when I worked at a bank."

He recommends a Pupuseria just around the corner for food, but he warns me to keep my eyes open and to go straight there and not to wander. Looking up to where he's pointing, I take a deep breath and make a beeline for the food shack, following a high wall of corrugated iron, its metal folds rusty and crimped as it bends with the corner. Ripped tarpaulin sheets shelter a clutter of wooden tables and chairs, where a round woman pats out discs of maize dough over a hot plate.

Returning to El Salvador in years to come, I learn that for every three Salvadorans there are two of these pupuserias – similar to Argentina's epidemic of pharmacies occupying every corner. A narrow street without one of these eateries just feels wrong. But I will learn all that years later. For now, this is my first experience and I'm hungry. The two women of this establishment eyeball me as I walk in as if I'm from outer space.

"Hola, chele. ¿Que te gusta?" one asks, querying what I'm after with a grill of gold teeth. She fills the middle of a dough ball with cheese and beans.

"Dos de estos, por favor," I say, pointing at the things she's patting into perfect discs ready to be fried.

"Un dólar," she answers. "¿Quiere bebida?"

Drink? Yes: "Una botella de Coca." I revel in my new language, in the easy back-and-forth ordering my food and drink.

Within minutes, two of these delicious looking Frisbees are plonked in front of me, along with a jar of an orange coloured sauerkraut mix called curtido. I rip the maize pockets open, and I find a web of sticky cheese and refried bean curd desperately holding the pieces together as a wisp of steam rises from it. Who ever thought food could taste this good beneath a plastic roof? I wash the delicious pupusas down with the cold bottle of Coke and return to my new friend at the hotel entrance, who is now joined by another guy. The two men are busy with ice cream cones that are melting quicker than they can eat them.

"Es mas seguro," the guard says, pointing at his friend's car and clogging his bushy moustache with the melted treat. "Vamos, cinco por media hora," the taxi driver adds, offering a half hour tour of the city for five dollars.

The Pupusa scenario has boosted my confidence and I oblige.

Grinding through the gears, he drags the wreck around the narrow streets as I watch the lifeblood of the city going about its daily business. Pavements spill over with open beach umbrellas shading rickety stalls. Weaving between the standstill traffic are the street vendors with whatever you want to buy stuffed in their backpacks: hairbands, sunglasses, boxes of matches, bunny ear TV aerials, ballpoint pens. Two soldiers with rifles sitting in the back of a pick-up truck in front of us stare back laughing.

"¿Por qúe se ríen?" I ask the taxi driver, curious as to why they are laughing at us.

"No acostumbrado a los cheles, amigo," he says. 'They're not used to white guys in the city.'

He continues circling the litter-strewn streets talking of his family and showing me the sights that end at the giant white cathedral standing at the head of the main plaza.

When we arrive back at the hotel, my friendly taxi driver claims he has no change when I pull out a ten dollar bill. Instead, he smiles and points at his watch.

"Mas tiempo hombre, quarenta y cinco minutos hombre." Ah. We've been longer than what he originally quoted for. I hand over the ten dollar bill, happy that I'm back safe, hoping that $5 extra will at least get him some beers or, better still, put a few meals on his family's table.

I'm comforted that my door's still locked upon my return to my room. I drift off to sleep reflecting on my afternoon here – dissatisfied that I've seen so little, and with the urge to one day return and experience it in the way I did Nicaragua.

CHAPTER SEVENTY-TWO
ANTIGUA

Sweet instant coffee in a disposable plastic cup from the hotel foyer downstairs: that's breakfast. The bus eases out of the sky-high iron sheeted gates at 04:30 sharp.

We head north.

An endless queue of trucks lines the side of the road as we approach the border. Sunbeams glint through the gaps between them as we pass. Camouflaged military soldiers surround them, searching in, out and around the cabs and cargo. But even the stern scene of border control is a good place for a pupuseria: smoky hot plates are loaded up kerbside by dumpy Salvadoran women in frilly bean-stained aprons. The smell of sizzling maize treats wafts on the dawn breeze into my window; this is as close as I'm going to get since we are not allowed off the bus. Meanwhile, our attendant collects our passports for the last time and alights the bus to have them checked through customs.

Less than two hours later, we pull in to the safe haven of the Tica bus terminal in Guatemala City and I face my next challenge: choosing a taxi. The cab drivers swarm around the bus door, yelling at the travellers to try to gain our attention. I choose a friendly face and walk with him in the direction of the shiny new Toyota Corolla I think he's pointing at. But as we cross the parking lot, that automobile pulls away, revealing the clapped-out death trap he's expecting me to get into, its multi-coloured panels complemented further by the shoelace tying down the bonnet.

"¿Tiene la fuerza a llegar a Antigua?" I ask him, inquiring if it's going to make the thirty-minute drive to Antigua.

"No hay problema, es carro muy fuerte," he replies, vouching for his vehicle.

Here we go again.

We hit the highway and talk about all manner of subjects. He's a friendly guy but just can't seem to grasp that New Zealand is not Australia.

When we reach the picturesque town of Antigua, we rattle through the cobbled streets trying to find the hostel where Trent has told me he'll be staying. Miraculously, I locate not only the hostel but also Trent. The driver takes the money and speeds off, leaving me at the roadside in what will be my new home for the next week or so.

"Hey, how are ya, mate?" Trent says, with a red face, hanging from the balcony and sounding the wrong side of tipsy.

"Yeah, good, man," I reply. "Is there a bed here?"

"Dunno, mate, go in and ask." Trent disappears into the top room.

I have no choice but to walk in – but as I do, the reality hits me like a train. The scene is all too familiar: backpackers in baggy hemp pants and woven bracelets sit smoking cigarettes and sipping beer.

"No hay espacio, amigo," the desk clerk tells me – to my relief. "Pero el hospedaje al otro lado, tiene."

She directs me to the hostel across the road. I'm worried that it will reveal travellers just as crusty and familiar, but I cross the road to check it out. The cool interior, colonial archways and quiet atmosphere are pleasantly surprising.

"¿Tiene habitación?" I ask the desk clerk, enquiring after a room.

The girl behind the desk is frantically texting on her phone. She barely looks up and hands me a key with a number 7 attached. I climb a set of stairs; I seem to be the only guest. The empty Spanish hotel has the atmosphere of a morgue, but I don't want to trawl the streets searching out my options – it's been a long day. So I find my room and throw my bag on an empty bed. A tall, slim, older English chap with a greying beard and a well-travelled face is already in my room and reading on his bed.

"'Ello," he says cheerily. "Morris," he introduces himself.

An independent traveller, Morris enjoys exploring different parts of the world for a month or so every year to escape the trappings of his fencing company that he owns back in the UK.

"I met this batty old woman in the plaza earlier," he tells me while

I unpack my belongings. "She's invited me and a couple of others to a macadamia farm tomorrow. You should come along."

I am surprised at how glad I feel for the invite.

I rummage through my pack. I'm slightly disconcerted that I seem to have misplaced the $50 that I'd stuffed into the bottom at the hotel in San Salvador. I assume I must've just misplaced it – but I hope this is not a bad omen for what's to come.

"Fuck!" I say angrily and out loud. "I'm sure it was here."

"What's the matter, lad?" Morris asks curiously.

"I thought I had fifty bucks stashed in here."

"Those Tica buses," he begins. "You know why they're a bit more expensive than the others, don't ya?" He can judge by my reaction that I probably don't know. "They're followed by an unmarked car of armed guards the whole way."

"No shit?!" I answer. "Really?"

"Yep," he says nonchalantly. "They've had too many hold ups in the past. It only used to be forty bucks, but that hotel they put you in – well, I don't know about that place."

Morris seems to be insinuating that my money was swiped at the hotel. I consider it and suppose it's as likely as it being swiped anywhere else. Even so, I'm pretty glad I chose the more expensive option over the three-day chicken bus.

Next day, we wait at the bus stop for the old lady Morris has met. We're joined by a couple of other random tourists that she's obviously lured into her trip to the macadamia farm. Two Ronald Reagan doppelgangers are dressed in pastel shades of golfing attire.

"What a beautiful day!" an old lady cries out cheerily as she meets us at the bus stop.

"'Ello Doris," Morris greets her. "This is Darren. I brought him along."

"Fantastic!" she says, clapping her hands together. "The more the merrier! You guys are going to love this place!"

Bubbly and – I soon learn – bursting with useless facts and figures, she's clearly excited about being our tour guide. Her attire can only be described as a tropical peacock, from her purple paisley cravat tucked into the top of a shimmering blue full-length floral dress to her bright red lipstick and yellow eye shadow. The colourful paintwork of the chicken bus that pulls up alongside us stands no chance against dotty old Doris' explosive outfit.

"All aboard!" she hollers, clapping her hands again.

We board the bus and start bouncing down the road. Our group is scattered amongst the locals. I sit halfway back, but I have a feeling I would be able to hear Doris even from the back of the bus. She goes into a full-blown speech at the top of her voice. Locals turn their heads. She's in fierce competition with the music blasting from the sub bass speakers tied into the roof. When we pull into our destination village, she's still talking but by then I'm not quite following. I'm glad for the momentary quiet as we shuffle off the bus and group ourselves in front of a peach-coloured church.

"Just a little walk up the road," she says in her shrill voice.

We arrive at the gates of the farm, and we're welcomed by the owner, an excited ex-pat American in his fifties. His long grey hair is banded into a ponytail and his open Hawaiian shirt reveals a hairy potbelly. He's accompanied by his wrinkly, collagen-lipped, Guatemalan glamour wife, who sports – uncomfortably, I imagine – tight, piss-wash jeans that pinch her plump crutch into a grotesque camel toe. She trots around in high heels with the jeans cinched up so high her shiny vinyl red belt is almost hidden by her deflated breasts that hang limply over it. Captain Ponytail shows us around his farm in a now not-so-excited, more half-interested, fashion. As if he didn't already seem self-congratulatory enough (*My wife! Just look at her!* you can almost hear him sing), he boasts the whole way through the orchard about his achievements and how many locals he has employed. Never mind that he no doubt pays them a pittance; he's got his spiel and he's sticking to it. The only guests who seem to really care are the two Ronalds; neither speaks but Ronald One makes astonished 'ooos' and 'aaahhhs' at the appropriate moments and Ronald Two nods vigourously to both Captain Ponytail and Ronald One.

Morris and I spend the tour smirking and sharing glances with each other. If I had any notion about the glamour of owning a macadamia farm, Captain Ponytail and his whole presentation has disabused me of that idea.

CHAPTER SEVENTY-THREE
LIFE IS CHEAP

Apart from the cooler climate and the abundance of traditional dress that the local women wear, Antigua is reminiscent of León. Its bright yellow alleyways, colonial architecture and cobbled streets are typical of the original Spanish towns that are spread throughout Latin America. Looming over the city like a giant pyramid stands the mighty peak of volcano Agua that provides a stunning backdrop for the many tourists roaming the streets with cameras at the ready.

"I'm pretty keen to do a couple more weeks' study," I mention to Trent over a beer. "What's your school like?"

"It's great," he replies, sipping from his bottle. "Come in with me tomorrow and you can meet the director."

The next day, I agree to eight days of lessons. I spend them studying the subjunctive tense, a confusing mix of clauses dealing with the subjunctive form of articulation. My teacher is a happy little lady by the name of Olga, her shiny black hair sculpted into a long plait hanging down her back. During classes she shares her horrific stories of the surrounding villages where kidnappings and lynchings have taken place. She tells her tales in the same manner as someone would talk about what was for lunch.

"The eight-year-old son of the local police chief was kidnapped and a ransom of two thousand dollars was demanded," she says one day, speaking in a slightly different Spanish to the Nicaraguan inflection and tone that I'm used to. "The parents, after several weeks of frantically scraping together and borrowing money from friends and family, were still two hundred dollars short of the figure asked when the final phone call came through." She pauses before continuing, as if to check my reaction.

"And?" I say, waiting for the cliffhanger.

"Well," she goes on. "Then they were given directions to a roadside clearing on the edge of the village where they eagerly made their way, expecting to reunite with their son." She pauses again, clasping her miniature hands together. "Instead, they found his lifeless body slumped in a ditch with eight deep puncture wounds in his side, one inflicted after each phone call where they'd begged for more time to come up with the money."

She relates the conclusion straight-faced, as if this type of thing happens all too often. I think back to the little peaceful village with the peach-coloured church near the macadamia farm and imagine it could have happened in a place just like that. I wonder if dotty old Doris and Captain Ponytail are aware of this underworld that surrounds them. Finishing the lesson, I cheer myself up on the walk home at the markets, returning to the hostel with a handful of new football shirts.

Life is cheap in this part of the world but ironically the people seem to live far happier, more contented lives. I wonder, after hearing Olga's stories, whether it's possibly because at any moment all the happiness can be taken away.

Morris leaves to return to his fencing business in the UK, and Trent is busy at the hostel across the street, latching on to new arrivals daily with repeat stories that appear to serve the sole purpose of boosting his ego. The scenario looks all too familiar. I do not want to succumb to an easy path – which will inevitably lead to the kind of loneliness that I felt in León.

I go to a park with my guidebook to map my next route.

CHAPTER SEVENTY-FOUR
VOLCAN PACAYA

I book in for a trip to Volcan Pacaya, an active volcano an hour from Antigua. A crowded minivan drags our group south, skirting the fringes of Guatemala City before finally arriving at a gravel car park in the tropical lowlands. Exiting the van, we're bombarded by a bunch of snot-nosed children arguing with each other over the price of the walking sticks they've snapped from surrounding trees. We are a motley crew, to say the least. I seem to be the only solo traveller amongst us: Israelis, Canadians and a few other misfits all part of separate groups. The two American couples – who are very, *very* large – have declined the children's offer of sticks and instead chosen the more expensive option of mules to lug them the first hour. They wobble unconfidently on the backs of the hired animals and duck under low branches as we climb the slippery volcanic mud tracks. The mangy nags are under-nourished and buzzing with flies. I watch the mules from behind, skinny legs and joints buckling under the weight as they miraculously carry the two fat American couples up the incline on their backs.

"Caaan't they go a little faaster?" one of the women says in a southern drawl as she rocks back and forth on the spine of her steed.

Can't you go on a diet? I think to myself.

As we exit the wooded area of the lower slopes, the path and landscape turn to scoria. Every footstep from here on up desperately tries to bite into loose gravel. The sticks we purchased at the base are now not such a bad idea – and at one dollar a pop a definite bargain. The lucky mules have reached their boundary and stand relieved of their cargo while the Americans, now on foot, huffing, puffing and wheezing in the intense heat, surely wish they'd never agreed to such a ridiculous day outing.

Volcan Pacaya is active. No: it's *extremely* active. Its violent eruptions close down the higher slopes on a regular basis. It's unnerving and exhilarating. We climb closer to the top and are rewarded with views of moody skies and countless other volcanic peaks jutting upward, shadowed by looming clouds. There! A huge plume of smoke shoots from a cone on the horizon! Seconds later a deafening boom travels on the wind. My heart thunders. But this doesn't faze the guides a bit.

"¡No te preocupes amigos! Es normal," they say, shrugging. *Don't worry – this is normal!*

We continue on up. Jets of steam emit from cracks in the volcanic rockside. It seems a dangerous bargain, going further up the hillside, but I follow our guide. And just around the corner we're suddenly surrounded by glowing red lava rivers that rush downhill at tremendous speed.

"¡Con Cuidado!" a guide shouts to us – *careful!* – before sitting down on a rock and lighting a cigarette. All around us, red hot boulders are thrown into the air crackling and spitting before rolling off down the hill. They burn paths of destruction just metres away from where we stand.

The terrain is incredible, the sounds ferocious. A small cluster from my group stand on a huge bubble crusted over with a thin layer. They try to poke holes in it with sticks while, directly below, hot molten lava rushes by. The guides look at them, roll their eyes and turn away, obviously seeing this a million times before. *Stupid gringos,* I can hear them thinking – except of course they'd be thinking *gringos estúpidos.*

I wonder if any of the *gringos estúpidos* have ever fallen in through the thin layer of crust keeping them safely on the surface.

Descending at dusk rewards us with amazing views back towards the bubbling crater. Against the dark night sky, its glowing lava rivers cascade into bright red lines on its slopes. This trek far exceeds the macadamia farm visit. This is a magical wonder provided solely by mother earth. I am overwhelmed and exhausted, but elated.

We arrive at the base, and the clever little snot-faced children swarm us, taking their sticks back to sell to the next group.

Two months after arriving back in New Zealand, a slot on the six o'clock news reports an active volcano in Guatemala, famous for tours to its lava rivers, has exploded, killing three tourists and leaving countless others with third-degree burns. I wait for the newsreader to name the hill, and am not entirely surprised when she confirms that it's the very same one.

CHAPTER SEVENTY-FIVE
SAN PEDRO LA LAGUNA

Arriving back from the day trip, I'm seeing the benefits of the quiet hostel. It may be lacking atmosphere, but it attracts a smaller, more mature crowd, and as the rabble from my volcano day-trip exit the bus and pile through the doors of the hostel opposite, I'm quietly relieved.

I push the buzzer and the gate clicks open. The foyer is deathly silent, and I head upstairs to my room to further plan my route north.

But upstairs I discover I am not alone; when I come to my room I find a blond-haired guy unpacking his bag on what was Morris' bed.

"Hey, how are you?" I greet him.

"Hi, I Marco," he says in quiet, broken European English.

When I ask what he's been up to today, he looks at me with an open mouth and a blank stare. "I speak German and Spanish," he informs me. "English, no much."

"¡Ah! ¡Que bueno!" I reply, happy for the opportunity to continue practicing my Spanish. "No problema, yo hablo español."

I learn that Marco has been travelling through Central America on a break from his physiotherapy studies in Switzerland. His language skills derive from his Swiss father and Spanish mother.

"What are your plans for Guatemala?" I ask him in Spanish, thoroughly enjoying using my newly-acquired skills.

"I'm going to Lake Atitlán on Wednesday."

Since I am heading north as well, I ask if he'd like a travel companion. He agrees with my proposal and we gear up to leave the day after tomorrow.

Wednesday arrives and a crowded minivan carts us out towards the lake but terminates halfway at a busy triangular intersection where the driver leaves us in a dust cloud. Sitting on our bags, we're unsure of where we are. The tickets we'd paid for took us all the way to the lake. We wait. Buses arrive and leave continuously, but none show signs of going our way. Fearing we've been scammed, a minivan screeches to a halt across the road.

"¡Panachajel!" screams the attendant, hanging out of the door and waving us over.

"¡Gallo tour! ¡Dale! ¡Dale!" he shouts again, pointing at us.

"That's us! Gallo tours!" I say to Marco, jumping up from the dust.

"Si, vamos," he replies in his soft, monotone voice.

We're bundled in to the cramped van and arrive twenty minutes later in Panajachel on the shore of Lake Atitlán, a small town of streets lined with blanket shops and travel agent windows full of faded yellow posters of the lake.

The town is shaped by deep escarpments surrounding it, and an armada of leaking boats bob in the orange foam at the water's edge, each boat guarded by its owner who waits to pounce on tourists. Marco and I stand out like sitting ducks as they move in.

"¡Tres dolares muchachos!" shouts one. His flustered nature is unsettling. "¡Rápido, rápido!" He hurries us on to his small wooden boat.

We pay him the money, and then wait while practically every other boat splutters out across the lake. Ours takes forty minutes to fill up with passengers – but by the time we leave it is the fullest of the fleet. The sly captain jumps aboard and we leave the shore, making our way across the peaceful surface of the lake to the tiny village of San Pedro la Laguna.

We arrive at the opposite shore, and the passengers slowly disembark one by one onto a dry dirt track that leads up to a row of bars and accommodation options. There are plenty of hostel touts crowding the streets, and music blares from inside the bars, but even with those familiar sights and sounds, I can see that the Mayan culture is still in full swing over here. Old couples walk hand in hand in traditional woven dress through the white, stone-walled, narrow dirt lanes of the village and speak with each other in a strange-sounding Spanish dialect.

"Es Mayan 'Quiche'," Marco comments, explaining the language.

We walk the opposite way from the disembarking crowd, avoiding the disco hostels in the little main street, and find a locally-owned establishment. The powder blue four-storey building is a simple concrete structure of square, windowless double rooms.

"Dos dólares cada noche," the young girl says, wearing a brightly woven dress as she climbs the stairs barefoot in front of us.

"Two dollars a night is perfect," I comment to Marco, noting the light bulb dangling from a wire fed through a chiselled out hole in the ceiling.

"Si," he replies in his uninterested tone – and I see him also gazing up at the hole.

The upside of the place are the large hammocks strung across each floor's balcony that command stunning views over Central America's deepest lake. We dump our bags and pick one each, and spend the afternoon watching local fishermen sieving out an orange algae that's covering huge sections of the deep blue water. Leaving the comfort of our hammocks to find food, we're talked into buying tickets for a hike to the dormant volcano San Pedro that towers over the lake.

"Vamos a salir en la manana a las quarto," the short Guatemalan says as he hands us two pink raffle tickets, informing us we leave at 4am.

At dinner, we choose a simple local restaurant overlooking the orange water. A young man joins us and nods towards the harbour.

"Todo el pez, se va a morir," he says, telling us the fish are all going to die. "La naranja es toxico." He goes on to explain that the orange algae is poisoning the lake and the villagers are constantly dredging it out with nets.

"¡¿Pollo o pescado?!" a man interrupts through a toothless mouth, standing at the end of the table in a chef's hat – chicken or fish?

Marco and I share a quick glance; there's no discussion over the menu after what he's just told us.

"¡Pollo, por favor!" we both say at the same time.

The chef returns in no time with our food, and he joins us, speaking in a bastardised Spanish / Quiche dialect through the remaining three brown teeth that poke from his large hippo-like gums.

"I have a chance with a lady in the village tonight, boys," he tells us in his language. "You have any condoms?"

Shocked at his question but pulling one from my wallet, I watch as his face lights up like all his Christmases have come at once.

"That's put a smile on your face!" I say, laughing. We leave him and his gummy smile, staring at the square foil condom packet with his tongue hanging out. Back at the blue tower block and swinging in the hammocks, children's kites flutter high in the air streams and birds chase each other, darting in the deep blue sky. The sky slowly changes to a burnt orange, a shade not too dissimilar to the poison algae covering the water, then fades completely before it finally bursts into a clear starry night. My thoughts drift to my family in the UK who right now have no clue as to exactly where I am in the world. I smile, thinking they'd be assured if they could see me so content in my swaying hammock, listening to the clapping and hymns of the rapturous congregation spilling into the night air from the tiny Catholic church across the lake.

CHAPTER SEVENTY-SIX
SANTIAGO ATITLÁN

While the village still sleeps the next morning, Marco and I creep out of the hotel and into the village to meet Juan, who'll be guiding us up the hill. We meet at the misty dock. He is carrying a machete longer than my arm, his short stature silhouetted against the layer of fog that carpets the lake. Also waiting beside him are two other travellers who have booked in for the walk.

"You guys speak good Spanish?" they ask, wearing earflap beanies and speaking in accents that clearly come from Spain. "We're from Madrid – and you guys?"

"New Zealand and Switzerland," I reply, then switch to Spanish.

After the introductions and general niceties we all follow Juan in the dark up through the back of the village to the beginning of a track that leads into thick forest. The three-hour, 2000-metre climb up a steep and laborious path passes through maize plantations and cloud forests where cacao grows abundantly.

"Hay muchas animales aquí en este tierra," Juan says in a slow voice, informing us of the varied species of animals that inhabit the surrounding dense bush. "Monkeys, armadillos and mouse deer." He says their names in English and assures us again these creatures are all abundant on these slopes. We continue on; we see none.

The cloud forest is drenched in lead weight humidity and as we climb higher into the clouds my ankle problem begins to resurface. I find it difficult to keep up with the group. The three months of shuffling about León, smoking cheap cigarettes and living off a diet of fried food probably hasn't helped the situation. When we reach the top I remove my boot; the swollen joint throbs with pain.

But the pain soon subsides as I look around me and take in where I am. The views are breathtaking. A stunning 2000 metres below, the silver speck that is the town of Santiago Atitlán twinkles at the shore as the misty green volcanoes of Tolimán and Atitlán dominate the ranges that jut out behind each other, battling for space in the oil painting view.

"Idiotas, perezosas," Juan mumbles as his machete blade 'tings' and hacks at an overgrown bush. "Los otros guias." He is complaining of the other guides. "Very lazy."

We sit in a tree, with our legs dangling, marvelling at the vista. The lake is huge and like Santiago Atitlán below, other towns and villages in the distance shimmer in the morning sun around its shoreline.

"We met a crazy guy from New Zealand in Mexico," one of our Spanish travelling partners says.

"Really?" I reply. "Curly hair, glasses and swears a lot?" I add, jokingly thinking of Dan.

"Yes! Do you know him?" the other says, surprising me.

After further investigation, we work out the guy can only be Dan.

"Holy shit, that's hilarious," I remark as they tell me of his extra-long lay-ins, smoking habits and foul-mouthed stories. Staring out across the mountain ranges and lake I think of Dan and what we've experienced together, from the Germans to the Buenos Aires robbery, from the Colombian nightlife to the Ecuadoran jungle village. I miss him, but not enough yet; his annoying traits of talking over me and correcting my Spanish still linger.

"¡OK! ¡Vamos a salir!" Juan says, snapping me out of my far away thoughts. Time to descend.

We follow Juan into the trees. Hiking back down the trail is less painful on my ankle than the climb but proves hard on the knees. Every step is a jarring one as my leg muscles tense up to support the weight of my pack. I'm starting to wince with every step when, just like with the view at the top, my pain is checked when a young boy passes us. He's dressed in torn clothing and bears a huge roll of logs on his back. The logs are tied with twine and connected to a rope that wraps across a rubber strap on his forehead that supports the weight.

As he disappears into the scrub, I reassess. Shit. I have it pretty easy.

༄

Back in town, we drink a couple of beers with the Spaniards. They hand me a flyer for a hostel in San Cristóbal de las casas, a town in Chiapas, Mexico.

"Hey, this where your friend was!" the taller one says, referring to Dan. "Es muy buen hostel."

I thank them, always glad for a recommendation. And with that we part ways.

We leave San Pedro La Laguna the following morning in a large wooden boat jam-packed with Mayan families. They huddle together in the bow of the vessel, sitting on wet algae dredging nets and sacks of beans. They fall asleep one by one before the boat even leaves the dock.

Soon we are spluttering across the glassy lake through the light fog. Our destination is the town of Santiago Atitlán, the very town we had looked down on yesterday, its foggy morning streets now alive with market vendors.

"Aquí esta," Marco says, informing me that the crumbling wall we are standing next to is the hostel in his guidebook.

We knock. The door opens by itself and we step inside.

"Buenas. ¿Quieres habitacion?" says a young girl in jeans and T-shirt.

"Si," Marco answers. "¿Cuánto vale?"

The room is by no means luxury: four walls, an electric fan and a roof. But at three dollars each for the night, it's perfect. Without eating, or talking for that matter, we sink off to sleep.

Waking early and hungry, we find the streets are already a hive of activity. Mayan women in woven purple dresses squat at the kerb bartering over neat stacks of fruit and vegetables in large wicker baskets. The lines of these women are seemingly endless, stretching all the way into the village.

"Debe de ser el dia Mercado," Marco mumbles, guessing it's market day.

"Sin duda," I reply, agreeing and buying a bunch of bananas.

Climbing a set of mossy stairs that lead into a misty plaza, we stand looking at the entrance of what looks like a gingerbread house from a derelict children's playground. An ornate but crumbling teal facade of a small Catholic church, with its grand exterior of bulbous royal blue trims and cornices, is both charming and dilapidated – or perhaps charming because it's dilapidated. We enter the church and are met with an eerie chanting that fills the hollow pitch of the roof. Flickering candle flames expose these ghostly moans to be a group of shawled women on their knees praying. Marco and I share a worried glance. We're not sure what's happening but it looks to be a private moment. A private, haunting moment. We return to the village.

The day crawls by at a snail's pace while we sit by the lake watching the little boats ferry passengers back and forth across the water to the various villages that dot the shoreline.

"Maybe we should leave this afternoon?" I propose to Marco, now bored and not seeing any point in staying the night.

"Si," he agrees in his monotone Spanish. Our conversation is certainly limited to a minimum, but for the moment, it works for us both.

Collecting our bags, we catch another wooden boat back to Panajachel in hope of buying bus tickets back to Antigua.

The minivan is already full when it arrives. Smartly dressed older people fill the seats, smelling of fresh soap and shampoo. They obviously hadn't banked on our company, judging by the disgusted glares they give us. But we hadn't banked on such fancy attire for the bus ride back to Antigua, so we stuff our bags in and select seats in the back of the bus, pushing past the well-dressed passengers in our typical cloud of scruffy traveller dust.

CHAPTER SEVENTY-SEVEN
ANTIGUA REVISITED

The old people in the minivan are obviously delighted when we're the first to jump out as we pull up at the side of one of Antigua's tiny streets. Marco and I wave goodbye – but it isn't reciprocated. We check back into the quiet hostel for one night, and I withdraw some more money and meet Marco back at the room. We throw in a load of clothes in the launderette across the street and grab some bean tacos in a noisy food bar down the street.

"¿Mañana, nos vamos?" I ask Marco, putting it to him that we head north tomorrow.

"Si, vamos," he agrees, void of any facial expression.

'Private minivan to Flores, $25. Accommodation in Lanquín incl.' A sign reads outside one of the many tour companies that line the streets.

"El bus publico es mas barato, pero mas lento." The greasy guy speaks to us from behind the desk, where he's eating a plate of pork. By now we get the difference between the expensive bus and the chicken bus – the chicken (public) bus is cheaper – but slower. *Mas barato* and *mas lento*, compared to the private bus he's trying to sell us. And even if I don't much like paying for the more expensive route, I also don't relish the idea of being stuck in the confines of an uncomfortably hot bus surrounded by squawking animals for hours on end. So we agree to the tour option and hand over the money. As I go to pay the man at the counter, I realise I only have $5 remaining in my pocket and become frantic. I search all my other pockets, my hands moving furiously in and out of my pants, my shirt, my jacket. I seem to have lost the large amount of cash that I'd drawn out earlier.

"Fuck! I've been robbed!" I say to Marco under my breath re-searching every pocket. "Fuck, fuck!" I repeat, trying to retrace my steps in my head and remember if anyone has bumped into me or seemed suspicious. And then it suddenly dawns on me.

"The pants at the launderette!" I cry. "The cash is in the pocket!"

Walking at pace back to the launderette, my mind is now conjuring scenarios. The guy who puts the clothes in the washer, does he check the pockets? I bet they do. I wonder how I'm going to handle the situation if the money isn't there.

When I walk in, the guy gives me a confused stare.

"No estan lista tu ropa, amigo," he says, telling me the clothes aren't ready and still in the wash.

"No, no," I say, still frantic. "Necesito buscar por algo en el bolsillo, por favor," I tell him, demanding I check the pockets.

I dip my hand in to the machine and pull out the pants and there, deep in the pocket, is the $200 I'd withdrawn earlier. The guy's eyes light up: missed opportunity! But I don't dwell long on what may have happened – I'm so grateful to have found my cash, I thank him profusely, even if he did nothing other than not steal the money he didn't know about.

I return to the hostel and sit on the rear balcony. I drape my US dollar bills over the handrails to dry in the sun. I check them every few minutes to make sure they don't flutter away.

CHAPTER SEVENTY-EIGHT
LANQUÍN

Our plan to catch the six-hour minivan that shuttles tourists door to door from Antigua to Lanquín seemed like the clever option. At least we would not ride eight hours on a partially unsealed road, with nothing but blown out eardrums (from the deafening music) and cramped knees (from the inevitable wedging that occurs in the chicken bus). At least we'd have a comfortable ride.

At least that's what we thought.

We couldn't have been more wrong.

Three hairy Israeli guys flirt with a couple of flabby American Peace Corp volunteer girls who insistently brag at the top of their voices.

"YEAH, THE WHOLE VILLAGE LOOOOVES ME, I'M LIKE, THE ONLY ONE WITH A TV," one of them says twiddling her dreads and obviously keen to be the centre of attention.

I'm in a foul mood by the time we pull into a gas station in smog-infested Guatemala City. But the mood of the whole bus shifts dramatically when the co-driver informs us we will not be allowed to disembark, as the area is too dangerous.

"HEY BUD!" shouts one of the American girls. "WE NEED TO PEE! DUDE, THIS IS OUTRAGEOUS!" They are desperate to be heard. They are enraged. They fly off the handle. They yell some more. The hissy fit that ensues has me almost in stitches, were I not so annoyed. They look like they have a swarm of bees trapped in their filthy clothes.

The bus driver, ignoring their fury, alights the bus and locks the door behind him to fill the tank.

"FUCK THIS GUY!" America's sweetheart says, directing it to the other passengers and clearly expecting us to take her side. I avoid eye contact with her and try to ignore their outraged babble. And I don't think I'm the only one who's relieved when the driver finally gets back on, engages the engine into gear and pushes out into the traffic.

Even after a toilet stop on the safer fringes of the city, the

Americans' high volume bullshit continues and is only escapable with stereo headphones or earplugs – neither of which I have. Marco, on the other hand, inserts his and drifts off to sleep with a smirk on face, leaving me with the bitches from hell. The verbal garbage continues for the next five hours. Peace corps workers bringing peace to our little jaunt up the highway. Bringing peace? Ha! Far from it. Spoilt American kids sent to Guatemala during their college breaks by their parents. Parents who have done an awful job of rearing them, who now send them out into the world to make it a better place. How lucky we are.

Finally, miraculously, they grow tired of their own voices and curl up in their seats, exposing rolls of white flesh from where tufts of armpit hair sprout. I try not to look but I am compelled to check on them every now and again – they're sitting just across the aisle from me, and it's almost impossible not to. There's a kind of morbid curiosity that takes hold of me. I alternate between closing my eyes and peeking their way. Sometimes the very sight of someone is enough to make you seethe. Even if they've finally shut up.

Then, eyes shut and mouth open, snoring and dribbling on herself, the noisier of the two shifts in her seat and twists her baggy vest. This twist (of fate) releases an unrestrained boob that flops out, bearing a hairy brown nipple that resembles a large wart. The nipple wart seems to be alive. I shouldn't be staring but I am. The nipple nestles itself in the fold of her equally hairy armpit. I don't know whether to smile or grimace.

I spend the next few bumpy hours averting my eyes and am relieved when we come to a halt in the highlands in a long line of semi-trucks and minivans. As if from nowhere, several Mayan women balancing baskets of chicken, tortillas and salsa on their heads appear from the dense foliage.

"YES!" The sweethearts pipe up, smelling the food. Pushing their way past the rest of us, they lunge at the window with money, desperately worried they will miss out on stuffing their fat faces.

"¡Tortillas! ¡Pollo!" the vendors cry, taking advantage of whatever's causing the hold-up and pocketing our loose change.

An hour or so later the road frees up and we continue on with the bitches talking shit again, now re-energised from the food. Their voices grate. Their content is just shy of useless. Their values seem not so Peace Corps to me. At least they keep their nipples to themselves.

As dusk settles, the bus winds down through a mossy green valley heavily shrouded in mist, and we eventually arrive at the hostel in Lanquín.

Similar to a Club 18:30 hotel in Ibiza, the place is firmly rooted on the gringo trail, and holds a monopoly over any other efforts of accommodation in the area. It processes tourists like a sausage factory. We are duly processed and shown to our room.

Situated on an absolutely beautiful site scattered with bamboo-clad cabins leading down to the idyllic banks of a fast flowing river, it is also, unfortunately, home to a log framed structure with a bar running along its back wall selling overpriced drinks and floppy microwave pizza. In the middle of this log hut sits a large table where a bunch of high-pitched spring break students drink beer and shout at each other. Competing for air space, they bark across the table trying desperately to get their points across and stories heard. It's perfect, of course, for the girls from the bus. They join in and the ego war grows while they all drink pitchers of brightly coloured booze like their lives depend on it.

Marco and I, still in the garden, share a disappointed glance and head to the village to find food. We sit down outside a busy little comedor on the main street: much more peaceful. This is reminiscent of the villages on the shore of Lake Atitlán. Traditional Mayan dress still rules the fashion and couples shuffle along the cobbled streets, hand in hand.

"Dos especiales, por favor," Marco asks the waitress, requesting the dinner special of grilled chicken, beans and tortillas. Two large plates of hot food are brought out to our little wooden table on the sidewalk. Grazing over my meal, I relish the absence of the soggy pizza bar back at Club 18:30.

Marco smiles before forking up some food while we're watched by a thousand village eyes.

CHAPTER SEVENTY-NINE
SEMUC CHAMPEY

A half-plucked chicken pecks around my feet while I sit at the kerbside in the mist. It's the crack of dawn the following day.

"El bus," Marco says, pointing at the wheezing vehicle that squeals to a halt inches from my toes.

Lanquín's closest attractions are Grutas Lanquín, a giant cave that stretches fifty kilometres underground, and Semuc Champey, a series of tepid waterfall pools further into the jungle.

We opt for the waterfalls and board the bus.

I'm surprised we're the only passengers, but as the driver starts slowly lapping the village, blowing his horn through the smoky market stalls and wooden framed pick-up trucks, I begin to understand why. We complete the same circle four times, picking up local passengers as we go. The whole tour around town lasts forty-five minutes with a stop halfway. Here, the driver departs, leaving the engine running and disappearing into the smoke and vegetable stacks. A few minutes later he returns with a squawking live chicken swinging upside down from his hand, which he stuffs into the glove box of the bus's dashboard.

The thirty-two-seater now contains around forty-five people and a chicken, Marco and I the only foreigners. My blond friend is pinned between two cowboy-hatted old men. I'm sandwiched between two ladies breastfeeding their offspring. Unable to move and just inches away, I can't help but watch. There you go again, Darío, I scold myself: spying on nipples! But this is different. Warm milk bubbles from the suckling babies' mouths, dribbling down the firm brown breasts of their mothers. Cramped and crowded, with a squawking chicken in the glove box, I can't help but smile at how much more pleasant – and, remarkably, peaceful – this bus ride is compared to the bus that brought us here.

The old wreck reluctantly heaves its rusty chassis up a steep muddy road shrouded in mist, barely missing an old woman on one blind corner and a wild pig laid out in our path on another.

"¡VAYASE CHANCHO!" the driver shouts at the pig and honking his horn as it squeals and rolls off the cliff, never to be seen again as we slide round the next corner. The road violently twists and turns around the green hillside before arriving at a large wooden archway where we squeeze our way off. Two mustached men brandishing pump action shotguns stand smoking cigarettes in the car park. In blue jeans and cowboy boots, one wears a Rambo T-shirt while the other proudly polishes his gun barrel. The dirt car park is empty. It occurs to me it might be better if we stay on the bus. I turn to Marco, who fires me a look – clearly thinking the same thing. But we are here, and we've made an effort to get here, so we throw caution to the wind and disembark.

The bus grinds into gear and within seconds disappears off around a corner, leaving us on the deserted road dressed only in board shorts and flip flops, and armed with towels. The two men, now leaning against a tree off to the side, eyeball us with hands on their shotguns as we start to walk towards the gates.

"Esta abierto," one says to us, indicating the place is open. "Adelante," he adds, welcoming us.

"Why does a waterfall need to be protected with armed guards?" I ask Marco, now inside.

"Hmm. ¿No se?" he replies with his usual abrupt answer. A man of few words. I begin to wonder if he's fed up with my company, or perhaps he's grown up in a 'speak when you're spoken to' environment. Whatever the case, I realise as I'm standing there with my towel and the armed guards that I'm looking forward to seeing Dan again. Where Marco says little, Dan would have a hundred jokes. And while those jokes wore thin, they still injected our travels with a kind of energy that I appreciated – even if I needed a break.

A sign on the path points skyward to a lookout.

"¿Vamos?" I ask Marco.

He nods.

We climb a treacherous cliff face and pull ourselves up over slippery bare tree roots that cling to the rocky surface, and, 100 metres up, we reach a muddy lookout. Peering down into the thin deep-cut gorge that slices into the thick green jungle, we make out seven tiered sandstone pools full of steaming turquoise water nestled at the base. This magical place is alive with the tweet and screech of jungle bird life as we descend from the lookout. We wallow and relax in the warm water for a couple of hours with the place all to ourselves. It seems we've found paradise.

The birdsong sounding so peacefully through the trees is destroyed by a group of tour buses skidding into the car park off in the distance, and we wait for what can only be an onslaught of day-trippers. Like a box of multi-coloured cereal poured into our bowl of quiet, a rabid crowd of gap-year students in fluoro swimwear fill the pools, splashing and shouting. Others in yellow life vests hang from ropes and abseil down the falls at the opposite end. Others, screaming at the top of their voices, are being bounced along in inflated inner tubes, turning what was a place that dreams are made of into a public water park during school holidays.

We don't really begrudge the schoolkids their pool fun – but we don't need to stay, either.

We exit our paradise and wait for what seems like an eternity at the gates. Our bus doesn't come. And it rains. And rains some more. By the time the bus arrives, the roads are so slick the return trip is like a 'World's most dangerous roads' YouTube video, albeit slightly more perilous as the death trap's bald tyres are now desperately trying to grip the slippery mud surface as we descend the twisted wet road – now more a brown river than a road.

With my heart still in my mouth, we make it to the bottom of the gorge, and, alive, we jump out just before the village at the road that leads to the caves of Grutas Lanquín. During our walk, two late teen lads eyeball us from across a field. I start to wonder about the walk back, along this stretch in the dark. The track is long but partially sealed and we need only walk a half hour to reach our destination – which turns out to be another car park.

"Hola." A greeting comes from a small wooden sentry hut.

We approach the hut and find a small woman sitting inside.

"Treinta quetzales entrada," she says, asking for an entrance fee. We pull the notes from our pockets, and she hands us a raffle ticket each.

The caves are pitch black. We're accustomed to attractions being closed for repairs or shut down altogether, so it comes as no surprise that the electricity supply to the caves is dead. The string of bulbs that once illuminated the brilliant colours of the giant rock formations are now mere decorations hanging in the still underground air. But we want to see the formations that tower over thirty feet tall and are five metres in diameter, and we've come prepared. We whip out our headlights and strap them on, wandering deep into the earth.

We soon lose ourselves amongst the red and yellow fossilised columns. The cave stretches into the earth's depths beyond the wire handrail that guides tourists – and we go deeper. The temperature drops. We continue on, with only our lights to show the way. Descending into what feels like a large hollow cave, we see bats hanging from the top curve of rock – lots of bats. They squeak as our lights connect with their eyes. Looming above us are pillars of rock the size of lighthouses. A shudder travels involuntarily through my body.

"Vamos a salir." Marco says it first, shivering and keen to get back up into daylight. I've seen enough and agree. Enough Indiana Jonesing for one day. We climb back out and wait for the highlight of the caves, which is to come at the close of the day.

According to the travel books, thousands of bats leave every day at dusk through the entrance arch in a thick black squeaking cloud. It seems we've visited at the wrong time of year, however, as we patiently wait while in dribs and drabs and in no particular hurry around twenty or so fly out.

An American family in the car park has arrived without head torches.

"You won't be able to see anything," I warn them. "Probably best to come back tomorrow if you can buy a flashlight from somewhere."

"Oh, OK – yeah, thanks, I guess you're right," the father says. And then he adds, "Hey, you guys want a ride? It's a little dark to be walking, dontcha think?"

We don't have to be asked twice.

As I climb into the car, I'm immediately transported into a different world. Clean upholstery and a pine air freshener scent bring back memories of a place I left eight months ago, where collecting rental vehicles for the various film companies I'd worked for was an almost everyday occurrence. I'm overcome with a feeling similar to the one I experienced on the side of the road waiting for my bus, just as I was leaving León. I stare into the dark. I am a tiny speck in the universe. I am happy.

"We'll jump out here, thanks," I tell the family as we pass the hostel.

They give a hearty wave as they drive away.

We arrive back at our cabin to find a note pinned to our door and signed by management stating that by not using their restaurant or shuttle services we're not supporting local business. I laugh, and look at Marco.

"After a day and a half of eating meals in the village and using local transport, they have the audacity to pin this on our door?!"

Marco tears the note off and looks at me. "Idiotas."

Sometimes Marco's singular way of summing things up with a word is spot on.

We smile. We're happy to have ruffled the feathers of the establishment. We're glad to disrupt the monopoly these money hungry foreigners have built. We're glad we actually contributed to the real local economy that in reality doesn't care if people from the outside world visit or not, and not given our money to this gringo hostel charade that relies on it.

"Vamos a comer en el pueblo," Marco says with a smug smile.

We crumple the note and head back into the village for dinner.

CHAPTER EIGHTY
FLORES

Six hours into the trip from Lanquín to Flores, I examine my map and realise we've been had. Or at least misinformed. The greasy guy back in Antigua who sold us the bus tickets said the drive took around five hours. "No mas amigos," he promised, eating his pork from a Styrofoam carton. But it's clear we have at least another three hours before arriving. Our driver, a shifty-eyed character wearing a gold chain and basketball vest, parks up in every village en route where a group of eager locals, obviously aware that he's coming, all queue for the SIM cards that he dishes out. Reaching the town of Cobán, he dumps us in the drizzle at a mini mall.

"Go inside, get coffee," he commands in Spanish from his seat. "I go pick up mattress, see you twenty minutes."

"A fucking mattress?!" I complain as he disappears into the wet fog. "What the fuck is up with this guy? He's taking the piss!"

I slump down next to Marco, and it dawns on me that my bag with all my belongings including passport and credit card are now roped down under a tarp on the roof of Mr. SIM Card's minivan at a Guatemalan mattress store.

"What are we going to do if he doesn't come back?" I ask Marco, feeling my stress levels rising.

"Hmm, no se," he replies in his usual fashion, appearing not overly bothered.

Forty stressful minutes drag by while the other passengers start to question if the driver's coming back. And then he pulls up outside. We notice the windows are steamy; the side door slides open revealing not the mattress that was supposedly picked up but instead the driver's whole family. They filter out one by one onto the footpath and disappear into the mall. Shoving us in like nothing has happened, we return to our seats and continue driving north through the mountains. Our next pit stop is for a late lunch at a small comedor in the middle of nowhere. We are dying of hunger. Tired dishes of chicken in a runny red sauce accompanied by tortillas and rice are limply spooned onto our plates from stainless steel hot trays by a woman who clearly wants us to hurry up so she can close her doors.

Outside, two small kids no more than five years old beg for money in the lay-by.

"Un quetzale, un quetzale," they squeak with hands out.

"No tengo nada," I tell them instead giving them a chunk of chicken each. Remembering the packet of balloons in the side pocket of my rucksack I'd taken from Malenita's party back in León, I set my food down and blow up a couple. They start to giggle, but it's not the balloons inflating that amuses them. I turn to where they point and see that a dog is now snout-deep in my food tray, pushing it around the car park.

The kids run off, still giggling, bouncing the balloons in the air. The dogs have eaten my dinner.

Even so, my mood lifts. A feeling of happiness washes over me; I'm actually glad my pockets were empty. The little street beggars trained to extort money have changed to joyous kids chasing balloons.

Tired and hungry and ten long hours after departing Lanquín, we cross the short causeway that links the dirty town of Santa Elena to the small island of Flores in Lake Petén. The van skids up outside a small iron gate in a narrow rocky street, where a sign hangs loosely: Hostel Tres Amigos. It seems every backpacker coming this way is staying at this hostel.

Marco and I inspect the dorms and discover an untidy mess: backpacks leaning against the bunks have exploded like party streamers, sending clothes in all directions, some hanging from furniture and door handles while other garments that have missed their target sponge up the puddles that speckle the floor. Marco and I don't imagine ourselves staying in such squalor; we rent a private room. We are walled in by bamboo, which is surprisingly pleasant. We spread out on our beds, exhausted from the day's travel. I'm relieved that I can sleep knowing that no other annoying dorm mates will disturb me during the night. We drift to sleep to the faint hum of the downstairs bar.

CHAPTER EIGHTY-ONE
EL REMATE

"There are no McDonalds for miles! It's crazy!"

We should be used to this by now, but I'm still shocked when I hear a frustrated backpacker splutter thus. This time, it's an obnoxious American guy issuing his complaint the following morning at breakfast as little chunks of egg tortilla spray all over the table. He chews and talks, chews and talks.

In no mood to deal with this shit anymore, I turn to Marco, who is quietly reading his book. "Let's get out of here, man, we can eat on the way," I say, grabbing a Styrofoam cup and filling it with free coffee.

A noisy tuk-tuk carries us back across the causeway from Flores and we are dropped at Santa Elena bus station where we switch to a minivan going to El Remate, a smaller community situated fifty-five minutes further round the shore of the lake. Minutes after leaving the station, the van stops in an enclosed market area crowded with household goods, mops, buckets, brooms and other cleaning sundries hanging from the rafters of the stalls. Hordes of street vendors shuffle their way up to the windows asking for money for the food and water bottles they're pushing in our faces. As a general rule, we know not to stop in the middle of a crowd of third world pedestrians, or you'll be buying Chiclets and cellphone covers for days. But we're trapped in the minivan, so we have no choice. We pass money out the windows and purchase water; we manage to avoid purchasing mops and sponges. After clawing our way out of the market, the minivan drops us on the edge of the lake in a dirt lay-by and we're hassled again by touts who urge us to follow them to the accommodation they're offering.

"Este," Marco says, pointing at one in his book. "Vamos." He walks off in the direction of it without saying another word.

According to his book, the hostel is owned by a lady called Doña Julia and located on a street that branches off the main road, skirting the eastern shore of the lake. We walk in what we think is the correct direction, while an old man in a red Hawaiian shirt and sandals circles us on an old squeaky mountain bike.

"Mi casa es muy barata, hombres," he says, desperately trying to sway our decision to stay at his place.

"Ya tenemos, amigo," we reply repeatedly, saying we're good. It takes several rounds until he squeaks off in the opposite direction.

When we come to Doña Julia's, we are instantly glad we didn't go with the man on the red bike. Built in a clearing cut in the jungle, our room is one of four; we are fortunate to land the top balcony with a view straight down the eye of a jetty. By day, we enjoy an unencumbered view over the turquoise lake; by night, the skies turn to burnt orange sunsets. Doña Julia and her family spend their days wandering around the property cooking, breastfeeding their snotty-nosed babies and tinkering on old cars that, judging by their looks, they should probably give up on.

On our first afternoon here, we jump in the warm lake from the end of the jetty where a crusty German hippy woman is de-flea-ing her dog. I tread water, watching from a safe distance while she picks at her pet on dry land. I say hello.

"I'm Nina, and this is Hashish," she says, referring to her dog and plucking at his fur. "So, you're on your way to Tikal, no?" *Pluck, pluck.* "I've been here for a long time. It was so different years ago." Pausing, she stares off into space. "We would take opium and mushrooms and sleep in the temples; it was a very spiritual time." She's deeply absorbed in her own memories and staring into space as she warbles on.

But then she grows serious and her tone shifts. "It's a great place here, but you must be careful of the police; they're very corrupt. My house and land were taken away by the authorities, but they had no proof."

"Proof of what?" I ask.

She changes tack once more, this time moving the conversation back to the more comfortable territory of the inviting landscape. Maybe she's worried she has revealed too much of her past life to a couple of strangers. I wonder how often she does that.

"Well, it's a lovely lake," I say, wondering if this feels as awkward to her as it does to me.

We swim a little further out. From where we are floating, we can see another jetty down the shore, and we can see a group of women washing clothes in plastic tubs and looking in our direction, giggling.

We turn and spot what they must be laughing at back on shore. A tall leathery-skinned guy comes sauntering towards us down the jetty in black Speedos and cowboy hat. He pulls a matchbox from his swimming trunks and a thin cigar from his hatband, strikes a flame and lights it.

"Mornin', Nina, mornin', fellas," he greets us.

"Morning, Hank," Nina replies.

We swim a little closer.

"I see you met some new friends, Hashish," he says to the dog, ruffling the fur on its head. We learn that he is based in Guatemala City and stays here every November in the room next to ours.

"Do you guys smoke pot?" he asks.

"A little, yeah," I reply, pulling myself from the warm water and slightly wary of his forward nature and choice of clothing.

"OK, well I'll be sure to come find you guys later on then." He sucks his cigar.

The evening sky is pure orange and fishermen stand silhouetted on their small boats out on the lake.

"I've never seen a sunset like this, Marco," I say, astounded at the intensity.

"Mmm," Marco replies, not moving his head.

At around midnight there's a knock at our door that wakes us. We are startled and open the door with caution. Hank is leaning on the balcony, still in the Speedos and with his back to us. Looking like a Marlboro cowboy swimsuit edition calendar model, he turns his head.

"You fellas wanna smoke?" he says, beckoning us over.

"Sure," I reply, though I am slightly weirded out by the situation.

We lean on the balcony and puff away on a giant joint, gazing at the thousands of stars that umbrella the lake.

"Get in there after 3pm tomorrow afternoon," he says, not turning his head.

"Tikal?" I ask, presuming he's talking about the pyramids.

"Yep, there's a bus at noon," he replies. "All the other tourists will be leavin' when you arrive." He passes me the joint. "You'll have it all to yourselves, and you can get in the next day on the same ticket."

Drawing a toke and passing it to Marco, we nod at each other in agreement. Hank's seems like a good suggestion.

"Vamos a quedar en hamacas," Marco says, telling him of our plan to stay in hammocks out there and blowing out a plume of grey smoke into the still night air.

CHAPTER EIGHTY-TWO
TIKAL

We wake with hazy heads. We jump in the lake before eating a taco breakfast cooked by Doña Julia: there's no other way to begin the day in this place. It's paradise. It's quiet, the water is warm, the sun is warm, the slight breeze off the lake is warm and Doña's food is delicious. It's a great find. Thanks to Marco.

"¿Quedamos unos dias en la vuelta?" I suggest to him, hoping he'll want to stay here an extra day or two after Tikal.

"Si," he answers shrugging and not overly excited.

"¿Podemos dejar las maletas aquí?" I ask Doña Julia, hoping we're able to leave our large backpacks with her while we visit Tikal.

"Si, allá," she replies, placing a stack of warm tortillas wrapped in a hand towel on the table. She points to the corner of the room, indicating the spot for our bags, and we leave them there to be tugged and poked by the snotty babies crawling around the lounge.

In the village we come to the local barber sitting in a worn out swivel chair in a rickety wooden hut, painted blue and loosely held together with rusty nails and twine.

"¿Quiere cortar?" he says desperately, looking up from his outdated *Time* magazine. A haircut? Well, no. I take off my hat, revealing a No.2 buzz cut. He repeats his question to Marco. But Marco also shakes his head and declines.

"Es mi negocio," he says, unprompted, informing us it's his business. We can see that – and by the looks of it a very old one. We examine the place further; it's a time warp to the 1950s. An old calendar on the wall is years out of date and hangs next to a large shard of broken mirror where customers are able to admire their finished haircuts. The barber's arsenal of tools laid out on the bench could easily pass as a sheep shearer's and the chequered linoleum flooring desperately tries to curl itself back into a roll from the edges of the room. The bus timetable on his wall is also years out of date, and there's a vine growing through it from the jungle outside.

"Los buses, nunca cambiar," he tells us, looking at the timetable claiming the buses never change.

"¿De donde son ustedes?" he asks, curious of our native countries.

"Suiza," Marco says, turning the old man's expression to a blank look.

"¿Alemania?" the barber says: Germany.

"Si," Marco confirms, a simple lie the easiest way to avoid a lengthy explanation.

We leave the old man with his magazine and sit across the road at a shady concrete plinth where a faded bus sign hangs from a wooden stake. There, we wait in hope for the afternoon chicken bus. Midday drifts by with the light breeze that blows up through the cluster of adobe buildings. Eventually, well after mid-day – actually, one hour later than scheduled – the rumbling sound of an engine grows stronger as the bus approaches us.

"¡Se viene el bus!" shouts the barber from across the street, still inside his shop with his *Time* and his old schedules. He seems determined to see that we are on the right bus, and we wave as we climb aboard.

We rumble off further into the dense jungle accompanied only by a couple of schoolkids and an old man holding a motorbike wheel.

Just as Hank had said, we arrive as hordes of daytrippers leave in a mass exodus from the site, jumping into the line of minivans and buses parked alongside the dirt road.

"Dos hamacas, por favor," Marco asks a smartly dressed man at the ticket desk.

"Quatro dolares." He takes our notes and hands us two neatly folded cotton hammocks and mosquito nets. "Dondequiera," he adds, pointing at a group of straw roofed concrete plinths in the paddock. "You choose," he repeats in English.

We string up our hammocks under our chosen straw roof. We are situated no more than thirty metres from the entrance that hides the Mayan city. The musical chatter of birdsong and the haunting screams of howler monkeys that call out to each other across the jungle are a constant reminder that we are now guests in their lost world.

But I am ready for the wild. I test my hammock, and relish the idea that we're spending the night in such a strange and wonderful place.

Suddenly, there's movement above. I'm startled and look up in the tree over my head. Just a metre away and sitting on a branch is a brown, pointy-snouted creature peering down at me. It's like nothing I've ever seen before – meerkat crossed with a baby bear, perhaps. It examines me with its shiny black eyes while wiggling its snout and curling its long tail around a branch before scurrying back up into the foliage.

"What was that?!" I ask Marco excitedly, forgetting to use Spanish.

Am I ready for the wild?

"Pisote," he says, obviously understanding what I've asked.

"¿Vamos?" I say, suggesting we head in for a look.

"¡Si, claro!" he says, with an excitement I haven't witnessed from him before.

Even if I'm a little skittish at the encounter with the wild critter, Marco seems fully ready.

The jungle trail and its parasite-tufted trees are empty for us to explore, our only company being the howler monkeys. As we go deeper into the forest, the only indication that Mayan temples from more than 1500 years ago once stood here are the intricately carved white stone combs that protrude from the summits of giant earth hills. Shafts of sunlight cut through the canopy and all around us are mini mountains of decaying leaves and mulch. The giant tiered bases of the excavated and restored temples stand among the trees in all their glory, silent and eerie. I'm struck by how alone this place feels, especially since Marco and I have timed the trip so well and have the place all to ourselves. I breathe in, full of wonder at a place so old, so barely a part of this world anymore. It's as if we're in a place nearly forgotten by the modern world. The only sign of life, besides Marco's and my breathing, is the chirping song of wildlife that surrounds the ruins.

As we continue to wander through the site, we come to two Guatemalan families who've also come late in the day. We cross paths with them from time to time. As the evening slowly darkens a pink glow fills the sky and casts a magnificent light on the temples. Climbing the giant stone stairway to the top of Temple Four, we sit at a dizzying height to watch the pink hue of the day's last light sink behind the green carpet of jungle as the abundant wildlife continues to chatter away across the canopy.

Marco and I can't believe our luck.

Back at our concrete pad, and swinging in the hammocks enveloped and protected in mosquito nets, we enjoy the bird life's conversation that continues to roll out over the forest. It's followed by a moment's silence, which is then replaced by the bloodcurdling screams of the monkeys, who continue throughout the night echoing in the darkness. We discern a certain pattern as one troop howls across the jungle and then receives the replies of other groups many miles away. It's a bizarre but strangely soothing sound in our surroundings. I don't know when we fall asleep but the monkeys seem to keep us company all night long.

6am and the birds are at it again. We wake and return to the paths leading around the temples, which are now shrouded in thick morning mist creeping through the dense wall of the trunks and vines. As the cloud burns from the air, the temple combs appear once again, majestically poking out of the green canopy and mapping out the city from above.

We have an excellent view from the top platform of Temple Two. Our quiet is disturbed when we hear people climbing the steps. I dread seeing people here, breaking into our peaceful surroundings. It's been a luxury to have this place to ourselves all night long – a privilege that I am loathe to give up.

"Hey! Fancy seeing you here!"

It turns out that the first head that appears is that of Julian, the

South African guy from the Caribbean crossing. Which I suppose is not so much a coincidence as an inevitability; this is a well-trod tourist trail, and it's not uncommon to cross paths with previous travel companions.

"Hey! No way!" He seems surprised to see us. "Did you stay the night?"

"Yeah, we hired hammocks," I say. "This is Marco."

"Hola," Marco says, shaking Julian's hand limply.

"How was the diving?" I ask, curious to know about Honduras.

"The diving part was great," he begins. "But getting there was the biggest hassle. It's a pretty corrupt place and they're not really used to tourists."

We nod.

"The islands were amazing, though – they just need to get their shit together on the mainland."

Julian enjoys the misty temple tops in silence and we descend and explore the ruins once more. Wandering through the dappled light of the trails, dwarfed by the sheer size of the structures, we continue to feel in awe. When the site slowly begins to fill with the tour groups arriving from Flores, we know it's time to leave. We bid Julian goodbye and the last I see of him is him climbing up a wooden staircase that leads to the summit of another temple.

Marco and I return our hammocks and venture out to the road in hopes of hitching a ride back. It's not long before a car stops. The vehicle is on its last legs and not surprisingly dies half way up an incline.

"¡Sale! ¡Sale!" the driver shouts, telling everyone to get out and push.

Lining up with the laughing family at the rear of the pick-up truck and pushing it to the peak, we gain momentum and jump in the back as it lets out a puff of grey smoke and bump starts with a jolt.

"¡¡Woooohooo!!" cries the family as we bump along the jungle road towards Flores. As we near the lake, the driver slows down to a safe-ish speed and Marco and I jump out, catching ourselves on our feet and running to slow down as they disappear off into the distance waving.

El Remate is as quiet as it was when we left. After our excursion into the wild, we are dying for a cold drink. We stop at a store on the way to Doña Julia's. The dirty white house has a hole in the front wall with 'Se vende' painted crudely above it in drippy red. We peer into the darkness, and a man barks at us from the back of the shop.

"¡¿Busca?!" he shouts, asking what we're looking for.

"Dos Coca-Cola, por favor," I reply politely, now slightly scared.

In the darkness of the interior, the man pulls himself out of his chair and hobbles to a chest freezer, where he pulls out two ice-cold Cokes before popping the caps with a bottle opener.

"¡Dolar!" he shouts unnecessarily, still using his lazy dialect.

Although the store ogre's manner leaves little to be desired, the Cokes he's sold us are a much-needed burst of ice-cold refreshment. Finishing my bottle in one tilt, I need another.

I manage to catch him before he sits back down. "Uno mas por fa," I say through the hole in his wall.

He stops mid-way back to his chair, grunts and turns around to glare. Then he hobbles back to the freezer.

"¡¿Algo mas?!" he shouts, staring at me like he wants to kill me.

"No, gracias," I say sheepishly, handing him over fifty cents.

Back at the lodge and smoking a joint on the balcony is Hank, still wearing his Speedos and cowboy hat.

"So how was it?" he asks.

"Man, it was incredible," I answer, savouring the last drops of the second Coke. We share our experiences of the last two days, re-living the mysterious, grand atmosphere of the mighty ruins that lie dormant in the jungle. I realise Hank has heard these same tales more than once before, but I can't help myself – in my enthusiasm, I must tell someone, and Hank and his Speedos happen to be the only person around.

The orange sky fades, revealing a million stars that glint over the shimmering surface of the vast lake. This is a place where Mother Nature has hidden some of her most precious treasures. It's a magical part of the world. Staring out into the darkness, I know some day I will return.

CHAPTER EIGHTY-THREE
FRONTERA COROZAL

Marco is bound for Honduras.

We leave the lake village together taking the crowded 7am bus to arrive back at the Santa Elena terminal. The busy station wipes away what tranquillity is left in my soul and Marco quickly bids me farewell and climbs aboard his bus. The bus backs out and I'm left alone. But I don't feel lonely. Losing Marco as a travel companion is not like splitting with Dan. For one thing, Dan and I go back. For another, I realise I actually know Marco very little, even after spending a week or so with him – and going to some memorable places together. In fact, I realise now that I really don't know a lot more about him than what I originally learnt in the first few minutes of meeting him.

Come to think of it, I will probably have more conversation with myself travelling alone.

I purchase a bus ticket to Palenque from a booth and grab a tuk-tuk back to Flores.

Back at the Tres Amigos hostel, I'm forced to take a dorm bed as the private rooms are all full. The whole hostel experience is hard to readjust to after having my own room in León and sharing with Marco. I am really not in the mood to mix with the other travellers downstairs, so I lie back on my bunk and study my guidebook before drifting off to sleep. All night long my sleep is interrupted as drunk guests come in and out of the dorm. Finally, my alarm wakes me at 4am and I leave.

I walk through the dark cobbled streets that lead me down to the edge of the lake where the ticket seller had instructed I wait. I sit in silence in the dark. The situation feels familiar. Soon two other travellers show up. One is a girl wearing baggy hemp clothing and another, from what I can make out in the dim light, is a local girl.

Simple "Holas" are exchanged and before long the headlights of a minivan come across the causeway towards us.

The vehicle is fucked. While my bag is secured on the roof, I get into a struggle with the broken folding side door to gain entry to the bruised and battered shit heap. With a windscreen spider crack, much like the Bolivian bus back in Uyuni, the bus does not inspire confidence.

It looks like I'm in for another adventurous ride.

The sheet of glass miraculously remains intact as the bus trundles along, letting out a grating squeal every time we bounce through a pothole. After an hour or so we stop in a small village. It's still dark outside. The driver leaves the engine running and exits to buy a coffee and food from a small store, without asking if we're hungry. The area we've stopped in is not giving me the confidence to follow him. A few guys mill around outside in cotton vests and jeans with revolvers in their belts. The other two travellers are fast asleep. I really want a cup of coffee, but, thinking better of it and going with my gut, I stay put. When the driver returns, he greedily munches from a Styrofoam takeaway box as he steers the bus with his free hand along a road flanked by maize fields. The smell of his food torments me.

When will we stop to eat? I think to myself, wondering how much longer I can go on.

Six hours – that's how long.

The potholes that have now become the size of bomb craters throw us into the air during the six hours of bumpy dirt roads that become progressively worse. I have a feeling we're driving to the edge of civilisation. But then, quite suddenly, we arrive at a descending track that opens out on to a river, and we are greeted with a scene that seems all too calm. Little motorboats putter across the slow flowing stretch of water while a small bell on a buoy softly rings as it sways in the wake created by the boats' choking outboards. The bus drives down a crude concrete ramp that joins two wooden planks spanning the length of an old wooden barge's floor and both set at axle width. The old vessel creaks under our weight as the wheels slowly ease their way onto the barge, and we float across the river. I am partly charmed by the scene and partly alarmed: we are trapped inside the vehicle as it's practically the same width as the floating platform. Our minivan seems ill suited to be crossing this river; everyone else seems so at ease. River people in giant inner tubes push themselves past with long branches. One is a girl selling baked cakes and snacks. I can't believe my eyes. I am almost faint with hunger.

"¡Si! ¡Si!" I cry from the window, beckoning her over with my hand. "¡Por favor!"

Choosing the three largest chunks of cake from her basket, I hand over ten quetzales before she floats off smiling. The square cakes taste divine. I stuff my face with the sweet, substantial treats.

Still eating cake, I feel a jolt as we ground on the opposite shore. Like an overweight pig that's chosen the wrong spot to drink and is escaping a crocodile, the screaming bus starts to bellow smoke while the tyres spin desperately trying to grip, spraying clods of wet mud into the air as it climbs up the opposite bank.

Back on land, we still have a fair distance to go. The potholes resume – this side of the river is in no better shape than the other. More potholes, more maize fields – while we suffocate in the heat of the bus's interior.

Springing up out of nowhere, a small community suddenly comes into view and we are surrounded by a clutter of adobe structures. The bus slows as the road ends and we're let out at a whitewashed wooden hut.

"Allí," the driver mutters, opening his mouth for the first time and pointing to the Frontera Corozal border with Chiapas.

The officer stamps our passports and points to a row of long motorised wooden canoes bobbing at the edge of the Usumacinta River. This is the river that divides Guatemala and Chiapas.

"¡Allí!" he says, repeating the only word the driver had muttered all morning.

So we climb aboard one of these vessels with all our gear, and the pull chord is yanked, bringing the engine to life. We splutter upstream while families of monkeys swing above us by their tails and look down eyeballing us attentively from jungle branches. The boat slows and steers into a muddy siding on the opposite water's edge.

"¡OK! ¡Vamos!" the captain shouts, leading us up a slippery bluff.

At the top is a modern, white, one storeyed building with a low-pitched brown roof, and, joining the line of other border crossers, I'm met with my first pair of stern Mexican eyes as I reach the officer at the hole in the wall. He carelessly turns the pages in my passport as if it's a document of little importance. Then his hard stare pans up to my face with a look of hatred. Why he's looking at me in this fashion I don't know. Perhaps he's having a bad day. Maybe he's confused by the amount of border stamps it contains. Do I smile? Do I look away? I feel asking him will end in a whole lot of trouble so I decide against it. Finally, he opens the last page, where he staples a 262-peso departure tax that will need to be paid when I leave Mexico.

A brand new Toyota van sits waiting on the verge, the driver just as talkative as the last.

"This is a bit better," the hippy girl says in a strong US accent as she jumps in. "That last bus was fucked!"

Seeing that she's now keen to converse, I reply. "Yeah, I thought that window was gonna pop out on every pot hole we went through. And how hot was it in that thing!"

"Yeah, crazy," she says, pushing her stereo buds into her ears and obviously not that keen to talk after all.

The other girl, a solemn, larger, blonde girl who also hasn't said a word the whole day, looks over to me with a sad face.

"You OK?" I ask her, hoping she'll keep me company with some conversation.

"No speak good English, sorry," she replies in a German accent.

The van's condition makes up for the shit heap we spent the whole morning in, and just as I'm beginning to think the remainder of the ride will be quite enjoyable, the driver pulls over at the end of a long road. A child sitting on a motorbike shouts something into the front yard of a house and speeds off helmet-less. Moments later, five overweight Mexican women trot over to our van, slide the door open and stuff themselves in like cattle. Glaring at us like we're not supposed to be here, the freeloading porkers cackle and snort while applying lipstick and make-up for the rest of the trip.

Two military checkpoints follow and officers in black jump suits interrogate us at each one, searching our bags but seemingly more suspicious of the freeloaders as they question them for quite some time. Finally we are sent on our way, and we arrive at a dirty bus terminal in a sea of roof-racked buses and minivans.

"Gracias amigos, aquí esta," our driver says, indicating we've arrived. He pulls away and leaves us next to our pile of bags. The hippy girl who has been with us since Flores realises we are still twenty kilometres from Palenque, and, seeing our minivan refuelling in the gas station, shouts after him when he pulls out.

"Fucking stop, you asshole!" she shouts, blocking his path and waving her arms. "We all paid to be taken to Palenque, and that's what you're going to do!" she demands in quick fire Spanish.

"No chica, no mas, no mas," he refuses.

"¡No puta! I call policía!" she threatens, rattling off more Spanish and arguing with him.

With a sudden change of heart, the driver reluctantly hands us all twenty pesos, and points to another van that will take us the rest of the way. I am grateful to get the ride, but I'm even more inspired by this girl's negotiating skills in Spanish. I relish the thought of being able to tackle a situation such as this someday.

We pile in the back of another overloaded minivan. We spend the last leg of our trip together squashed against the windows surrounded by sacks of corn and beans.

CHAPTER EIGHTY-FOUR
PALENQUE

The second minivan that the hippy girl had bargained for us pulls over at the side of the road in the town of Palenque and we pile out and head our separate ways. The guidebook speaks of a complex of bamboo cabins nestled among thick jungle, haunted by the sounds of giant insects, hummingbirds and monkeys. It's situated two kilometres away, and it seems like a better option than the dusty bus connection hub I'm standing in. So I flag down another minivan, and it drops me at the gates of the complex.

My clothes are drenched. It's humid here; everything is soaked in a blanket of wet and the sounds of giant insects and frogs chirrup through the trees. I find my way to reception and check in. The guidebook doesn't lie; the buildings are made entirely of bamboo. Following a vine-flanked path to my room, I drop my bag and make fast work of a chicken leg and rice at the small comedor within the complex.

I collapse on the bed after a long hot day of travel, little food, and interrogation. I sink into a deep, sweaty sleep.

A deafening tropical bird chorus at the crack of dawn wakes me. Grabbing a plate of scrambled eggs and a sweet, piping-hot coffee, I head out early to avoid the crowds.

With my thumb up, I stand out on the road. An open top brown Buick stops and a thin, old Caucasian lady looks over her shoulder at me.

"¡Venga!" she says, leaning across and opening the passenger door.

"¡Gracias!" I thank her, jumping in confused by her appearance and native dialect.

"¿A donde va?" she says through wrinkly puckered lips before smiling.

"Las ruinas, por favor." I am excited to get to the ruins. "¿A donde eres?" I ask her, curious about her heritage.

"¡Soy Mexicana!" she answers with glee. "Pero mi Padre era Estados Unidos."

Ah, American Dad. That explains it.

Less than five minutes later, my Buick grannie drops me at the end of a long lane lined with hedgerows.

"¡Adios!" she calls out, waving her hand and driving off.

I follow the lane, the fields either side slowly growing into thick jungle while butterflies spanning every colour of the rainbow flutter in abundance. I reach a large car park where a few tour buses are parked, and I'm immediately bombarded at the entrance by teenagers dressed in pastel shades of fake Abercrombie and Fitch t-shirts, clutching guide maps.

"¡Cinco dolares, hombre!" they shout, pushing each other and pointing at their flaps of paper, promising to take me off the beaten path to see hidden ruins that are not shown on the map.

"No tengo dinero," I say, politely pushing through them, declining. I'm sure they're harmless, but it's far too early to be fed information while being dragged through the back of beyond.

Along the side of the main plaza stand two giant temples constructed from white stone, each with an impressive flight of stairs leading up to small rooms on top. Landscaped paths skirt the neatly mown lawns and guide visitors around the bases of the giant white temples, majestically contrasted against the dark green jungle foliage that grows uncontrollably behind them. The facades are littered with well-preserved wall carvings depicting skulls, animals and gods adorned in long headdresses. The carvings are meticulously done and the site is impressive, but I can't help but feel it lacks a certain something in comparison to the previous ruins I've visited. Further, the extensive repair work seems to detract from some of the original charm. There's a tower that has been added, for example – later century archaeologists and historians imaging what might have been and placing it in amongst the ruins. For me, that could be left out. For me, the grown-over ruins speak across centuries, without any added modern interpretative work. I explore the grounds and buildings twice, capturing as many photos as possible, before a mist of rain sets in. I near the end of the main trail on my second loop and reckon my exploring has come to an end. Here, I pass a strip of red 'do not cross' tape tied across a path that disappears into the tangled foliage. Looking around me, I don't see anyone else and decide to investigate what's on the other side. *I'll probably never return here,* I think to myself, justifying my actions and ducking under the tape. Those modern archaeologists and historians would kill me if they saw me, but I am careful to stay on the trail and not disturb anything hiding in the rough ground foliage. I follow the trail further in, trying to be as quiet as possible, and I arrive in a ruined plaza of rubble constructed of mossy green rock where small dwellings and temples are strangled by the roots of large trees. No modern interpretive work here. Being in here alone, I marvel at the tiny settlement that once would have been a thriving neighbourhood. Nearby is the sound of rushing water. I follow the sound and come face to face with a waterfall that cascades over brown moon-like rocks carpeted in lichen. In addition to the off-limit ruins I've just walked through, this offers a complete contrast to the manicured grounds of the main site.

But I do not want to overstay my welcome. I snap off a few photos and retrace my steps back to the main path. Just before I reach it, I'm startled by the sound of footsteps crunching on the gravel.

"¡¿Que hace aquí?!" demands a Mexican gardener pushing a wheelbarrow and asking my business here.

I pretend not to understand. "No speak Spanish, sorry," I say apologetically, noticing the giant machete lying in the wheelbarrow.

Angrily, he tells me that I'm not allowed to be here and that I'll be fined for trespassing.

I apologise again and walk away at pace. I daren't look back as I make a beeline for the car park.

CHAPTER EIGHTY-FIVE
CHIAPAS

I exit through the gift shop of the ruins, and it's not long before I'm back out on the main road with my thumb up. I feel a car slowing behind me and turn around. It's another Mexican grandmamma, driving another late model American car.

"¡Sube!" she shouts, beckoning me in with her old, wrinkly hand.

Obliging, I hop in.

The car's interior is immaculate. Red and white leather features adorn the dashboard and door panelling and seats are upholstered in the same material. The old lady is as chatty as the last and we make pleasant small talk as the pristine beast glides us through the jungle. She tells me she and her husband ran a gas station in Palenque for thirty-five years and retired a few years ago. Her three boys and two girls are all grown up and live in the US with their own families now. Pulling in to the hostel's lay-by, I don't want to get out. This is the most conversation I've had since travelling with Dan and the Germans.

The lady wishes me luck and with that, is gone.

I try to spark up several conversations with different people over dinner to no avail, and retire early to my large empty dorm. It's nice to have the space to myself. But it's also a big space with no one to talk to. I look inside myself. Am I putting up walls with other travellers when it comes to interacting? I'm fine with anyone local, as the two car rides with the old ladies has proved, but if I am completely honest with myself, I know my approach and disinterest in fellow travellers has alienated me somewhat.

I attempt to kill time by studying my schoolbooks but my mind drifts back to the pressing subject at hand.

I brood.

The Palenque terminal resembles the interior of a KFC fast food joint. Red plastic chairs sit side-by-side in rows, and at the back there is a red-and-white painted wall with a series of square holes where tickets are dispensed. I purchase my ticket and slouch back to my chair. A small Mexican boy in dirty clothes sits down next to me and falls asleep on my shoulder with his hand down his pants. Looking down at him, I see he's content and comfortable by my side. Great. This is the first warm-hearted interaction I've had since leaving Eva and her family back in León, and the boy's gone to sleep with his hand in a compromising position. The boy is sweet, and I am glad to offer my shoulder for him to lean on, but I'm far from comfortable with the placement of the boy's hand. I worry I'll be identified as a paedophile, that I'll be thrown in jail for illegally trafficking a child north. Me, a sex slave trader. I try to move away but the boy settles in deeper on my shoulder. I can see the newspaper headline now –

BACKPACKER SEX SLAVE TRADER GETS TEN YEARS FOR TRAFFICKING MEXICAN SCHOOLBOY

Fortunately, he doesn't join me on the bus. When I get up to leave, he slides down into his chair, still asleep and fondling his crotch.

The Palenque / San Cristobál bus is a six-hour gut-churning roller-coaster that twists at breakneck speed through the highlands of Chiapas. We pull over at the halfway stop to grab some food. I stuff my face with a cheese tamale and watch from my seat as a line of passengers disembark and throw up their breakfasts on the roadside. Admittedly, I feel a little queasy after the greasy tamale, but not enough to share it with the lay-by.

The next stop is clearly unofficial. The bus screeches to a halt when a long plank embedded with nails attached to a length of rope is slid in front of us from the thick undergrowth. The tension of the passengers increases when a group of men in black ski masks and red bandanas and clutching automatic rifles surround the front of the bus and converse with the driver through his side window. Unable to understand what is being said, the passengers sit in scared silence – me included. Then, as suddenly as the plank appeared across the road, it is pulled away and we are allowed to pass. The men disappear with their impromptu roadblock back into the bushes.

I am confused by the situation and grateful to have come through the roadblock so easily. It's my first such encounter. What the men wanted I'll never know – but the whole scenario leaves me a bit rattled. The other passengers, all of Mexican descent, seem to be unperturbed by what we all just witnessed so I decide not to question it. Sometimes ignorance is bliss.

The bus continues on, hurtling through highway bends at breakneck speed and delivering us, miraculously, to our destination in one piece.

CHAPTER EIGHTY-SIX
SAN CRISTOBÁL DE LAS CASAS

Although rainy and cold, San Cristobál de las Casas has a familiar layout, colonial and colourful. There is a lazy welcoming feel to the town, similar to Antigua in Guatemala and León in Nicaragua. I take a taxi to the hostel that the two Madrid guys – the ones we hiked Volcano San Pedro with – recommended.

When I push open the large wooden gate to the reception area, I can't believe what I see. Shaggy-haired, stinking of booze and leaning against the desk is a traveller who has clearly just woken up. He's enquiring about the wallet he lost the night before. He's in rough shape and in a dark mood – and a sight I've never been happier to see.

"Heeeey!" I say.

Dan turns around. "How d'you know I'd be here?" he says without saying hi.

"I didn't!" I reply, hugging him and getting an unwanted whiff of booze. I mention the two Spanish guys I hiked San Pedro volcano with, the ones who had spoken of him. He doesn't recall them.

"Let's eat!" he says. "I know a sweet taco stand up the street. Cheap as, bro."

After all of our petty squabbles and the unspoken ill-feeling that results from two people travelling too long together, saying I'm elated to see Dan is an understatement. My lonely feeling vanishes with our first taco meal. My time in León and Guatemala were amazing, but there is no substitute for the company of old friends who understand each other.

We tuck into a pile of the fifteen-cent street tacos, and Dan goes into detail about a recent nightclub shooting that happened where he was present.

"We were all pissed up and dancing when two loud bangs filled the air, sending everyone to the floor," he starts. "Then the music shuts off and the lights go up."

"Fucking hell!" I exclaim. "Anyone die?"

"Hold on, hold on," he stops me, wanting to stretch out his story. "We're all led in single file out of the entrance, where we have to step over – get this – two bodies.

"No way!"

"Their heads were floating in pools of dark red blood."

"Jesus," I say, starting to wonder about how safe this town really is.

"Turns out the two victims were plaintiffs testifying against a narco trafficker who had put a price on their heads. The hired hit man had somehow got his weapon past nightclub security and shot them both at point blank range in the face before slipping out with the crowds."

"Bro, that's nuts," I say, worried about travelling in Mexico. "Anyway, what have you been doing since you left León?" It occurs to me I don't have a clue where he's been.

"Just chilling," he says. "Stayed in Estelí in Nica for a bit but it was too fucking hot." He thinks back. "A local dude took us on a camping trip for a night in his canoe though – that was cool."

We talk on, Dan recalling things he did between bouts of hostel drinking.

"That chick Kim from New York stayed with me in Xela in Guatemala. We went and checked out Tikal."

"What did you think?" I ask him, excited to recall my own recent experience there.

"Yeah – cool, man, just didn't get enough time there really." He seems not overly impressed. "Those day trips are too rushed."

"Yeah, I know what you mean," I say. I decide against telling him about staying the night with Marco, how we had the place to ourselves.

"El Salvador was dodgy," he starts. "Kim and I got stuff nicked from our bags at that shitty Tica bus hotel."

"No shit! I knew I hadn't lost that money!" I say, now

remembering the cash I frantically rummaged in my bags for in Antigua, and what old Morris had told me about that place.

"Yeah, bro, for sure. They know by the time you realise the money's gone, you'll be nine hours north or south. Perfect crime. Sly bastards."

When we return to the hostel after our catch-up lunch, we find a group of people crowding the foyer readying to leave on a boat trip.

"What's all this about?" I ask a girl fossicking in her bag.

"It's a boat ride through a canyon," she says in a strong Canadian accent.

Dan retires to a hammock to cure his dreadful hangover with a cold beer and I join the over-zealous backpackers in a minivan going west for the river trip. Slipping yellow life vests over our heads, we climb aboard what looks like an ex-lifeguard boat. We are strapped into rows of plastic orange chairs.

"We are about to take a trip through the mighty Cañón Sumidero," the guide says in broken English. "It's over a kilometre high on each side! Look out for crocodiles!"

Floating down through the jaws of the colossal Sumidore canyon, its towering moss-covered rock formations reach up either side, I realise that this experience feels too contrived, too staged. For one thing, the layout of the boat's seats and the bright yellow vests really take something from the beauty of what I'm seeing. The stark contrast of all this plasticky colour is disruptive, to say the least. Strapped in and feeling uncomfortable in the life vest and bicycle helmet, I feel out of place with these thrillseekers. I'm not one to chase these extreme attractions on a daily basis. The simple life I'd had in León is something so far from here, so *foreign* to this kind of experience. I suppose it's a kind of immersion many travellers will never experience (or want), and I feel lucky – again – to have been a part of something detached from the gringo trail.

The crocodiles mentioned by the guide have obviously moved on to greener pastures – or muddier waters– as the only glimpse of a reptile is the scaly tail of an iguana that slithers off into the bushes when the guide shouts and points. I think we are supposed to be impressed.

Back at the hostel, the group settles into the evening activity – sinking beers at the bar and reliving the exhilaration of their motorboat adventure. Dan joins them, eager as always for drinking buddies. I escape, wandering down through the town to the rusty framed stalls of the markets to grab some vegetables for dinner back at the hostel. Ornate churches dominate the town and several groups of people waving black and red flags hand out flyers. The black ski masks and red bandanas across their faces are reminiscent of the plank roadblockers that stopped the bus from Palenque. What's most interesting are the wooden rifles they are holding. Reading one of these leaflets, I understand that they are a Mexican indigenous armed revolutionary group based in Chiapas resisting control by the Mexican government. The masks are quite worrying but their picket sites seem peaceful enough and I continue on.

Down among the markets women in traditional woven dresses sit behind their various wares – including stacks of carrots, racks of fake football shirts and piles of cellphone covers.

"Hola. ¿Cuánto vale este?" I politely ask a young man at his stall, enquiring about the price of an onion. He glares. He's clearly not happy about my interest in the onion. Thinking he's not heard me correctly and positive I've pronounced my sentence correctly, I try again. For the second time, my words fall on apparently deaf ears and his glare intensifies. Now feeling scared, and wandering what his problem is, I turn and walk away empty-handed, feeling like I don't belong, but happy I haven't been shot in the face.

CHAPTER EIGHTY-SEVEN
MEXICO D.F.

With only nine days left in our Latin American odyssey, and tired of constantly shifting after nine months of our nomadic lifestyle, Dan and I decide to make only one more big move after San Cristobál. Mexico City has more than enough going on to keep us occupied for the remainder of our stay.

"How's your bank balance looking?" I ask Dan, while we wait for our last bus of the trip and curious to know if he's spent as much as me.

"It's all good, man," he says with a contented smile. "That stop in Nicaragua and the one in Guatemala were cheap as fuck." He adds, looking like he thinks I've spent more. "You? That school and the home-stay must've set you back a bit?"

"I've spent about NZ $17,000, including all our flights so far," I answer, not one to be cagey about financial matters.

"What?!!" Dan exclaims, clearly surprised. "How?" He looks utterly confused. "That's about where I'm at too. How'd I spend as much as you?"

I turn to him as he follows me up onto the bus, and give him his answer. "Beer money."

The previous day, we'd decided to splash out and make our last bus ride a good one, buying the gold class tickets with the ADO bus company. Like the dream liner buses of Argentina, the giant beast has fully reclining seats and a food and drink service. Even better, it only stops once, in Oaxaca, during the fifteen hours it takes to whisk us smoothly to Mexico City. In keeping with our style, we leave early afternoon and travel during the night.

We slow down during morning commuter traffic as we enter the sprawling city, but soon we arrive at the terminal. Mexico City has an extensive subway system, so we descend from our bus depot into an underground passageway. And what we find is not what I expected. If first impressions count for much, we are about to be very impressed:

this place is spotlessly clean, and there is clear signage to direct us whichever way we choose. People are immaculately dressed, toing and froing as metros arrive and depart. Men with briefcases, women with smart suits. Schoolkids and grandmas, all proceeding with great intent while the echo of scruffy buskers who sit against the tiled walls strum guitars. No stray dogs down here. No beggars down here. Definitely not what I expected.

"Do we look that bad after being on the road for nine months?" I whisper to Dan as we stand on the subway platform waiting for a train to Zócalo.

"Why's that?" he asks, looking around.

We feel a number of stares. We try not to stand out.

But we do stand out – and we soon discover why. The strange stares we're getting from the women surrounding us soon make sense when we're escorted by security to the other end of the platform – where all the men are standing. Separated by crowd barriers, males and females are kept apart in carriages due to one of Mexico's central cultural issues: men, apparently, cannot keep their hands to themselves.

Built on the foundations of the ruined Aztec city that the Spanish completely destroyed in 1519, Mexico City sits at 2400m, which, combined with the terrible smog problem, makes it feel like we're a lot higher. The thin and oxygen-deprived air feels similar to that in La Paz, Bolivia. The original foundations were built on a swamp, which has helped the buildings withstand the countless earthquakes that have rattled this region. You can still see remnants of past earthquakes in the crooked rooflines of the buildings that line the narrow streets of the old town.

Our hostel is located in Zócalo, the city's main square, and looks over the huge charcoal grey cathedral that stands crooked and sinking in the vast rectangular plaza. All around the square circulates a busy four-lane street of stand-still traffic – which produces a continuous rising cloud of smog. The upside of the congestion is that we are able to cross the roads on foot without fear of speeding cars.

Much like our first stay in Santiago, this hostel is full of backpackers raring to get going on their adventures. Mexico City is, for many, the starting point; from here, many will head south, some making a route similar to ours, but north to south. Some will stick to the gringo trail, some will venture off. It's fun to see the buzz of the new travellers. I feel like I've come a long, long way.

Others here are like us: tired and ready to go home. And ready to start saving for the next one.

Settling in to our dorm, I open my bag locker. On the inside of the door is a graffiti slogan written with a marker pen. It reads: Welcome to Mexico City USA.

"Haha!" I laugh to myself, understanding all too well the implication. "Spot on!"

At a guess, I'd say eighty percent of the guests at the hostel are from the US, the other twenty probably from Europe. There's no avoiding the Americans here. Some are loud like the Peace Corps beauties from the bus. Some cling together, looking fearful of what they might find a little further afield. Some play loud music. Some play pool. They are all about to set off on the adventure of their lives. I don't really feel like talking to any of them.

But I'm open-minded when one approaches us. We're sitting at a communal area that looks out over the Zócalo.

"Hey I'm Grant, how you doing guys? I'm planning on living here," he tells us in a Californian accent and looking over the top of his thin reading glasses. I guess he's in his late thirties, and he looks sincere, and friendly. I figure he's singled us out because of our uninvolvement with the crowds. "I'm a writer for Fodor's guidebooks," he adds, handing me his card.

He's not so much full of himself, but he exudes a confidence. And he keeps us entertained with his rich knowledge of Mexican history and politics, going into great detail about an area of the city known as the Plaza of the Three Cultures.

"If you'd like, I'd love to take you there tomorrow," he offers.

"It's somewhere that doesn't get visited too much by tourists." He pushes his glasses up. "I've also got to deliver a book to a restaurant I've recently included in the new issue of Fodor's, so we can tie the two together."

Dan is busy drinking his beer, but I agree for both of us.

"Hey, I wasn't trying to eavesdrop, fellas," an old man with beige shorts, knobbly knees and a yellow cap says from out on the balcony, "but that sounds like a great idea. Could I join you?" His accent is similar to Grant's.

"Sure! The more the merrier!" Grant answers, happy he's got another follower.

"Great! I'm Bert," the old man says, shaking all of our hands.

"Are you here alone?" I ask him, wondering how a man of his respectable age comes to be in a city like this, and relating to backpackers like us.

"Too much excitement for an old fella like me, you think?" he says with a smile.

"No, not at all!" I quickly reply, hoping I haven't offended him. "Just curious as to your story and why you're here."

"Well, I've been travelling for a long time now," he says, and I know we're about to settle in for his life story. "But I won't bore you guys with the long version."

Much to our relief, we get the short version: Bert is a sprightly New Yorker of seventy-six with the attitude and energy of a twenty-five-year-old, who's been exploring the globe for the last ten years since his wife died.

"No point in moping around waiting to die," he says in a hard knock fashion. "That's the last thing she would have wanted."

The conversation continues until the early hours. Bert is a pleasure to be around. We make a plan to meet downstairs around midday.

Grant shows up at noon in the hostel foyer and takes us all on a forty-five-minute walk through some poorer neighbourhoods of the city. I worry at first whether Bert will be able to keep up, but he soon puts Dan and I to shame as we struggle to follow behind him in the heat. Fit as a fiddle and unfazed by the humidity, he bounds up stairs and chats to random pedestrians on the way while we wheeze like a pair of unfit losers. To add to my state, my nose begins to bleed.

"That's from the air pollution – it happens to us all," Grant says, as I wipe the blood from my nostril.

"Come on, boys!" Bert calls back to us, winking and rubbing it in.

We arrive at the Plaza de las Tres Culturas, in the Tlatelolco neighbourhood. It is surrounded by sky-high blocks of yellow flats dotted with TV satellite dishes. It is ugly. I wonder why we've come this far to arrive here. It does not seem a tourist attraction at all. But the ugly plaza takes on a different meaning after Grant's detailed description of the shooting massacre that took place here in 1968.

"Two days before the Olympic opening ceremony commenced across town, a thousand protesting students gathered here, and were fired upon in broad daylight by the military," he explains. "This was quickly followed by the government disposing of the corpses overnight – and the story was conveniently covered up like nothing ever happened."

We can tell Grant thoroughly enjoys his position as history guide. He does an excellent job of bringing meaning to the square where we talk four decades later. I can almost sense all the terror that occurred right where I'm standing, and a strange feeling sends a shiver down my spine. Adding to the atmosphere is the area behind the plaza, behind the domineering block of flats in front of us. There, we come to Tlatelolco, another Aztec city and scene of earlier violence and terror, its walls razed by the Spaniards and reused by the enslaved Aztecs to re-form them into a crooked Catholic cathedral that sits behind the ruins and stands still today, dark and monolithic between the modern office blocks like a constant reminder of the colonisation that we've seen almost every day during our trip. The three structures – the apartment block, the cathedral and the ruins – remind us of three completely different eras and are a bizarre juxtaposition of architectural and human atrocity. Although not exactly a photographer's dream, the plaza is memorable, and the way Grant has shared its history has made for an interesting day.

As the afternoon draws to a close, our guide leads us to the place he'd mentioned yesterday, a place that has a write up in his new guidebook. But we get lost along the way, and even Grant is unsure if we're in the right neighbourhood. My paranoia starts to talk to me. I recall getting mugged in Buenos Aires those many months back. I figure we've had a long run of good luck, and something is bound to happen in our last few days. I walk on, winding myself up for no reason.

"¡Hola, Señora!" Grant calls out to a young woman in the dimly lit lane he's led us to. "El Pulque bar. ¿Donde esta?" At least I'm reassured he's inquiring if she knows of the place.

"Ah, siii," she answers, smiling and washing away my paranoia. "Es por allá." She points at a barred door from where a neon glow shines.

"*Yes!* ¡Gracias, chica!" Grant says excitedly. "I knew I was right!"

Stepping through a tiny entrance, we find ourselves in a vibrant neon-lit bar specialising in pulque, a frothy, milky, viscous drink made from fermented agave plants. It's high in alcohol content and deceptive in its kick.

"¡Hola!" Grant greets the portly bar owner, who clearly doesn't know him from a bar of soap. "¡Tengo un regalito!" he continues, passing him the new edition of the Fodor's Mexico City guidebook, which now, thanks to him, includes this bar.

The owner, now remembering him, is ecstatic, and, accompanied by a beaming smile, claps his hands and shouts to a waitress to bring a round of the strange drinks. The waitress obliges, wobbling across the white tiled floor in a pair of high heels and a frilly dress. She arrives at the table where we've made ourselves comfortable. The pink beverages slosh around in pitcher-sized, handled glasses.

"They taste sweet, but they're really strong," Grant warns us, holding up his glass and toasting us. While we sit and swig back one pulque after another, the bar comes alive, and soon patrons are dancing on the tables, singing karaoke and pulling us up to join in.

A small stage of red velvet is lit up and Bert, now well inebriated, slaps his thighs, dancing like his life depends on it, much to the elation of the crowd who clap and cheer him on.

Catching the last train across the city, I think about our day's achievements. Activities that for any local resident would be the mere goings-on of daily life in this gigantic city.

I smile – content, fulfilled.

CHAPTER EIGHTY-EIGHT
CITY LIFE

It's past 11am when we finally drag ourselves out of bed the next morning, and, judging by the lack of noise that usually filters up through the centre shaft of the hostel, it seems the majority of the other guests have already departed for the day. The cafeteria downstairs is empty and we pull up a couple of chairs and drink a coffee while the hum of the city's pedestrians go about their daily business.

We finish our coffees and venture out into the plaza in search of food. Just outside our door, we're confronted by a dirty-skinned street midget covered in an array of home-made tattoos.

"¡Hombrrrreee puuuto!" he shouts, singling Dan out for no particular reason and lunging aggressively. We try not to make eye contact with him. We try to ignore him as we pick up our pace, weaving through the crowded sidewalk, desperately trying to lose him and hoping he'll give up chase.

"I think we lost him," Dan says, exhausted and panting in the heat.

"¡Oye! ¡PUTO!" comes a cry from the sea of bodies, jostling for space on the path.

"Fuck! What's his problem?" I say, confused and pissed off that he's followed us this far.

We pick up our pace again, and his shouting finally becomes fainter as he loses interest and latches on to another random victim, disappearing in the opposite direction, trying his luck to ruin their day instead.

"What a fucking weirdo," I exclaim, relieved that he's left us alone. Then, I look around and wonder, "Where are we?"

"Who cares?" Dan answers, not bothered by the fact that we are in a completely unfamiliar street. "Let's just have a wander." My mind flicks back to Buenos Aires and the crackheads.

Around every corner a new scene springs out at us, but these are scenes so different to that ill-fated day in Buenos Aires. From street artists drawing on the pavement to a film crew shooting a TV commercial between Aztec ruins and tall office blocks that sprout in alternating rows from the earth. The contrast hits me. The life I'm going back to is, by now, *foreign*. My work in film – orange vested uniforms, fifteen-hour days, catered meals, TV adverts worth millions – seems almost surreal after travelling with no more than a 40L backpack, living by the seat of my pants and not knowing what each day will bring. After the things I've seen on this trip, First World problems seem insignificant. And the daily conundrums, I can barely fathom anymore: which shampoo to purchase, which jeans to wear Friday night…

"Aye! Come on!"

Dan, now up the street, snaps me out of my thoughts. I'm still staring at the film crew.

I turn and catch up with him. We follow signs to the Aztec Museum, and turn into a plaza where we come upon five men in feathered costumes who leap from a platform at the top of a pole, towering above the buildings that surround it. It's astounding to watch, even if we can plainly see how the cord that's wound up and attached to their ankles slowly unravels from the pole. They circle and swoop, much like birds. It's a sight to behold. These men, we learn, are Voladores, or pole flyers, performing an ancient Mesoamerican ritual that goes back to a time when men, dressed in colourful birdlike attire, found the tallest tree of the forest and climbed it, fasting and praying to the gods for relief from a long-lasting period of drought and famine. The story goes that the men stayed in the tree all night then felled it the next day, carrying it to their village and erecting it with the base firmly in the ground and the top reaching upwards to the gods. The ceremony has grown over the years to represent a kind of thanksgiving to the gods – with incredible acrobatic performance of the five flyers who carry out the Danza de los Voladores in city squares in various parts of Mexico. We're lucky to have happened upon it.

When the fliers reach the ground, they bow and run around with hats asking for money. I gladly chuck a few coins into the hat, astonished by what I have just seen. We leave them with their unwound rope and enter the museum. Incredible artefacts from the times of the Aztecs fill the rooms of the building, including giant carvings of Olmec heads and a life-sized replica of a temple side at the Teotihuacán site that sits outside the city.

By the time we make our way through the museum it's quite late in the day.

"I'm over walking. Let's go back to the hostel," I say to Dan, hoping he's feeling the same way.

"Yep, it's beer o'clock." Dan is reliable, that's for sure.

The hostel is its usual hive of activity. And old friend Bert seems particularly alive tonight, too. We find him sitting on a couch trying to chat up a young woman – who has her hand on his knee!

"Bert, eh?!" Dan says, offering him a beer. "Can't see it, but I hope I've got his energy when I'm that old."

"Same," I reply, admiring the old man's stamina and confidence.

I revel in the happy mood tonight but I feel a touch sad that our journey is coming to an end.

"Only a few days left, bro," I say to Dan, swigging my beer.

"Yeah, we should probably do something worthwhile then," Dan says, swigging his beer but not offering any suggestions.

"Teotihuacán," I propose. "We have to."

CHAPTER EIGHTY-NINE
TEOTIHUACÁN

Teotihuacán: the largest pre-Hispanic city in all of the Americas.

We arrive after a two-hour rumbling bus ride that drags us along the choked up highway. Staring out the window into the dusty streets, I lose myself in my daydream: the Bolivian bus to Potosí with the puking child; the little Lanquín bus circling the village for an hour; the fishtailing Peruvian bus to Machu Picchu; the bullet holes in the window of the Guayaquil bus in Ecuador.

I'm snapped out of my thoughts when we stop for lunch. I'm starving.

Included in the tour is a stop en route for a meal of mole, a Mexican dish, usually chicken, cooked in a chocolate-chili sauce. The village where we stop is built in the traditional colonial style, but it feels like it's been overly dressed up for the tourist trade. Stores selling trinkets that only foreigners would buy outnumber the food stalls that clog the streets of previous places we've been. We're ushered into a room where a Mexican woman in traditional dress explains the versatility of the agave plant, its many uses including thread, needles, soap and tequila. Then we are led to a store that sells these products at sky-high prices.

"This is bullshit," Dan whispers under his breath.

"Yeah, where's the food?" I reply, keeping my voice down but becoming irritated that we're being hustled. My stomach growls in agreement to my whining.

Finally, we are led around the perimeter of the village square, where we are seated at a long table and served the promised meal. Good things come to those who wait, they say, and this is no exception. I'd almost put up with more tourist bullshit for another plate of this. It's beyond tasty. Plump juicy chicken is slathered in a thick sauce, hinting at chocolate and mildly biting, and served with a mountain of rice and black beans.

"Fuck yeah," Dan mumbles, wolfing down the delicious food and forking another dollop of beans in before finishing his mouthful.

We arrive at the ruins full-bellied. The unmistakable Pyramid of the Sun dominates the view. Everything around it appears miniaturised. Compared to the previous temples I've visited, this is colossal in size. Our informative guide leads us through the first complex, a series of tunnels and rooms cool in temperature, where he explains the intricate and immaculately preserved murals that adorn the walls. Depicting everyday scenes of Aztec life and still clearly visible in their red and white hues, they are rare indeed.

"Creo Teotihuacán y Copán de Honduras se tienen, pero solo los dos," he says, stating that only this place and one other site in Honduras have such well-preserved murals.

When we exit this area, the light blinds us and illuminates an overwhelming panorama.

The Avenue of the Dead, a wide, dry, red dirt causeway which runs for over a mile, is flanked by the main temples of the Moon, Sun and Feathers that proudly stand on either side of it. The avenue, littered with clusters of smaller ceremonial platforms where pushy vendors selling hammocks and slogan t-shirts hassle the public, stretches out before our eyes and disappears off in the distance. The scale is beyond description – to say it is huge is an understatement.

Standing at the base of the gigantic Sun Pyramid, I'm not at all looking forward to climbing its 248 steps that lead up into the sky. But I spy several larger Mexican tourists beginning their ascent, so I join them. This man-made mountain is so big, there is only one way to climb it: one step at a time. I soon discover that looking up at the backsides of other tourists struggling to reach its summit is more detrimental than helpful, so I put my head down and get on with it, focusing on my feet and each step they take.

Dan and I eventually arrive, exhausted, at the crest. Sitting down and still gasping for air, we take in the 360-degree views of the vast plains. Spectacular. To the north is a tall jagged mountain range; this is my favourite direction in the vista – nature at its most beautiful, punching up at the sky in a kind of defiance. The view makes the day trip worthwhile – and the best possible end point for our trip.

I've been at higher altitudes during the last nine months than ever before in my life. I've surprised myself at my endurance levels climbing to these mountain summits, whether created by Mother Nature or man-made. The sheer excitement of making it to the top and staring out over a continent and its incredible landscape never interested me until a few years ago. I've endured both freezing and sweltering temperatures. The people, the families, the companions, the poverty, the music, the crimes – all carved into my body, my heart, my being, never to be lost. All from a place where I, at the beginning, felt so lost. That little stray dog, that perrito callejito, following his master. Dan has been a good guide, for the most part. Dan, who's seen most of this with me, a friend who knows me better than anyone now, a friend for life, stories for life, stories to tell to our childr…

"BUUUURP!!!!!"

Startled from my daydream, I turn to see Dan holding his stomach.

"Fuck, bro – that chocolaty chicken. *Jesus*."

The other sightseers at the summit giggle at Dan's giant belch.

We head down.

Back at the southern end of the Avenue of the Dead and within the Ciudadela complex stands the Pyramid of the Feathered Serpent. With its carvings still largely intact, its sides are adorned with Feathered Serpent heads carved from large blocks of stone that decorate the six-tiered temple.

"This is that one from The Doors," Dan says, referring to a classic photo of Jim Morrison used for one of the band's album covers.

The sheer history and beauty of this site, not to mention the sleeping tombs still under its foundations, stands in great contrast to the spirit of modern business – whose development pressures the existence of such landmarks as they encroach and change the landscape. Nearby is a proposed site for a Mexican Walmart, granted government permission in 2004. Incredible that such an important part of world history is a mere blot – and a potentially removable one – on the landscape in the name of Progress.

"¡OK! ¡OK! ¡Vamos, amigos!" Our guide claps his hands, rounding us up like cattle. "The bus is outside! We go now please!"

We are deposited back in the Zócalo, where we buy our last bottle of rum to share with Bert and Grant.

"Here's to nine months on the road!" I declare, toasting them as we overlook the Zócalo, now adorned with thousands of coloured light bulbs that twinkle huge nativity scenes. It's the festive season; it's the perfect season to say our farewells, such cheer and goodwill palpable in the mood around us. Leaning over the balcony, I sip my rum and stare down at the nativity lights reflecting on the wet streets. The trip flashes through my mind in fast forward. Fourteen countries travelled in nine months, all of the same language but each unique in culture and experiences. From the wind-burnt faces of the shy mountain people of the Bolivian Alti Plano to the happy welcoming smiles of Colombia and the desperate demands of the gun-toting thieves in Argentina – they are all unforgettable.

"Good luck, guys," I say, toasting Bert and Grant and raising my glass to them. We shake hands for the last time.

"Until we meet again, eh?" they both answer.

And we pour another glass.

CHAPTER NINETY
BENITO JUÁREZ AIRPORT

The cab arrives at 5am.

Dan and I are whisked to the airport before the morning traffic grinds to a halt. The thirty-five dollar fare is a harsh reminder of the world we're about to re-enter, but considering the importance of this flight we hand the driver the money without question and smoke one last cigarette outside the terminal.

Then we stroll into the airport.

At the check-in desk, we're first in line. We watch as our backpacks disappear through the rubber flaps on the baggage conveyor belt. We are handed our stamped passports and boarding passes.

"Let's just go straight to the gate," I suggest to Dan, eager to sleep for a while before we board.

"Yep, good idea," he agrees, pre-occupied with something in his passport. When we sit down, he says, "Did you get this tax slip stapled to yours when you crossed the border into Chiapas?" He shows me the strip of paper that's torn from where it was stapled.

I tell him not to worry about it: there is so much paperwork with every border check, I have learned that you just go with the flow.

Unfortunately, my flow is not Dan's flow, and we are soon met with a snag at the boarding gate. The check-in desk clerk who takes my passport overlooks the paper slip and hands me back my boarding stub. I head off towards the gate, almost forgetting Dan. Looking back over my shoulder, I see he's being questioned and is now holding up the line of passengers so turn on my heel to see what the problem is.

Holding the slip of paper, the flight attendant looks at me. "¿Ya ha pagado, no?" she asks me sternly, referring to my departure tax payment.

"No," I reply. "¿No es necesario, si?" I try playing dumb.

A few more words are spoken before Dan turns to me.

"Yeah, it is necessary," he says. "We can't leave the country until it's paid."

Which leads to the most idiotic series of events.

It begins when one attendant, now speaking perfect English, says, "The bank opens at 09:00, so you'll be fine."

"Our plane leaves at 09:00 – so we won't be fine!" Dan counters in a raised voice – still in Spanish.

The girls standing behind the desk look at us with gormless expressions as if we are stupid. Like puppets from a *Thunderbirds* movie, the whites of their almond eyes bordered with thick black eyeliner flick from left to right while their little blue hats sit tilted on their heads.

Dan's voice steps up a level. "You're not making any sense – do you understand what you just said?" He is clearly beginning to get frustrated.

Realising their mistake, they frantically tap away on their keyboards and secure us a flight at 14:00 before directing us to where we can pay the tax.

So we sit outside the doors of the bank. At 09:05 there is still no sign of life inside and the doors are still locked. At 09:30 – well past the designated time of opening – the place is still in complete darkness

"Must be late," Dan says. "Typical Mexicans."

10:30 rolls around and still there's no sound from inside.

"This is fucking ridiculous!" I say, now irate. "What's going on?!"

I peer inside the dark interior and I can just make out a sandwich board set up below the tellers' desks. It bears a sign telling customers that it's a religious holiday weekend and the bank won't be open again until the following Tuesday.

"What the fuck is wrong with these people? Why are they telling us to go to the bank?!!" I say, laughing now at the absurdity of our situation.

Apparently, Mexico does not want us to leave.

But there's anger in Dan's eyes.

We stomp back to the airline desk. The discussion gains heat.

"We'll give you the money and you can pay the fee on Tuesday," Dan offers, still speaking in Spanish.

"We cannot do that, sir." They clearly do not want the nearby passengers to hear the escalating situation. "You can speak in English," they say to Dan – in English. "It's easier."

This only infuriates Dan more as he kicks off and raises his voice again. "I speak perfectly good Spanish and I will continue to speak it, until this is resolved," he tells them, his voice still increasing in volume.

Seeing that this isn't getting them anywhere and apparently not wanting to encourage any more of a fuss, they remember a military bank in Terminal 2 where we can pay. Conveniently.

"Thank you!" Dan says, switching back to English before we jump on the airbus that takes us around to the other terminal. The bank has one teller working behind a small barred window. He is dressed in military uniform. He looks efficient. We can only hope.

The teller takes our last notes and loose change and we return to the boarding gate with our stamped strips of paper. We are checked in by new attendants. Apparently our earlier helpers are on a coffee break. We are unable to thank them for their help and the marvellous last impression they've given us of the dance around Latin American paperwork.

Finally sitting in our plane seats, we're met with the disapproving glares of the smartly dressed businessmen who surround us. I am literally wearing the same outfit I arrived in nine months ago. I'm feeling very out of place. Fourteen countries by bus obviously shows. We are shaggy-haired and bearded. The mud-stained laces of my leather boots are untied and lying lifeless on the floor. My t-shirt is stiff and only has two holes – not bad, from my view, but possibly an affront to the nattily dressed business flyers. My needlework on the camo pants has changed in colour at each repair and the pants are attracting attention. They've been through a lot – I don't think the Suits could stand a recount of the Lima liver story.

Ignoring the stares, I pull a crumpled copy of the *New York Times* from the back of my seat and only then realise how long it's been since I've seen (or cared) about world news and, more so, how insignificant it seems. If I imagined nine months ago that I'd stepped through the looking glass into a world of unknowns, I'm *really* through it now. *Buckle up: going home is going to be a strange trip.*

The plane leaves Latin soil and we reach maximum altitude in no time. Soon we are presented with plastic trays that are placed neatly on our fold-down tables. Looking down at the foil lid, I'm intrigued to see what's inside. It occurs to me that I'm famished – we missed breakfast due to the morning's departure tax shambles. I peel back the lid, hoping to find an aviation version of the typical Latin breakfast – maybe a tortilla and beans?

What sits before me is nothing like the meals I've enjoyed in recent months. On my Styrofoam plate is a thick yellow slab resembling a dishwashing sponge, which I presume is meant to be an omelette.

I've become accustomed to a simple life. My wants and needs have been boiled down to basic nutritious food, shelter and the odd bottle of rum. The reintegration into First World life will not be easy. I can already sense a worry growing in my gut. The omelette is practically an affront.

But I eat it, every last bite. The clammy, dry sponge does not go down easily, but this is the life I'm going back into – the transition happens here.

I place the lid back, close my eyes and prepare myself for what's to be the biggest culture shock since I entered Chile back in April. Drifting off to sleep as we fly northeast across the United States, I dream, restless. I am back sleeping on the sticky vinyl seat of an old bus; I am being bounced along a potholed road. A man carries a baby goat in the aisle.

The reggaetón that blasts from the speakers next to me stirs me from my dream-state. I turn to my left, and my cheek connects with an old woman's snoring head resting on my shoulder. To my right, a child pukes green bile into a plastic bag.

ABOUT
DARREN HOWMAN

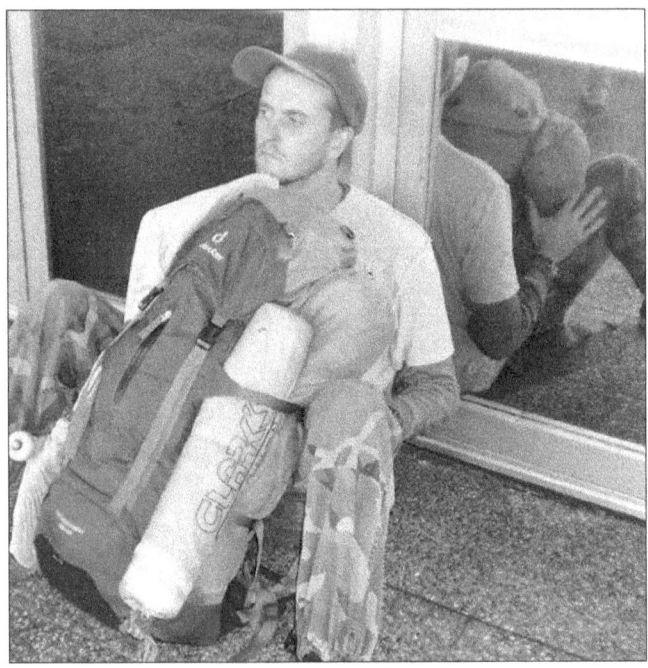

Born and raised in the Berkshire countryside, Darren Howman had a wanderlust from an early age.

His lifelong passion for skateboarding was the original impetus to explore the world – which then ignited a burning curiosity to explore lesser travelled and inhabited routes.

Darren now resides in Auckland, New Zealand, and works in the film industry.

Also from EVERYTIME PRESS

https://www.everytimepress.com/everytime-press-catalogue

Travel & Memoir

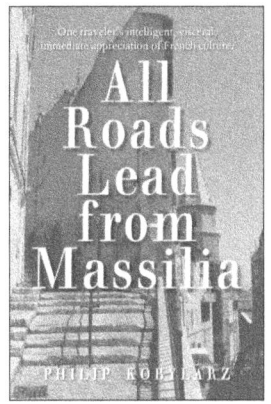 

- *All Roads Lead from Massilia* by Philip Kobylarz
    978-1-925536-27-0 (paperback)   978-1-925536-28-7 (eBook)
- *Lenin's Asylum* by A. A. Weiss
    978-1-925536-50-8 (paperback)   978-1-925536-51-5 (eBook)

 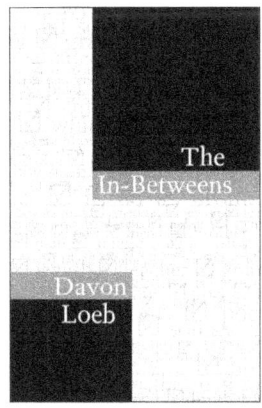

- *Sydneyside Reflections* by Mark Crimmins
    978-1-925536-07-2 (paperback)   978-1-925536-08-9 (eBook)
- *The In-Betweens* by Davon Loeb
    978-1-925536-56-0 (paperback)   978-1-925536-57-7 (eBook)

Also from EVERYTIME PRESS

https://www.everytimepress.com/everytime-press-catalogue

Resource & How-To Books

- *all you need is ... a whiteboard, a marker and this book!*
  by Matt Potter   (available in paperback only)
  978-1-925101-82-9 (Book 1)   978-1-925101-96-6 (Book 2)

- *The Pointless Revolution!* by Paul Ransom
  978-1-925536-74-4 (paperback)   978-1-925536-75-1 (eBook)
- *It's About the Dog* by Guilie Castillo Oriard
  978-1-925536-19-5 (paperback)   978-1-925536-20-1 (eBook)

www.ingramcontent.com/pod-product-compliance
Lightning Source LLC
Chambersburg PA
CBHW031418150426
43191CB00006B/314